ESSAYS IN
BRITISH BUSINESS HISTORY

ESSAYS IN
BRITISH
BUSINESS
HISTORY

EDITED

for the Economic History Society

BY

BARRY SUPPLE

CLARENDON PRESS · OXFORD
1977

Oxford University Press, Walton Street, Oxford OX2 6DP

OXFORD LONDON GLASGOW NEW YORK
TORONTO MELBOURNE WELLINGTON CAPE TOWN
IBADAN NAIROBI DAR ES SALAAM LUSAKA ADDIS ABABA
KUALA LUMPUR SINGAPORE JAKARTA HONG KONG TOKYO
DELHI BOMBAY CALCUTTA MADRAS KARACHI

British Library Cataloguing in Publication Data
Essays in British business history.
  1. Great Britain—Industries
I. Supple, Barry   II. Economic History Society
338'.0941   HC255   77–30196
ISBN 0–19–877087–1
ISBN 0–19–877088–x   Pbk

Printed in Great Britain by
Richard Clay & Co Ltd, Bungay, Suffolk

Acknowledgements

IN most cases the chapters in this collection are based upon published work. The relevant publication is indicated below, and in more detail in the first note to each chapter. The contributors to and publishers of this volume are most grateful to those concerned for permission to use the material. The editor also wishes to acknowledge the constant encouragement of the Publications Committee of the Economic History Society, which gave helpful advice throughout our preparation of the collection.

The following chapters are largely based on material published in the sources indicated;

Chapter 2: S. B. Saul, 'The Market and Development of the Mechanical Engineering Industries in Britain, 1860–1914', *Economic History Review*, 2nd ser. XX (1967).

Chapter 3: B. W. E. Alford, *W. D. & H. O. Wills and the Development of the U.K. Tobacco Industry, 1786–1965* (Methuen, London, 1973).

Chapter 4: Barry Supple, *The Royal Exchange Assurance: A History of British Insurance, 1720–1970* (Cambridge University Press, Cambridge, 1970).

Chapter 5: D. C. Coleman, *Courtaulds: An Economic and Social History*, vol. 1 (Oxford University Press, Oxford, 1969).

Chapter 6: Roy Church, *Kenrick's in Hardware: A Family Business, 1791–1966* (David & Charles, Newton Abbot, 1969).

Chapter 7: Charles Wilson, *History of Unilever* (2 vols., Cassell, London, 1954)

Chapter 8: Peter Mathias, *Retailing Revolution, A History of Multiple Retailing in the Food Trades based upon the Allied Suppliers Group of Companies* (Longmans, London, 1967).

Chapter 12: W. J. Reader, *Imperial Chemical Industries: A History* (2 vols., Oxford University Press, Oxford, 1970, 1975).

Contents

Introduction: Approaches to Business History

THIS latest volume in the Economic History Society's series of essays on various aspect of economic and social history is, like its predecessors, designed primarily for the convenience of students (using that ambiguous term in its broadest sense). In this respect, it has two related aims: to obviate a good deal of hunting and gathering in a somewhat scattered literature, and to introduce newcomers to the scope and content of a specialist aspect of the study of the past. In this instance, however, for reasons which will be more fully discussed below, it did not seem appropriate to attempt to achieve these ends by reprinting articles or other material in the form in which they had already been published elsewhere. Instead, nearly all the essays were specially written for this collection, in most cases on the basis of material which had already appeared in full-scale company histories. Some distinctive method of compilation was in fact necessary, partly because of the relative novelty of the subject, but principally because of the characteristics of that version of business history chosen for particular emphasis in this volume.

There is perhaps no longer any serious need to defend the autonomy of business history as a field of study in Britain. The journal *Business History* was launched in 1958; the first university post explicitly in the subject was created in 1959. These institutional innovations, like much else of a substantive nature in the field of business, occurred a generation or so after comparable developments in the United States. But since another generation has almost passed, we can assume that the field has entered the realm of academic respectability. Indeed, it is now generally accepted that systematic historical studies of business behaviour, structures, and policies, and of their consequences for the economy as a whole, not only comprise a proper activity in themselves, but are also of considerable relevance to a broader understanding of economic processes. Of course there is a sense in which this recognition has never been withheld. Economic historians have always assumed that business activity and business men have played critical roles in economic evolution. Nevertheless, it is still possible to make the point about the relatively recent institutionalization of business history, if only because of earlier variations of, and vicissitudes in, the standing of the subject-matter as a distinct specialism or sub-field. This has in large part no doubt been based on good methodological reasons (the difficulty of studying business behaviour apart from the larger corpus of economic theory or economic history). But it has also been a function of changes in the academic perspective on Britain's economic past. It is this factor which, perhaps above all others, has influenced the conceptual frame-work within which business and business men have been studied—has helped to determine whether the business man's economic role has been considered innocuous or positive, malevolent or benign; whether business activity has been seen as 'enterprise' or 'administration'; whether attention has been concentrated on innovation or on management; whether the individual or business structures, the enterpriser or market forces, personal or impersonal factors, have occupied the centre of the stage.

From the present point of view—i.e. assuming that business history is concerned with the study of an important and conceptually distinct economic and social activity—there are two main perspectives which, although closely related, are worth distinguishing.[1]

In the first perspective business activity is seen in terms of enterprise and innovation, and therefore involves specific points of decision-making. This naturally leads to a concern with the individual risk-taking entrepreneur, and is certainly the tradition mode for the study of business in the past. It shaped the first approaches to the origins of the Industrial Revolution and its characteristics as a heroic process. And at another level, it was represented in a highly systemized form in the work of various social scientists, and notably in the theory of economic growth associated with J. A. Schumpeter.[2] In the 1950s these presuppositions about the importance of enterprise and the individual were responsible for the flowering of work on the entrepreneur in various of the social sciences. As far as historical studies were concerned, its most important manifestation was the establishment of the lively and productive Centre for Research in Entrepreneurial History at Harvard University; and the tradition and styles which lie behind such work are still very much in evidence in economic history on both sides of the Atlantic.

The second perspective on the study of the past is a much more recent development. It is best, though (as we shall see) not exclusively, represented by the idea of *company* history—the history of particular formal enterprises in terms of their organization, policy, and purpose as well as of the people who guided them. But it also involves broader perceptions: of over-all business structures in the economy, for example, or of the relationship between business activity and structure on the one hand and the performance of the economy on the other.

There is, of course, no need to emphasize that this type of approach is, in some form or another, also as old as economic history itself, nor that it is, or can be, intimately related to the first (entrepreneurial) version of business history. But in its self-conscious, specialized, and more fertile academic form it really only goes back to the 1930s in the United States,[3] and to the 1950s in this country. This modern phase of business history was decisively opened in the United Kingdom with the publication of Charles Wilson's *The History of Unilever* (2 vols., 1954) which has been followed by a host of other substantial company histories.[4] The difference in chronology between the booms in American and British business history is also associated with a difference in the degree of self-consciousness involved. In the United States the distinction between business and economic historians was strongly marked. In the United Kingdom, on the other hand, although the widespread development of company history was slower in coming, when it did arrive, not only was the intellectual climate different, but those who wrote business histories were largely recruited from, and frequently returned to, the ranks of economic history. The resulting closer connection between 'general' economic history and the specialized study of business history has helped to extend the latter away from the preoccupation with administrative structures, which characterized many of the initial American approaches to the subject, towards a broader concern with the economic and social context of business activity. In fact, British business history is characterized not only by a somewhat closer integration of the two themes—entrepreneurial and institutional—but also by a concern with questions about performance and efficiency of the economy as well as the firm. This is no doubt related to the maturing of industrial economies in general and the diffused anxiety about the performance of the British economy over the last one hundred years.[5]

This logical relationship between business history, broadly defined, and the study of the evolution of a mature economy has helped to shape the three main interrelated models used by business historians. The first of these is the conventional approach: the detailed examination of the history of individual companies in what amount to institutional or business biographies with a variable analytical or theoretical emphasis. By definition, the result is usually an individual case-study. The second approach, which flows logically from the first, pays particular attention to the development of comparative business structures and over-all business policies. Here too it would be possible to exaggerate the novelty of recent scholarship: economic historians have always been interested in 'industrial history', as it used to be called, which necessarily involves some perception of over-all patterns of business organization and policy.[6] Nevertheless, in recent years there have been more systematic and rigorous attempts to study the evolution of such patterns—derived in part from the obvious need to generalize on the basis of comparative rather than individual case-studies, and in part from the increasing interest in the corporate or managerial character of modern economies, and the associated dominance of large-scale companies.[7]

Both concerns—with explicitly comparative studies and with 'big-business' structures—have been exemplified in recent work on the relationship between corporate size, business policy, and internal organization. This somewhat specialized field was pioneered in the United States by Alfred D. Chandler, who extended his work on the nineteenth-century origin of large-scale firms

('The Beginnings of "Big Business" in American Industry', *Business History Review*, xxxii [1959]) into a detailed study of organization in the twentieth century (*Strategy and Structure: Chapters in the History of the Industrial Enterprise*, Cambridge, Mass., 1962). With some time-lag, the same theme has been employed to illuminate the British scene—notably in Derek F. Channon, *The Strategy and Structure of British Enterprise* (London, 1973) (for the postwar period), and Leslie Hannah (ed.), *Management Strategy and Business Development: An Historical and Comparative View* (London, 1976).[8]

The third mode which might reasonably be categorized as business history —even though some of its practitioners might be surprised to find themselves placed in such company—results from the systematic examination of the role of entrepreneurship in the performance of the British economy. It has particular relevance to the apparent slowing-down of Britain's growth rate in the late nineteenth century, for this has given rise to a variety of explanations and counter-explanations, including some fairly sharply contrasting views of the role, or guilt, of British entrepreneurs.[9] At the same time, however, the range of questions and concepts involved has been used for other periods of British history, and marks one of the important interconnections between business history and the analytical aspects of economic history.

The multilayered character of business history raises obvious problems of selection and definition for a collection of this sort. In the event, it seemed neither feasible nor useful to attempt to cover the general analytical questions of entrepreneurship and its relationship to British economic progress. In addition to leading us away from areas most central to what is generally understood by 'business history', this would have involved the consideration of material which (at least for the critical period 1870–1914) is already widely available. Admittedly, it was judged useful to include Professor Saul's essay on the mechanical engineering industries, which provides an important survey of an industry and its business problems to serve as a corrective to too easy generalization about British economic decline. But apart from this there are no comparative studies of entrepreneurship in the now conventional sense— except, of course, in so far as all case-studies of business behaviour implicitly deal with the relevant issues, and often explicitly comment on them.

It was even easier to exclude case-studies specifically devoted to the macro-economic, 'structural' history of business (again, with the proviso that many of the chapters necessarily, if incidentally, touch on relevant issues). This is because the question is so recent and the literature so compact that its coverage here would have involved duplication. Instead, it seemed that by far the most useful purpose of such a collection might be served if it provided primarily a variety of case-studies of business organization and behaviour—thus exemplifying the 'characteristic' product of business history in a variety of ways.

This meant that a majority of the contributions would be drawn from work on the history of individual companies. And this was the case in nine out of the thirteen essays. Of the remaining four, two deal with important industries (which would otherwise have been neglected) at significant moments in their history: that by Professor Saul by an adaptation of his important article on mechanical engineering; that by Professor Church and Dr. Miller by an original essay on the inter-war motor industry. In addition, the essay by Dr. Garside, on industrial relations, was commissioned to help fill what is too often a large gap in company histories; and in the first chapter the editor attempts to provide a framework for the subsequent case-studies, in the form of a general survey of the important aspects of British business in the late nineteenth and twentieth centuries.

As far as the essays on individual firms were concerned, a problem arose which is more or less distinctive to business history. In other fields it is usually possible to find a large number of fairly concise articles which can adquately represent the principal types of work and conclusions in the field. Business historians, however, rarely publish articles comprising broad-based studies of individual companies. Rather, in the nature of the subject-matter, they have tended to embody the results of their research in large and detailed books— from which it would normally be very difficult to select, say, a chapter which would deal with a 'rounded' issue in a fairly concise and self-contained way.

The solution for this particular difficulty was something of an innovation: eight contributors were asked to provide essays of an appropriate length and unity, directly based upon the published company histories, but concentrating on specific themes, episodes, and periods. The result, it was hoped, would be to provide the narrative detail essential for a proper grasp of business history, but at the same time to highlight themes with a general relevance. This process involved cuts, rearrangements, and the rewriting of existing material. And, although it did not entail the provision of entirely original studies or of previously unknown information, there is a sense in which these essays *are* new products, to be assimilated at a different level from the substantial company histories which were their starting-point.

Once this decision had been taken, and been shown to be feasible, the question of the choice of case-studies was less forbidding. It was also made so by the prior decision to confine the scope of the collection to fairly modern British business history—essentially between the last quarter of the nineteenth century and the Second World War. This was partly a matter of avoiding a scope so great as to make it impossible for the individual essays to reinforce each other and provide some coherent pattern. But the restriction of period was also a function of the aim of the collection. The mode of business history chosen for major emphasis—the detailed treatment of individual companies— has been best exemplified in more modern studies; while the themes which are currently of greatest interest—organizational innovation and changing scale of operation, the role of markets and technology in the evolution of modern business, the influence of the state, etc.—were all best represented in company histories concerned with the modern period. It was also felt, again in the interest of coherence and because of the ready availability of appropriate material, that the chronological scope of the volume should end roughly with the Second World War. Professor Church's study of Kenricks takes the story down to 1950 for purposes of thematic continuity. The one large exception to the rule is Professor Barker's essay on the development of the Float glass process. This was considered to be a sufficiently rare example of a case-study of technological change from the inside to warrant inclusion. It is also the one case-study of an individual enterprise not drawn from an already published work.

As with all other fields of history, it is not possible (at least without considerable duplication) to divide material both chronologically and thematically: the same themes and problems recur again and again, albeit in different guises and patterns, in *all* periods of business history. Indeed, this is a marked characteristic of this volume precisely because we have chosen themes relating to pervasive aspects of business enterprise: its scale, structure, administration, technology, and marketing. On the other hand, to give at least a preliminary shape to the collection, the main essays have been divided into three sections, which obviously contain overlapping material. In the first part have been gathered together the four essays whose subject-matter is located squarely in in the period 1870–1914. As already emphasized, this is not because it was decided to give prime attention to the debate about the quality of British entrepreneurship at that time. It is true that the gathering-together of some actual case-studies may in part provide a firmer empirical framework for the easy generalizations which too often characterize that debate. But the main point is that the period does have something of a coherence, and its business history, although anticipating topics which were to be even more significant in the twentieth century, is interesting precisely because those topics first manifested themselves in their modern form during these years. The second part, which develops many of the same themes, is concerned with substantive aspects of British (private) business in the twentieth century, primarily in the inter-war period. The third part is concerned with aspects of the growing role of the state and the question of industrial relations in business matters. It is separated not because its contents are separable from private business activity —on the contrary—but as a reminder of their special, and rapidly growing, significance.

The compilation of a collection of this sort is, in one sense, a very unsatisfactory task: twelve case-studies can never represent an entire field of study; and the problem of deciding what to put in is soon overshadowed by the problem of deciding what to leave out. In the end, the striking feature is the number and importance of the unavoidable gaps in the topics covered. Thus with the exception of Chapter 4 on insurance, there is nothing on the direct sale of services to the consumer (even though services accounted for over 30 per cent of personal consumption by the 1890s); with the exception of Chapter 8 on Allied Suppliers, there is nothing on distribution; and, in effect, there is nothing on financial enterprise. All this will appear surprising and it is not entirely explained by the fact that much less work has been done on the history of services. But rather than spread material too thinly it was decided to deal more adequately than might otherwise have been possible with manufacturing industry. At another level, it is a matter for regret that space could be found for only one chapter explicitly concerned with smaller-scale enterprise, and one on industrial relations. The friendly, as well as critical, reader will also no doubt quickly note the absence or shortage of material on changes in commercial law and government policy; on profitability, investment, and productivity; on the rise of mass manufacturing; on mergers and monopolies; on the staples of Britain's long industrial history: cotton, wool, iron, steel, coal, shipbuilding, railways; and on a host of other aspects of business activity.

Yet all this is in the nature of the beast. Any collection of essays from such a broad and variegated field is bound to give only a partial view of it. Its aim is to be representative rather than comprehensive; stimulating rather than finally satisfying; an introduction rather than a conclusion.

NOTES

1 For other, more detailed, treatments of the historiography of business history, see Roy Church, 'Business History in Britain', *Journal of Euorpean Economic History*, v (1976); B. E. Supple, 'American Business History', *Business History*, i (1959); T. C. Barker *et al.*, *Business History* (London, 1971); P. L. Payne, 'Business History', in P. L. Payne (ed.), *Studies in Scottish Business History* (London, 1967).

2 J. A. Schumpeter, *The Theory of Economic Development* (Cambridge, Mass., 1934); *idem*, *Business Cycles* (New York, 1939).

3 See Supple, art. cit.

4 These include: P. G. M. Dickson, *The Sun Insurance Office, 1710–1960* (Oxford, 1960); W. G. Rimmer, *Marshalls of Leeds, Flax Spinners, 1788–1886* (Cambridge, 1960); T. C. Barker, *Pilkington Brothers and the Glass Industry* (London, 1960); R. H. Campbell, *Carron Company* (Edinburgh, 1961); A. E. Musson, *Enterprise in Soap and Chemicals, Joseph Crosfield & Sons Ltd., 1815–1965* (Manchester, 1965); Peter Mathias, *Retailing Revolution, A History of Multiple Retailing in the Food Trades based upon the Allied Suppliers Group of Companies* (London, 1967); D. C. Coleman, *Courtaulds: An Economic and Social History* (2 vols., Oxford, 1969); Roy Church, *Kenrick's in Hardware: A Family Business, 1791–1966* (Newton Abbot, 1969); W. J. Reader, *Imperial Chemical Industries: A History* (2 vols., Oxford, 1970, 1975); Barry Supple, *The Royal Exchange Assurance: A History of British Insurance, 1720–1970* (Cambridge, 1970); B. W. E. Alford, *W.D. & H.O. Wills and the Development of the U.K. Tobacco Industry, 1786–1965* (London, 1973).

5 By way of contrast it could be argued that the preoccupation of some historians with the possibly heroic role of the entrepreneur was a product of the concern—so characteristic of the 1940s and 1950s—with initiating growth and industrialization in relatively underdeveloped economies.

6 Examples of industrial histories are: G. C. Allen, *The Industrial Development of Birmingham and the Black Country* (London, 1929); T. S. Ashton, *Iron and Steel in the Industrial Revolution* (2nd edn., Manchester, 1951); S. J. Chapman, *The Lancashire Cotton Industry: A Study in Economic Development* (London, 1974); D. C. Coleman, *The British*

Paper Industry, 1495–1800 (Oxford, 1958); W. E. Minchinton, *The British Tinplate Industry: A History* (Oxford, 1957). Many of the company histories mentioned above are also concerned with the over-all development of the relevant industry.

7 In this respect, see Leslie Hannah, *The Rise of the Corporate Economy* (London, 1976), and the literature there cited.

8 Comparable themes are explored by Peter Mathias and Charles Wilson in essays in Harold F. Williamson (ed.), *Evolution of International Management Structures* (Newark, 1975).

9 See, e.g., P. L. Payne, *British Entrepreneurship in the Nineteenth Century* (London, 1974); D. H. Aldcroft, 'The Entrepreneur and the British Economy, 1870–1914', *Economic History Review*, 2nd Ser. xvii (1964); D. C. Coleman, 'Gentlemen and Players', *Economic History Review*, 2nd Ser. xxvi (1973); Donald M. McCloskey and Lars G. Sandberg, 'From Damnation to Redemption; Judgements on the Late Victorian Entrepreneur', *Explorations in Entrepreneural History*, ix (1971); Charles Wilson, 'Economy and Society in Late Victorian Britain', *Economic History Review*, 2nd Ser. xviii (1965); Donald M. McCloskey (ed.), *Economic Maturity and Entrepreneurial Decline: British Iron and Steel, 1870–1913* (Cambridge, Mass., 1973).

1

A Framework for
British Business History

BARRY SUPPLE

THIS chapter is designed to complement and link the case-studies which follow. However, it is cast at a much more general level, and does not purport to be a business history of the period. Its aim is not to 'summarize', let alone 'analyse', the evolution of British business, but to highlight the context within which it developed and to emphasize some of the central issues involved in an analysis which still has to find its author.

(A) ECONOMIC PERFORMANCE AND ECONOMIC STRUCTURE[1]

The starting-point for a study of business development must necessarily be the evolution of the economy—at once the basis and the outcome of business activity.

A popular and conventional image of Britain's economic performance over the last century or so is one of only intermittently relieved gloom: after the heroic period of the Indistrial Revolution and the presumed 'mid-Victorian boom' of the 1850s and 1860s, it is generally assumed that the economy suffered retardation, from about the 1870s, which was transmuted into the vicissitudes of the inter-war period and the uncompetitive vulnerability of the post-1945 era. Such a superficial picture is, of course, literally erroneous, even if its implications still have to be taken seriously as an indication of the 'shape' of Britain's modern economic development.

In fact, the available statistical data—even allowing for the ambiguities which invariably attach to the measurement of economic change—present a different historical pattern. The Industrial Revolution and the middle decades of the nineteenth century were characterized, in terms of cosmopolitan standards, by respectable rather than spectacular growth rates. Initially, total output increased by 2 to 3 per cent annually and *per capita* output by about 1 or $1\frac{1}{2}$ per cent. These rates rose slightly in the early Victorian period. Subsequently, there was undoubtedly a check to the progress of the British economy, but that check amounted to slower growth rather than to decline— and there is in any case considerable disagreement about its timing as well as its extent. Indeed, the controversy which surrounds the very concept of the 'climacteric' in the last quarter of the century (the idea of a genuine 'Great Depression' has long since been abandoned) is itself an indication that the putative slowing-down of the economy could hardly have been statistically very significant. Admittedly, prices and profits were under pressure, the rise of exports definitely slowed down, and in some industries productivity growth faltered. But the home market expanded, there were important developments in terms of the balance of production of goods and services, and foreign investment and the sale of services overseas boomed. Only with respect to the period from the 1890s to 1914 is there *general* agreement among historians that the economy had slowed down sufficiently to speak of a critical phase. And even so, after the First World War the peacetime growth performance, including the performance of the economy after 1945, was at least as good as, and in many respects better than, that of the classic period of 'rapid' industrialization in the nineteenth century, as is indicated in Table 1.1.

TABLE 1.1

Annual Percentage Rates of Growth, United Kingdom

	Real Gross Domestic Product	Gross Domestic Product per man-year of employment
1856–1899	2·0	1·1
1899–1913	1·1	0·1
1924–1937	2·3	1·1
1948–1962	2·2	1·9

Source: R. C. O. Matthews, 'Some Aspects of Post-War Growth in the British Economy in Relation to Historical Experience', *Transactions of the Manchester Statistical Society* (1964–5), reprinted in Derek H. Aldcroft and Peter Fearon (eds.), *Economic Growth in Twentieth Century Britain* (London, 1969).

The true statistical picture hardly matches the image of economic decline portrayed in some of the more pessimistic comments on Britain's economic (and business) history. Yet it also has to be said that the *relative* growth rate— relative to conscious aspirations as well as to the achievements of other economies—was disappointing. Certainly, other leading industrial nations, in all but the inter-war years, have generally tended to do better than Britain. And this is both the more obvious and the more serious in light of the fact that the British economy has been more dependent on world trade and, therefore, on explicit competitiveness. (On the eve of the First World War the export of domestic goods and services was equivalent to roughly one-third of gross domestic product.)

In any case, however, the idea that an economy's performance can be adequately indicated, or even accurately measured, by an over-all rate of growth of the output of goods and services, is intrinsically unsatisfactory. We should be at least equally interested in the direction and extent of changes in the *structure* of economic activity. Such changes—linking shifting patterns of consumption, output, and employment—are integral aspects of the process of economic maturity. Thus the proportion of personal consumption devoted to services rose from roughly 25 per cent in the 1870s to about 33 per cent in the 1890s, thenceforth remaining at more or less the same relative level, although the types of service demanded continued to change. On the side of production, the proportion of the national income derived from the various main sectors of economic activity changed most markedly in the late nineteenth century: between 1871 and 1901 the share in British national income of agriculture, forestry, and fishing fell from some 14 per cent to just over 6 per cent; while that of manufacturing, mining, and building rose slightly, from 38 to 40 per cent; and that of services went from about 48 to 54 per cent.[2] Aggregate changes in the twentieth century were somewhat less significant.

Clearly, during the entire period under consideration business was operating in a more or less 'mature' economy: an industrial society with a vast amount of its resources in the service, or tertiary, sector. Indeed, measured by such aggregative statistics, the extent of structural change appears less than might otherwise be supposed, even in the late nineteenth century. Yet, as often happens, aggregation is the enemy of accuracy. The foregoing data conceal very important alterations in the pattern of economic and business activity. At one level this has been reflected in extremely important shifts in the scale and organization of enterprise (below, section (C)). At another, structural change in the economy in the years after 1870 in response to alterations in income, technology, and taste involved substantial changes in the 'mix' *within* the service and manufacturing sectors: the growth of financial and commercial services in the late nineteenth century; the decline of domestic and the rise of government services in the twentieth; the growing importance of the manufacture of vehicles, electrical and electronic equipment, chemical products, and artificial fibres and materials; the varied satisfaction of the growing demand for goods and services in leisure activities; the relative decline of such 'staples' of industrialization as coal, cotton, wool, heavy engineering, and shipbuilding.

It should, however, be remembered that for much of the period the economic structure was so complex that we are in fact dealing with large changes in relatively small percentages. Thus the rapid decline in the proportionate significance of textiles and clothing entailed a fall from about 8 per cent of the national income in 1907 to just under 6 per cent in 1935; and the doubling of the importance of chemicals meant a rise from 1·1 to 2·1 per cent in the same period. Indeed, the over-all economic structure changed relatively little in the first decades of the twentieth century: it was only in the next generation that the most dramatic shifts took place.[3]

(B) ECONOMIC PERFORMANCE AND BUSINESS ENTERPRISE

In spite of the growth and structural changes which have taken place over the last century, it is often assumed that the achievement of the economy in both respects has been seriously deficient. As a result, the questions of whether, and how far, the responsibility lay with the business man have been widely canvassed, particularly with respect to the late nineteenth century. Lack of enterprise, misplaced investments, technological naïvety, complacency about marketing, the 'irrational' pursuit of non-economic ends—all, and more, have been attributed to British business.

Although it is not the intention here to enter into a substantive discussion of these issues, it is important to emphasize that the quest for an understanding of the precise causal relationship between business activity and economic growth is fraught with methodological difficulties. One reason lies in the fact that the growth of output and of productivity are indications both of economic efficiency *and* of the demand for the products of enterprise. Hence the 'poor' performance of a particular industry or firm *may* be attributable to inadequacies on the side of supply (among which entrepreneurial failings are one —but only one—possibility). But it can also derive from an 'exogenous' cause —namely the slow rate of growth of the market. Thus it has been argued that the relatively slow development of the British steel industry in the late nineteenth century derived from the fact that it 'had access to a market for steel that was growing less rapidly than those served by its competitors' (Germany and the United States), with the result that its rate of growth was less, its capital investment slower, and its equipment older and less productive.[4] Yet even here there is a strong possibility of circular argument, whatever side one takes, because the expansion of the market for a product can itself be a function of changes in productivity and, *inter alia*, of the acumen of entrepreneurs. Nevertheless, it is significant that, in the case-studies which follow, there is a distinct tendency to emphasize 'objective' factors relating to the size and nature of markets, or the availability of advanced techniques, rather than the autonomous potential of entrepreneurship. This is particularly so in the studies of mechanical engineering, insurance, the tobacco industry, and the motor industry. And even where, as in the case of Professor Coleman's study of rayon, business success is primarily associated with 'enterprise, opportunism, and luck', the context for that success is held to lie in 'markets' rather than 'chemistry'.

It is also important to note another and similar conceptual problem concerning the relationship between entrepreneurial and macroeconomic performance. This involves the specification of what is *meant* by a 'poor' performance—of the economy, an industry, a firm, or a business man. It is certainly not sufficient to identify a 'low' rate of growth of output or productivity. As we have seen, for example, at the level of economy, a low growth rate in relation to other countries may be a high one in relation to the economy's own history. Within an industry, a rate of growth, of (say) productivity, which is low relative to the same industry in other countries may merely reflect the prior attainment of a higher absolute level of efficiency. It has been argued that this was the case with the British iron and steel industry in the late nineteenth century.[5] More pertinently, it is not easy to attribute responsibility to business, merely because technology was less sophisticated, or the rate of growth slower, or productivity less than in enterprises elsewhere (at home or abroad). Rather it would be necessary to show that available technology, existing resources, realistically attainable market prospects, etc. all provided opportunities for faster growth or higher productivity *which were systematically neglected*. Business men are only to be judged feeble business men when they fail to do things which successful business men might reasonably be expected to do in the same circumstances. Hence it may well be that in the late nineteenth century Germany and the United States enjoyed faster growth rates in some newer industries (for example, heavy electrical engineering, new steel products, organic chemicals, artificial dyes), while Britain lagged in these sectors and remained relatively more dependent on older industries such as textiles, shipbuilding, coal, or on the less sophisticated segments of growth industries (cables and telegraphic equipment, rails and pig iron, traditional acids and alkalis). But to 'prove' business sloth even *within* these so-called neglected sectors—i.e. ignoring the instances of substantial growth and profit in service and some consumer goods industries[6]—we should really have to show that the neglect was a neglect of profits and productivity; that the business man would have been better off by doing things differently or doing different things.

But in order to demonstrate, or disprove, that this was the case it is necessary to do more than to deduce from a combination of the performance of the economy and contemporary complaints that business enterprise was somehow lacking. Instead, one of two related lines of argument are necessary. The first alternative is to adopt the methods of counterfactual history—deriving aggregate measures of productivity and profitability and comparing them with equivalent, hypothetical measures which 'should' have obtained if business men *had* used the 'superior' methods or adopted the 'better' pattern of activity posited by their critics. This is obviously a daunting prospect. But such research as has been done suggests that the answer to the charge of entrepreneurial 'irrationality' is not yet proved. And leading proponents of this method have argued that work undertaken has been 'damaging to the hypothesis of entrepreneurial failure, rejecting repeatedly the presumption of missed opportunities underlying the hypothesis'.[7]

The second method of genuinely appraising the hypothesis of entrepreneurial failure is allied to the first. It is to investigate, in detail, specific instances of business operations. To study individual firms or groups of firms, and to attempt to understand their functioning, is in one sense a more microscopic and, potentially, a less rigorous analytical task. Yet, as an approach it has analogies with counterfactual or hypothetical enterprise in that it attempts to answer the question 'How well did business men perform?' by looking at what they actually did and considering the alternatives. Thus Professor Saul, in his study of the mechanical engineering industry (Chapter 2), redresses the balance of views on entrepreneurship by emphasizing the technical and commercial success of British business and acknowledging the effective market constraints on technical and organizational progress in the period before 1914. On the other side, Professor Church's examination of the history of Kenricks (Chapter 6) exemplifies the inhibition of entrepreneurial conservatism in a close-knit family firm. At another level, studies of outstanding business frequently emphasize the entrepreneurial factor—for example, in the case of Courtaulds and rayon (Chapter 5) or the development of Float glass (Chapter 10). Yet this is not always the case. Dr. Alford, for example, concludes his study of Wills' growth in the tobacco industry (Chapter 3) on a note which places market, technological, and institutional factors in the forefront of the explanation of success, while not denying the importance of the skills which could take advantage of them. Of course, the very individuality of case-studies means that we can know relatively little about their representativeness: the literature of entrepreneurial performance in 1870–1914 is littered with examples and counter-examples. Yet any exploration of the actual processes which comprise business policies and structures cannot fail to shed light on a debate about the dynamics of economic growth or decline. And the scope of many case-studies is often sufficient to create a legitimate basis for generalization.

Of course, it could be argued that individual British business men were behaving perfectly 'rationally' in the late nineteenth century—maximizing profits and adjusting with smooth effectiveness to the spur of the market— but that the successful pursuit of private gain was inimical to the maximizing of a *social* return. So far the only version of this argument to be widely accepted is the one which holds that British business men were too slow to adapt staple industries, too half-hearted in the expansion of chemical, electrical, and vehicle industries, too content with good profits and neglectful of the long-run competitive future, too reliant on overseas investment and the international sale of services. Yet the view that it may have been profitable to avoid a radical restructuring of the economy, but that it was ultimately weakening, may not tell us very much about the quality of business decisions and attitudes. After all, even though Britain's reliance on staple industries and overseas investment proved inappropriate later on in the twentieth century, this was by no means obvious in 1870–1914. And just as it is no part of the individual business man's role to anticipate unpredictable developments, so it would hardly have been 'natural' for him to forgo opportunities of substantially profitable enterprise in the production of textiles, shipbuilding, and coal at a time when he could do these things supremely well—and profitably. Nor for that matter would it have been 'rational' to ignore the potential of overseas investment which led to the accumulation of over £4,000 m. of capital outside the domestic economy by 1914, and to an income equivalent to one-third of the value of commodity exports.

In any case, depending on one's focus of attention, the presumed evidence of 'lack of adaptability' in the British economy is still a matter of dispute. Within the critical period of the late nineteenth century, for example, there is very extensive evidence of structural flexibility: the rise of large-scale units in food-processing and the manufacture of inexpensive household goods; the transformation of retailing through grocery chains like Liptons, chemists like Boots, newsagents and booksellers like Smiths; the creation of entertainment and leisure industries; the worldwide success of British financial institutions (between 1870 and 1913 while national product rose by about 150 per cent the real output of insurance and banking and the financial sector increased eleven-fold)[8]. Even at the level of manufacturing industry (and there were equally striking changes in the supply of services) the change was strongly evident, and are exemplified here in Chapters 3 and 5. As Professor Wilson has written in his well-known vigorous defence of the late-Victorian economy:

Increasingly, therefore, in a more diversified and variegated economy, the industrial-commercial revolution rolled on. The years of the 'Great Depression' saw great volumes of goods previously supplied (if supplied at all) from craftsmen of village or town move into the factory stage of production. From machine to shop there flowed the branded, packaged, standardized, advertised products newly characteristic of the urbanised, industrialised society that was setting itself new patterns and standards of social life.[9]

That British business endeavour was more 'appropriate' for the pre-1914 economy and its market structures than it is sometimes given the credit for, is at least rendered the more likely by the course of events when the First World War and its aftermath effectively transformed the realities of the country's economic situation. Admittedly, from many viewpoints the inter-war period was a gloomy and disturbed era. Yet, as we have seen, in terms of over-all growth rates the economy's performance was far from negligible. Even more significant, there was a notable advance in the effort devoted, and the return to research and development, while the continued development of the home market was associated with impressive expansion in 'old' as well as 'new' industries (the latter including motor cars, radios, and domestic appliances, electricity and electrical equipment, and new fabrics).[10] If British entrepreneurs were responsible for Britain's lack of industrial adaptation before 1914, they made a surprisingly rapid improvement in subsequent years!

Having made these points, however, we should be careful not to leap to the immediate conclusion that the more sprightly performance of the economy in the inter-war period, or the rapidity of its structural change, were necessarily 'caused' by able entrepreneurship—any more than it would be reasonable to assume that because growth or adaptation were slower before 1914, business must have been at fault. This *may* have been so, but if we are attempting to

assess the influence of business skills on the over-all performance of the
economy it is a mere tautology to *assume* that the measure of those skills is the
level of that performance. The business history of changes in economic output
and structures cannot be confined to questions of entrepreneurial ability. It
should, ideally, embrace a host of other factors on the side of supply: the
availability of natural resources, for example, or the quality of labour skills, or
technical knowledge, the access to capital, the nature of social institutions,
government policies, etc. Moreover, even consideration of the circumstances
which directly control the ease and cost of production and distribution
is not enough. We must also take account of the role of changes in
the level and pattern of demand throughout the period covered by this
collection.

The relation between demand and supply raises similar methodological
problems to those raised by the relationship between business activity and
economic performance. Thus changes in demand are of course themselves
influenced by business decisions and policy: by advertising, innovation,
greater efficiency, competition, and the like. And in the last resort the growth
of the market can be seen as the consequence of economic expansion and
aggregate production. Yet demand is also shaped by changes in purchasing
power, income distribution, and tastes and consumer habits which are not
directly the outcome of business activity—which, indeed, transform the
opportunities for business activity. Thus in the period under consideration
there were significant increases in private disposable income brought about
not only by growing production and productivity, but also by a fall in the
price of imports, particularly food. This happened in the last quarter of the
nineteenth century and for much of the inter-war period. At the same time,
there was a long-run tendency (itself no doubt influenced by changes in
economic and business structures) to increase the proportion of the national
income going to wages and salaries: this was about 45 per cent in the 1860s,
47 per cent in 1910–14, and 59 per cent in 1935–8.[11] (The share of salaries increased particularly rapidly: from 6·5 to 10·8 to 17·9 per cent.[12]) Both these
trends in distribution were underpinned by the over-all growth in national income: aggregate consumers' expenditure rose, in real terms, from just under
£1,000 m. annually in the early 1870s to some £1,850 m. on the eve of the
First World War, and by a further 25 per cent in the next twenty-five years;
per capita increases in consumption for the same periods were 40 and 20 per
cent respectively.[13] And the obvious result was that more consumers had a
greater amount of purchasing power above that needed for essential or conventional consumption. Taken together with shifts in consumer tastes, these
increases helped shape a new context for business enterprise.

In the late nineteenth century such changes in income created new demand
for packaged and processed foods, for simple consumer goods and services
just above the level of bare necessity, for greater convenience in distribution

and transport, and for the services and goods associated with leisure-time activities. They thereby established the basis for business expansion and innovation in such fields as multiple retailing in food, clothing, and the sale of tobacco and newspapers; in biscuits and confectionery; in the manufacture of soap and clothing; in entertainment, sport, and journalism; insurance and public transport; gas lighting; etc. All this was perhaps most striking among moderately well-paid wage-earners and the lower middle classes (rather than among those at the bottom end of the scale of contemporary income distribution). At a different, perhaps overlapping, level of income, there was an analogous growth in the demand for ordinary goods and services in a more sophisticated, mass-produced, or commercialized form. In addition, the wealth of the middle classes helped establish the beginnings of the large-scale purchase of what we have come to call consumer durable goods—bicycles, stoves, sewing-machines, pianos, and even, by the opening years of this century, motor cycles and motor cars.

It is, of course, for this reason that the more spectacular, or at least notable, examples of business success in the period 1870–1914 are drawn from the new or newly important sectors supplying consumer goods and services: Lever Brothers, Boots, Liptons, Home and Colonial Stores, Rowntrees, Cadbury, Harmsworth, Rothermere, the Prudential Assurance, and so forth. And certainly it was in such fields that the possibility of business growth from scratch was the greatest. Yet, as some of their names imply, the 'new' consumer markets of the late nineteenth century were in part the consequence of the evolution of already existing staple industries—as was the case with the demand for tobacco, for example (below, Chapter 3), or insurance (Chapter 4), or textiles (Chapter 5). Moreover, while our attention is naturally caught by the novel and the heroic, it should not be completely distracted from those large areas of business activity in traditional fields—engineering, shipbuilding, cotton and woollens, coal-mining—which were still, collectively, much more important.

Nevertheless, a new shape of business activity was beginning to emerge. And the trends in income and expenditure which had helped to form it in the two generations before 1914 continued to operate through the otherwise troubled decades between the world wars. Indeed, by the 1930s the growth in demand—at least from those who were fortunate enough to remain in employment—for chemical products, electricity, radios, household equipment, motor cars, petrol, the cinema, professional sport, rayon, and the like, had given a familiar appearance to an important part of the business scene. This was so even though it is easy to exaggerate both the relative significance and the distinctive growth rates of the 'new' industries: the two fastest-growing industries between the wars were electrical engineering and vehicles; but prominent in the next rank were timber and furniture, food and tobacco;[14] and 19 out of the 50 largest companies in 1930 were engaged in the 'traditional' food, drink, and tobacco industries[15]—although the first of these, at least, frequently involved the sale of novel products in novel ways.

In any case, with respect to both 'old' and 'new' industries we are here beginning to encounter that slightly ambigious concept, the rise of the mass market: a nationwide demand, quickly responsive to changes in price or income, for more-or-less standardized consumer goods and services above the level of mere necessities. (The nature of such commodities—the degree of fabrication or sophistication involved in their production or sale—also entails an elaborate development of the capital or intermediate-good industries needed to sustain their production.) At the same time, extensions in the demand for services engender, *pari passu*, similar changes in their market situation. It is of course true that the trends towards this form of mass consumption came later, slower, and less decisively in the United Kingdom than in the United States. And it is at least worth considering whether the combination of a smaller absolute market and an apparently greater differentiation of taste and demand in Britain so reduced the market for standardized products as to inhibit the evolution of mass consumption and mass production.[16] But, reasonable as such an hypothesis seems, it is still based on a *relative* judgement. Once the comparison with the American market is dropped, one can speak with greater confidence of an enormously significant qualitative change in the pattern and extent of the British consumer market from the late nineteenth century.

The importance of all this for business history lies in the fact that the development of a mass market is not independent of business activity. Firms soon adapt not only to its existence, but to its potential for further development. Mass markets (like any other sort) are created as well as discovered—or, rather, they simultaneously shape and are shaped by business policies and structures.

These themes are well illustrated in the various case-studies in this volume. The new mass markets for tobacco, insurance, rayon, soap, groceries, and motor vehicles moulded the structure and success of businesses in those industries. But the hallmark of success was also an ability to devote attention to marketing and distribution, to the implications of a national or international demand, to the technological aspects of low costs and high volumes, and to the forging of direct links with consumers through branding, advertising, packaging, and so on. To be denied a mass, standardized market (as was the fate of some sectors of the mechanical engineering industry: Chapter 2) or to resist its possibilities (as did Kenricks in hardware: Chapter 6) was to be distinctly less successful as success is normally measured in the cosmopolitan world of business.

At the same time, the lessons of business history occasionally point in a direction at once more subtle and more realistic than the popular vision of universal mass markets for standardized, cheap products. Admittedly, that is sometimes the most appropriate perspective: Courtaulds' marketing of rayon, of which it had an effective monopoly, as an inexpensive substitute for, rather than a quality version of, silk was an important element in its huge financial success; while Wills' 'discovery' of the penny cigarette and its effective use of branding as well as modern technology and distribution structures created a virtual prototype of a mass-production firm. Collaterally, the development of the national grid by the Central Electricity Board (Chapter 11) was an excellent example of the structural implications of technology designed to satisfy a standardized national market. Yet some of the essays also remind us that even large markets could be highly structured (for example, Chapters 2 and 3), and that even in such a 'typical' modern industry as motor manufacturing the role of the economies of scale may have been less important than is imagined. Thus Professor Church and Dr. Miller argue (Chapter 9) that whereas Fords were relatively unsuccessful in the inter-war pursuit of a low-price, high-volume, standardized market for cars, other companies better appreciated the importance, as far as the British market was concerned, of mixing design with price-competition, and of adapting policy to the pattern and outlook of their consumers.

It was naturally easier to do this at home than abroad. And such considerations are possibly related to the importance of the domestic scene in the history of Britain's business successes in the period. There were, of course, exceptions such as the supply of financial and shipping services, or the boom in the sales of rayon in the United States with patent protection, or shipbuilding in the late nineteenth century (it is interesting to note how few of these sold directly to the final consumer). But the outstanding examples of successful enterprise catered heavily for the growing domestic market for consumer goods and services. Certainly, Britain's relatively poor export performance indicated either a lower sensitivity to overseas demand or an inability to compete—and was in either case associated with less sophisticated or market-orientated business.

Finally, we cannot leave the question of the quality of British enterprise without commenting on technology. As various chapters suggest, technical innovation and quality were present throughout the period. And there is an abundance of literature on the successes of British technical innovation—more than matched by an abundance of complaints about a widespread inability to apply its results. This may be so, but it is a marked feature of some of these essays that advanced production techniques are seen as logically indispensable, but nevertheless secondary, to commercial and organizational considerations (for example, in Chapters 3, 5, and 9). Moreover, and more curiously, in some important instances—cigarettes, rayon, motor vehicles, electricity generation—the successful adoption of a technique was essentially a derivative process. Indeed, at times, as Dr. Hannah points out in Chapter 11, the process reverses the conventional picture: Britain is the technical late-comer, benefiting from the process of catching up other industrial societies.

(C) BUSINESS AND THE CORPORATE ECONOMY:
SCALE, STRUCTURE, ORGANIZATION

The growth of a national market in Britain, as in every other industrialized economy, set the scene for the dominance of the large-scale company as a unit of production and a form of business organization. This was so, even though the scale and success of such firms as Lever Brothers, I.C.I., Courtaulds, Commercial Union Assurance, and Dunlop Rubber necessarily entailed a multinational spread of operations. Of course, the complexity and proliferation of economic activity have continued to spawn varied opportunities for small-scale businesses to provide specialized goods and services, either directly to the consumer or to other firms. But the long-run structural trend, although by no means smooth, has been decisively clear. In manufacturing industry, for example, the share of the largest 100 firms in total net output rose from 16 per cent in 1909 to 24 per cent in 1935, sagged slightly for the next two decades, and then increased sharply to 42 per cent in 1970.[17] In distribution, large-scale enterprise has also been conspicuously successful: co-operatives, department stores, and multiple shops increased their share of total retail trade from 10 to 13 per cent in 1900 to 33 to 39 per cent in 1950.[18] And in finance and insurance the trend to concentration was even more rapid: the 121 English joint stock banks of 1880 were reduced by amalgamations to 43 in 1913, and by 1920 to a handful, of which the leading 5 were absolutely dominant; and in insurance the most rapid concentration came in the late nineteenth century (Chapter 4): on the eve of the First World War the 12 largest companies in life and in fire insurance controlled just over 50 per cent and 80 per cent of the relevant business.

As the following case-studies suggest, the specific factors responsible for this trend to large-scale enterprise have varied markedly. The economies of scale in their conventional sense—the unit-cost reductions derived from large accumulations of capital equipment, advanced and expensive technology, specialization of function, bulk purchasing and distribution—played an obvious part. And the importance of the positive attainment of economies, particularly in the twentieth-century growth of big business, in such industries as chemicals, engineering, motor cars, food-processing and drink, tobacco manufacture, transport, and financial services, needs little emphasis. At the same time, however, the emergence of the giant firm was also a function of financial considerations (stock-market buoyancies in particular increased the probability, and profitability, of mergers and floatation) and of market vicissitudes and ambitions. The desire to protect investments and market shares, the ambition to secure market control and stability of sales, the pressure to mitigate competition and to expand sales and profit margins—all illustrate the range, from defensive to offensive, of policies involved, as well as the over-all importance of market strategies in the history of large-scale enterprise. And, in the event, many of the most spectacular instances of big business (with Courtaulds, Lever Brothers, Austin, Morris) rested as much on product differentiation as on 'pure' cost advantages.[19]

The influence of the market also helps to explain why increases in the scale of enterprise and degree of business concentration have tended to take place as the result of merger and acquisition. There were, of course, exceptions: W. H. Smith, Boots, Dunlop, and Morris Motors are among the firms to have grown predominantly by 'internal' expansion. But amalgamation was by far the quickest and most effective way of attaining marketing objectives: eliminating surplus capacity and 'excessive' competition, rationalizing output, meeting foreign competition or adapting to a change in demand, extending a product range or attaining greater geographical coverage. Indeed, it was the diverse nature of such commercial considerations, as well as the multiplicity of other causes, which is relevant to the fact that merger activity was unevenly distributed over time.

As has already been implied, the first substantial merger boom in British business history occurred in the late nineteenth and early twentieth centuries. The transformation of the structure of banking and insurance came about essentially through amalgamations. In manufacturing industry in the period 1888–1914 almost seventy firms on average disappeared in mergers each year.[20] The large firms which resulted from the most important amalgamations tended to be in the older, traditional industries: textiles, brewing, tobacco, cement, sugar, and the conventional sectors of the chemical industry. Moreover, in many of these instances the dominant motive was frequently to defend a market position or to eliminate competive instability: of the 52 largest companies in 1905, nine were in textiles (where problems of surplus capacity generated a far from expansive outlook) and 18 were in brewing (as brewers sought to defend their market position by forward integration into tied houses).[21] It is indeed significant as well as symptomatic that many of the pre-1914 mergers were little more than cartel-like federations of (frequently family) firms, which then made little if any effort to promote an integrated business policy or unify their operations.[22] On the other hand, amalgamation also exemplified a more 'positive' policy, with dominant partners taking the lead in response to heightened opportunity as well as competition. It is significant that in at least two industries—life insurance and tobacco (Chapters 3 and 4)—a threatened American business 'invasion' played an important part. At another level, however, it was obviously possible to grow in a more coherent fashion and by other means: the Royal Exchange Assurance expanded without any significant acquisitions, and William Lever built up Lever Brothers without the help of mergers until 1906—although in each case continued growth necessitated mergers at a later stage.

Before 1914 firms in the new industries—motor cars and electrical engineering, for example—where size was ultimately to be associated with vigorous growth, mass production, and a more novel technology, were not yet large by national standards. The inter-war story assumed a different shape. Throughout the 1920s there was a powerful merger movement, the high spots of which were the creation of I.C.I. (Brunner, Mond, Nobel Industries, British Dyestuffs, and United Alkali) in 1926 and of Unilever (Lever Brothers and the Margarine Union) in 1929. Amalgamations, together with the 'internal' expansion of firms, raised the share of manufacturing output of the top 100 firms from about 17 per cent to some 26 per cent (the degree of concentration lessened slightly in the subsequent two decades). And by now concentration was particularly marked in such new industries as non-ferrous metals, rayon, margarine, dyestuffs, petroleum, and rubber tyres, as well as in the manufacture of more traditional products in iron and steel, explosives, matches, soap, and sugar. Indeed, perhaps the most important point of categorization is that those industries which grew rapidly also showed a high degree of concentration. Hence, although in 1930 most of the 50 largest firms, in terms of capitalization, were in traditional sectors (19 were in the food, drink, or tobacco industries), the advance of firms in motor vehicles, electrical engineering, newer chemicals, rayon, etc. had been perhaps even more striking. Moreover, and related to this point, while much of the inter-war attitude to mergers and 'rationalization' was determined by caution in the face of competition and shrinking or unstable markets, the most vigorous and successful examples of amalgamation and growth contrasted with many of the late-nineteenth-century examples, in so far as they were based on diversification of product range and/or integration of process and function.

Consistent with the more 'progressive' character, the larger business units of the inter-war period also attained more formal economies of large-scale production: advanced production engineering, the systematic use of resources in research and development, internal specialization. But the influence of the market and marketing remained powerful even when, as often happened, it was intermingled with other factors. Thus I.C.I., which was a firm based on science and technology which greatly expanded its research effort, was formed in large part as a defensive alliance of enterprises to counter the market influence of the newly formed I.G. Farbenindustrie; and marketing problems rather than technical economies shaped the outcome of investment decisions such as the expansion of its Billingham plant (Chapter 12). Even more striking was the extent to which motor-car manufacturers such as Morris attained a degree of mass production by innovations in marketing as well as in manufacturing techniques (Chapter 9). On a broader front, large-scale enterprise was generally dependent on the securing of advantages in the costs and effectiveness and marketing and distribution. And these skills not only served to expand business activity in terms of a single product line, but facilitated diversification as the relevant skills were transferred. Thus Unilever was created to secure, among other things, the effective co-ordination of raw material purchasing. Yet the associated integration of activities in the fields of fats, oils, soap, and margarine also led to expansion into other foods and proprietary products. Moreover, through its subsidiary, Allied Suppliers, and under the pressure of competition in margarine, Unilever came to control a substantial network of grocery shops (Chapter 8).

The growth of large-scale corporate enterprise has had a number of important implications and consequences. The enormous increase in capital requirements was among the more obvious of these and in the long run, in terms of business control and policy, it ultimately produced that division between ownership and control which is generally supposed to distinguish the capitalist structure of modern industrial society. Yet in the earlier part of our period, even though the high capitalization of new amalgamation often necessitated a wider diffusion of share-ownership, the result was not always a disruption of family control, let alone the immediate creation of a new class of professional managers. Thus, from the case-studies published here, one can cite Wills, Courtaulds, Lever Brothers, Morris Motors, and Pilkington as firms in which personal or family control continued for many years. And Dr. Hannah has pointed out that before 1914 the three largest British companies —J. & P. Coats in cotton, Imperial Tobacco, and Watney Combe Reid in brewing—'were not built up around a new corporate management at all, but around old family firms with their senior management and directors recruited principally from among the founding families'.[23] Certainly compared with the United States, big business in Britain was for much longer distinguished by the dominant presence of family managers.[24] This could work to the disadvantage of the firm where the family influence was conservative and resistant to change or growth (this happened at Kenricks: Chapter 6); but elsewhere close family ownership was associated with rapid and very profitable expansion. Indeed, some of the most successful of the large British enterprises —Boots, Lever Brothers, Morris Motors, Austin, for example—were dominated by their owner-founders long after they had attained spectacular national status. Yet the fact remained that not merely size but also administrative complexity inexorably shaped a new managerial style. The professional executive (often with a stake in the business, but rarely a very important one), sometimes alone, but increasingly in teams, came to assume control of business institutions. These developments occurred early in the railways and in banking and insurance, somewhat later in many manufacturing industries. Even such a giant as William Lever had to succumb in the early 1920s (Chapter 7) while in the 1940s William Morris's personal influence gave way to that of a now more orthodox organizational team. But already, and certainly for most of the inter-war period, the higher reaches of British business were peopled by managers rather than owners, administrators rather than entrepreneurs. And the basis of success was often a willingness to allow inherited hierarchy to give way to specialists and systematic administration, Of course, 'personalities' still abounded. Indeed, the centralization which accompanied enhanced professionalism often gave a more, rather than a less, striking role to the powerful and dramatic personalities (as happened early on with General Managers in insurance: Chapter 4). Nevertheless, the institutional constraints upon them were growing in intensity and effectiveness.

As already implied, the twin evolution from family to profession and from individual to collective in the management of British business had its parallel in terms of the basic institutional structure. For the emergence of a managerial class is obviously a function of the introduction of formal bureaucratic structures into business enterprise. Hence the continuity of 'non-professional' management in many of the large firms of pre-1914 Britain was closely related —as cause as well as effect—with their loose organization. Sometimes this was because the dominant influence of the entrepreneur—William Lever or Jesse Boot or Thomas Lipton—centralized decisions and precluded the need for formal structures. More often, and particularly in many of the merged firms in manufacturing industry, it reflected a conservative attitude to size and competition: being responses to price-cutting on the part of groups with strongly entrenched interests, the mergers did not always make any effective moves to tackle the question of surplus capacity and, even more significantly, rarely made any decisive attempt to streamline and integrate their organization. (In the case of the 4 largest textile combines in 1898–1900, the *average* number of Directors drawn from the constituent firms was 41.[25] In such instances the defensive search for size was rarely matched by the development of new strategies or structures within the new firm. In contrast to the contemporaneous growth of big business in the United States, centralization and functional departments had to wait for a later period.[26]

The continued growth in the scale of enterprise after the First World War led to a greater degree of centralization and, in the case of firms which had been dominated by entrepreneurial individuals or families, a more systematic *structure* of policy-making. Once again, British business lagged behind the U.S.A. in terms of organizational enterprise. But some at least of the elements of a centralized and functionally departmentalized structure, with systematized techniques of control and separate division for different products, which Professor Chandler has identified as the type of modern corporate organization, began to make their appearance in such firms as Dunlop Rubber, Brunner Mond, Boots, Courtaulds, Maypole Dairies, Bowater Paper, Morris, Nobel Industries, Vickers.[27] As was only appropriate, however, the only two industrial companies which in the 1930s and early 1940s developed 'a multidivisional structure comparable to that set up by General Motors and Du Pont after World War I' were the two largest: I.C.I. and Unilever.[28] I.C.I.

looked specifically to the American experience and created distinct quasi-autonomous product 'groups', controlled by a strong central general executive using sophisticated budgeting, forecasting, and performance measurements. Unilever's adaptation to 'managerial enterprise' had begun in Lever Brothers, before its merger into Unilever—indeed, even before its founder had died (1925) and was replaced by the man who had already begun to reform the control and operation of its subsidies: Francis D'Arcy Cooper. His advent, in Professor Wilson's words, 'signified nothing less than the complete metamorphosis of Lever Brothers from a private empire owned and controlled by one man into a public company administered by a professional management'. From then on the process of centralization and rationalization accelerated.[29]

The general significance of these developments for one's perception of British business history naturally depends on the perspective used. Advance and change in the structure as well as the scale of enterprise in the inter-war period no doubt marked a considerable improvement on the looser, perhaps more complacent, bases of corporate enterprise in the manufacturing industry of late-nineteenth-century Britain. And certainly they appeared to be associated with more decisive developments in the 'modernization' of the economy's pattern of output. Yet from the viewpoint of American business the sophistication of British practice and structure was still fairly low.[30] Moreover, the achievement both of distinctive improvements in productivity and of managerial systematization was unevenly spread among the different industries and sectors of the economy. Some of the most rapidly growing industries also exemplified the most decisive organizational changes—but it is not always clear which way the causal relationship ran. Indeed, although there are strong indications that the larger scale of operations involved facilitated the attainment of internal economies and greater productivity, there are still ambiguities about the balance-sheet of giant enterprise. In part, these arise from the possibility that the potentialities of the new scale of operation, in terms of structural and decision-making reforms, were not fully realized. But they also stem from the likelihood that the higher degree of market control or monopoly entailed generated high social costs. Analogously, it is at least possible that larger units of production might outrun the managerial skills of those in charge, while there must be some question of the effectiveness with which managerial decision can replace the market as a means of allocating resources —which inevitably happens as individual enterprises grow larger.[31] In the last resort, however, difficult as it is to measure the costs and benefits of large, corporate enterprises, the supposition must be that their contribution to sustaining output and productivity growth have been considerable.

The trend towards large-scale enterprise and the associated erosion of 'pure' market forces were not merely reflected in the appearance of huge private corporations. Indeed, the very concept of a 'corporate economy' has much more general implications than this: parallel to the growth of big business

Barry Supple

came the growth of 'big government'. As the example of I.C.I. shows (Chapter 12), this was partly because the sheer size pf modern companies has given them a strategic economic role: and in the case of I.C.I. this role in a period of high unemployment was reinforced by its importance in terms of defence strategy in the late 1930s and early 1940s. In the case of Anglo-Iranian Oil Company, strategic considerations led to a large government investment. Yet this need for the state to support as well as control did not derive solely from the vicissitudes or power of private enterprise. It was also related to the dynamics of modern economies, in which the social (i.e. often generalized economic) return to certain activities inexorably attracts the attention of the sovereign power. This happened with the building of the national grid in the late 1920s and 1930s (Chapter 11), when the 'externalities' to a unified system of providing cheap electricity could not be neglected, and led to the creation of a public corporation. It was also exemplified with the London Passenger Transport Board, the BBC, and overseas airline operations. The characteristics of industrial and social maturity, as well as the evolution of political pressures, have increasingly involved the state in direct economic activity and in a multiplicity of forms of economic control and guidance. Only the spectacular pace of this development since 1940 has obscured its operations in the inter-war period. The corporate economy was, inevitably, a mixed economy.

The final essay in this collection (Chapter 13) concerns an aspect of the corporate economy which has possibly loomed as large as the economic role of the state in the last generation. Dr. Garside here considers aspects of the inter-war history of industrial relations. And even though, as he rightly laments, available sources make it impossible to generalize about important areas (for example, industrial relations at the level of the firm or many of the newer and more prosperous industries), his essay emphasizes the extent to which, in modern societies, industrial relations have been conducted at the level of the industry or the economy. It also shows the complexity of the relationship between the economic position of an industry and the harmony or disharmony which characterized it. This symbiotic link between context and object, between action and environment, is, indeed, a fitting reminder of all those other areas in which what business men *do* and the 'objective reality' with which they are faced and which they help to create, are indissolubly related in a reciprocal, fascinating, and frequently inexplicable way.

NOTES

1 Some parts of this section are derived from material in Barry Supple, 'Aspects of Private Investment Strategy in Britain', in Herman Daems and Herman van der Wee (eds.), *The Rise of Managerial Capitalism* (The Hague, 1974), pp. 73–95.

2 Phyllis Deane and W. A. Cole, *British Economic Growth, 1688–1959* (Cambridge, 1962), p. 166.

3 Ibid., p. 299. Among the most significant structural changes involved were the following:

	Percentage shares in national income		
	G.B.	U.K.	U.K.
	1907	1935	1955
Engineering and metal manufacturing	8·2	9·4	19·5
Government and defence	3·0	4·7	9·4
Domestic service	3·8	3·4	0·6

4 P. Temin, 'The Relative Decline of the British Steel Industry, 1880–1913', in Henry Rosovsky (ed.), *Industrialization in Two Systems: Essays in Honor of Alexander Gerschenkron* (New York, 1966), p. 142. Cf. Donald N. McCloskey, *Economic Maturity and Entrepreneurial Decline: British Iron and Steel, 1870–1913* (Cambridge, Mass., 1973).

5 McCloskey, *Economic Maturity and Entrepreneurial Decilne*, p. 125: 'The rate of productivity growth [in iron and steel] in America did finally come to exceed the rate in Britain, but only because Britain had earlier achieved high levels of productivity.'

6 See below, p. 15–17.

7 Donald M. McCloskey and Lars G. Sandberg, 'From Damnation to Redemption: Judgements on the Late Victorian Entrepreneur', *Explorations in Entrepreneurial History*, ix (1971), 103–4.

8 Approximate calculations, derived from C. H. Feinstein, *National Income, Expenditure and Output of the United Kingdom, 1855–1965* (Cambridge, 1972), Tables 54 and 55.

9 Charles Wilson, 'Economy and Society in Late Victorian Britain', *Economic History Review*, 2nd Ser. xviii (1956), 191.

10 Derek H. Aldcroft and Harry W. Richardson, *The British Economy, 1870–1939* (London, 1969), pp. 239–88; R. S. Sayers, 'The Springs of Technical Progress in Britain, 1913–39', *Economic Journal*, lx (1950), 275–90; Derek H. Aldcroft, 'Economic Growth in Britain in the Inter-war years: A Reassessment', *Economic History Review*, 2nd Ser. xx (1967), reprinted in Aldcroft and Fearon (eds.), *Economic Growth*; J. A. Dowie, 'Growth in the Inter-War Period, Some More Arithmetic', *Economic History Review*, 2nd Ser. xxi (1968), reprinted in Aldcroft and Fearon (eds.), *Economic Growth*.

11 Income from employment as percentage of gross national product. C. H. Feinstein, 'Income Distribution in the United Kingdom', in J. Marchal and B. Ducros (eds.), *The Distribution of National Income* (London, 1968), pp. 116–17.

12 Ibid., p. 119.

13 Feinstein, *National Income*, T.14–15, T.42.

14 Dowie, art. cit. 76.

15 Leslie Hannah, *The Rise of the Corporate Economy* (London, 1976), pp. 120–1, Table 8.2.

16 See the discussion in Leslie Hannah, 'Business Development and Economic Structure in Britain since 1880', in Leslie Hannah (ed.), *Management Strategy and Business Development: An Historical and Comparative Study* (London, 1976).

17 S. J. Prais, *The Evolution of Giant Firms in Britain: A Study of the Growth of Manufacturing Industry in Britain, 1909–70* (Cambridge, 1976), p. 4.

18 J. D. Jefferys, *Retail Trading in Britain, 1850–1950* (Cambridge, 1954), p. 73.

19 Professor Prais also emphasizes the importance of 'spontaneous drift' (the tendency to increased concentration as a result of the variability in the growth rates of individual firms; op. cit., Ch. 2), while questioning the significance of 'technical' economies of scale and (in the period since the 1950s) of marketing forces (Ch. 4).

20 Hannah, *Corporate Economy*, p. 23.

21 Peter L. Payne, 'The Emergence of the Large-Scale Company in Great Britain, 1870–1914', *Economic History Review*, 2nd Ser. xx (1967), 539–40.

22 See Alfred D. Chandler, 'The Development of Modern Management Structures in the U.S. and the U.K.', in Hannah (ed.), *Management Strategy and Business Development*, p. 36.

23 Hannah, *Corporate Economy*, p. 26.

24 See Chandler, 'The Development of Modern Management Structures', p. 28.

25 Payne, 'The Emergence of the Large-Scale Company', 539–40.

26 Chandler, 'The Development of Modern Management Structures', pp. 40 ff.

27 Alfred D. Chandler, *Strategy and Structure: Chapters in the History of Industrial*

Enterprise (Cambridge, Mass., 1962); 'The Development of Modern Management Structures'.

28 Chandler, 'The Development of Modern Management Structures', p. 44.

29 Below, Ch. 7.

30 For an assessment of the British lag in terms of strategy (diversification) and structure (multidivisional) see Leslie Hannah, 'Strategy and Structure in the Manufacturing Sector', in Hannah (ed.), *Management Strategy and Business Development*.

31 For a discussion of these issues, see Hannah, *Corporate Economy*, pp. 140–1.

I

2

The Mechanical Engineering Industries in Britain, 1860-1914[1]

S. B. SAUL

(A)

British engineering in the 1860s was still dominated by those sectors which had emerged from the Industrial Revolution earlier in the century—textile machinery, railway rolling-stock, steam-engines and boilers of all kinds, and the relevant, most heavy, machine tools. The largest firm was undoubtedly Platts of Oldham with 7,000 men employed in two works in 1875. The most important as a group were the manufacturing and repair establishments of the railway companies. The manufacture of agricultural and hydraulic machinery were two fast developing sectors. Certainly, there were areas where others were beginning to lead the way but this was in no sense a surprising or undesirable development: a virtual monopoly could not persist for long. The critical question is to ask in what sectors Britain continued to lead the way and how ready it was to follow up the innovations of others. Table 2.1 shows the relative importance of these trades in 1907.

TABLE 2.1

Gross Output of Selected Engineering Industries in Britain in 1907 (£ m.)

Textile machinery		13
Railway locomotives:		
Private builders	4·5	
Railway company (construction and repair) ..	7·9	12·4
Steam-engines (excluding locomotives and agricultural steam-engines)		6·9
Boilers		4·1
Machine tools		2·9
Agricultural machinery	1·1	
Agriculture steam-engines	1·3	
		2·4
Cycles, motor cycles, and parts		5·6
Motor vehicles and parts		5·2

Source: First Census of Production (1907).

Textile machinery was the largest single branch and an overwhelmingly dominant force in world trade. In 1913 about 40,000 men were employed, over three-quarters of them by six very large manufacturers of cotton machinery in Lancashire. It was, too, an industry apparently kept vigorous by the infusion of new blood—Howard & Bullough and Brooks & Doxey, only founded in the 1850s, were in many ways the technological and commercial leaders after 1870. In 1894, for example, Howard & Bullough set up an American subsidiary, and their reputation and their ability to offer a full line of equipment for a spinning mill made them fearsome competitors in that market. The large home market was a clear advantage, but by 1907 45 per cent of the industry's output was exported, and only a quarter of that went to the British Empire. After India, the main markets were in Europe—Germany, Russia, France, and Belgium. By 1914 the U.S.A. was the only area in the world not dependent on Britain for a major part of its textile machinery. Even there Keighley firms monopolized the market for worsted machinery. *The Times* suggested in 1913 that, except for those in the United States, Austria, and Switzerland, the world's cotton spindles had been mostly bought in Britain. Platts of Oldham had an output in 1914 equal to that of the whole American industry put together. Each week they turned out 20 mules, over 100 ring frames, 320 looms, 80 carding engines, as well as many other ancillary machines. In some parts of the world Platts' machinery was standard for all cotton mills. Unlike the American industry, which had grown so customer-conscious in its fight for the orders from the southern mills that it was prepared to grant all kinds of design concessions to individual millmen, the British were in a position to insist on standardized products. Chinese spinners, for example, stated that they preferred British to American machinery as the latter changed so often that there was great difficulty in securing new parts for replacement.

Gibb describes American development to 1900 as the combined result of original thinking and copying from the British, while Navin writes of the traditional American way of catching up in this technology—purchasing British machines through a third party, copying them minutely, and advertising them as such. This was how Lowells attempted to break the Keighley monopoly of worsted drawing and spinning machinery in 1898, for example, though with little success.[2] On the other hand, two of the main technological advances of the later nineteenth century were pioneered in the United States— ring spinning and the Northrop loom. As for ring frames, the great productive power of the British industry enabled it to improve on ring spinning techniques and sell in the American market itself despite the freight and duty. American-made ring frames were not exported at all before 1914. The Rabbeth spindle, which made ring spinning a commercial success, was introduced into England by Howard & Bullough in 1878. In seven years they sold $1\frac{3}{4}$ m. spindles—less than half of them at home—and another 2 m. in the next four years. Employment boomed from 350 in 1870 to 2,000 in 1892. Platts reached a similar level of output in the early 1890s. Brooks & Doxey matured under the same influence: by 1892 they were employing 2,000 people and making 2,000 ring spindles a week as well as preparatory machinery and some machine tools. Tweedale & Smalley of Rochdale, only founded in 1892, were already employing 1,700 workers, largely on ring frames, in 1900. All this indicates an industry which had fully retained its virility and competitiveness. Nor should it be forgotten that for most of this period extensive improvements were being made to the mule. Indeed, one technical expert has suggested that the 1870s and 1880s were outstandingly productive in this respect.

On the more specific question of standardization and interchangeability, almost all the credit for developing these techniques has gone to American engineers—the principal exception being the Portsmouth block-making machinery of the beginning of the nineteenth century. Undoubtedly, their contribution was enormous through the creation of new types of machinery to machine small parts accurately in mass—turret-lathes, milling and grinding machines—but what of the British role? In so far as Britain's pre-eminence lay in heavy capital goods the opportunities for mass production were limited, but once specialist manufacture became the rule, and where the market existed, or could be created, to warrant investment in using these techniques, there is little evidence of technological shortcomings. The major firms in the textile machinery trade were specialists and in no sense general engineering firms, though all the big companies produced a wide range of textile machines. Spindles were certainly made interchangeable from at least the middle of the nineteenth century, and by the end of the century were being turned out by individual firms in very large quantities—in batches of up to 100,000. It appears, however, that right up to 1914 they were not produced on modern machinery but were made by extremely skilled and experienced workmen using a grindstone and achieving an accuracy of up to 0·0005 inches on what were small diameters, with the use of emery cloth. They were, of course, using the 'go, no go' gauges required for interchangeability rather than seeking dead accuracy. It seems primitive, but it is by no means clear that it was economically unsound, especially when one reads of the difficulties experienced by American firms in matching with machinery 'the superb work of the English fitters'.[3] As for the rest, textile machinery parts were not altogether truly interchangeable without a certain amount of fitting. By and large the technology was one of skilled repetitive work using conventional machine tools combined with considerable numbers of special-purpose tools designed and made by the textile machinery firms themselves. Despite the size of their output their machining techniques were a mixture of the conventional—not to say old-fashioned—and the highly specialized. The industry did little after 1850 to advance engineering technology in general, nor was it an important centre for general engineering training.

More interesting perhaps is the production of locomotives, the second largest of the engineering trades and one where Britain's performance was not quite as satisfactory. Standardization and interchangeability were certainly not confined to, or originated by, American builders. Sharp Roberts built interchangeability to templates and gauges at a very early date, and theirs was one of the first works in the world to use the system. To ensure interchangeability for his first series of standard locomotives for the Great Western in the early 1840s, Daniel Gooch sent out full specifications and templates to the builders employed, this being the first attempt at standardization on an extensive scale for an individual railway. 'These drawings I took great pains with, giving every detail much thought and consideration . . . When I had completed the drawings I had them lithographed and specifications printed, and thin iron templates for those parts it was essential should be interchangeable, and these were supplied to the various engine builders with whom contracts were made. One hundred and forty-two engines were let, and all the makers did their work well.' How accurate all this was, and how much hand fitting was required in assembly is not known, but the principle was there. It reached its peak when John Ramsbottom was Chief Engineer at Crewe. Having been trained at Sharp Roberts, he had absorbed their technological ideas. Between 1858 and 1872 a total of 857 goods engines were constructed at Crewe for the London and North Western Railway, and another 86 between 1871 and 1874 for the Lancashire and Yorkshire Railway—943 locomotives identical in almost all respects, a record which was not subsequently surpassed.

But if all this was so, why was it that an American firm such as Baldwins was able to take the technique to its logical conclusion, building standard engines for stock on a very large scale and employing 19,000 men in 1907, whereas the largest company in Britain employed less than half that number and the largest single private establishment employed 3,400? The answer lies largely, I think, in a study of the market. Unlike most other countries— Germany and the U.S.A. in particular—in Britain the major railway companies made and repaired their own engines in what were some of the largest engineering establishments in the country. These company workshops were private empires largely isolated from the market. The strong individuality of the chief engineers meant that there was little interchange of information or uniformity of practice. Some were brilliant designers, some definitely were not. F. W. Webb, for example, Chief Engineer at Crewe from 1871 to 1903, was a man of the most extreme dogmatism and prejudice, and suffered from increasingly serious bouts of insanity during the last years of his career. The best works were very advanced in equipment and practice. Those at Horwich were described in 1891 soon after their opening as possessing 'some of the finest milling plant we have yet seen'. Great strides were made there and elsewhere in standardizing rolling-stock and ensuring interchangeability of cylinders, valves, axle-boxes, springs, wheels, and so on. Milling was introduced into the Stratford works of the Great Eastern Railway in 1878. The Gateshead works were reorganized in 1883 and 1884, and with the arrival of T. W. Worsdell as Chief Engineer the following year there was a marked increase in the use of milling machines for all kinds of heavy work and for finishing processes. G. J. Churchward took charge of Swindon in 1902. With a strong functional outlook and little interest in aesthetics, he launched a major programme of re-equipment through standard types of engine with many parts common to all—piston-rods, cross-heads, valves, axles, springs, and a standard bogie too.

However, the railway companies were unable to capitalize on all this and manufacture locomotives for others—the sale of engines made at Crewe to the Lancashire and Yorkshire Railway resulted in the private builders successfully applying for an injunction in 1876. The private builders were relatively few in number in 1914. The best private works were as well equipped and organized as those of the railway companies. Dubs' machine-shop was described in 1887 as one of the finest in Britain, using milling techniques extensively and 'the result of this ensures such absolute uniformity of dimensions that the firm can at once duplicate any part of any engine ever made by them', and the organization such that 'no man ever leaves his machine to grind his cutting tools, there being a squad of men who do nothing else all the year round'. A visitor to the Beyer Peacock locomotive works in 1886 reported that 'all holes are drilled through templates: in fact everything is machined to templates so that corresponding parts are interchangeable'. The amalgamation of three companies in the Springburn district of Glasgow to form the North British Company in 1902 was certainly in part a response to overseas competition, but the prime difficulty remained that the market structure gave the private builders little opportunity of building up quantity production of relatively cheap general-purpose engines. The home market was limited for the reasons I have mentioned. Of 937 engines sold from 1872 to 1914 Nasmyth Wilson placed only 7 per cent on the home market. The Vulcan foundry sent 70 per cent overseas from 1894 to 1905, and from 1906 to 1914 sold at home only 17 of 948 engines produced. Compare this with the experience of Baldwins who in 1906 sold 292 engines overseas and 2,374 at home, or the Hanover locomotive works which from 1846 to 1907 sold only one-fifth of the 4,000 engines turned out overseas. When they did give orders, the home railways often refused to take stock patterns, but insisted on what suited them and fitted best into their own repair and maintenance patterns. The private builders got their bread-and-butter orders overseas, and these came from railways in the Empire and South America run by British railway engineers. These men, too, rarely ordered from stock, but designed in detail precisely what engines they wanted. The chairman of the North British Company told the Tariff Commission in 1905 'it is practically impossible to make parts to stock: we never know what the next orders will be'. And he added ruefully, 'in our work as contractors'—note the term—'there is not much scope for men of an inventive turn of mind'. The builders complained bitterly too about the army of inspectors who invaded their shops whenever orders involving the Crown Agents were being fulfilled. They also argued that their costs were raised by the consulting engineers' practice of forcing them to obtain bought-out parts from specified firms who took advantage of their position to inflate their prices.

This institutional framework therefore resulted not only in the market being created in an entirely different manner in Britain and America, but in the building of entirely different technical products. The British engine was a high-quality product with a long life, relatively expensive and difficult to service, closely tailored to the needs of the line for which it had been specifically designed. It was not necessarily very suitable for other purposes, and was particularly unsuited to poorly constructed tracks. For their type of engine the British makers were unsurpassed. Their works were well equipped: standardization within the runs they were given was a commonplace, but by the last decade of the nineteenth century not only had they no sound market basis for producing standard engines cheaply for stock, but the engineering traditions which they had built up in response to market conditions would have made it well nigh impossible for them to adopt the practice anyway. Unfortunately, by 1914 more and more countries were beginning to wonder if the British type of locomotive was what they wanted. German competition was particularly serious in South America, American in Japan. British trade was becoming more and more narrowly based geographically.

The manufacture of railway carriages and wagons was more important than that of locomotives and though the same institutional structure faced them, a few large firms, centred upon Birmingham, were able to enjoy considerable economies of scale especially after a major amalgamation and rationalization of production came about in 1902. This was perhaps the first true assembly industry, less at the mercy of the whims of its customers than locomotive machines. In 1913 its exports were considerably larger than those of locomotives and the industry's competitive position in the difficult South American market much stronger.

Knowledge of production techniques in the manufacture of steam-engines —stationary and marine—is scarce, but when the market was right, interchangeability was aimed at and achieved from an early date. An outstanding example of interchangeable marine-engine construction arose out of a rush Admiralty order for shallow-draught gunboats during the Crimean War. One hundred and fifty sets of engines were successfully built by Penns and Maudslay to that principle—the first example of mass production in marine engineering. There were, of course, innumerable makers of small stationary engines, and in general at the international exhibitions of the 1860s and 1870s their products came under severe criticism for their poor fuel economy, something which might not matter too much at home but made them unsaleable overseas. However, already in those decades one or two outstanding makers were striking out into new directions. Hick Hargreaves of Bolton sponsored the American Corliss engine here, and in 1867 began making it simply and to a standardized design. In the late 1860s James Tangye had a huge success when he brought out a simple engine manufactured interchangeably and built for stock in large numbers. He created a separate machine-tool section to build the tools for the purpose, and then went on to sell such machines to industry generally. Even more significant was the work of Peter Willans who introduced the principle of standardization between engines of different sizes. The high-pressure cylinder of one size was the same as the low-pressure cylinder of the next smaller size but one, and so forth: interchangeable cylinders, pistons, rings, valves, were made in quantity for stock. An American engineer commented in 1897: 'I do not know of an American shop building engines which carries the principle so far.' James C. Peache went to Willans's works at Thames Ditton to take charge of the system of interchangeable manufacture in 1885. In 1891 he invented his own high-speed engine to the same pattern, and it was later extensively manufactured by Davey Paxman. Savory's of Birmingham made small, very high-speed marine engines to the same principle too. These were pioneers, but their output became large, their fame great, their works became models, and many came to see and learn there. So far had things gone that the British Navy had six cruisers built with interchangeable main and auxiliary engines in 1903—the first navy to do this —using as chief contractor Hawthorn Leslie who had fifteen years' experience of the work with smaller naval craft.

A related sector of the engineering industry where the market complicated the position was the manufacture of agricultural machinery. Several large firms in the eastern counties achieved striking success both at home and overseas in those lines most in keeping with British engineering traditions— portable steam-engines, threshers, ploughs, and, later, oil-engines for farm use. Their business expanded rapidly after the mid-century. Marshalls of Gainsborough, the most important, founded in 1856, employed 550 by 1870, 2,000 in 1892, and 5,000 in 1913. Clayton & Shuttleworth established a general iron foundry in Lincoln in 1842, employed 1,400 in 1885 and 2,300 in 1907. Ransomes of Ipswich, a much older firm dating back to the eighteenth century, employed 1,500 in the mid-1880s and grew fast largely on the basis of exports during the 1890s to reach 2,500 in 1911. Rustons of Lincoln, founded in 1857, employed 5,200 in 1911. Less than half of their work-force was engaged on agricultural machinery, though perhaps a third of their oil-engines were for farm use. Howards, plough-makers of Bedford, and Fowlers with steam-plough equipment, were also major exporters. These firms dominated the international exhibitions of the late nineteenth century in their own specialities just as much as the Americans did in theirs. Clayton & Shuttleworth were described at the Vienna Exhibition of 1873 as having machines all over the Austro-Hungarian Empire, and in fact had a factory in Vienna, set up in 1857 and soon employing 700 men. They had another at Pesth where Robey of Lincoln also had a works. It was fortunate that they did too, for tariffs and government subsidies to the state manufactory of portable engines had largely eliminated imports by 1900. Up to 1914 Russia was the big market for Ransomes and also for Marshalls and Garretts, and all lost heavily on account of money lodged with Russian banks when the revolution broke out. The selling mechanism was particularly highly developed. The organization included a staff of travellers, mechanics, spare-part depots, and repair shops, and in most cases a complementary organization which bought grain from the farmer, thereby allowing a purchase of machinery and sale of produce to be carried out conveniently in one transaction.

So much, in this field at least, for the poor British reputation for salesmanship. The home trade was negligible: output of steam threshing sets in 1913 was above 100 a week of which, on average, only two were sold at home. By weight, fully half the exports in 1913 went to Europe, an unusually high proportion. Between two-thirds and three-quarters of the total output of agricultural machinery were exported—a high proportion, especially when one recalls that very few binders or reapers went overseas. The works were apparently modern and well equipped, though considering the range of equipment all produced and the large size of much of it, they were in no sense engaged in mass production—at their peak Clayton & Shuttleworth produced 25 threshing sets a week. Marshalls, as early as 1885 were extensive users of milling machines, twist drills, and the like; Clayton & Shuttleworth employed as Works Manager to 1914 H. F. L. Orcutt, who had helped plan Loewe's machine-tool works in Berlin and was a constant advocate of American production methods. Ransomes' factory in 1905 had a great deal of American machinery, and J. E. Ransome himself commented that 'firms with antiquated tools generally go down. It is a very bad sign when a works is full of old tools; it does not pay to keep them.' When questioned on interchangeability he was somewhat contemptuous. The firm had been using standard interchangeable spare parts since before he was born: they could not service machinery supplied to farmers in remote parts of the world in any other way.

But of course British agricultural-machine production failed in the one area where the American mass interchangeable techniques were so relevant—in reaping and binding machinery. In 1900 the entire British output of harvesters was not a tenth of that of McCormick. It is true that during the 1870s, when the Americans seized the whole of world trade, British makers failed to appreciate what was happening until too late. They were too confident that American machines were too light and applicable only to the United States home market, whereas the machinery was in fact quickly and intelligently adapted to local requirements. But the market was again a difficult one. The problem was not one of lower labour costs as is sometimes argued, for the higher yield per acre in Britain tended to make mechanization of the harvest on improved land a profitable undertaking.[4] The difficulty was that the new machinery could only be used on large, level fields with no boggy patches or land-fast stones. This and the drastic fall of the arable acreage after 1870 made it extremely difficult to establish a strong home market and to cut down the American lead which was itself in part a reflexion of her favourable home market conditions. To all this had to be added the conservatism of the British farmer himself. Discussing this point, an official report noted the suspicion and often undisguised hostility of farmers to all innovations, and commented, 'manufacturers have had to contend with much inertia and prejudice in bringing their appliances to the notice of the farming public'.

In their own specialities the British firms carried out with marked success what was largely an export trade, producing their equipment by up-to-date methods and selling it vigorously. The market, however, played a significant part in limiting the extension of Britain's output of agricultural machinery. This is not to argue that it was the only factor: a report on the Paris Exhibition of 1900 stated, 'It is useless to deny that amongst the jurors there was a feeling that amongst British agricultural implement makers there was a certain want of progress and they were too much inclined to rely on their undoubted triumphs of the past.' This comment, however, almost certainly applied to the industry's inability to move into the harvester market, rather than to any weaknesses in the traditional fields. It may have been this sense of despair which caused an observer to comment on the number of American machines shown at the Maidstone Agricultural Exhibition of 1899 that 'some of our leading firms were becoming implement agents rather than implement sellers'. We shall see later that the work of importing agents had a more stimulating effect on the machine-tool industry in the more favourable market conditions obtaining for that sector after 1890.

(B)

So far there has emerged a pattern of the classic engineering industries continuing to enjoy marked commercial and technological progress, moving into new fields such as the manufacture of ring frames, adopting new techniques of standardization, but with their success being limited here and there by peculiar market problems. It is, however, possible to go further than this. The most influential branch of all engineering production is the machine-tool industry, for it is there that new skills and techniques are acquired and diffused. Several writers have attributed a major role in the development of the American system of manufacture to the inventiveness and productive skill of its machine-tool firms, and the spread of the understanding of these new methods to other industries through engineers trained in them. How then did the machine-tool industry in Britain fare? How was it affected by the differences in the fortunes of the various branches of the engineering industry, and how did it, in its turn, determine the nature and rate of technological innovation?

Again, market forces can be seen to have been a major significance. With the exception of the textile machinery firms, which in any case appear to have made many of their own machine tools, the industries already discussed—locomotive, steam-engine, agricultural-machinery makers, and to this list one should add shipbuilders—brought a demand for the highest quality and most up-to-date machine tools of the heavier kind. Many of the works, as we have seen, were superbly equipped. They generated a machine-tool industry second to none. Buckton, Muir, Hulse, Richards, Asquith (in England) and Shanks and Lang (in Scotland) were possibly the most famous, and the most outstanding of all was Cravens, who became probably the finest firm in the world supplying heavy machine tools. To give but one example of Britain's superiority: although the American industry pioneered the use of milling for light work, in Britain its use, and the production of such machines for heavy work, was by 1900 generally acknowledged to be very much more advanced. The traditional centres of British engineering became heavy users of milling machines; Brooks & Doxey had 160 in their textile machinery works by the mid-1890s, for example. Orders for heavy machinery were too small to allow a firm normally to specialize in one type, but even here the British industry was in the van of developments. After 1880 Langs of Johnstone began to concentrate solely on lathes, and were described in a report of 1908 as the only European firm specializing in the American fashion: they were, however, rather special, being also the first company in Europe to supply machine tools with cut rather than cast gears. The impression is inescapable that the home investment boom of the 1890s witnessed the first full realization of the new machinery techniques then available throughout the whole engineering trade. Locomotive makers re-equipped extensively with British and American machinery as did the machine-tool makers themselves. As for foundry machinery an American observer, referring to the state of the British industry in 1911, wrote, 'in power and hydraulic presses, welding and brazing equipment, cranes, power plant machinery, pressure pumps and nearly everything for the foundry, Europe leads'.

But in medium engineering, where the Americans made most spectacular progress, the home machine-tool industry got less support. It could be argued that Britain was not missing much by abstaining from interchangeable manufacture of guns before 1850, given the troubles the Americans experienced. After all, the golden rule of mass production is not to tool up until you have got things right. At the appropriate time the relevant techniques were quickly adopted here, first in the government factory at Enfield, and within four years by two private firms—the Birmingham Small Arms Company founded in 1861 and the London Small Arms Company who were already manufacturing inter-changeably rather earlier than this. Sir John Habakkuk has pointed out that the arms factories here did not become centres of learning as those in America did, but one does not need a deep knowledge of Western history to realize that the Colt Armory was not just turning out military rifles. The American market advantage was considerable. Colt's own revolver factory in London was short lived because there simply was no business available when the Crimean War ended. The government doled out declining orders for rifles between three or four firms to an agreed proportion, and all market and technological initiative was lost. In office machinery little progress was made until American firms set up branch plants in Britain. The watch industry, still entirely a handicraft trade, came under most severe pressure from Ameri-can and Swiss makers during the 1860s. In 1888 the Lancashire Watch Com-pany was set up to buy out most of the hand workers at Prescott, and began manufacturing by the interchangeable principle. It was soon employing 500 men and the works were said to be entirely equipped with American machinery. Even so, in 1902 some 225,000 watches were made in Britain compared with $2\frac{3}{4}$ m. in the U.S.A. and 6 m. in Central Europe.[5] In the lighter sector of the agricultural-machinery industry Britain was left far behind, and the lag in electrical engineering was a serious disadvantage too. All these were the in-dustries which in the United States became the main outlets for the makers of the new machine tools for mass production.

But even where interchangeable manufacture of what we now call consumer durables was successfully carried out, the impact on the machine-tool makers was sometimes negligible. The history of the Singer company is particularly interesting in this respect and little known. The company, founded in the United States, began assembling parts in Scotland in a small way in 1867, and switched to actual manufacture of sewing-machines three years later. By 1885 it was making 8,000 machines a week, rather more than the parent factory at Elizabethport, New York. At the turn of the century 7,000 employees were producing 13,000 a week, and the Clydebank factory was by far the largest sewing-machine works in the world. Whatever the original motives for the move to Scotland—the president of American Singer was an emigrant Scot—the existence of relatively cheap labour did not inhibit the use of the most modern machinery. Contemporaries described the factory with open-mouthed enthusiasm: 'probably the finest monument of a sound invention properly developed that the present age has produced', said one. Unit costs in 1885 were reckoned to be 30 per cent below those in Singer's American plant. There was no other factory like it in Britain in the 1880s. A large number of modern machine tools were employed, but detailed statistics show that well over three-quarters of them were made by Singer itself, and a very high pro-portion of those brought out consisted of straightforward lathes. The accounts of the purchases of milling machines show that very few indeed were supplied from outside the Singer organization before 1900. The firm therefore had a negligible impact on machine-tool demand; it did nothing towards the building-up of capacity and know-how in modern machinery methods in the British machine-tool industry, but simply began to buy once that capacity had been created—largely by the cycle industry.

The tradition of the general workshop making its own tools died hard. The textile machinery firms certainly made many of their own tools. The same can be said of locomotive makers such as Nasmyth, Sharp Stewart, and Beyer Peakcock. Tangyes, as we have seen, began their machine-tool business in this way. More famous still was the Birmingham firm of Nettlefold & Chamberlain, which utterly transformed the wood-screw industry, using techniques acquired by buying in 1854 patent rights to American automatic machinery. As early as 1869 they were employing milling cutters to shape all six sides of nuts simultaneously, but a report of 1876 significantly noted that 'all the machines and tools are made at the works'. For all these reasons the commercial production of new medium machine tools—milling machines, turret lathes, and later, grinding machines—got off the ground only slowly. Their value was appreciated by the best shops: importing agents such as Churchills did much to make them known. Many of the new machine-tool firms took up their manufacture. A report on the Vienna Exhibition noted that 'the workshops of certain leading firms in England are being filled up with tools of a special kind, possessing great originality with regard to fitness for a purpose in the manufacture of general machinery, agricultural engines, small arms, etc.' But the breakthrough of mass demand was slow to come. The machine-tool firms remained small in size and limited in resources. Specialization was found to be impossible even by makers of outstanding brilliance such as Smith & Coventry, very highly praised by the American, Charles Porter, and by Alfred Herbert, the firm which introduced twist drills to Britain in 1876 and did more than any other to popularize milling. Long runs were essential to cover the cost of the special machine tools, the elaborate jigs and templates, and the time taken to set them up—and this applied as much to the makers as to the users of machine tools. It was, too, a vicious circle, for these small firms were inadequate training-grounds from which engineers could go out and spread the gospel of the new production methods. There was a wide gap between the best practice as represented by firms such as Singer and Nettlefold and that of the average user of machine tools, between the efforts of the pioneer machine-tool makers and the mass of Yorkshire shops.

The breakthrough in demand came from the cycle industry. The arrival of the safety bicycle and the pneumatic tyre created such a boom that the big makers in Coventry and Nottingham were forced to reorganize their methods completely to meet the demand. Small men began to assemble and specialist component makers grew up to supply them. A firm such as the Birmingham Small Arms Company, which had trifled with cycle making in the 1880s and abandoned it altogether in 1888, came back into the trade. By 1896 they were making 2,000 sets of cycle components a week and buying in large quantities of machine tools—giving even a small firm like Holroyd a single order for 124 milling machines in 1896. Vast capacity was created by the large cycle makers and rows of the best machinery installed as a result of the heavy investment of the early 1890s. The financial bubble burst, but now the pressure was on: the need was to use this machinery to the full, to standardize and to extend the market, and this they did remarkably well. Above all, they abandoned the high price/high quality market which had limited growth potential. They looked to the wider market for low-cost cycles and the consequent need for standardization and more automatic manufacture.[6] In 1913 Britain exported 150,000 cycles, Germany 89,000, and the rest of the world almost none at all. Much of the early machinery was imported, but quickly new firms such as Ward's and Herbert's arose in the Midlands and older firms flourished as a result of the new impetus. Interchangeable batch production and production for stock for the first time became standard machine-tool-making practice. Nor was it just the demand of cycle makers. The belated development of electrical engineering and the exacting requirements of builders of steam-turbines and gas- and oil-engines all helped to spread the advanced techniques.[7] Then, too, there was the influence of the motor car. One must not be tempted to underestimate this development simply on account of the more spectacular progress made in the U.S.A. Table 2.1 shows that by 1907 motor-car manu-facture was already a sizeable part of the engineering industry and in the next six years output was to increase almost threefold. Nor was the running all made in the medium sector of the machine-tool industry. Many makers of heavy machinery, too, rose brilliantly to the market opportunities offered by the development of high-speed steel, taking advantage of their reputation for strength and rigidity, and redesigning their tools to transmit the greater power now required. Tangyes, with huge high-speed lathes, Hetheringtons with high-speed radial drills, and many Halifax firms were leaders in this area.

In this way the machine-tool industry reached its maturity. Such figures as we have of the output of machine-tool firms suggest that in this field British industry was re-equipping at a rate far in excess of that shown by those indices we have for total industrial investment after 1900.[8] Of course, not every problem was solved, not all the leeway was made up. Specialization remained rare: except for Herberts and Cravens, the average size of firm was low. As Professor Rosenberg has pointed out, the degree of specialization and of size achieved in the United States was possible only because of the simultaneous growth of several industries sharing certain technical processes.[9] The American advantage, once established, was difficult to break. In specialized lines, world demand can easily be satisfied by one firm enjoying considerable economies of scale—indeed, much of world trade in machine tools has been, and still is, of this kind. Simply for this reason, unlike many other new engineering industries, no American machine-tool firm found it worth while establishing a branch plant here, but concentrated on arranging agencies for the sale of their special-purpose machines. It is significant that Herberts, who were the largest manufacturers before 1914 (as they still are), were also major agents.

The development of the machine-tool industry after 1850 can be seen, therefore, to reflect partly a discontinuity of growth and partly the pattern of demand for heavy and medium machines. Of course, demand is not just something objective faced by a manufacturer, but something that he can, at least to some degree, seek to fashion to his own liking. One must therefore also blame the machine-tool makers for not doing enough to take up, develop, and force new ideas on their customers. Similar criticisms have been made of other sectors of the engineering industry.

We can hardly argue in terms of the market without at least a passing reference to selling techniques, though there is no space here for a detailed analysis. Even a superficial examination of the sources, however, indicates that the usual complaints about British methods are too general to be convincing. Some writers argue that not enough was done to determine and satisfy the needs of particular markets: others bemoan the lack of standardization. We cannot be too dogmatic on this: in the case of agricultural machinery differences in physical environment required considerable product variation and British firms apparently responded well. In much textile machinery, such was the reputation of Lancashire and so unimportant the physical environment that standardized equipment was the rule, though of course this could only be created by extensive sales efforts. A firm like Mather & Platt had its resident staff of engineers in India; senior members of the firm travelled extensively in Europe and South America; in Russia their agent was Ludwig Knoop. This reflected an outstanding achievement. Yet this did not apply to loom making, most of which was carried out on a small scale and was quite unstandardized largely because local specialization in weaving had encouraged local loom-makers to cater for their own districts, and many different types gradually emerged—a pattern only broken when an entirely new form of loom appeared such as the Northrop, which was standardized from the first.

Of course, one faces a serious problem of contradictory patterns of behaviour. There were the textile machinery makers imposing their standardized equipment on buyers, but making it in a conservative manner; the locomotive builders more advanced in an engineering sense, but having to conform to customer preferences. Some of this has been explained by way of institutional and market patterns, but we are still left with the problem of distinguishing between the best and the average, of discovering how representative is the pattern established in this chapter.

(C)

My aim has been to depart from vague generalizations about British industrial performance and to point out differences between the various sectors. I have tried to show that some sectors of British engineering—makers of textile, steam, and sewing machinery, for example—were very advanced commercially and technologically, and that where in others—agricultural machinery, locomotives, and above all in that most critical sector, machine tools—the degree of success varied, it was in part at least conditioned by the nature of the market. Much remains to be explained the weaknesses in those mass-production industries I mentioned before, watches and office machinery. The gun makers may have been at a disadvantage in their own field, but why did it take them so long to apply their techniques elsewhere in the way that Remington did? As for motor cars, I have elsewhere questioned the adequacy of the market as a complete explanation. In other sectors—electrical machinery, for example—the market has been cited as a factor in slow growth, though here too it is obviously not the whole answer in view of the striking successes achieved in the north-east in a more helpful institutional environment. Peter Temin's study of the steel industry takes the pattern of demand as a neglected factor, but does not deny the stupidities and failings of the industry itself.[10]

Clearly, the market is not a complete answer to all our questions. To understand more fully the lags and successes of British engineering there is need for more detailed examination of its training and institutional patterns. The usual, and often justified, condemnation of the system of formal technical education must be modified so as to distinguish between the needs of different products—the bicycle essentially the product of practical men; the steam-turbine which was inevitably the province of the trained engineer; the early internal-combustion engine developed by professional engineers but improved in major aspects by practical men. It is significant, perhaps, that by 1914 French engineers with their superior training in scientific principles were producing far more 'efficient' locomotives than the British practical men. Yet there were brilliant successes too. What more theoretical discovery was there than the steam-turbine and who better trained than Parsons? One American student of engineering has written of Willans as the leading figure of a new school of engineers in Britain in the 1880s—men with an adequate knowledge of mathematics and mechanics, familiar with the laws of thermodynamics, and adept at applying theoretical principles to practical problems. But the marriage did not always work well. The consulting engineer was all too often deprived of the chance of combining his theoretical knowledge with a practical understanding. He was called in to do the calculations but if he tried to give the maker a free hand in the interests of economy the cry was, 'What does he get his fees for?'

Most engineers to 1900 still came up through an apprenticeship, and the machine-tool firms developing the American methods after 1870 were too small to be an effective training-ground; this is the one outstanding contrast with American experience. Importing agents such as Churchill's and Buck & Hickman played an important role in spreading knowledge of the new techniques, but it was not the same thing. You do not learn from talking to an agent as you do from working with a maker. In Britain the railway workshops and the big-steam-engine shops were typically the places where young men served apprenticeships. It is not without significance that Stoke City Football Club was founded by a group of public school boys serving their time in the local railway workshops; Royce, Bentley, Austin, and A. V. Roe of aircraft fame were also trained in this way; Singer, Hillman, the Starleys, Willans, were among the many apprenticed at Penns, marine engineers of Greenwich. These were first-generation men, first-class engineers, men of drive and enthusiasm, but trained in a traditional environment and finding it hard to break with the past. The American motor-car industry, on the other hand, was fertilized not by college graduates but by engineers trained in modern machine-tool shops and consequently capable of appreciating the complete reorganization of the production processes that the new machine tools required. Here, it was slow to come. The leading firms in the British motor industry, controlled by these men of high ability, their shops packed with rows of the latest machinery, still operated without comprehension of what modern engineering implied. Love of the technical product was slow to give way to love of the technique of production.

This is not to argue by any means that no direct transference of interchangeable skills took place. We have mentioned B.S.A. and Bradbury's. As one report said of the latter, 'For over 30 years the firm have turned out their famous sewing machines in the system of interchangeable parts and they have now applied the same principle to the construction of cycles.' They also turned out automatic and capstan lathes, drilling and profiling machines for cycle-makers. Harry Lea of the Lea & Francis Cycle Company was formerly employed by Singer, and Graham Francis had worked for both Pratt & Whitney and Ludwig Loewe. More interesting still was the career of George Accles, apprenticed at Colt's works in Hartford and engaged later in establishing works for manufacture of cartridges and of the Gatling gun in many parts of the world. He set up his own works in Birmingham in 1888 but soon turned to the manufacture of cycles and of labour-saving American-type tools for the industry. It is not without significance that there were no major railway works in Birmingham and the Black Country to impress their traditions of engineering there. Mr. Trebilcock has written more generally about similar indirect benefits that were derived from the armaments industry. The greater availability of government contracts towards the end of the century was accompanied by greater freedom of design, and this, together with the rather special demands of weapons manufacture, resulted in a host of innovations which produced 'spin-off effects' for other industries. Where armaments firms such as Vickers moved into the civil field with motor-car manufacture they were also able to use their old arms-selling networks.[11] But this was all very much the exception, not the rule.

(D)

This chapter is not intended to be a general apologia for British industry.If it has played up the successes, technologically and commercially, it is because they are generally underestimated. If it has largely ignored entrepreneurial explanations of Britain's relative decline, this is to readjust the emphasis and seek more precision, rather than in any way to cast it aside completely. Here we have looked for that precision by analysing the environment in which firms operated, seeking to define more closely the extent to which the residual factor of enterprise must be called upon for explanation. It may be that mechanical engineering differs in important respects from other industries, but in that field at least I would argue that the slowing-down of British industrial growth after 1870 is more due to objective economic factors than has previously been recognized.

NOTES

1 This chapter is a revised version of S. B. Saul, 'The Market and the Development of the Mechanical Engineering Industries in Britain, 1860–1914', *Economic History Review*, 2nd Ser. xx (1967). Detailed footnotes can be consulted in the original article and in S. B. Saul, 'The Engineering Industries', in D. H. Aldcroft (ed.), *The Development of British Industry and Foreign Competition, 1875–1914* (London, 1968).

2 G. S. Gibb, *The Saco-Lowell Shops* (Cambridge, Mass., 1950), p. 260; T. R. Navin, *The Whitin Machine Works since 1831* (Cambridge, Mass., 1950), pp. 375, 391.

3 Gibb, op. cit., p. 345.

4 P. A. David, 'The Landscape and the Machine', in Donald McCloskey (ed.), *Essays on a Mature Economy: Britain after 1840* (London, 1971).

5 Professor Church has suggested that the slow technological development of watchmaking in Britain compared with Switzerland was due to the fact that the Swiss with their limited natural resources simply had to respond effectively to the destruction of the native textile industry, whereas Britain faced no such crisis. The textile crisis is surely much exaggerated and in any case he suggests no mechanism to explain why Swiss entrepreneurs should have been so moved. See R. A. Church, 'Nineteenth-Century Clock Technology in Britain, the United States and Switzerland', *Economic History Review*, 2nd Ser. xxviii (1975), 630.

6 A. E. Harrison, 'The Competitiveness of the British Cycle Industry, 1890–1914', *Economic History Review*, 2nd Ser. xxii (1969), 295.

7 Floud, in criticizing this analysis, created a model in which the sudden rise of U.S. imports because of the cycle boom overcame, in a year or so, the conservatism of decades in the machine-tool industry. (R. C. Floud, 'The Adolescence of American Engineering Competition, 1860–1900', *Economic History Review*, 2nd Ser. xxvii (1974), 64.) The model grossly distorts the argument for it misses the stress I have placed on the gradual build-up of experience, albeit of modest proportions, during the previous decade. That the surge of growth came from cycles in particular can hardly be denied but I have also emphasized the growth in demand in other industries at much the same time. There may be more validity in Floud's other point that prices of U.S. machinery fell during the home depression of the early 1890s and thus stimulated her exports of machine tools.

S. B. Saul

8 S. B. Saul, 'The Machine Tool Industry in Britain to 1914', *Business History*, x (1968), 32.

9 N. Rosenberg, 'Technological Change in the Machine Tool Industry, 1840–1919', *Journal of Economic History*, xxiii (1963), 424.

10 Peter Temin, 'The Relative Decline of the British Steel Industry, 1880–1913', in Henry Rosovsky (ed.), *Industrialization in Two Systems: Essays in Honor of Alexander Gerschenkron* (New York, 1966), pp. 140–55.

11 C. Trebilcock, 'Spin-off in British Economic History: Armaments and Industry, 1760–1914,' *Economic History Review*, 2nd Ser. xxii (1969), 480.

3

Penny Cigarettes, Oligopoly, and Entrepreneurship in the U.K. Tobacco Industry in the Late Nineteenth Century[1]

B. W. E. ALFORD

ON its formation in 1901 the Imperial Tobacco Company (of Great Britain and Ireland) Ltd. was capitalized at £11,957,022 which, in financial terms, made it the largest company in the U.K. at the time. In common with companies involved in the so-called merger movement, Imperial had been formed by the amalgamation of a number of previously independent businesses; though in this case the reason for the amalgamation was somewhat unusual, since thirteen firms had agreed to combine in order to beat off a challenge from the American Tobacco Company, operating through its subsidiary Ogden's, which threatened to corner the U.K. market for tobacco goods. Moreover, of the thirteen firms one stood out above all others: W. D. & H. O. Wills of Bristol. Indeed, it came as something of a shock to Wills' new associates when, at the final meeting arranged to agree the basis on which the new company was to be capitalized, it was revealed that Wills' annual net profits were running at a level of £750,000, representing a return of just over 60 per cent on the existing total capital employed in the business. Accordingly, Wills was valued at £6,992,221, representing nearly 60 per cent of the total capitalization of Imperial. The next largest firm in the group, Lambert & Butler of London, was valued at £751,306. Even Ogden's was capitalized at only £1,500,000, and this figure was the product of optimistic accounting.

In short, by the end of the nineteenth century Wills dominated the U.K. tobacco industry and, in effect, exercised a high degree of oligopoly control over the market. No better testimony to this could be given than that of James Buchanan Duke, the Napoleonic president of the American Tobacco Company, at the signing of the 'peace' between the British and Americans in 1902: 'I did hope that I should be able to force you to reduce your prices, and if you had I should have had you, but you refused to do so and I was therefore beaten.' It is the purpose of this essay to examine the factors which determined Wills' rise to dominance.

(A) THE TOBACCO MARKET AND INDUSTRIAL STRUCTURE
IN THE MID-NINETEENTH CENTURY

Up to the 1840s the tobacco industry developed on a regional basis: basic labour-intensive methods of producing a limited range of smoking and chewing tobaccos and snuffs reinforced limitations on the market imposed by the local character of product loyalties and the restrictive nature of inland transport. And as part of this pattern tobacco was sold mainly through small specialist tobacconists, who blended tobaccos to match local tastes, and to a lesser extent through other small shopkeepers, including apothecaries, who had some knowledge of the trade. Manufacturers in a given region were largely insulated from outside competition. But with the advent of railways the possibility of a transformation arose. Goods could now be distributed easily over long distances. However, selling smoking tobacco and snuff on anything approaching a national scale involved additional problems of marketing. Some manufacturers, such as Wills, were certainly able, by this time, to achieve a high degree of standardization in production, but it was still difficult for them to reduce their dependence on local retail outlets possessing specialist knowledge of local tastes. Some means was required for enabling the manufacturer to appeal directly to consumers, thus reducing the role of retailer to one of simply providing a point of sale.

In an effort to achieve this, in 1846 Wills hit upon the idea of giving special names to certain of its smoking tobaccos. Now, tobacco had always been sold under names which described the type of leaf and/or its region of origin and sometimes this was linked with the name of the retailer who made a speciality of blending tobaccos; but Wills' new names—which were introduced in 1847 —were contrived to emphasize the uniqueness of the manufacturer's product. For all its longer-term importance, nevertheless, branding was not a revolutionary innovation in the sense of immediately changing the whole nature of the market. Wills' brand-names were reserved mainly for loose tobaccos, since, in addition to the fact that consumers had to be educated to acceptance of brands, no one had yet invented an efficient packing machine; until that day came tobacco had to be weighed, wrapped in paper packets, and labelled by hand, and this tended to restrict the volume of production. But allowing for these limitations, branded tobaccos could now be sold by retailers with no special knowledge of the product, and this was a big step forward.

From the 1840s to the 1860s the market grew steadily, and an indication of this is given by the number of licensed retailers and dealers in the U.K. which rose from 186,000 in 1840 to 245,000 in 1860; and by the latter date most tobacco was sold for pipe-smoking since the fashion of chewing tobacco had virtually died out, while cigar-smoking was almost exclusively a pastime for the well-off and snuff-taking had never been very popular. And although smoking became something of a vogue among the middle and upper classes in the mid-nineteenth century, by far the main market for tobacco was among the working class who accounted for 80 per cent of consumption. Moreover, the spread of pipe-smoking was stimulated by two developments. The first was the gradual introduction, from the 1850s onwards, of briar pipes which were easier to handle and more durable than clays or the much more expensive meerschaums, and certainly more hygienic than clays. The second development was the increasing use of milder 'Virginia' tobaccos after their discovery in the 1860s, since they were ideally suited to briars. And the spread of pipe-smoking provided a marvellous opportunity for employing the techniques of branding and advertising. Furthermore, independently of their own efforts, tobacco firms were greatly helped in promoting standard-quality branded tobaccos by public concern over adulteration and by a general tightening-up of legislation governing tobacco manufacture, promoted by Gladstone in the early 1860s.[2]

The tobacco industry thus became a pioneer in popular marketing of cheap consumer goods. There were, of course, other industries—for example, food-processing and pharmaceuticals—where similar developments were occurring throughout the latter part of the nineteenth century, though none of these would appear to have rivalled tobacco closely in extent or ingenuity.[3] The clearest indication of this is provided by the quality of advertising materials used by leading tobacco manufacturers: their packet labels, showcards, and posters almost certainly included some of the most effective and outstanding examples of commercial art of the late-Victorian period. And this was backed up by Press advertising and a variety of more permanent forms of display which nowadays have become collectors' items. Yet for all its importance, successful application of branding and advertising depended fundamentally on a firm's selling organization. Wills was particularly skilful in this field. By the 1860s it had built up a national selling network staffed by carefully selected travellers who were highly paid by contemporary standards. A traveller's job was not simply to open new accounts and to push new brands, but also to provide a flow of market intelligence which would help the firm to tailor its products and selling methods to match variations in demand. Moreover, in 1864 Wills opened a London warehouse so as to secure the advantages of centralized distribution from the capital.

In 1871 Wills introduced its first branded hand-made cigarette, appropriately named Bristol. Soon other brands followed and this provided further opportunities for extending the use of elaborate packaging and colourful advertising. However, because of the high costs of production of cigarettes in relation to other tobacco goods, they were necessarily sold to a limited, luxury market; and significantly enough Wills produced these cigarettes at a newly opened London factory, mainly for the London market which traditionally set tastes in smoking habits.

These features of the market for tobacco goods were a major cause of significant changes in the structure of the industry between the 1850s and the 1880s. And between 1870 (the first year for which detailed figures are available) and 1880 U.K. sales of tobacco goods rose from 53·5 m. lb. to 63·5 m. lb. In terms of sales volume and value, by the early 1880s six firms—W. D. & H. O. Wills (Bristol), Cope Brothers (Liverpool), Lambert & Butler (London), Hignett Brothers (Liverpool), John Player and Sons (Nottingham), Stephen Mitchell & Son (Glasgow)—probably accounted for between 20 and 25 per cent of the industry. Behind them were another half-dozen or so which could claim some importance in national terms, but whose combined sales amounted to no more than 10 per cent of the total; while the remainder was produced by between 200 and 300 firms.[4]

Until the 1870s there was a high degree of competition between firms and, moreover, those beginning to gain a stronger hold on the market were doing so by means of innovations in selling and distribution as against techniques of production. Certainly, tobacco manufacture was not immune to the ubiquitous application of steam-power; it had made possible adoption of larger, faster, and more powerful presses and cutting machines—in turn, this directly reduced costs of production and, furthermore, if such innovations could be combined with careful organization of manual processes within purpose-built factories, further savings could be made. Yet the most efficient application of these techniques yielded a firm a cost/profit advantage rather than a competitive selling advantage, largely because of the somewhat special cost/price structure of the tobacco industry. This will be examined shortly.

In 1880, however, the Rose packing machine was invented and in 1885 the Williamson airtight tin was patented; and Wills acquired exclusive rights to the use of these in the tobacco industry. The packing machine broke a major bottle-neck in the production of smoking tobaccos, and airtight tins enabled Wills to guarantee the quality of its products over long periods and under varying climatic conditions. Even more importantly, these innovations did not simply produce certain costs advantages, they also provided very effective means of product differentiation—this was particularly so in the case of airtight tins—which gave a strong impetus to the switch in consumption to branded packet tobaccos. Moreover, acting strongly in conjunction with these technical innovations were longer-term government regulations and the development of more effective means of detecting adulteration, which have already been noted. This worked particularly to the advantage of the bigger manufacturers serving a national market.

Further, Gladstone's regulations concerning the export of tobacco goods worked directly in favour of firms which could afford to build purpose-designed bonded factories. However, it was the excise tax on raw leaf which, indirectly, had a very powerful effect on the structure of the industry. In 1880 the rate stood at 3s. 2d. per lb. as compared with an average prime cost of 7d.

A manufacturer had to finance the tax from the moment he withdrew leaf from a bonded warehouse until he received final payment from his customers. On average the minimum period involved was between five and eight weeks; though when allowance is made for seasonal fluctuations in demand, unusually heavy withdrawals of leaf because of hedging against duty rises, and the need to carry stocks of manufactured goods against losses in production, a firm such as Wills was doing well to turn over its capital three or four times a year.[5] In consequence of all these factors, financing the duty accounted for approximately 60 per cent of Wills' total capital employed, for example; and for every increase in sales there had to be a corresponding, proportionate increase in the amount of capital employed. Therefore, as the scale of operations of leading firms increased, the *absolute* size of this capital requirement grew, to such a level as to form a kind of threshold barrier confronting a smaller firm which might see an opportunity for challenging firms such as Wills in the national market; unless, that is, it could secure unusually easy access to capital and was willing to accept a high degree of financial risk. As leading firms increasingly developed their sales of nationally branded goods, so this threshold became clear cut and marked the extent of a growing gap between them and the rest. For example, in 1880 Wills employed a capital of £300,000 and by 1885 this had reached £471,000. For the large, established firm, however, the cost of financing such a big capital requirement was by no means necessarily high, since the firm's very size became a source of security through its market power. All Wills' capital needs were financed by the partners and by relations, friends, and acquaintances at a fixed rate of 5 per cent per annum—and as Wills' position within the industry strengthened the partners moved towards financing all their needs by themselves out of rising profit returns.

Possession of, and access to, large capital resources was also of advantage to a firm in its operations in the leaf market. With the necessary skill it was possible to gain significant cost advantages in the purchase of leaf.

Growing concentration in the structure of the industry was reflected in the changing pattern of pricing of tobacco goods. At the mid-century price-competition was strong and, as might be expected, involved periods of considerable price instability resulting from fluctuations in duty rates, leaf prices, and demand. During the 1860s and 1870s, however, both supply and demand conditions became much more stable, and this produced a pattern of conventional prices which was determined by the size of monetary units and the level of duty in relation to the quantities in which tobacco was sold to a predominantly working-class market; the most popular sorts of pipe tobaccos being retailed at 3d. per ounce. When branded tobaccos were introduced their trade prices were set on the comparative basis of adding a mark-up to prices of existing tobaccos such as would give an even-money retail price;[6] and this higher price for branded packet goods became an important element of product differentiation. Moreover, as firms gained experience of selling branded goods the quality range of tobaccos offered was widened. For Wills, and almost certainly for other firms, mark-ups were added on the principle of what the market would bear within the constraint of having to charge even-money prices. Thus the pricing of branded goods amounted to monopolistic pricing. Correspondingly, as sales of branded goods increased in proportion to total sales the tobacco industry became more monopolistic in organization.

One of the clearest signs of changes in the structure of the industry between the 1850s and the early 1880s was growing collusion between a small group of large manufacturers. From time to time they met together, on an informal basis, to discuss issues of pricing and terms of trading; and before long these meetings began to produce informal policy agreements. Not surprisingly, the effectiveness of these agreements was variable, but there is no doubt that on major issues a handful of firms was seeking to impose its will on the industry as a whole and that its efforts were meeting with a growing measure of success.

(B) BUSINESS STRATEGY AND GROWTH
IN THE LATE NINETEENTH CENTURY

By the mid-1880s Wills was *primus inter pares* among U.K. tobacco firms and it appeared set to consolidate this position. Yet within a decade the firm came to dominate the industry. In order to understand this development it is necessary to examine the firm's strategy in a little detail.

From the mid-century onwards the main operational objective of the firm had been to maximize the sales weight of tobacco goods, on the assumption that this would produce an increasing stream of profits. Furthermore, it is important to note, accounting procedures employed by Wills (and by many other firms in a whole range of industries in the nineteenth century) defined profits as residual rewards to management and not as returns on capital employed; and this naturally tended to direct attention to searching for, and then exploiting, new sources of profit, rather than to making calculations on alternative uses of finance in different sectors of the market, which would have been consistent with the objective of profit-maximization. Moreover, this immediate objective was interrelated with the more fundamental one of securing the survival of the firm in order to serve the financial and social needs of a large and strongly committed nonconformist family; and when, eventually, this aim was secure the partners became intent on building up a national and international reputation for their business.

Such business objectives gave a powerful and continual thrust to the search for new markets, and this included searching for new techniques which might provide new types of goods or, at least, contribute to further brand differentiation of existing ones. In all this, however, there was never any question of the partners looking beyond their own industry, even if only as far as related ones. Therefore, in the Penrosian sense, by the 1880s Wills had increasing spare resources; it possessed such ample financial reserves that it began to experience a measure of overcapitalization;[7] More significantly, it had potentially spare management resources, since the partners could well have reduced their involvement in the business by giving up a range of routine tasks and limiting their activities to major management functions. In one sense, of course, this could be regarded as a measure of inefficiency, but to do so would be to ignore the Wills family's positive opposition to developing business activities outside tobacco. In part this was simply a matter of choice but in part, also, it was founded on a shared belief that extension of the firm into new fields would lead to divided, and therefore destructive, loyalties in what was essentially, and necessarily for them, a family firm.

The task of finding new markets in the tobacco industry was a very difficult one because of the basic nature of the finished product. And within the broader context of distribution and retailing of consumer goods in the late nineteenth century it was difficult to imagine how, short of quite revolutionary changes in the pattern of consumption, the firm could expect to achieve a significantly larger share of the market than it held by the 1880s, through existing selling techniques. It was natural, therefore, that considerable attention should have been given to discovering and acquiring new production techniques. And it has already been noted how the acquisition of the Rose packing machine and the Williamson airtight tin served both selling and production objectives.

By the early 1880s, however, cigarettes offered the most obvious opportunities for new sources of profit. Neverthless, mechanization of cigarette production presented formidable technical obstacles. A number of inventors had been grappling with the problem for some years without much success; indeed, from time to time Wills received information about prototype cigarette-making machines (and other technical developments) from inventors who were keen to sell their patents to a leading tobacco manufacturer. Successive partners had always taken a close interest in technical developments but when, in 1878 at the age of 22, Harry Wills was formally appointed the firm's engineer, the quest for new techniques was given stronger impetus.

After school at Mill Hill and Clifton College, Harry had served three years as a pupil engineer at the Avonside Engineering Company, which he completed by taking a number of examinations in engineering subjects at Bristol University College. Harry was, by temperament, attracted to any new mechanical gadgetry and he was a keen amateur inventor. His enthusiasms in this area sometimes outran his judgement—which was somewhat unreliable—though within the firm this was balanced by his more sober-minded brother, George. Born in 1854, George has been educated at Mill Hill and after he left there in 1872 he spent three years in different departments of the firm. In 1875 he was formally appointed a manager of the Bedminster factory. George proved to be a man of very shrewd and sound business ability who, with enormous energy, devoted himself to mastering every branch of the business.

George became a partner in 1882 and Harry in 1884; and by this latter date these two members of the fourth generation were, in effect, joint Managing Directors of Wills. And the combination of George's and Harry's talents were ideally suited to the special opportunities which opened up in the tobacco industry in the mid-1880s. Moreover, George enjoyed a close relationship with his uncle, William Henry Wills, the leading member of the third generation who had been mainly responsible for building up the firm in the 1860s and 1870s. Although William Henry no longer worked full time at Wills, he was Chairman of the Board of partners and he exercised a genial, astute, and strong influence over policy-making. Thus his relationship with George was of some importance, since the younger partners could make no major decision of policy without the consent of the senior partners of whom two, Frederick and Edward, were still very active in the firm. The remaining and largest partner was Henry Overton Wills III—father of George and Harry—though he had completely retired from active business and was happy to leave matters to George.

Harry was largely responsible for the acquisition of the Rose and Williamson rights, but in between these activities he was involved in acquiring the exclusive U.K. rights, for Wills, to the Bonsack cigarette-making machine. This machine was to prove the most fundamental technical development in the history of tobacco manufacture. James A. Bonsack of Salem, Virginia, patented his invention in this country and in the U.S.A. in 1881, but it was not until 1883, by which time he had been able to make certain improvements to the prototype, that he decided to advertise it. He did this by setting up a working model in Paris. Wills heard of Bonsack's arrival from its continental agent and Harry immediately went over to Paris to inspect the machine. He was very impressed with what he saw and, on returning to England, with his brother George he persuaded the senior partners to invite Bonsack to set up his machine at Wills' Redcliff Street factory in Bristol, where it could be subjected to rigorous testing. This crucial first move was in direct accordance with the firm's general policy and owed much to Harry and George. The next move was equally crucial and was, from the firm's point of view, to a significant degree dependent on luck operating through family relationships.

It so happened that some cousins of the Wills family, John Hopkinson and his son Charles of Manchester, were consultant engineers whom the partners had referred to in the past on a number of quite minor matters; and it was the natural thing to turn to them again for advice. Charles Hopkinson made a thorough test of the machine and then submitted a report. Certainly, with the advantage of hindsight it is clear that the report was of outstanding quality. Hopkinson listed certain mechanical faults and explained how they could be remedied. He estimated the saving in costs made possible by the machine, and although this was done on a conservative basis even then he showed that it amounted to a reduction of 80 per cent (from a cost of 5*s*. to 1*s*. per 1,000 cigarettes). But the really striking thing was that Hopkinson did not confine himself to purely technical matters: he included clear and penetrating advice on the potential market for mass-produced cigarettes, in particular for cheap cigarettes. He also spelt out the possible alternatives open to Wills and the reasons why, in his judgement, the firm should purchase exclusive rights to the Bonsack at once. Again it was Hopkinson who was responsible for calling in J. Harry Johnson, one of the leading patent agents of the day. At first Johnson expressed doubts as to the strength of the Bonsack patent but, after very detailed investigation, he accumulated sufficient evidence to enable leading counsel to be certain that the patent could be defended if the need arose. And the ability to establish exclusive rights to the invention was of fundamental importance to Wills and to the development of the U.K. tobacco industry.

Exclusive ownership of the Bonsack cost Wills £4,000 in 1883—each new machine cost approximately £200. There was no royalty payment. This must rate as one of the best buys in British industrial history.

Wills introduced its first machine-made cigarettes in either late 1883 or very early 1884, and production was confined to the more popular of its existing brands. Of course, at this time cigarette consumption was negligible. Besides, the novelty character of cigarettes had meant that, from their introduction in the 1870s, pricing had been very much a secondary factor. Because of smoking requirements cigarettes obviously needed to be within certain size limits and to be sold in convenient quantities. Within these requirements it was simply a matter of fixing a trade price which would allow even-money retail pricing; and given the relatively very high rate of duty this left plenty of room for a healthy profit margin. Wills therefore priced cigarettes on the principle of adding a fairly substantial mark-up to conventional tobacco prices, on a weight for weight basis; and the relatively high price for cigarettes, as with packet tobaccos, became a feature of product differentiation. Further, profit on trade prices of cigarettes appeared modest in relation to total costs of production, including duty; but when this is translated into either a return on true costs (i.e. when the duty element is calculated in terms of the costs of financing it) or on total capital employed, cigarettes rated at between five and ten times as profitable as ordinary pipe tobaccos. Nevertheless, it is important to stress that cigarette prices were not fixed in relation to these considerations because of the nature of the product and its market; cigarettes were viewed as making a useful, but necessarily very minor, contribution to total profits.[8]

The impact of the Bonsack machine on the profitability of cigarette production was therefore dramatic. Yet still Wills did not reckon the profit potential of machine-made cigarettes as very substantial and consequently made no effort to press home its potential competitive advantage along the lines urged by Hopkinson. Why?

For a start there was no obvious evidence here, or abroad, of a large unsatisfied demand for cheap cigarettes. And under any circumstances the senior partners were cautious and determined to proceed slowly; especially as they were concerned to maintain and enhance the firm's reputation as the leading manufacturer of quality tobacco goods—this after all had been an important element in their success to date. A reputation as a manufacturer of cheap cigarettes might truly prove penny wise and pound foolish. Finally, though less importantly, concern was expressed by one senior partner over the possibility of machine production putting people out of work; an attitude which again betrayed a low estimation of the potential demand for cigarettes.

These views were not shared by George and Harry who were keen to follow up their cousin's advice, but in 1883 they were still very much junior partners. Over the next four years, therefore, machine production of cigarettes was limited to existing brands at relatively high prices. Nevertheless, it soon became clear that even the market for these brands was expanding and trade in it had in no way damaged the firm's reputation—quite the reverse! What is more, as turnover of machine-made cigarettes grew their contribution to profits could not be ignored—particularly as gross profits per lb on cigarettes were running at seven times the rate for smoking tobaccos. Further, other firms were showing growing interest in the cigarette market. This knowledge proved a powerful solvent to the resistance of the senior partners. Meanwhile, George and Harry had been assuming greater responsibility, and therefore influence, in the firm, and by 1887 they felt strong enough to press their demands once more.

Eventually George persuaded his uncle, William Henry, of the need for the firm to make the experiment with cheap cigarettes. Having secured this support, the other senior partners quickly acceded to George's plans. Final details would have been settled in 1887 had it not been for a duty alteration in that year which necessitated various price changes. Thus Wills introduced two new brands of cheap cigarettes—Woodbine and Cinderella—in 1888: an event which, in retrospect, can be seen clearly as marking the beginning of the modern cigarette industry in this country.

Given the existing range of brands, the specification of a cheap brand was partly predetermined, but this still left room for choice and there can be little doubt in the light of its subsequent success that Woodbine at 1*d.* for 5 achieved the optimum. The critical factor was almost certainly price: it defined and differentiated Woodbine as the cigarette everyone could afford. And conventional pricing and costing methods automatically endowed even a cheap brand with very healthy profit margins. Once again, however, while penny cigarettes were expected to do well it was never thought that they would rival, let alone supplant, pipe tobaccos, so healthy margins on such fractional units were justified by the need to produce satisfactory levels of profit.

The scale and speed of success of penny cigarettes astounded even George and Harry Wills. Booming sales produced soaring profits. Fractional profit margins on penny cigarettes took on a completely new order of significance

TABLE 3.1

Wills' Cigarette Sales by Number and Type, 1888–1891 (to nearest 100,000)

Year	Ordinary cigarettes	Penny cigarettes	Total
1888	21 600 000	4 800 000 (5 months)	26 400 000
1889	23 600 000	27 800 000	51 400 000
1890	24 500 000	48 900 000	73 400 000
1891	41 500 000	84 500 000	126 000 000

when multiplied by large turnover. Between 1887 and 1890 Wills' annual net profits rose from £46,500 to £85,000; in 1891 profits passed £100,000, in 1896 £300,000, in 1898 £500,000; and in 1901 they reached £750,000. These vast increases were due entirely to cigarettes. As Table 3.2 indicates, sales of smoking tobaccos had even begun to fall by the end of the period; and since this was associated with some slimming of margins the profitability of cigarettes is even larger than the figures suggest.[9] The firm's over-all position in the U.K. industry, in terms of sales weight, is shown in Figures 3.1 and 3.2.

TABLE 3.2

Comparative Analysis of Wills' Sales by Weight, 1885–1901

Year	Wills' cigarette sales as % of Wills' total U.K. sales	Wills' cigarette sales as % of total U.K. sales	Wills' cigarette sales as % of total U.K cigarette sales	Wills' cigarette sales (lb)	Wills' tobacco, snuff, cigar sales (lb)
1885	0·7	neg.	n.a.	28 952	3 980 007
1890	4·3	0·6	59·2	204 126	4 495 663
1895	25·6	5·0	55·4	1 709 277	4 967 185
1900	57·5	13·8	54·6	5 793 757	4 285 812
1901	63·7	14·5	55·2	6 870 842	3 921 709

Wills thus came to dominate the cigarette market and, as will be shown shortly, this meant effective dominance of the whole industry. Moreover, Wills maintained this position even though by the early 1890s other firms had entered the machine-made cigarette market and were making vigorous efforts to expand their sales. The key to Wills' success was its head start with penny cigarettes since this gave Woodbine the supreme market opportunity to establish itself as *the* universal brand of cigarette. And Wills' other brands benefited from the firm's reputation as the originator of machine-made cigarettes. The early defence of the Bonsack rights was therefore crucial for the firm and, furthermore, this machine remained superior to other competing ones which came on to the market in the 1890s.

B. W. E. Alford

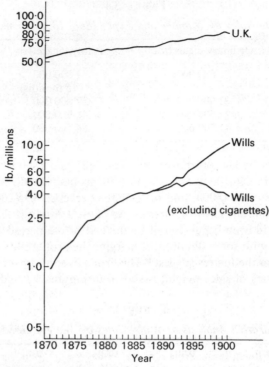

FIG. 3.1. Total Domestic Sales of Tobacco Goods, 1870–1901: U.K. and Wills compared (log scale)

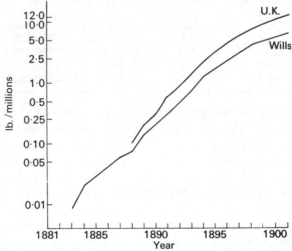

FIG. 3.2. Domestic Cigarette Sales, 1883–1901: U.K. and Wills compared (log scale)

(C) RESPONSES TO COMPETITION

Before examining the more general nature and significance of Wills' development, it is necessary to consider briefly the reaction of the firm to two developments in the industry since this will reveal a great deal about its behaviour over these critical years: these developments were price-cutting and the invasion of the U.K. tobacco market by the American Tobacco Company.

During 1894 large, multiple wholesale/retail tobacconists, following the lead of Singleton & Cole in Birmingham and Salmon & Gluckstein in London, began widespread price-cutting, mainly of retail prices: and it was taken up by chain and department stores as a form of loss-leader selling.[10] Over the following year the practice spread; furthermore, Salmon & Gluckstein began producing their own brands of cheap cigarettes. Matters came to a head in the Wills company in 1896. From 1894, however, there had been a fairly clear division between those partners who wanted some form of strong action to regulate prices and terms and those who were in favour of allowing matters to rest: this was mainly a division between the Bristol and London managements. Those in London were quite happy to let things alone as they were aware at first hand that sales of the firm's branded goods—especially cigarettes—were booming in the metropolis under the stimulus of retail price-cutting; whereas the Bristol managers, who dealt with the country as a whole, were concerned lest small retailers be driven out of business, thus strengthening the bargaining position of large wholesaler/retailers who might well then exert pressure on manufacturers for more favourable trade prices. Since policy was finally determined at Bristol, it was decided to renew earlier discussions with other leading manufacturers with a view to setting up machinery for enforcing a schedule of prices and terms.

After a number of meetings in early 1896 arrangements for a schedule were settled between the six leading firms, together with separate agreements with certain large wholesaler/retailers aimed at stopping cutting at source. Within Wills, however, there were growing misgivings over this policy and these were voiced strongly by Sir William Henry in a letter to his nephew George a little later in the year. He considered the firm to have acted unwisely in agreeing to price control and that it should 'get free at first opportunity and be able to act independently'. He was doubtful whether the schedule could be made to work, was concerned about public reaction, and apprehensive of other firms breaking ranks and stealing the march on Wills. And, in a final comment, he summed up perfectly what became the guiding principles of the firm's business strategy as it accustomed itself to its new-found prodigious prosperity: 'We are doing well now. Don't let us take a leap in the dark. Let us wait where we are quite still, till daylight dawns. One false step now may ruin our whole business and turn its growth into decay.' And, taking up Sir William's metaphor: when day dawned for the partners they could see it was a very sunny

i

one and they decided to take advantage of it by making hay while the sun lasted.

By early 1897, therefore, Wills was giving little more than token support to efforts to control prices and terms. Over the next three years the firm was involved in discussions about price-cutting and actually became party in 1900 to a very limited arrangement with other manufacturers concerning pipe tobaccos. But none of this amounted to much for it was clear to the partners by the late 1890s that there were two fairly distinct markets for tobacco goods: one for cigarettes and strongly branded pipe tobaccos which the firm dominated and which was highly profitable; one for weaker brands of packet tobaccos and loose tobaccos which was intensely competitive as trade prices and manufacturers' profit margins were being continually squeezed. Nevertheless, Wills strongly believed contact with other firms to be necessary in order to enable it to exercise a degree of control and market leadership—and, more fundamentally, the partners were convinced that cigarettes would remain a minor section of the tobacco market, and they were therefore concerned to keep a close eye on sales of pipe tobaccos while doing everything to maintain their dominant position in the cigarette trade.

Thus Wills still pursued a somewhat cautious policy, reflected by the manner in which it did not exercise the full extent of its market power: while it certainly aimed to maximize sales through its production and marketing advantages it was, in strict economic terms, unduly co-operative with other manufacturers and unnecessarily conciliatory towards retailers. In short, although Wills had all the required qualifications, its strategy did not conform to the precepts of what would now be defined as oligopolistic behaviour. Now, in terms of sales and profitability it is doubtful whether this made much difference. But in terms of the firm's broader business strategy this caution and lack of understanding of its true market position did have important consequences in relation to the second development. This will be discussed in a moment.

Before the American invasion is considered, however, it is necessary to expand our analysis of Wills' market position as defined in terms of sales value, by adding an account of what this meant in terms of profits. It has been shown how, by weight,Wills accounted for 12 per cent of U.K. domestic sales of tobacco goods in 1901. Against this, the firms which formed the new Imperial Tobacco Company in 1901 produced 40 per cent of total U.K. sales. Moreover, Imperial was capitalized on the basis of the net profits of each constituent company, and on these terms it was necessary to allot Wills nearly 70 per cent of the ordinary share capital. Therefore, on the assumption of Imperial being no more profitable than the industry as a whole, Wills alone accounted for roughly 30 per cent of the industry's net profits. But Wills' extraordinary profitability arose directly from producing over 55 per cent of U.K. cigarette sales; and about 25 per cent was produced by other branches of Imperial. It follows, therefore, that Wills' share of the industry's profits must have been significantly above 30 per cent—an informed guess would put it upwards of 50 per cent.

By the end of the 1890s the partners were left in no doubt as to the profitability of their enterprise. When the firm was formed into a company in 1893 its capitalization had been nearly doubled by the introduction of a large element of goodwill. The return on this expanded capital roughly tripled between 1893 and 1901 to 39 per cent. On the original accounting basis (i.e. excluding goodwill) return on total capital employed rose from an average of 20 per cent to just over 60 per cent by 1901–2, and this makes no allowance for a measure of undistributed profits retained in the business. Yet in some ways this success was viewed by the partners as practical confirmation of their cautious policies. And these attitudes were similarly displayed over the most serious challenge ever faced by the firm: the American invasion of 1901–2.

The early stages of the 'tobacco war', as it became known, including the formation of Imperial, were outlined at the very beginning of this chapter. After a fierce struggle peace was signed; Woodbine and, somewhat ironically, the American Bonsack machine were the rocks on which the American Tobacco Company foundered. But when Duke had first announced his warlike intentions there was a strong body of opinion within Wills for selling out to him on the best possible terms. And this view did not spring from a desire to give up business in favour of other, possibly more gentlemanly, pursuits; it arose from a genuine belief that this was the only way to secure the firm's position in face of such an overwhelming threat. Moreover, all the partners were extremely agitated over the possibility of the American Tobacco Company cornering the U.S.A. leaf market. In the event, the dominant characters of Sir William Henry and George Wills ensured that the firm would stand and fight in combination with others; though their decision to pursue this course derived mainly from their assessment that it would be extremely difficult to get any sort of satisfactory terms from the American Tobacco Company, and not from a clear understanding of the strength of Wills' market power.

On this reasoning, the possibility of Wills standing alone was ruled completely out of court. Yet with the advantage of hindsight this appears to have been not only a feasible alternative but might possibly have led, also, to Wills securing an even more dominant position within the U.K. market; and the firm would certainly not have become involved in the unsatisfactory structure of Imperial which remained after the 'war'.[11] The main beneficiaries from the formation of Imperial were the other constituent firms since, relatively, they stood to lose most from a battle between the American Tobacco Company and Wills.

Nevertheless, even if the partners had fully understood the nature of the firm's power it would have been a perfectly understandable strategy for them to have opted for combination. It was a less risky course than going it alone, as it probably brought about an early resolution of the conflict because leading U.K. firms could not be used as pawns in a drawn-out campaign; and there was every indication that Duke would use this tactic if possible, since he had already made what proved to be an abortive attempt to acquire the Nottingham business of John Player & Sons. In short, there is no way of precisely determining which was the optimum course, given Wills' objectives and necessarily imperfect knowledge.

In turn, however, this raises what is in many ways a more fundamental issue in this context: the manner in which Wills actually made the choice of policy. In effect, the partners did not adopt a strategy to meet this radical change in market conditions, they simply adopted short-term tactical policies which squared with their somewhat cautious, pragmatic approach. In the by then traditional manner they consulted with the few other leading firms in the industry. Moreover, as early as 1894 Wills had become alarmed about a possible threat by the American Tobacco Company to corner the leaf market in the U.S.A., and had gone into the matter so thoroughly as to prepare a contingency plan; naturally enough, at that time and because of the nature of the issue, the plan was based on an amalgamation with the other leading U.K. manufacturers. When Wills' fears proved unfounded the plan was dropped; it was, after all, no more than a tactical response. Four years later, when Wills' earlier fears revived, the plan was resuscitated but, once again, fears receded and no action was taken. When the ultimate threat from the American Tobacco Company finally materialized the 1894 plan was, yet again, resurrected and this time it provided the detailed design for the new Imperial Company. In the immediate situation this policy might appear reasonable enough, but when it is seen against its longer-term consequences it reveals a great deal about the formulation of business strategy. The full significance of this will be considered in the final section but, for the moment, it can be noted that once the dust of war had settled and peace had returned to the market, Imperial remained as a mammoth corporate oddity.

(D) ENTREPRENEURSHIP IN THE DEVELOPMENT OF THE TOBACCO INDUSTRY

The purpose of this chapter is to explain how oligopoly developed within the U.K. tobacco industry in the latter half of the nineteenth century and the elements underlying Wills' emergence as the dominant firm. In the latter respect certain factors stand out fairly clearly from the foregoing analysis. First, there was Wills' early adoption of branding and advertising. Secondly, the firm's acquisition of exclusive rights to certain technical innovations enabled it to steal the march on competitors in a manner which gave it rapid and commanding market advantage. Above all, Wills' success depended on the Bonsack cigarette-making machine. Moreover, the central importance of these factors focuses attention on the role of entrepreneurship. Now, one of the general problems in this regard lies in taking account of relationships between various levels of management within a firm, in the process of entre-preneurial decision-making.[12] Fortunately, the Wills business was at a stage of development in which the partners not only directed over-all strategy but, also, were involved in the whole range of managerial functions.[13]

In examining entrepreneurial performance it is important to note that, in this case at least, while oligopoly theory is useful in helping us to distinguish certain dominant features of the tobacco industry over this period, it does not provide anything like an adequate basis for explaining business behaviour. At no time did the partners have a clear understanding of the firm's market power. Their immediate objective was not to maximize profits but to increase sales as the means of increasing the flow of profits; and although this involved some notion of a satisfactory level of profits, until the 1890s at least, this was very elastic in accordance with contemporary accounting practices. And, as has been shown, this immediate objective was further conditioned by succes-sive partners' concern to preserve the long-term existence of the business in order to meet the financial and social needs of a large, nonconformist family.

More generally, formal theory does not provide a basis for realistic *ex post* evaluation of business performance, since there is no satisfactory means for relating measures of short-term maximization to the requirements for longer-term growth. Therefore, an analysis of entrepreneurship as against other factors determining a firm's performance cannot be quantitatively precise. For this reason it is necessary to rely on qualitative evaluation of the role of individual business men. But this needs to be done with extreme care because it is usually possible to obtain a sharp focus on certain, allegedly major, business decisions and by this fact alone entrepreneurship can be easily elevated in the analysis to the position of the central dynamic factor which responds to a range of other, given conditions. And such an approach is often elaborated with colourful accounts of leading figures and underwritten by apparently revealing evidence of deeper psychological motivations.

The particular talents of the Wills partners have been briefly described. Collectively, they combined shrewdness in exploiting available markets and techniques with patient, conscientious application to the detailed working of their business. Together with an infusion of philistine, nonconformist beliefs this probably made them duller than most contemporary leading business men; and they are certainly not ideal subjects for business biography. But they had sufficient flair for taking risks with new ideas. Thus, in terms of profit or loss, the firm probably benefited from the virtues of the partners' dullness without suffering unduly from its vices. At the same time, however, it is pos-sible that the competitive opposition faced by the firm was mediocre; or, alternatively, other manufacturers' objectives might have been such that they did not seek the same kind or level of expansion as did Wills. Yet there is ample evidence to show this not to have been so and, in the 1890s in particular, the other leading firms in the industry were vigorous in their efforts to match Wills' technical and market performance. Furthermore, in 1901 Wills proved its ability to stand comparison with the mighty American Tobacco Company.

For all their success, however, the partners never adopted coherent strategies as conditions altered. Their response was always one of short-term tactics, albeit in accordance with their basic objectives. The formation of Imperial has been shown to be an example *par excellence* of this approach. And as one of the leading examples of the amalgamation movement it is of more general significance: it stands as a warning against assuming that firms necessarily operate on the basis of a prepared strategy, however well or badly defined; in fact, what might appear as a strategy *ex post* might well have been the outcome of a series of short-term tactical manœuvres.[14]

Up to this point, nevertheless, our analysis at least bears out the view that entrepreneurship was of crucial importance in securing Wills' dominance over other tobacco firms. But at the same time this does not imply a correspondingly crucial role for entrepreneurship within the development of the industry; yet it is in this latter respect that by far the most significant assessment of its economic role has to be made. In other words, was Wills' superior entrepreneurial performance in relation to other firms as unique and influential in the industry's performance when judged against other factors external to Wills? Moreover, it is essential to examine such factors in terms of their independent and dynamic effects, and not to view them as a range of given conditions within which the entrepreneur necessarily performs the central role.

We have analysed how the changing structure of the industry was a necessary response to market and technological developments. So far as the market was concerned these developments involved a complex range of elements including rising incomes, population growth, urbanization, and the revolution in transport. Indeed, this last element can be used to illustrate the direct effects of external factors. For rail transport not only opened up much wider markets than existed before, but it actively forced manufacturers to expand their selling networks for fear of others breaking into their previously insulated regional markets. Furthermore, the ubiquity of rail transport affected general patterns of retailing and distribution in ways which, in effect, made it impossible for tobacco manufacturers not to alter the structure and organization of their firms. As for technological changes, by providing the means for mass producing basically simple products they determined that certain firms would develop into relatively large-scale enterprises within the industry.

Market and technological factors were directly and powerfully augmented by two institutional factors: taxation and patent law. As to the former, the proportionately very large amounts of capital required to finance the duty on tobacco leaf actively promoted growing concentration of production, and it greatly facilitated the establishment of patterns of monopolistic pricing. As to the latter, it enabled whichever firm acquired rights to crucial manufacturing processes to defend its exclusive use of them in a manner which directly accelerated and accentuated the process of concentration. Moreover, because of the capital requirements of the excise tax, innovation and the defence of patents involved comparatively minimal financial risk. In 1895, for example, investment in plant and machinery accounted for only 4 per cent of a total capital of £890,000 employed by Wills.

The nature of these external factors together with what is known of Wills and other tobacco firms provides support for the hypothesis that if Wills had not come to dominate the industry some other firm would have done. Entrepreneurship was obviously a necessary condition of the industry's growth, but the level required was not such as to make it a factor in short supply. And beyond that level entrepreneurial ability determined the degree to which individual firms secured a share of the industry's expanding fortunes; while the expansion itself was determined by factors beyond the control of individual business men. In other words, the Wills family was by far the main beneficiary of the Wills partners' special talents. However, in so far as the timing of innovation is an important factor in an industry's development, then the unique combination of chance elements and the business abilities of the Wills partners might well have been of special significance. A plausible hypothesis would be that if Wills had been unwilling to make the production and marketing experiment with machine-made cigarettes then, in the short run, cigarette production would have been more evenly spread—and possibly lower—a situation which would have made the industry far easier game for the American Tobacco Company. But while this would have resulted in different ownership of the industry it is difficult to see how it would have resulted in any change in structure: a foreign oligopolist would have simply supplanted a domestic one. Moreover, this hypothesis ignores Wills' delay of five years before taking full advantage of its patent rights, so an alternative British firm might simply have replaced Wills and have developed to a similar position. Whichever way various alternatives on this counterfactual theme are developed it seems to make little difference to the probable outcome.

It is, of course, impossible to generalize about the development of British business enterprise over the latter half of the nineteenth century on the basis of this one case. But, at least, the tobacco industry is of some general significance as a major example of a consumer-goods industry; in some ways it could be defined as a new industry of this period. Its expansion was associated with buoyant demand and new products; and it was not hampered by an old industrial structure or by traditional patterns of labour supply and organization. Yet its expansion was not mainly the achievement of a sparkling new generation of entrepreneurs. It was more directly the result of market, technological, and institutional factors. In short, our analysis provides some grounds for suggesting that discussion of the performance of British business, over this period at least, should concentrate primarily on such factors and only secondarily on the particular virtues or vices of individual business men.[15]

NOTES

1 Further details on particular aspects of the developments covered by this chapter can be obtained by consulting B. W. E. Alford, *W.D. & H.O. Wills and the Development of the U.K. Tobacco Industry, 1786–1965* (Methuen, London, 1973).

2 See G. L. Apperson, *The Social History of Smoking* (London, 1914); Arthur Hill Hassell, *Food and its Adulterations* (London, 1855); J. D. Burnett, *Plenty and Want* (London, 1966).

3 For a general analysis of the retailing aspects of these developments see J. B. Jefferys, *Retail Trading in Britain, 1850–1950* (Cambridge, 1954).

4 This is necessarily a *rough* estimate, but, in addition to the business records of W.D. & H.O. Wills, it is based on the business records of Lambert & Butler (in the possession of the Imperial Group Ltd.) and on various miscellaneous company reports and records in the possession of W.D. & H.O. Wills. Furthermore, significant indications can be discovered from the contemporary trade Press: *Tobacco* and *Tobacco Trade Review*.

5 It is important to note that these operations had always required considerable skill on the part of the tobacco manufacturer.

6 Trade prices were those prices charged by the manufacturer to either wholesalers or retailers. Wholesale and retail prices were arrived at by successive mark-ups on trade prices. In addition, manufacturers offered a series of terms related to quantities purchased. Just over 2*d.* out of the retail price of 3*d.* was accounted for by duty and the prime cost of leaf (having made allowance for moisture gain in manufacture) so other costs and profit margins on an ounce of tobacco turned on fractions of a penny. To put it another way, an increase in retail price to the next even money unit, i.e. to 3¼*d.* per ounce, while costs remained constant, would produce a huge increase in profit margin for distribution between manufacturer, wholesaler, and retailer. The full implications of the peculiarities of this cost/price structure are taken up below. Detailed specifications are provided in Alford, op. cit., pp. 243, 244, 415, 416.

7 See E. T. Penrose, *The Theory of the Growth of the Firm* (Oxford, 1960). For example, as early as 1889 the firm's Board minutes record: 'That looking at the way in which capital is increasing it is considered desirable for the partners who have more than £100,000 each in the business to reduce their capital to that amount as early as they conveniently can.'

8 Again the cost/price structure is crucial (see n. 6, above). In this case the percentage rate of profit on the true trade cost of cigarettes could be fixed at a high level without any effect on retail prices because it was in terms of fractions of a penny.

9 Wills' position in the growing export trade of tobacco goods was correspondingly strong.

10 For a general discussion of developments in retailing during this period see Jefferys, op. cit.; B. Yamey, 'The origins of retail price maintenance', *Economic Journal*, lxii (1952), 522–45.

11 For a detailed analysis of this see B. W. E. Alford, 'Strategy and Structure in the U.K. Tobacco Industry', in Leslie Hannah (ed.), *Management Strategy and Business Development* (London, 1976).

12 For an examination of this and other, related issues see B. W. E. Alford, 'The Chandler Thesis—Some General Observations', in Hannah (ed.), op. cit.

13 A stage which has been defined as the personal enterprise. For the development of this and other terms in this connection see Alfred D. Chandler and Herman Daems, 'The Rise of Managerial Capitalism and its Impact on Investment Strategy in the Western World and Japan', in Herman Daems and Herman van der Wee (eds.), *The Rise of Managerial Capitalism* (The Hague, 1974).

14 For the classic statement of the strategy/structure approach to business development see Alfred D. Chandler, *Strategy and Structure: Chapters in the History of the Industrial Enterprise* (Cambridge, Mass., 1962); also Alford, 'The Chandler Thesis'.

15 For an elegant statement of a somewhat different view of the role of enterpreneurship generally over this period see Charles Wilson, 'Economy and Society in Late Victorian Britain', *Economic History Review*, 2nd Ser. xviii (1965), 183–98.

4

Corporate Growth and Structural Change in a Service Industry: Insurance, 1870-1914[1]

BARRY SUPPLE

THIS chapter is concerned with the growth of the insurance industry, and with the associated adaptations of its business structures, in the period 1870-1914. Whether or not the four or five decades before the First World War comprise an era in Britain's economic and business history with coherent and distinctive characteristics is a question which is still controversial. In the case of non-marine insurance,[2] however, the late nineteenth century was a time of such substantial and specific developments—in terms of scope of activities, scale of operations, and organization of enterprise—that it must necessarily be treated as the beginning of a new phase.

Of course, as with all economic and business activity, these developments built on what went before. Fire and life insurance in particular had evolved substantially during the Industrial Revolution, when the value of private and commercial property grew, the habit of rationalizing risks developed, and the middle classes paid increasing attention to the virtues of prudence and thrift which were catered for by new modes of life insurance. Thus between 1790 and 1870 the sums insured by fire insurance policies in England and Wales rose roughly from £150 m. to some £1,500 m., while during the same period the equivalent value of life policies increased from perhaps less than £5 m. to almost £300 m. Structurally, there were similar spectacular developments. In 1800 there were only about 6 companies doing life business and less than 20 underwriting fire risks (some companies were involved in both sorts of insurance). By 1870 there were about 100 life insurance companies and perhaps half that number of fire insurance companies (again with a considerable overlap). Yet the developments of the first half of the century were somewhat limited in scope: they largely affected traditional underwriting in fire and life; they were mainly restricted to the domestic market; and the business enterprises involved were relatively simple in structure and orientation. In the decades after 1870 this situation was transformed. Just as in other sectors of the economy new products (steel, chemicals, electricity) were evolved, so in insurance the complexities and risks of a modernizing society stimulated new types of cover: against railway and industrial accidents, theft, legal liabilities, and the hazards of travel by motor car and aeroplane. Moreover, in the decades immediately before 1914 traditional as well as these novel modes of underwriting both grew and penetrated new levels of society and economic activity until, in terms of their popularity, relative cost, and the means used to sell them, they became items of mass consumption. At the same time the opportunities offered by worldwide economic development led to a rapid and ultimately spectacular growth of overseas business for British companies, which thereby came to play a substantial role in the new international economy. Even more significantly from the present viewpoint, these patterns of expansion, the pressure of competition, and the structural imperatives of growth led to the emergence of large-scale, amalgamated companies with far-reaching implications for management structures and techniques. The interrelationship between these developments is what concerns us here. And its general significance should be obvious: in terms of the scope and new variety of their business, the scale of their operations and its organizational problem, and the techniques needed to maintain the momentum of growth, the history of insurance companies in the decades immediately before 1914 anticipated, in microcosm, the larger development which dominated so much of the twentieth-century business economy.

The subject-matter of this chapter is therefore the general nature of business expansion in insurance and its structural implications in the period 1870–1914. However, detailed information will be drawn largely, although not exclusively, from the experience of one company: the Royal Exchange Assurance Corporation (R.E.A.). The first section deals with the extent and pattern of growth, and with the development of the R.E.A. In the second and third sections we shall turn to consider the impetus to expansion, the rise of large-scale companies, and the organizational aspects of growth and scale.

(A) THE DEVELOPMENT OF BRITISH INSURANCE BUSINESS,
1870–1914

Although new types of insurance (notably accident insurance of various sorts) and the widespread diffusion of life insurance as a form of investment radically changed some of the basic characteristics of the industry in this period, fire underwriting remained the backbone of its organization and profitability. Thus in 1913 fire insurance premiums were some £29 m.; life insurance premiums were almost the same amount, but the element of running costs and profits involved were significantly less; and all accident policies brought in premiums of something over £7 m. In fact, it seems that by the 1860s the habit of insurance against fire was so well established in the United Kingdom that its subsequent growth was largely a function of the increase in the value of buildings and other insurable assets. (In 1862 it was estimated that in England and Wales some £1,000 m. of property was insured, leaving about £500 m. uncovered. But much of this last category was in too small quantities to be insurable.) Yet in spite of the fact that the home market for fire insurance was increasingly dependent on the growth of property values rather than on any change in the habits of potential policy-holders, total premiums exhibited a very marked rise—from less than £4 m. in 1870 to £29 m. in 1913. This sevenfold increase, at a time when reproducable capital at home little more than doubled, is easily explicable in terms of overseas expansion: the approaching saturation of the British fire insurance market forced British companies to turn their attention to South America, Australasia, South Africa, the Far East, and, above all, the United States—which alone accounted for 40 per cent of total fire premiums for British companies in 1900. Other non-European markets probably generated at least a further 20 per cent of premium income. Property-owners and business men in developing economies overseas turned to Britain for the experience, stability, and funds of its companies in their search for security of physical capital and stocks. In the vanguard of Britain's penetration of the new international economy, the characteristic U.K. insurance company now had branches or large agencies in Melbourne, Cape Town, Bombay and Manila, Buenos Aires and New York, Chicago and San Francisco. A further striking point is that much of the impetus for this growth came from relatively young and thrusting offices. By 1901 the five leading fire insurance companies were the Royal, the Commercial Union, the Liverpool & London & Globe, the North British & Mercantile, and the London & Lancashire (their total fire premium income was about £9 m.). Four of these had been established after 1844, and three originated in Lancashire. Old-established companies like the R.E.A., the Sun, and the Phoenix (all eighteenth-century creations) were still modestly important at home, but lagged in overseas development. As we shall see, such developments were also associated with a general trend towards industrial concentration. On average in the period 1900–15 the ten leading companies earned some 70 per cent of all fire insurance premiums.

The domestic market for life insurance was by no means as limited as was the case with fire insurance. On the one hand, the practice of life insurance, like the consumption of so many other former luxuries, began to penetrate into new, poorer social strata. Industrial assurance (life insurance for the 'industrial classes' at this time catered for by specialist companies)[3] grew remarkably; premium rose from £1·5 m. in the late 1860s to £16 m. in 1912 (by which time sums assured, at £350 m., were about half the amount insured under 'ordinary' policies). Even more remarkable was the domination of industrial business by large companies: in 1905 the Prudential was responsible for half of all the premiums paid, and it was backed up, if not closely rivalled, by such other giants as the Refuge and the Pearl. On the other hand, the extension of ordinary insurance and (by means of the endowment policy) the investment habit among people of middle or high incomes still had enormous scope for expansion—as exemplified, in the period 1870–1914, by the growth in sums assured (almost all of it in the U.K.) from £293 m. to £870 m. and in premiums from £9·8 m. to £29 m. The figure for sums assured was even more impressive in the light of the growth of the more expensive, if rewarding, endowment policies from a negligible amount to £339 m. By 1913 almost two-thirds of life policies and over one-third of sums assured were endowment contracts. A response to public need under the pressure of genuine competition (some of it, as we shall see, from invading American firms), the growth of endowment policies reflected an increased emphasis on life insurance as a form of productive savings—the accumulation of funds for old age or retirement or, in the words of one company brochure, for 'school expenses, the support of sons at college, the dowry of daughters, the entry of sons into professions or businesses'. In this respect the 1890s were a crucial decade: endowment policies quadrupled—reflecting, no doubt, not merely the general pressure of middle-class savings but the falling rate of return on the more traditional investments. And, as with fire insurance, extension of business also brought concentration: between 1881 and 1914 the share of total life premium enjoyed by the ten largest companies rose from 33 per cent to 43 per cent (of which the five largest enjoyed no less than 35 per cent).

As we shall see, competition, sales pressure, and the 'education' of the public played important roles in the contemporary expansion of life insurance. So did improved actuarial practice, which combined with market forces to extend the range of attractive offerings while standardizing and cheapening the most popular types of policy. In its new maturity, life insurance had assumed some of the characteristics of a mass-production industry, particularly with respect to its drive for large turnover and its use of intensive marketing arrangements. At the same time, however, its total bundle of 'products' was becoming less standardized precisely because, in order to expand, it had to cater for an increasing variety of needs. In the last resort it was the element of demand and social change which did most to shape life insurance as a whole. For from the cheapening of postal and transport services (which enormously facilitated the control of agency and branch systems) to fundamental developments in income distribution and middle-class attitudes, life insurance could not escape its environment. It was, indeed, itself a powerful expression of social as well as economic development.

The third area of expansion, accident business, contrasted with the growth in fire and life insurance in that while their expansion was a logical extension of earlier developments, the new growth point related to risks which had not previously existed, or which had hardly before been the object of insurance. These entailed a proliferation into a multitude of separate fields of insurance, each with its own specific characteristics—into insurance against personal accident and disease, employers' liability, fidelity guarantee, burglary, plate-glass damage, public liability, and loss of liquor licences, culminating in that most typical of twentieth-century ventures, motor insurance. In spite of this apparent fragmentation, however, there are good reasons for considering all these branches together, quite apart from the historical convention by which they were grouped under the collective name of 'accident insurance'. The first is that in organizational terms (precisely because they appeared after fire, life, and marine insurance had settled into an established structural framework) offices tended to group them into a single department for underwriting and administrative purposes. Secondly, the coincidence of their development suggests that they were all influenced by a common set of economic and social factors at work in late-nineteenth-century Britain. As the nation matured, so its maturity demanded new sorts of services. As capital grew more abundant and technology more sophisticated, so quite new types of costly hazards— railway and motor-car accidents, plate-glass breakage, boiler explosion and other engineering risks—became increasingly frequent to the point at which systematized insurance was both feasible and mutually profitable. The continued expansion of professional and middle-class incomes, together with the extension of insurance as a social habit, naturally turned men's minds to the need to protect those incomes against the consequence not merely of their deaths, but also of injury, sickness, and disablement—and against the possibility of theft, of damage to their or other people's property, and of claims by injured third parties. Continuing change in the technical, economic, and social systems also raised questions of social and legal responsibility with regard to the injury of industrial and other sorts of employees: and these, as much the outcome of economic maturity as was the evolution of a substantial class of professional and business men, were resolved by a series of laws (1880, 1897, 1906) which, creating an explicit liability, led immediately to the creation of a new type of insurance.

Of the three principal examples of the new form of insurance, personal accident insurance began in the 1840s with the era of railway travel and from then on grew fairly steadily; employer's liability (workmen's compensation) grew dramatically in the 1880s and 1890s (100 new accident companies were formed in 1881–97 and accident premiums rose from £520,000 in 1884 to £5·2 m. in 1905); and motor business, starting at the end of the 1890s, attracted at least £1 m. in premiums by 1914. As in the other branches of insurance, general accident tended to be concentrated in a relatively few hands —initially the specialist firm which had ventured into the new fields. Thus personal accident business was at first dominated by the Railways Passengers Company, the Accidental Insurance Company, and the Ocean Accident Company; by the mid-1890s liability business, and accident business in general, was dominated by four companies: the Employer's Liability Assurance Corporation, the Railways Passengers, the Ocean Accident, and the London Guarantee (together accounting for about half the national premium of £1·75 m.); and motor business was originally in the hands of specialists who could oversee the new risks: in 1914 the Car & General Insurance Corporation and the Motor Union Insurance Company accounted for about a third of national motor premiums. However, by this time, although motor business remained fairly specialized, the other fields of accident insurance had begun to attract the more established companies which were already extensively committed to fire and/or life business. With this development in the early twentieth century, and with the associated trend towards amalgamation, we enter a new era of industrial structure in insurance: the era of the large-scale composite office combining fire, life, and accident departments, each benefiting from the economies and interlocking connections which only a single organization, a single network of agents, and an overlapping set of markets could bring.

Since, in the following sections, the structural and administrative implications of these various changes will be examined primarily in terms of the experience of the Royal Exchange Assurance, it will be appropriate in the first instance to indicate that company's pattern of development in the period.

The R.E.A. had been established in 1720, but entered the twentieth century as a leading example of the new breed of composite companies. After a period of relative stagnation a new vigour on the part of its management spurred it to fresh heights in the late nineteenth century. This is shown by its record of premium income (see Table 4.1).

TABLE 4.1

R.E.A. Premium Income (Annual Average)

	Fire (£)	Life (£)	Marine (£)	Accident (£)
1871–1874	138 200	141 100	145 200	—
1891–1895	241 200	160 300	101 600	—
1911–1915	859 900	404 000	426 100	c. 275 000

It is worth noting that the abruptness of the recovery was widely associated with the introduction of new managerial talent and new business ambitions in the Corporation in each of its three main non-marine departments. Thus the transformation of its fire underwriting was generally associated with a change in the office of Fire Manager in April 1890: before then the Corporation's fire business was said to be characterized by 'caution and timidity'. At home there was reluctance to establish domestic branches, while the corporation almost completely ignored the booming area of overseas insurance: in 1885 its foreign fire premium accounted for about 2 per cent of its total, whereas the young and enormously vigorous Commercial Union earned almost £600,000 in foreign premiums out of a total premium income of £867,000. After 1890, however, with the appointment of an enterprising and active Fire Manager (O. H. Duncan, formerly of the Royal Insurance—the most formidable of the relatively new fire insurance companies) all this changed. By 1900 total fire premiums had more than trebled, and overseas income exceeded home premiums. On the eve of the First World War about 70 per cent of fire premiums came from overseas, and even the United States total exceeded that of the United Kingdom.

Life insurance business, which had long stagnated and been unresponsive to mounting competition and innovation in the industry at large, was also overhauled with the appointment of a new young Actuary (Gerald H. Ryan, aged 29) in 1888, and of his successor, Harry E. Nightingale, in 1893. Conditions for policy-holders were improved, premiums were reduced, bonus payments extended to endowment policies, interim bonuses declared, agents' commissions made more attractive, and a new, thrusting, and commercialized attitude was adopted. By the late 1890s new business (sums assured) averaged £605,000—compared with £212,000 in the early 1880s. As in manufacturing business, the doctrines of mass production—high volume, low margins—proved more profitable than a small turnover with high profit margins.

Finally, stimulated by the arguments of its Actuary and the subsequent appointment of a young and driving Accident Superintendent (Arthur W. Wamsley), the R.E.A. was one of the first of the established companies to enter the field of accident insurance—hitherto in the hands of specialized enterprises. This included personal accident (1898), employers' liability and fidelity guarantee (1899), and burglary (1900). By 1907 accident premiums were some £165,000 and among composite companies this was exceeded only by the London & Lancashire and the Commercial Union, both of which (unlike the R.E.A.) had grown by amalgamation with very large specialist accident offices.

(B) MARKETING AND THE DRIVE FOR EXPANSION

During the period 1870–1914 British insurance business was transformed. The pressures which produced large-scale, worldwide offices can now be considered.

The first point to be made is that the era was characterized by an intensification of competition which placed a new emphasis on marketing for all insurance businesses. The competitive eagerness which extended fire (and subsequently accident) underwriting even affected the staider field of life insurance. Advertising expenditure soared, premium rates were cut and bonus payments increased (at the expense of profit percentages), policies were simplified and liberalized, pushing salesmen were employed. 'We are *traders*', said the President of the Institute of Actuaries in 1892. Significantly, the rise of mass marketing coincided with the invasion of the British market by American life offices. For in the United States in the late nineteenth century native companies had perfected a host of high-pressure selling techniques. As a result, in Britain the impact from the 1880s of offices like the Equitable Life Assurance of the United States, the New York Life, and the Mutual Life of New York was said by one professional journal to be like the effect of an 'electric shock . . . on a body of low vitality'.[4] Quantitatively the American companies were not very significant, but their impact—on sales techniques and on the transformation of the market by the development of investment—was very considerable.

Compared with the situation in life insurance, competition for fire business took somewhat different forms. This was largely due to differences inherent in fire underwriting itself: the contract was essentially short term, the habit was widespread and ingrained, its outcome (even on the average) was unpredictable, and the most important consideration for the policy-holder was protection against the contingency for which the policy was taken out, rather than any hope of gain through savings. For these reasons not only was fire underwriting a riskier venture than life insurance, but competition was more likely to be concentrated on premium rates. Yet although competition was potentially very fierce in fire insurance, it was (perhaps for that very reason) substantially mitigated by agreements on premiums (tariffs) by the Fire Offices' Committee. By 1900 the so-called Tariff Offices accounted for over 90 per cent of the domestic and more than 95 per cent of all the worldwide business of British offices. As a result they were criticized (by *The Economist*, 30 April 1881) for having 'banded themselves together into what is virtually a great trades union, having for its object the restraining of competition and the upholding of rates', although in practice market forces continued to exert a strong pressure on insurance enterprise. A similar association operated in the field of accident insurance. Even so, in both fields competition still had a powerful role to play, for the public was in a position of great strength. As the Royal Exchange Assurance's House Magazine put it in 1910:

Schemes regarded as chimerical in the nineteenth century are the commonplaces of the twentieth. For the insurance companies the vox populi is the Vox Dei. The public has only to hint a need for cover for some particular contingency and its letter boxes are post-haste crammed with beautiful prospectuses offering full facilities. Dignified insurance companies, heavy with the weight of years, hustle one another in the insurance market place for the nimble half-crown of your domestic servant insurance, or the favour of replacing your broken plate-glass window.

For both the industry in general and the R.E.A. in particular one of the most critical responses to new market problems and opportunities lay in the adaptation of organization and the application of effort. Insurance, if it was to expand, had to be *sold*, and the effective point at which business was done was therefore the contact between agent and policy-holder. 'The magic of personal influence', in the words of a President of the Institute of Actuaries, meant that 'the Head Office manufactures the article, but has to look to its middleman to get orders'. Whatever else was important, an effective and vigorous agency network was indispensable to growth. 'It is not the goodness of the office,' said one M.P. in 1870, 'but the energy of the agent which secures the largest business.'[5] As a result of all this, the growth in the number of insurance agents was to some extent an index of both industrial expansion and competition. One estimate for the first fifty years of Victoria's reign held that the number of life agents alone had increased from about 6,000 to 100,000; while the R.E.A., whose growth by no means exceptional, increased the number of British and Irish agents from less than 600 at mid-century to about 5,000 in 1900 and over 15,500 in 1912.

The very great extension of the number of agents also led to important changes in organization. For the concentration on the point-of-sale, together with the need to control the new armies of agents, led inevitably to a rapid decentralization of sales policy and control. In the first instance, this trend was represented by the appointment of professional, salaried officials—inspectors (also known as 'superintendents' of agents or 'canvassers') whose task it was to supervise and instruct agents, to follow up their contacts and economize on their time, and to press for business in a continuous and systematic way. Inspectors first appeared in their modern role about 1850, and by 1907 it was estimated that fire, life, and accident offices employed about 2,000. The appointment of salaried canvassers, however, inevitably posed the need for a further extension of systematic control. Their expansion was therefore directly associated with the creation of district and branch offices. These were more suited than distant head offices for the tasks of general supervision—besides being needed to relieve some of the pressures of clerical work which had naturally mounted at head offices when inspectors had first been appointed. Finally, the proliferation of branches and of inspectors itself produced new problems of control and supervision for the head offices. This, in turn, led to a third stage of structural development in the late-nineteenth-century insurance industry: the appearance of agency managers.

The Royal Exchange Assurance appointed its first Inspector of Agencies in 1881 and in the next few years the system was broadly extended by the Corporation. At the same time the R.E.A. also created district and branch offices; the district office at Manchester became a branch in 1886; other branches were opened in Birmingham, Bristol, and Liverpool in 1887; and Newcastle, Leeds, and Glasgow followed within two years. These various moves meant that by the 1890s the R.E.A. relied on two relatively new types of official—the inspector and the branch manager, both of whom were really products of the new climate of insurance enterprise is the late nineteenth century. With the increased complexity and heightened competition of contemporary insurance, such professionals soon came to play a crucial role in securing business. As the R.E.A. Actuary put it in 1910, 'the actual procuration of assurance business, especially life, is drifting more and more into the hands of experts, the agents merely furnishing introductions'.

Changes in markets and in marketing structures therefore involved a

substantial measure of devolution. But branches also had to be fitted into a co-
ordinated (and, in the last resort, central) plan of action. Indeed, it was envisaged that as new forms of central control (for example, agency departments)
were fashioned, branch managers might have to assume a somewhat more
routine task. The new man, it was felt by some, would be the agency
manager:

To him will be entrusted the visions of the Directors in regard to new business, and
they will look to him to give them practical effect. To him will fall the duty of formulating the general plan of campaign, and of providing the means to carry it to a
successful issue . . . his advent seems to point to a greater homogeneity in the agency
work of the office and to a more general uniformity of practice, which will increase
the demand on the administrative rather than the initiative ability of the branch
manager.[6]

At the Royal Exchange, although a corporation Agency Manager was
appointed in 1903, his role was somewhat ambiguous. His department was
organizationally part of the Secretary's Office: and, while he had the task of
providing general supervision, advice, and help in matters relating to agents
and branches, he had no responsibility for technical matters concerning insurance or the supervision of the indoor staff of the various branches. Put another
way, the branch organization was still the basic charge of the Secretary and,
even more important, of the managers of the various underwriting departments. Thus, where there was reason to be dissatisfied with, say, the fire business at a particular branch, it was the Fire Manager and not the Agency
Manager who would take the initiative—as happened at Leeds in 1913 when
the Joint Fire Manager sent a man from Head Office to help increase the
branch's premium income: 'He will not hold any official appointment at the
Branch, but will act as the Fire Managers' representative, and under their
direct instruction.'

This situation was perfectly understandable, for the R.E.A. was still a
highly departmentalized corporation; there was as yet no General Manager
(although a Committee of Management was established in 1911) and the
authority and initiative of Departmental Managers was unquestioned. The
result, however, was that no *unified* control was effectively established over the
growing branches before the interwar period. Each was subject to pressures
(which were not always consistent) from Fire, Life, and Accident Managers.
In this respect the R.E.A. offered a sharp contrast to other leading insurance
companies which had already centralized and unified their management structures. In part this was because the Corporation was still relatively conservative. But it was also because, in spite of its genuine growth and success, it still
did not rival the other giants of the industry (it ranked twelfth in 1914). And
in this context, then, it is relevant to turn now to the factors shaping the
emergence of large-scale companies.

(C) THE RISE OF LARGE-SCALE OFFICES

The intensification of competition and the extension of branch structures and agency inspection in the late nineteenth and early twentieth centuries led almost inevitably to an increase in the cost of doing business. This was particularly marked in the case of fire insurance—commission and management costs rising from 28 per cent of premiums in 1877–8 to about 38 per cent in 1907.

The increased cost of doing business was associated with a very substantial increase in the size of individual offices. And it occurred to contemporaries that the rising costs of underwriting might in fact be one cause of the appearance of very big insurance companies, seeking to minimize cost increase by securing some economies of scale. In fire insurance, however, the cost advantages of large-scale operations were not obvious. Indeed, there was relatively little variation in the expense ratio of different companies: in 1906, for example, the average expenses ratio of 27 leading fire offices was 34·6 per cent, but 17 of these had ratios between 33 and 36 per cent. In the case of life insurance there were other factors than size which might determine expense ratios, and therefore make valid comparisons very difficult.[7] Nevertheless, in contrast to the situation in the fire business, the cost of transacting life insurance was in some measure related to the scale of operations. In the early 1880s, for example, an investigation which ranked 95 companies by the size of their premium incomes showed that the proportion of expenses to premiums fell steadily from one-third for the 14 offices with incomes below £10,000 to 10·4 per cent for the 9 offices with incomes between £200,000 and £250,000. Oddly, however, in the case of the biggest offices, with premium incomes exceeding £250,000, the expense ratio rose again, to 13·3 per cent.[8] The apparent anomaly concerning the very largest companies was, however, challenged by a distinguished actuary, T. B. Sprague, who argued that the most recent data, for 1887, showed that the biggest offices were, after all, the cheapest to run: 'It appears to follow that, in life insurance, as in so many other matters, there is an irresistible tendency to consolidation; and that, in life insurance at all events, this tendency is beneficial.'[9]

Whatever the role of rising costs and the economies of scale, the indisputable fact about the structure of the insurance industry in this period was, indeed, the 'irresistible tendency to consolidation'. Insurance, in every sense, was becoming 'big business'. For not only was its social and economic role being enlarged, but both the average size of firms and the relative importance of the very largest companies were increasing. Throughout this period fire underwriting was overwhelmingly in the hands of between fifty and sixty comapnies, and their average premium income rose from just over £160,000 in the late 1870s to over £500,000 in 1908. Meanwhile, the share of total premiums of the 10 largest offices, which had remained at just over 60 per cent for most of the late nineteenth century, rose to over 70 per cent in the period 1900–15. (Between 1899 and 1904 the share of the 9 leading offices rose from 54 to 66 per cent.)[10] In the case of life insurance, between 1881 and 1914 the average ordinary premiums of British offices increased from £116,583 to £308,503, while the share of total premium earned by the 10 largest offices rose from 33 to 43 per cent. Even more spectacularly, the 5 largest life offices increased their share from 21 to 35 per cent.

The growth of large-scale enterprise was not, of course, confined to insurance; it was a trend which increasingly characterized much of British industry in the generation or so before 1914. To some insurance men it seemed the result of a new business psychology—the 'passion for bigness, for big things' —which could be seen not merely in insurance but in 'every other department of life', and which operated 'apart altogether from corresponding profits'.[11] More generally, however, it is clear that market forces—particularly the fears and opportunities of competition—were largely responsible for the emergence of giant new combinations. Constant growth and geographical extension became indispensable means of self-defence. The momentum of expansion had to be maintained; and large offices, especially in so far as they diversified into a composite business and thereby develop mutually strengthening departments, were inevitably in a position of some advantage. In the search for new business, as one journalist pointed out, 'the most potent factor is connection'.[12]

It was for this reason that the most crucial period for the rise of large-scale insurance companies was the first decade of the twentieth century. For it was then, by a process of growth and amalgamation, that modern composite offices made their appearance. Admittedly, the trend towards very large-scale insurance enterprise was already strongly marked in the late nineteenth century with such offices as the Royal, the Commercial Union, and the Liverpool & London & Globe in fire insurance, and the Scottish Widows', the Standard, and the Gresham in life business. But the formation of very large composite offices was essentially the result of a wave of amalgamations after 1900. And the main occasion for sweeping structural change was apparently the 1906 Act, which extended employers' liability to all workers, including domestic servants, and thereby persuaded both accident and fire companies that the markets for various types of insurance were too intimately related to be kept separate. On the one hand, the economies of scale, especially in so far as an extended system of agents and branches had become essential, made it logical for individual offices to cater for *all* the main needs of the insuring public. On the other hand, apprehension as well as ambition was at work: offices increasingly found that they could only defend themselves against competition by offering both agents and clients a wider range of services. At the same time, too, the extension of the functions of the broker into non-marine business gave an added and very powerful incentive to offices which could provide varying sorts of cover.

In general, therefore, it could be said that the rise of composite companies was 'probably as much due to a desire to maintain valuable connections as to provide facilities for covering all risks in one office'.[13] This movement was particularly marked in the joining of accident and fire business, for it was in this respect that the importance of 'connection' was most marked: the property-owner who needed to insure against fire also needed to insure against claims from his employees—whether factory hands or domestic servants—and would naturally favour the agent and the company which provided both services. As with the middle-class family, so with the industrialist; as with the new department stores of fashionable London, so with insurance in Edwardian Britain: 'all the shopping could be done under one roof'.[14]

There were various reasons why this process was brought about by amalgamation rather than the steady evolution of individual offices. First, where a company wished to undertake a new line of business it obviously made more sense to acquire a going concern with an established management, agency network, and connection. Second, amalgamation was the quickest, and often the easiest, way to increase the size of operations. Third, the new partner brought in more business of the old type as well as new. And fourth, amalgamation automatically reduced the potential area of competition. In addition, of course, there was the prospect of economies resulting from the avoidance of duplication. In fact, however, amalgamation rarely led to significant cost reduction by the effecting of speedy economies. As later experience was to show, the nature of the insurance industry—the tenacious loyalty of agents and policy-holders, the sense of corporate momentum and institutional inertia —meant that these economies could only be achieved slowly, because they involved the sinking of corporate identity, the closing of branches, the reduction of staffs, and the like. *The Economist* saw the situation as follows:

The saving of expenses which must be the ultimate result of amalgamation is a gradual process. This cannot be otherwise if fair consideration be given to the moral, if not legal, rights of the staff taken over, and it is to the credit of our insurance companies that this side of the question has always been scrupulously kept in view. The immediate advantages are the consolidation of forces for forward movement, the fact that there is one competitor the fewer, the acquirement of new connections, and those additional opportunities which do not admit of exact description, but which always comes to a business as it grows in magnitude without loss of financial strength.[15]

Amalgamations had, of course, taken place throughout the nineteenth century. But, although the relatively unstable years of the 1850s and early 1860s had been marked by the absorption of large numbers of small and insecure companies, it was only in the last two decades of the century that a more modern type of amalgamation movement reached significant proportions. In the period 1886–1900, for example, an average of 9 offices annually amalgamated with others. In the five years 1906–10, however, the average number

reached 13, and in 1910 alone no less that 19 offices lost their separate iden-
tities in this way.[16]

Some of these amalgamations involved the joining-together of very large
fire offices, as when the Atlas acquired the Manchester (1904), the Alliance
acquired the Imperial (1902) and the Law Fire and the County Fire (1906), or
the Royal acquired the Lancashire (1901). But a more significant element was
the amalgamation of fire and accident offices. Thus of the 24 largest accident
offices in 1899, 15 were acquired by fire, or fire and life, offices before 1914—
8 of them in the brief period of 1906–10. Nor did the process of amalgamation
stop there; of 16 specialist marine insurance companies which had existed in
1899, half had been absorbed into composite companies before 1914; and of
the 29 relatively substantial proprietary offices doing only ordinary life business in 1899, 9 had been acquired by composite offices by 1914 (and 16 by
1919).

To some extent this last development was a consequence of the attraction
of life offices for fire companies seeking extended connections throughout the
country, and access to the potential fire business of their mortgage and other
investments. But the disappearance of specialist proprietary life offices was
also the outcome of the struggle for life business itself. In his report on the
critical quinquennium 1906–10, the R.E.A. Actuary cited various examples of
this trend and predicted that ordinary life business would eventually be controlled by 'influential "composite" companies transacting all classes of business' and by 'a few large mutual offices, who, by maintaining a high rate of
bonus in the future, will be enabled to support a separate existence'.

In one respect, of course, the R.E.A. had anticipated the most significant
feature of this process; for the Corporation was, in fact, a pioneer of composite business. By 1900 it included fire, life, marine, and accident departments. To this extent, therefore, it had been both fortunate and prescient. On
the other hand, however, although the momentum which had transformed its
situation in the 1890s continued (with the help of new accident premiums) to
push up its income in the first decade of the twentieth century, the fact remained that its growth was hardly at all characterized by the combinations
which other companies used as devices for rapid and dramatic expansion.

In avoiding any extensive participation in the amalgamation boom, the
Corporation was expressing satisfaction with, and even jealousy of, its own
traditions. As a result, it did not attain the spectacular size of the new combinations. (In 1914 the biggest firm, the Commercial Union, had total premiums in excess of £7·5 m., as against the R.E.A.'s £1·9 m.) In fact, however,
the R.E.A. differed in degree, rather than in kind, from the very substantial
composite offices of the pre-1914 insurance industry. And this meant that it
shared with them most of the difficulties which were the result of growth and
the diversification of underwriting departments. In particular, it encountered
the problems of management and control implicit in rapid growth. We have

already seen how this affected the structure and administration of agency and branch systems. Comparable problems soon emerged in relation to other areas of corporate organization—in particular departmental management.

(D) SCALE AND MANAGEMENT

Even before the mergers of the twentieth century the growth of insurance enterprises had created administrative problems which, in turn, had produced increasing managerial professionalization. In only one area did insurance Directors tend to retain a traditional role as against company officials: that was in the administration and investment of assets. Hence there emerged a basic distinction between Directors who supervised a company's business and managed its funds, and the officials who were responsible for the management of its underwriting activities. To knowledgeable contemporaries this difference was vital, and was associated with the increasing technicality of insurance. As one professional put it:

Any great interference on the part of the members of such an association, or even of the small body selected from among them to act as directors, will as a rule be of questionable advantage. No doubt the bringing together of men of business having varied knowledge and experience secures a valuable contribution to the aggregate skill that is needed; and their shrewd observations brought to bear on the capacity and character of the experts whom they employ, on the general conduct of the business, and even on some of its details, are of measureless value. Still it remains that between the knowledge of the most able director and that which is possessed by the officers of a fire or life insurance company, there is, or there ought to be, a wide gulf; and, consequently, its success or failure depends more upon its executive officers than in the case of almost any other business.[17]

This distinction was the administrative counterpart of the growing size and complexity of the business of insurance, which increasingly demanded skilled and full-time management and specialized departments. The very forces which produced an urgent demand for 'general management' by the early part of this century also explained the more independent role which Departmental Managers could, and had, to play. Thus if we compare the Royal Exchange Assurance's structure in 1915 with what it had been seventy five years earlier, the contrast is striking. In 1840 there were merely 39 clerks and chief officials in the 5 main departments (Secretary's, Sea, Fire, Life, and Cashier & Accountant's). By the First World War, quite apart from the technical transformation of insurance and the rise of the Corporation's national and worldwide branch system, there were over 400 clerks and chief officials at head office, organized into 8 departments (the above-mentioned 5, together with Accident, Agency, and Trustee and Executor). Some of these were further divided into sub-departments: by 1915 the Sea Department embraced separate Underwriters, Sea Claims, and Foreign Marine Offices, and the Fire Department included Home, Foreign, Agency, and Guarantee Offices.

It is obvious that the resulting increase in specialization of insurance management (which, of course, characterized all insurance companies in the nineteenth century) meant not only new roles for the Directors, but also a sharpening of the distinction between the different departmental heads. The same specialization of function which made it almost impossible for members of the Corporation's Court to assume managerial duties, also eliminated the overlapping of duties and the plurality of office-holding which had sometimes occurred in the nineteenth-century management of the Royal Exchange.

In the long run, of course, the specialization and strengthening of individual departments raised new issues about general management and the need to co-ordinate and control their operations. But for the R.E.A. the emergence of strong and relatively independent departments did not bring any particularly severe administrative problems until the end of the period. This was because the size and scope of the Corporation's business did not really reach critical levels until the 1890s or the opening years of this century. For most of the nineteenth century the organization was still sufficiently small to attain co-ordination in informal and personal terms. On the other hand, there were potentially very severe problems of organization and control on the border-land, and sometimes even in the no man's land, between existing departments. The main reason for this was, of course, that at the official administrative level the inherited structure gave a very considerable degree of independence to the individual departments. There was no built-in tendency to active co-operation. In some instances co-ordination could be imposed from above, but there remained serious problems of growth which could not be so easily resolved, because no institutional arrangements existed for their resolution. Among the most important of these was the question of control on a non-departmental basis as the Corporation extended the geographical scope of its activities through agents and then branches, throughout this country and then abroad. In the case of the Royal Exchange Assurance, the confusion and potential inefficiency inherent in such expansion with no clearly defined means of central co-ordination of agents and branches—who were responsible at various levels to the Secretary, the Fire manager, and the Actuary (and later the Accident Manager)—persisted for some time. And although an Agency Manager for the Corporation was finally appointed in 1903, he continued to work within the Secretary's Office, with no separate Agency Department, for some years.

In this and other respects, however, the R.E.A. lagged behind developments in the industry as a whole—which was quicker to recognize the need for what is now called 'general management'. The growth of the Corporation's business had been associated with the emergence of strong, vigorous, and independent departments. Paradoxically, however, those departments, precisely because they were independent, posed a mild threat to the continuance of growth. By the opening of this century the lack of active and firm central guidance and co-ordination was becoming increasingly obvious. A worldwide and very large-scale composite insurance business could no longer be run without the formal co-ordination of departments. In July 1911 the R.E.A. Court appointed a special committee to consider 'whether in view of the increased and increasing operations of the Corporation the existing system of management is best suited to the requirements of the business'. This committee proceeded to take verbal and written evidence from all the principal officers of the Corporation and in its interim report in August indicated that there was 'a consensus of opinion that the present system is not entirely satisfactory, and your Committee consider that some central authority for General Management should be created'. For this purpose the committee recommended the appointment of a Committee of Management consisting of the three Governors, which should meet weekly, at which times different Department Heads should be present— with a regular meeting at least once a month at which all the Heads of Departments should collectively meet the Governors 'to consider any business affecting the Corporation'.

These recommendations were informally adopted in the autumn of 1911 and when they were considered by the General Court of Proprietors the new Committee was seen as a means of 'concentrating and more effectually supervising the management of the various classes of business conducted by the Corporation'. It was acknowledged that the R.E.A. suffered through being 'probably the only insurance company of any importance in the City of London which has no [General] Manager or Management Committee'. The idea of a General Manager was rejected on grounds of 'consideration of internal arrangements'—presumably the prospect of difficult relationships if a new and senior official post were created above the existing semi-independent and senior Managers. In the event, the formation of a committee was a poor substitute for the appointment of a General Manager, in terms of his positive function and of providing a focus for managerial representation at the centre. The Corporation suffered by not making the sort of explicit appointment that had already greatly influenced the managerial evolution of other insurance companies. To take merely four examples, the Royal of Liverpool owed much of its early success to the appointment of Percy M. Dove (recruited from the Royal Exchange) as Manager in 1845; the Liverpool & London & Globe nominated its Secretary (John M. Dove, Percy's son) as General Manager in 1876; the Atlas, having chosen a powerful new Secretary, Samuel J. Pipkin, in 1884, appointed him as its first General Manager in 1896; and the Commercial Union recognized the new needs of its international business by appointing a General Manager in 1901. Nor was this trend towards a single executive head merely a corporate fashion; it is clear from these and other examples that the drive, unity, and purposefulness which were essential for profitable growth could best, and perhaps only, be obtained by a concentration of authority and responsibility. The period around the turn of the century was an 'Age of General Managers' as far as the development of insurance was concerned. It was almost as if the rise of huge new corporate personalities could only be sustained by the efforts of outstanding and powerful individuals. It was this element which was lacking at the Royal Exchange Assurance. Admittedly, its transformation from the late 1880s could be attributed to new and influential Departmental Managers who broke away from inherited attitudes and pushed the Corporation into advanced modes of business behaviour. But in spite of this, and in spite of the efforts of its various Secretaries, there could be no effective alternative to an explicit decision to create a new and much more powerful post. Until then, and even taking the Committee of Management into account, the Corporation, compared with most of its leading competitors, lacked a clear line of organizational authority.

The Committee of Management was an anomalous development, precisely because it was charged with a management, as well as an over-all policy-making and supervisory, function. As a result, the Corporation, in contrast to most successful insurance companies, avoided rather than confronted the problem of twentieth-century organization (in fact, the first R.E.A. General Manager was appointed in 1929). Indeed, the postponement of radical change only aggravated the problem by continuing and enhancing the independent authority of individual departments. Even with the new arrangement the Governors could not be expected to accumulate the necessary knowledge of detail or continuously devote the necessary amount of time to the tasks of management. There was still, therefore, a gap between the chosen instrument of general management and the departmental officials. And in the last resort this gap could only be closed by the creation of another management level. In the industry at large that level had been created in the two or three decades before the First World War as a logical and necessary complement to the growth in scale and scope which had transformed one of Britain's most important service industries.

NOTES

1 This chapter is based on the material in Barry Supple, *The Royal Exchange Assurance: A History of British Insurance, 1720–1970* (Cambridge U.P., Cambridge, 1970), Chs. 10–12, where references to sources will also be found.

2 In light of its quite distinctive and generally traditional character, the detailed growth and organization of marine insurance will not be considered in this chapter.

3 The distinguishing features of industrial life assurance were: relatively small policies, weekly payment of premiums, and the collection of premiums by agents who visited the policy-holders' homes.

4 *Journal of the Federation of Insurance Institutes* (*J.F.I.I.*) (1909), 80.

5 *Journal of the Institute of Actuaries* (*J.I.A.*), xxviii (1890), 177; *Hansard*, 23 Feb. 1870.

6 *J.F.I.I.* (1900), 425.

7 For example, whether the office was a mutual company not employing agents; the importance of new as against renewal premiums; the extent to which an office transacted other sorts of insurance.

8 *J.I.A.*, xxiii (1882), 362.

9 *J.I.A.*, xxviii (1889), 136–7, 149–51.

10 *Finance and Insurance Chronicle*, 2 Oct. 1905.

11 *Post Magazine* (1907), 260.

12 *Times Financial, Commercial and Shipping Supplement*, 29 Apr. 1913.
13 *The Economist*, lxvi (25 Jan. 1908).
14 *Royal Exchange Assurance Magazine*, iii, 7 (Dec. 1911), 235.
15 *The Economist*, lxix (18 Dec. 1909).
16 See data in *Insurance Directory and Year Book* (1966–7), pp. 256–72.
17 *J.F.I.I.* (1919), 60–1.

5

Courtaulds and the Beginning of Rayon[1]

D. C. COLEMAN

On 19 February 1904 a curious little concern called the Viscose Spinning Syndicate Ltd. was visited at its works in a back street in Kew, on the outskirts of London, by H. G. Tetley, a director of the silk-manufacturing firm of Samuel Courtauld & Co. Six months later the Syndicate, together with its set of patent rights covering the making of 'artificial silk' (later, in the 1920s, to be known as 'rayon'[2]) had been bought by Courtauld & Co. for approximately £25,000. By 1920 Courtaulds Ltd., with a capital of £12 m. and with a massive American subsidiary (later to be called the American Viscose Corporation), was easily the world's biggest rayon-manufacturing organization. What had happened and how had it happened?

(A) TECHNICAL ORIGINS OF RAYON

A point to be stressed at the outset is that rayon—the first of all man-made fibres—was not the product of a conscious search within the textile industry to find a substitute for silk. It owed much to professional chemists working on the chemistry of cellulose; and its development was initially related to problems in the quite different industries of electric lamp manufacture, papermaking, and explosives. A diverse collection of chemists, engineers, and professional inventors in France, Germany, and Britain evolved a product which by chemical accident looked like silk. In Britain it was then taken up by enterprising men who were looking, not for a silk substitute as such, but for a new source of profits.

Between the 1830s and 1850s early research in organic chemistry brought an awareness of the substance which came to be called cellulose $(C_6H_{10}O_5)$n., the essential component of all plant tissue. Various experiments in treating cellulose with acids and caustic alkalis then resulted in the discovery of the explosive material, nitro-cellulose or gun-cotton, which in turn led, via dynamite and Alfred Nobel, to the explosives industry. A different but related line of inquiry led to the 'nitro-cellulose' process of making rayon. In Britain the first effective demonstration of this possibility was made in 1883 by Joseph (later Sir Joseph) Swan who, seeking a uniform fibre from which to make a carbonizable conductor for his newly invented electric lamp, patented a method of making a nitro-cellulose filament and extruding it as a fine thread. Swan was not particularly interested in textiles; and the textile industry was not at all interested in Swan. In France, however, a very similar nitro-cellulose process was patented a year later by the Count de Chardonnet. A scientist and professional inventor, Chardonnet has a good claim to be regarded as the technical father of the rayon industry; for his invention was indeed the product of a conscious search for a silk substitute; and he set up a factory which from 1892 onwards began to manufacture the new product commercially. Another method of treating cellulose to produce an artificial fibre, the 'cuprammonium' process, was developed in Germany; at first wholly connected with electric-lamp filaments, its originators successfully started a company, Vereinigte Glanzstoff-Fabriken, to make cuprammonium silk. Meanwhile, in England, yet another process was emerging. It came by a complex route of patents and co-operation in which the two men chiefly responsible were C. F. Cross, a partner in a firm of consulting chemists much concerned with another cellulose-based industry, paper making; and C. H. Stearm, ex-bank clerk, amateur scientist, and manufacturer of electric lamps. Cheaper than the cuprammonium and less dangerous than the nitro-cellulose, the 'viscose' process used caustic soda in its treatment of cellulose in the form of wood pulp. On the basis of patents taken out in 1892 and 1898, and with the aid of capital from a variety of sources including some from a rich German nobleman-cum-business man with the name of Count (later Prince) Guido Henckel von Donnersmarck, Cross and Stearn incorporated the Viscose Spinning Syndicate Ltd. in 1899. Its plant at Kew had two main purposes: to make spun viscose filaments for Stearn's electric-lamp factory nearby; and to demonstrate that it was possible to make artificial silk from the spun viscose so that all the national patent rights (other than those for Germany, already bought by Donnersmarck) could be profitably sold off. Between 1899 and 1904 they were; and one firm after another, in Germany, France, America, Belgium, Russia, and England, discovered how unreliable the process still was and how much development work had yet to be done.

(B) COURTAULDS AND THE COMMERCIAL DEVELOPMENT OF RAYON

When Tetley first visited the Kew works in 1904 Samuel Courtauld & Co. was a private company, with a total paid-up capital of £337,200, which had reached a plateau of profitability after recovery from depression in the 1890s. With the exception of a mill at Leigh in Lancashire, the firm's plant was concentrated in and around the three contiguous Essex towns of Bocking, Braintree, and Halstead. The interrelated families of Courtauld, Warren, and Nettlefold— families whose nineteenth-century Unitarianism was giving way to orthodox Anglicanism—owned most of the capital, but control of the company's operations rested largely in the hands of the two managing directors: Henry Greenwood Tetley, a vigorous, bullying, dynamic, and far from even-tempered Yorkshireman; and Thomas Paul Latham, a smooth, quiet, and calculating Lancashireman. These two northerners were outsiders to the close-knit family group of southerners. Tetley had been imported in 1893 to solve the firm's production difficulties after the collapse of the trade in silk mourning crape which had earlier made massive profits for the Courtauld family; and Latham had come in as the new sales manager in the following year. By the turn of the century most of the output consisted of coloured silks —crêpes de Chine, voiles, and the like—as well as a declining amount of mourning crape.

Tetley played the dominant role in Courtauld & Co.'s entry into the new industry. In April 1904, after having paid a number of visits to the Viscose Spinning Syndicate and to the plant which Donnersmarck had set up in Germany, he told his fellow Directors that the company could not hope to maintain the profits of the last two or three years 'unless we can find some new source of profit'. Impressed by Chardonnet's venture, though troubled by its high costs, he suggested that the answer to the firm's problem lay in the viscose process which had lower costs and vast promise. The Board did not initially agree to Tetley's proposition but it did sanction a move already considered the previous year: the flotation of the firm as a public company. The subscription list closed on 8 July; the issue was a success; and the £600,000 paid-up capital (divided equally among ordinary and preference shares and mortgage debenture stock) of the new company was secured in such a way as to provide a good margin of cash. A week later, despite opposition from some of the older members, the new Board agreed to the purchase of the British rights to the viscose patents—a move which had certainly been dependent on the successful public flotation.

Land for a new factory in which to work the process was bought in September 1904 at Foleshill, then on the outskirts of Coventry, by the side of the Coventry canal. No reliable evidence has been discovered to answer the obvious question: why Coventry? Water-supply, good communications, the availability of both male and female labour, the remnants of a textile tradition from the old ribbon industry, coal—all were relevant and present. But what weight was in fact put upon them by Tetley and the company's engineer remains unknown. Machinery was ordered, buildings erected, staff recruited. The latter included a young man appointed to the post of chief chemist at £200 per annum; and a few key people were transferred from the Kew works and from the company's existing textile mills, including the manager who had been a chemist at Bocking. In July 1905 the Coventry plant started up; in August the Kew plant, which the company had also bought and continued to use for experimental purposes, was closed down. Thus equipped, and led by a Board of directors totally ignorant of chemistry, Samuel Courtauld & Co. embarked upon their new venture.

They soon began to discover that the first big obstacle to be overcome was the technical one of how to make the viscose process work. It demanded solutions to problems in chemistry, which were found by trial and error with little or no contribution from theoretical expertise in the chemistry of cellulose; and in chemical engineering, likewise tackled in a thoroughly empirical fashion. The filaments broke, stuck together, were too hard or too soft, would not dye evenly, or were in some other way blemished. In April 1905 they were reported as useless for weaving; in August Tetley was complaining that the yarn was not suitable even for embroidery; in May 1906 all the output was still only of poor quality; even by the summer of that year when sales commitments were beginning to grow, less than a quarter of the output could be classified as first grade. Some technical collaboration with the purchasers of the French patent rights had been negotiated by Tetley as early as September 1904 and bought from the French company (Société Française de la Viscose) for £2,500. Subsequent pooling of technical experience and reciprocal visits to factories presumably provided some help in tackling their common problems; but it did not solve them. The purchasers of the German rights (the company led by Donnersmarck) had meanwhile appeared as aggressive competitors, for early in 1906 they took out a patent (in the name of Dr. M. Müller) in Britain as well as in continental European countries, for a particular chemical composition of the 'spinning bath', i.e. the solution into which the extruded filaments were precipitated. Donnersmarck made it clear that he saw the Müller patent as a decisive weapon in this new international business battle. After consultation with the French, Swiss, and Belgian viscose companies, Courtauld & Co. decided to oppose the patent in Britain. The case was heard in May 1907 and, after a week of arguing, the petition for revocation of the patent was dismissed. But the probable and obvious consequences did not follow. For in order to cut through the confused and contradictory evidence given by the expert witnesses marshalled by both sides, the judge construed the patent in such a way that instead of its acting as a blocking patent over the wide zone of chemical possibilities which it had originally appeared to be, it blocked only one small, and not very useful, position in that zone. Consequently, in Britain though not of course elsewhere, Courtauld & Co. were left effectively untrammelled in their adoption of a Müller-type spinning bath, to the use of which they had been moving before the patent was taken out.

The accident of patenting and a patent judgement, together with the continuing vigour of empirical endeavour at Coventry, put Courtauld & Co. in a strong position. This favourable outcome was helped by further improvements to the chemical composition of the spinning bath; and by engineering advances affecting the design of pumps, the efficiency of filters, the machinery by which the yarn was spun, and the control techniques by which consistency was achieved in the viscose solution and hence in the ultimate product. Most of these achievements came within the years 1907 to 1910.

Technical advances do not in themselves guarantee improvements in the efficiency and productivity of a factory. That is the business of management. By the spring of 1906 the manager of the Coventry plant was a sick man, overwhelmed by a tide of difficulties. His place was taken by the then manager of the company's Braintree mill, Harry Johnson, who was to become a director of Courtaulds in 1914 and to leave a long-enduring impression on the running of the company's rayon factories. Johnson, wholly different in personality from his predecessor, was a roughish diamond, ignorant of chemistry, an admirer of Tetley, a textile man of the old school, a hard-working leader and driver. He succeeded in bringing order, cohesion, and a sense of purpose to the faltering Coventry factory just when it badly needed those qualities. In the longer run his attitude—essentially that of the 'practical man', suspicious of science and hostile to innovation—was to prove unfortunate in various ways. But in the pioneering days of rayon it was invigorating and invaluable. There was a good deal of rough-and-ready justice and not much regard, in the early years, for the rights of workers and the conditions in which they worked. The immediate results, however, were only too welcome to the Board. As employment—which included over 50 per cent of female labour—rose, so did output, productivity, and profits at Coventry.

TABLE 5.1

Rayon Output, Physical Productivity, and Gross Trading Profits, Coventry 1907–12

	1907	1908	1909	1910	1911	1912
Output (000 lb) p.a.	157	554	1216	1852	2176	2547
Ann. average total employees	330	691	1277	1930	2044	2220
lb of yarn per spindle per week	6·9	9·3	10·5	10·7	11·3	12·3
lb of yarn per worker per week	9·1	16·0	18·2	18·5	20·4	22·0
Gross trading profits (£000)	—10·3	24·5	147·9	183·0	250·5	304·9

By 1909 the profits of the new Coventry enterprise had already overtaken those derived from the company's textile manufacturing and selling activities.

Although that much older side of the firm's business was thus being overshadowed, its role in furthering the advance of Courtauld & Co.'s success in rayon was of vital consequence. Technical achievement, effective organization, improved productivity: none of these would have reaped the rewards without expansion of sales at profitable prices. It was here that the company's textile experience and marketing expertise told.

Because rayon, by whichever method it was produced, superficially resembled silk (though its physical properties were different and mainly inferior), it was initially sold as a silk substitute and its price thus set in relation to the highest-priced of all natural fibres. During the first decade of the century the products of both Chardonnet and Vereinigte Glanzstoff were being marketed, in Britain and Europe, with much emphasis on sheen and lustre; they were bought for manufacture into fringes, tassels, ribbons, embroidery, braids, and similar ornamental items—very much in vogue in current fashions of interior decoration. Samuel Courtauld & Co.'s new viscose yarns soon made an impact on this market because of lower costs and thereby their ability to undersell the other products. But such a market, narrow and restricted, held no great promise of expansion. The full harvest of profits could be reaped only by those who succeeded in making not simply low-cost yarn but yarn which was fit for weaving into ordinary fabrics with a mass use. It was precisely because Courtauld & Co. overcame this double challenge that, within a few years of buying the viscose patent rights, they emerged as the most successful of the rayon pioneers; and they were able to do this because they used their existing textile experience and plant for continuous experiment with the spinning, dyeing, and weaving of viscose yarn, alone or in combination with other fibres. The textile men at Bocking (and the manager at Coventry) knew the qualities which the yarn had somehow to be given: the chemists at Coventry had somehow to find them. At first fabrics were woven using cotton in both warp and weft but with rayon stripes; gradually the difficulties of so dyeing the Coventry product that it could be successfully woven and dyed with other fibres were solved; from about 1908 onwards fabrics with a cotton warp and a viscose weft were being produced in increasing quantities. The use of viscose rayon for making lining fabrics was developed and proved to be important and enduring; in 1911–12 a special department was set up at Bocking to make 'lining fabrics constructed partially of viscose'. As the quality of the yarn continued to improve it began to be used for warps and had no longer to be confined to wefts or to stripes. The proportion of Coventry's yarn output going to the Essex mills fell as more and more was sold to other weaving firms. The demonstration that viscose rayon was fit for ordinary textile uses had been made. In 1912 one of the main outside customers pioneered its entry into the hosiery industry, though in Britain the big expansion of its use in the knitting of women's stockings did not come until after the First World War.

In these marketing and promotional activities, Tetley's fellow managing director on the sales side, T. P. Latham, played a vital role as collaborator and organizer. He built upon the company's existing sales organization, trade contacts, and goodwill, promoting new outlets for the new product. In 1905 an advertisement appeared saying simply 'Artificial Silk:—salesman wanted by Samuel Courtauld & Co. Ltd., Coventry to visit manufacturing centres . . .' The successful applicant was appointed in February 1906; many more followed. In addition, a network of yarn agents was set up, at home and overseas, including one in the U.S.A. As the initial prejudices of buyers were overcome, as quality improved, and as viscose yarn emerged as the only type of rayon suitable for weaving, so did Latham pursue a policy of maintaining or raising prices for top-quality yarn and of seeking out the textile users. Meanwhile, competitors, still making the other types of rayon, had perforce to cut their prices in order to stay in the race even for non-weaving sales. Price discrimination by type and size of consumer was explicit; for weaving, as Latham observed in 1910, 'viscose alone is satisfactory'. He drew the corollary: 'it seems clear to us that the weaving trade can take viscose silk in constantly increasing quantity on the present basis of prices'. It was to prove only a little optimistic. The widening gap between production costs and selling prices brought big profits. While Courtauld & Co. prospered in the new viscose venture, their German counterpart, bristling with chemists, failed to do so. By 1911 Donnersmarck had not succeeded in making successful textile yarn, and Vereinigte Glanzstoff, appreciating the superiority of the viscose process, bought them out. But by that time the British company was not simply enjoying monopoly profits at home; it was just beginning to enjoy them in the U.S.A. as well.

(C) THE AMERICAN MARKET

Because a complex of patent rights, granted and sold internationally, provided the legal bases of early rayon enterprise, it is hardly surprising that international associations under various names—cartels, consortia, *ententes*, and the like—made an early appearance on this industrial scene. Samuel Courtauld & Co. were actively concerned with two such consortia between 1904 and 1914. The life and death of these bodies are not the concern of this chapter,[3] but their existence has to be noted because it was, in part at least, as a consequence of the firm's involvement with them that Courtauld & Co. acquired the American rights to the viscose process.

In 1905 the American rights were owned by Silas W. Pettit, lawyer and chief shareholder in a firm called Genasco (General Artificial Silk Co.), set up in 1901 as a result of the enterprise of a leading American chemist and a Philadelphia business man. Financial difficulties and the failure of the firm to produce any significant quantities of viscose yarn had resulted in Pettit buying the rights and trying his hand at this perilous but inviting game. He had scarcely more luck than his predecessors; by the time that the Courtauld venture started up at Coventry, Genasco's output was very small and barely saleable. In May 1907 Pettit got into touch with both Samuel Courtauld & Co. and the Société Française de la Viscose, seeking co-operation; in reality, of course, this simply meant technical help in making the process work. By this time the British and French firms had joined with the Swiss, Italian, and Belgian in negotiating the first of the international consortia. The crucial elements in this undertaking were the avoidance of competition and the establishment of technical collaboration. Pettit's inquiry was discussed by the members of the consortium and Tetley was entrusted with the task of negotiating with him. In July Pettit was informed by Tetley that 'our friends of the other companies seem disposed to welcome you as a member of our group'. But viscose horizons were still cloudy at that time. So negotiations continued. In

February 1908 Pettit was offered membership at a price which included an undertaking to allow the importation into the U.S.A. of the viscose rayon yarn of any of the members on payment of a commission to Pettit. Hoping for better terms, Pettit stalled and arranged for a friend to visit the Coventry factory on his behalf. In the summer of that year, however, Latham and Tetley persuaded Pettit to sign an agreement licensing Samuel Courtauld & Co. to import into the U.S.A. on payment of the agreed commission. In October Latham visited the U.S.A. and appointed as the company's yarn agent an English merchant resident in New York, Samuel Agar Salvage; he had earlier acted as Pettit's intermediary, for it was he who, visiting London in May 1907, had conveyed Pettit's wish to secure Courtauld's co-operation. So, while formally negotiating on behalf of the consortium, Courtauld & Co. had secured for themselves an exclusive entry into a potentially vast market.

This was only the first step, however, of a process in which Tetley skilfully exploited the growing strength of Courtauld's position and the continuing weakness of his continental partners in the consortium. In November 1908 Pettit died; negotiations about membership continued with his son, John R. Pettit. Tetley, in communication on the subject with the Société Française de la Viscose, played on their fears of the Donnersmarck enterprise: Pettit might be in league with the Germans; it was necessary to ensure that he was not 'playing a double game'. But the confidence of the British company was now growing fast; the once frightening vision of Donnersmarck and the Müller patent had receded; the American market beckoned and was not to be ignored. Courtauld & Co. alone had secured access to it, so they alone became vitally interested in a new factor: the level of the U.S. tariff. At the time of their importing agreement with Pettit, senior, this had stood at 30 per cent *ad volorem*. In January 1909 news came of a proposed increase. Pettit, junior, spelt out the obvious implications in a letter to Courtauld's in February 1909: we now enjoy a protection of, roughly, say 40 cents a pound. Suppose it was raised, will you not almost be forced to come over in order to compete? We expect it to be raised.' The matter was growing urgent. In May Tetley wrote to the French company blandly telling them that Courtaulds' were now 'disposed . . . to negotiate with Pettit on the basis of getting his patents, etc., for ourselves— and if that succeeds, to offer to you people a part'. He suggested a possible figure for their share, a figure which he must have known they could not possibly afford. A non-committal reply pleaded the pending outcome of financial re-arrangements. On 21 June Tetley wrote again. He assured them that this American transaction had nothing to do with the consortium; once everything had been settled, 'we will write you officially whether we find we are able to invite you to subscribe a part of the capital'. The sinister name of Donnersmarck was mentioned; it had been 'necessary to act promptly'. Prompt action there certainly had been. For what Tetley did not say was that five days previously, at a meeting in London, Pettit had sold out to Samuel

Courtauld & Co. for $150,000 (at then prevailing rates, approximately £31,000).

The French were aggrieved and said so; Tetley admitted the situation was 'rather a delicate one'. Some rights of import into the U.S.A. were conceded to the other members of the consortium (Courtauld & Co. could readily afford that in their confidence of technical and economic superiority); Salvage was to act as agent for the consortium; Latham dispatched a good supply of his usual soothing letters. And that was that. Courtauld's had now won the biggest prize and proceeded to enjoy it for themselves. Tetley's piece of sharp opportunism was second in importance only to his original purchase of the British viscose patents five years earlier. The £25,000 for the British rights and the £31,000 for the American were to prove investments of extraordinary profitability. One pertinent example will suffice. Pettit was offered as an alternative mode of payment $100,000 and £4,000 of Samuel Courtauld & Co.'s ordinary shares. He decided to take it all in cash. If he had taken and retained the shares, the market value of the holding in 1929 would have been about £2,500,000.

Within a few months land for the American factory was purchased at Marcus Hook, Pennsylvania, and the American Viscose Company incorporated. Early in 1911 A.V.C. began production. It started with the enormous advantage derived from its parent company's six-years' experience at Coventry. A high technical productivity was rapidly obtained. The marketing arrangements which the home company had set up for its own yarn exports were extended to provide outlets for the products of the American plant. As in Britain it could set its own prices; and the high American tariff ensured high U.S. prices. So by importing the newly developed Coventry production techniques over the tariff barrier, very high profit margins were achieved. In 1912 both Samuel Courtauld & Co. and their three-year-old American subsidiary were each earning net profits representing over 77 per cent on their issued ordinary and preference capital.

(D) THE RAYON BOOM AND COURTAULDS' PROSPERITY

This rapid accumulation of profits was thus accruing to a firm which enjoyed a legal patent monopoly in both Britain and the U.S.A., and was also protected by a high tariff in the latter country. The issued capital was rapidly becoming inappropriate to the earning power which was producing gross rates of return of around 100 per cent on issued risk capital in both countries. Samuel Courtauld & Co.'s shares were not quoted on the Stock Exchange, but during 1911–12 the £5 shares began to change hands privately at rates which represented a growing awareness of what was happening in Coventry and Marcus Hook: from £15 in April 1911 they had risen to £35 by February 1913. In April 1913 a new company, Courtaulds Ltd., was incorporated with an issued capital of £2 m. The method by which this was done made it effectively a 10-for-1 bonus issue to the existing holders of the £200,000 ordinary share capital. There was no public flotation and the holders of the outstanding debentures and preference shares had no opportunity to participate in the ordinary share allotment. The ownership of the ordinary capital of the new Courtaulds Ltd. thus represented in part the historical ownership of Samuel Courtauld & Co. and in part the effect of private dealing before 1913. The resulting distribution, set out in Table 5.2, illustrates what had been happening.

TABLE 5.2

Ownership of Share Capital in Courtaulds Ltd., 1913

	£	%
Courtauld family	651 600	32·5
Nettlefold, Browne, and Warren families	508 051	25·5
H. G. Tetley and T. P. Latham	373 852	18·5
Foreign holders connected with the artificial silk industry	138 500	7·0
Others, including employees of Courtaulds Ltd.	328 004	16·5
	2 000 007*	100·0

*The £7 represents shares issued to Directors and certain officials of the firm.

On the other side of the Atlantic the subscribed capital of A.V.C. was also increased in 1913: from $837,000 at which it stood in 1911–12 to $1,600,000 against a nominal capital of $2 m. This was done entirely by various internal transactions with Courtaulds Ltd. But this capital soon proved inadequate to deal with the astonishing profitability of A.V.C. In 1914 the gross return on subscribed capital had reached 156 per cent; and worries about high monopoly profits in the context of current anti-trust legislation seemed to call for further reconstruction. A.V.C. might be thought to be making more money than was good for it. So in 1915 A.V.C. was again reorganized, this time becoming The Viscose Company, with an authorized capital of $10 m., all but $500 of which continued to be held by Courtaulds Ltd. With the outbreak of war in Europe this remarkably profitable investment was rapidly to prove its worth to its British parent.

During the war years the textile side of the firm continued to be outpaced by the new rayon enterprise. In 1917–19 annual gross profits from yarn sales averaged £1,542,000, more than four times those arising from the firm's fabric sales, running at a mere £359,000. The company could sell all the viscose yarn it could make, and did so at prices which rose at roughly the same rate as prices generally. Although the basic patents expired at various dates between 1911 and 1917, the circumstances of the war effectively accomplished what the second of the international consortia had failed to do: prevent

competition. Courtaulds' *de facto* monopoly of the British market continued
and it was not until 1919 that new firms moved in. The company's yarn-
producing capacity was increased in 1917 by the acquisition, as enemy property, of a mill which had been set up in Flint by Vereinigte Glanzstoff in 1908
to work the cuprammonium process. Nevertheless, the war brought real
difficulties to the company's home operations. In 1913–14 yarn sales averaged
3·5 m. lb annually; they rose in 1915 but fell to a low point of 2·9 m. in 1918,
recovering only thereafter, to reach 5·8 m. in 1920. Numbers employed,
output, and productivity at Coventry all fell in 1916–18. Sharp increases in
taxation bit into gross profits from 1916 to 1921. It was the vastly increased
contribution from its American subsidiary which sustained the growth
of Courtaulds Ltd. in these years and brought the financial results which
necessitated still further capital reorganization.

In 1915 both the British and the American ends of the rayon business
produced 3·5 m. lb of yarn. Then came the change: output from Marcus Hook
went ahead rapidly and by 1920 whilst Coventry and Flint had together
reached 6·3 m. lb, American production (which by then included a new factory set up at Roanoke in Virginia in 1917) had soared to 10·1 m. lb. Prices
and profits had soared still more; in 1917–19 gross turnover margins on yarn
sales averaged 62·6 per cent in Britain and 76·1 per cent in America. By 1919
The Viscose Company's gross profits at $30 m. were three times the issued
capital. Although American taxes also increased, it was still possible in that
year to pay a 60 per cent dividend and carry forward a surplus of $21 m. The
widening gap between manufacturing costs and selling prices rested in part
upon a demand which was buoyed up by the entry of viscose rayon yarn
not only into weaving but also into the hosiery knitting industry. American
hosiers may not necessarily have been, as Tetley claimed, 'more intelligent',
but they certainly seem to have been more enterprising than their British
counterparts. One of the consequences of all this profit-making in America
was a renunciation of some degree of formal control of the American company by its British parent in order to ensure that American profits were not
subject to British taxes. Some American-based directors were appointed,
including Salvage, later to become the dominant figure in the American rayon
business; and some more of the American profits were remitted to the parent
in the form of capital transactions, thus avoiding English taxation. Between
1913 and 1920 Courtaulds' gross annual income from its American subsidiary
rose from £58,000 to £1,488,000; by the latter year the revenue from America
accounted for 38 per cent of Courtaulds' gross cash income (i.e. trading
profits *plus* investment income, before tax and depreciation). Not surprisingly,
yet another capital reorganization had to happen. Certain legal cases, on both
sides of the Atlantic, had made it clear that stock dividends did not attract
tax. So in 1919 a 1-for-1 issue brought Courtaulds' capital to £4 m.; and in
1920 after a revaluation which put The Viscose Company's assets at £7,800,000,

a 2-for-1 issue brought Courtaulds' capital to £12 m. all in ordinary shares. The American company's assets were brought into the balance-sheet; they were certainly undervalued and their true value was allowed to remain a mystery to shareholders. Suffice to add that in 1922 a further reconstruction of the American business proved necessary: the name by which it was to become generally known, American Viscose Corporation, made its appearance; and the authorized capital rose to $100 m.

Meanwhile, back in Britain, it was not perhaps wholly surprising that in 1920 the President of the Board of Trade was asked whether Courtaulds were known to the committee looking into wartime profiteering. The reply he gave was non-committal; nothing particular happened. Would the M.P. have put the question had he known that in the eight years 1913–20 85 per cent of the amount by which Courtaulds' issued capital was increased and 31 per cent of the company's total gross income were attributable respectively to capital gains from the U.S.A. and operating profits on manufacture in the U.S.A.? The fortunate and the enterprising had certainly done extremely well. New employment, for men and women, was created; the rewards for special skills had risen—the £200-a-year chemist of 1905 was earning £2,000 in 1920. The managing directors got handsome commissions: those paid to Tetley and Latham in 1904–7 averaged just under £4,000 annually, in 1912 they drew between them over £107,000 in commissions alone. And the ordinary shareholders received, in addition to their capital bonuses in 1913, 1919, and 1920, dividends which shot up from a mere 6 per cent in 1904–8 to an annual average of 24 per cent for the years 1910–14 and nearly 32½ per cent for 1916–20.

(F) SOME ELEMENTS IN SUCCESS

Thus, in the fifteen years from 1905 to 1920, a sound and unexciting Essex silk firm, worth about £300,000 in 1904, was transformed into a £12 m. business. Even that capitalization undervalued the true worth of a concern which included an American subsidiary that was itself the largest rayon producer in the world whilst its parent was the biggest in Europe. A British business had become the world-leader in a new chemical-textile industry, despite the much-advertised British lag in scientific education and the pre-war deceleration of its economy. It had been achieved, as this chapter has tried briefly to show, by a mixture of enterprise, opportunism, and luck.

This account is offered neither as a guide to future industrial behaviour nor as a generalization about the British industrial past. But it is perhaps worth emphasizing a few of the points which have emerged from this picture of a particular historical experience. First, the technical basis of the invention was not developed within the textile industry but by independent scientists concerned with other matters. Second, at the time when Courtauld & Co. took it up, their policy was directed by outsiders to a family firm; and the immediate purpose was not to acquire a replacement for an expensive input but to rejuvenate sluggish profits. Third, there were few established textile firms amongst those who tried to develop any of the 'artificial silk' processes; and amongst the international purchasers of the rights to the viscose process, Courtauld & Co. were the only such firm. Fourth, despite the novelty of the new enterprise, dependent on chemistry and chemical engineering, nobody on the Courtauld Board had any professional knowledge of, or training in, either of those subjects, a state of ignorance as true in 1920 as in 1905. Fifth, managerial and marketing skills, based on successful experience in producing and selling an end-product made from textile yarns, proved to be of greater consequence in achieving success than comprehension of the relevant chemistry. Sixth, and last, although these seem to have been the major conditions of success, it was the possession of the monopoly rights in the American market as well as the British which brought the big profits in a brief time.

NOTES

1 This chapter is a drastic abridgement of Part I of Volume ii of D. C. Coleman, *Courtaulds: An Economic and Social History* (2 vols., Oxford U.P., Oxford, 1969).

2 For the sake of brevity the term 'rayon' is used throughout this chapter, although it is strictly an anachronism for the period covered here.

3 For a detailed account see Coleman, *Courtaulds*, ii, Ch. 4.

4 The £7 represents shares issued to directors and certain officials of the firm.

II

6

Family and Failure:
Archibald Kenrick and Sons Ltd.,
1900–1950[1]

ROY CHURCH

ADOPTING a conservative definition of a small business as one with fewer than
200 employees, in 1935 small manufacturing enterprises accounted for 38 per
cent of total employment in the U.K. and 35 per cent of total net output.[2]
However, it is not only size that distinguishes small firms: privacy, owner-
management, and family control are equally central to an analysis of the small
scale enterprise.[3] In certain industries, notably those experiencing stagnation
or decline, large clusters of small firms have persisted and continue to survive,
apparently in defiance of the purgative effects of market mechanisms normally
associated in the textbooks with profit-maximization and competition. Our
knowledge of small firms was enlarged considerably by the report resulting
from the Bolton Committee's Inquiry on Small Firms, which charted the
general differences between large and small enterprise. But scant attention
was paid to causal relationships (apart from superficial statistical association).
Yet Sargent Florence, referring to Britain's inferior industrial performance
between 1880 and the 1930s, and Richard Caves, referring to the years since
World War II, both drew attention to the apparently greater resilience of small
family firms in the U.K. compared with the United States, drawing the conclusion that differences between the performance of identical industries in the
two economies could be explained partly by this fact and partly by the barrier
to progress, through resource misallocation, for which small firms were
responsible.[4] If such generalizations are to be accepted or discarded, research
must both explore the evidence for the extent of small firms in different
countries and identify the internal dynamics involved. This essay on Archibald
Kenrick & Sons seeks to contribute to our understanding of the behaviour of
family firms by a detailed examination of one unenterprising business which,
while unsuccessful in economic terms, nevertheless managed to survive.

(A) THE ORIGINS OF DECLINE

Owned, controlled, and managed by the Kenrick family since its foundation in 1791, Archibald Kenrick & Sons Ltd. of West Bromwich emerged as one of the largest hardware manufacturers in Britain. Even so, at the peak of the company's history at the end of the nineteenth century the company's paid-up capital was still only £301,000, with a work-force numbering fewer than 1,300, a figure never again to be exceeded. The firm's development had been dependent upon the growth of population and house-building, and from the mid-nineteenth century upon British expansion overseas, particularly in Australia. Beginning as a supplier of a range of relatively cheap cast-iron products, as the century progressed Kenricks became identified as the leading manufacturer of high-quality hollow-ware and domestic and builders' ironmongery. Only the buoyancy of Empire markets early in the twentieth century obscured and temporarily delayed the eventual erosion in the demand for cast-iron hollow-ware and for a number of other consumer goods in which pressed steel was fast replacing cast iron. This situation brought the firm face to face with problems identical to those facing other metal manufacturers whose cast-iron hardware was eclipsed in markets where articles made of steel, and subsequently in some cases aluminium, became the preferred substitutes. As the types of cast-iron products with which the name of Archibald Kenricks had been so long associated lost favour, the company's continued growth came to depend more than ever upon the Kenrick family's ability to recognize the signals of change and to adapt to altered circumstances in both home and overseas markets.

The independent response to competition had taken the form of the acquisition of several small firms with similar manufacturing output, of cast-iron hollow-ware and hardware.[5] Complementary to the take-over of competitors was a collusive strategy through membership of numerous manufacturers' associations which controlled the prices of particular articles made of cast iron. The most important of these bodies was the Cast Iron Hollow-ware Manufacturers' Association in which Kenricks was one of the two major firms, accepting higher prices than other members. During the final decade of the nineteenth century the company achieved its peacetime peak in sales, profits, and numbers employed, and, despite falling profits, the customary 10 per cent annual dividend was maintained. However, directors' salaries were little more than token sums, since the adoption of limited liability in 1883 had not altered the extent to which the interests of the family were identified with the fortunes of the firm. Although limited liability had removed the ultimate risk, family incomes were sensitive to business failure, whether resulting from external factors or owing to lack of enterprise. Such vulnerability posed a potential threat to the Kenricks as the climacteric phase of the company's history ushered in a period of decline, following the intervening booms associated with World War I and the post-war expansion.

Munitions contracts for the armed forces, followed by the pent-up demand for domestic hardware when the war ended, provided a financial basis which, supplemented by substantial bank overdrafts and family resources, enabled the directors to invest in new steel-stamping and die-cast aluminium plant in 1922. But the conjuncture of increased productive capacity together with a general collapse of overseas markets left the company with problems of over-capitalization, as overhead charges rose and prices and sales fell. From that time low levels of demand and falling product prices provided a discouraging business environment. The collapse of international trade was reflected in the decline in Kenricks' exports, for whereas in the early 1920s they accounted for between 30 and 40 per cent of turnover, by 1930 this had fallen to 15 per cent, and to 7 per cent in 1933, these proportions relating to substantially lower sales. Whether the sale of Kenricks' products were regulated through the company's affiliation to trade associations, or whether they were sold without restrictions on prices, almost every product experienced falling sales. Apart from gas and electric irons, which were the most successful of the new products introduced in the mid-1920s, exceptions to falling sales were cast-iron ranges and stoves, cisterns, and, above all, cast-iron enamelled baths. The latter was the major feature of Kenricks' somewhat limited policy of diversification by supplying fitted goods to the building trades—a decision which was precipitated by Kenricks' first trading loss, suffered in 1926, followed, in 1927, by a nil dividend, which was also unprecedented.

The optimism engendered by a modest increase in sales during the late 1920s, following the capital investment programme commenced in 1926, was soon dissipated in the collapse of sales in the ensuing slump. During the economic recovery of the mid-1930s only baths, ranges, and cisterns showed a rise in sales. By 1936–7 these three products accounted for 45 per cent of the total sales from Kenricks' West Bromwich foundry, baths alone accounting for 39 per cent. Yet in this branch of the light-castings industry the advantage lay more and more with the specialized, fully mechanized, continuous systems of production, the effective utilization of which depended on large-scale production like that of Allied Ironfounders' subsidiary, British Baths Ltd., of Greenford, where the weekly capacity of 2,000 baths in 1935 was nearly four times that of the Kenricks' foundry. Furthermore, the British Bath Makers' Association, to which the Kenricks belonged from 1931, would not concede the quota levels necessary to turn Kenricks' bath foundry into a profitable enterprise. From 1935 the company's bath sales began to decline. The three small subsidiary companies—Baldwins, then manufacturing builders' hardware, Anglo-enamel Ware, still making stamped steel hollow-ware, mainly mess tins on government contracts, and United Hinges—fared slightly better than the parent company and helped to offset Kenricks' losses, but in each case the trends in sales and profits were downwards after the post-war boom. In 1929 three of the associated companies had experienced trading losses for the second consecutive year (the fourth consecutive loss for Kenricks' West Bromwich foundry), and for the third time in three years no dividends were declared;

the year 1929 also saw the Directors denying themselves remuneration, a gesture repeated annually until 1934. In 1931 the company sustained its biggest trading loss (£26,000) and the years between 1931 and 1933, when in each year the cash/current liabilities ratio fell below 1 to 1, constituted an important phase in the firm's financial history, culminating, as it did, in capital reconstruction. On the insistence of Lloyds Bank in return for an overdraft of up to £42,000, the Kenricks issued a first debenture to that amount. Even so, the Directors considered the firm's financial plight to be so critical that depreciation allowances were suspended altogether from 1932. Taking this into account, the adjusted net trading profits reveal losses in every year between 1926 and 1933 inclusive, and again in 1936 and 1937, though the profits of the Kenrick group taken together show losses in 1928 to 1932 inclusive. Between 1925 and 1942 less than £20,000 was distributed in dividend payments and the Directors' remuneration was nominal throughout the period. Nil dividends and token remuneration of Directors were repeated for more than ten years after the intervening wartime boom.

While the Chairman, W. Byng Kenrick, attributed the company's deteriorating position to external factors of changing consumer demand away from cast-iron hardware, and to the general ill health of the British economy, the demonstrable success of some of Kenricks' competitors, similar in history, size, and resources, suggests that Byng's was an inadequate diagnosis. This was the view forcibly expressed by A. Wyndham Baldwin in 1935, when he joined the Board of Directors as the representative of the Baldwin family's substantial minority shareholding in Archibald Kenricks. He it was who persuaded the Kenricks to engage the leading firm of accountants, Peat, Marwick, Mitchell & Co., to investigate and report on the company's position.

(B) MANAGERIAL MALAISE: DIAGNOSIS AND RESPONSE

The accountant who led the investigation had difficulty in finding data adequate for an analysis of costing. Indeed, the accountant subsequently appointed in 1938 on Peat Marwick's recommendation later remarked that Kenricks' cost figures had been on such general lines that the allocation of expenses to the company's individual products when costed had adopted the principle of 'what one loses on the swings one gains on the roundabouts. Unfortunately,' he added, 'customers are sufficiently discerning as to choose those articles on the "swing" principle, leaving the company with the fixed charges which were hopefully loaded on to the "roundabout" products, the net effect being to reduce the company's profit-earning power.' Peat Marwick's report had also criticized the lack of accurate and detailed information which might reasonably have been expected of modern offices and factories of importance, finding it virtually impossible to identify costs of articles of diverse types and size. The report was equally critical of the absence of any adequate system of stock control, and argued that without much fuller and more reliable monthly information concerning trading results, sales, orders, wastage, liquidity, and capital expenditure, it was too much to expect the Board to be in a position to give proper consideration to the management of the company's business. Inquiries into the technical and productive aspects were hampered by Clive Kenrick, the temperamental Works Managing Director who refused to co-operate, but the paucity of cost data underlined the difficulties of assessing the costs of alternative productive methods and organization. Kenricks' sales policy was criticized for lack of vigour and possible under-representation leading to infrequent personal contact with customers.

Following from the conclusions set out in the report, five recommendations were listed. The first was that on the assumption of a continuance of the post-war fall in sales, Kenricks should rearrange the layout of the works so as to concentrate production in a limited location and thereby free land for sale or rent. Most of the unprofitable products should be dropped, some retained to maintain sales revenue, and Clive should present detailed specifications of his plan for modernizing the foundry in which capital costs should be related to savings and earnings expected to accrue on the basis of current turnover. Sales should be invigorated by a more aggressive policy which would be promoted by the establishment of a more effective sales organization supported by relevant statistical information. On the question of membership of a trade association, the consultants' view was that in cases where a strong association existed, a policy of co-operation was usually well advised, thereby confirming the long-standing Kenrick policy. A further recommendation was for the introduction of proper budgeting combined with effective stock, stores, and production control on a continuous rather than annual basis. These and similar reforms were intended to transform the office function from that of merely a repository for sundry information to one of providing a storehouse for a systematic collection of data on a large scale, where it would also be processed in such a way as to provide a comprehensive and thorough basis for managerial decision-making.

After referring to other firms in similar lines of business which were conducting profitable business, the report was explicit in its assessment of the Kenricks' grasp of business methods:

As is natural in a family business, the whole of the capital of which is privately held, practically all the important administrative posts are filled by members of the family, and there are no employees in positions of real authority. The impression we formed was that these members of the family had probably grown up in the concern and had a very great knowledge of their own business, but they did not appear to have acquired a knowledge of business methods as practically applied in modern industrial organizations. The reorganization of management would no doubt prove a heavy and responsible task, and those who carry it out would need to be ruthless in altering much in the way of methods and practices which have grown up for several generations and continued until they have become deep-rooted. We are satisfied that this cannot be done by existing personnel and that the administration needs to be strengthened from outside. The present chairman is, we understand, largely occupied with public duties. The company needs the vigorous full-time attention of its executive officer and accordingly it seems to us that Mr W. Byng Kenrick would be well advised to retain the chairmanship, in which capacity his wide knowledge of the business would be invaluable, but retire from active executive work.

The consultants recommended the appointment of a qualified accountant and a Managing Director to act as a joint Managing Director with Clive. It was envisaged that the new Managing Director would be a full-time appointment at Board level from outside the family, 'a man of energy and determination with a wide commercial training preferably experienced in the same or a kindred trade, but with a sound knowledge of modern sales organization and control'. Unequivocally, the report concluded that the possible alternatives to this plan of reorganization from within was either amalgamation with another company in the hardware industry, or outright sale of the business as a going concern.

How did the family respond to all this? Sir George Kenrick (a Director and formerly Chairman) indicated to Baldwin that he considered it to be a very good report, but that no action should be taken. Clive rejected the criticisms of the production side of the business as exaggerated, denying the need for substantial investment in modernization and defending his long-held position that rising turnover should precede investment in productive plant and equipment. Without such a sequence the company's financial position would not permit a policy of expansion. Byng likewise stressed the need to raise turnover as the immediate priority, together with closer attention to costs and prices. The result of the Kenricks' deliberations was the adoption of the proposals relating to improvements in sales organization, the appointment of an accountant, and the introduction of machinery for monitoring production costs continuously and systematically. Byng's document containing these recommendations to the Board also referred to the management issue raised by Peat Marwick: 'On the information at present before us I am not inclined to assent to a radical change from the original practice of retaining the management in the hands of the principal owners of the business.' Byng's recommendations were accepted by the Board, which recorded the rejection of any notion of altering the character of the business as one controlled and managed by the Kenrick family. Thus the newly created position of Sales Manager was given to William E. Kenrick, Byng's elder son, who, while assuming this responsibility—though with limited authority—received neither direction nor guidance as to his precise functions in this new role.

(C) KENRICKS AND CONTEXT

While the consultants' strictures on the company's lack of statistical data was fully justified, the same defect characterized the majority of firms in the light-castings industry, as contributors to the *Foundry Trades Journal* frequently remarked. The judgements relating to productive efficiency, therefore, were to some extent intuitive, based on observations of contemporary foundry practices. Compared with many other medium-sized foundries, Kenricks was mechanized to some considerable degree, and given the company's attempt to produce a variety of products, remarks made by the author of *Foundry Organization and Management* published in 1937 are relevant. In his view automatic and continuous production, which by this time the term 'mechanization' had come to denote, was only justified under conditions of large-scale specialized production. Comparing the types of equipment which he favoured (i.e. under conditions of diversified medium-scale production), it would appear that Clive's decisions in this connection, at least in the foundries, were probably the right ones. However, as he was the Director chiefly responsible for increasing diversification rather than specialization in the potential growth products, he must shoulder a major share of the responsibility for dispersing and dissipating effort, instead of concentrating managerial resources both in production and sales. The Kenrick Directors, even Clive who showed a thorough understanding of new techniques, including their limitations, had agreed to postpone heavy capital expenditure until sales rose to a level which could sustain complete mechanization.

How significant were the company's financial difficulties? Ultimately, of course, the capital expenditure of a business depends upon its ability to acquire cash resources and to pay for them. After the immediate high post-war expenditure the low profitability of the West Bromwich firm, especially from 1926, virtually eliminated profits as a source of finance, either for replacement or new developments. But by eventually waiving dividends, by departing from a regular depreciation policy, and by persuading Lloyds Bank to extend sizeable overdrafts, the Kenricks succeeded in securing resources sufficient to enable Clive to carry out the investment projects of the middle and late 1920s. Referring to that period, William later remarked that 'those who survived, survived largely because their credit was better than that of the others'. As a general observation this leaves room for disagreement, but the remark is relevant inasmuch that it suggests that the Kenricks did not find difficulty in obtaining financial assistance during the interwar years. Moreover, he considered the bank's support to have been crucial in enabling the company to embark on fresh capital expenditure at that time. That there was no economic justification for such preferential treatment from Lloyds is plain from much of the foregoing discussion, though it can be argued that the company's assets provided the bank with ample security. What seem to be relevant factors here relate partly to the company's very long-standing personal connection with Lloyds, and partly to the social position of the Kenrick family in Birmingham, West Bromwich, and Stourport. For it is entirely plausible that the Temple Row managers were reluctant to compromise the positions of such leading public figures as Sir George and Byng, similar considerations perhaps deterring a squeeze in Stourport where Gerald, inexpert in business, was immersed in the affairs of Worcestershire County Council. This factor may also have deterred the senior Directors at West Bromwich from the closure of the Stourport subsidiaries.

Compared with a notional best practice in the larger, thoroughly mechanized foundries, Kenricks' plant was, as Peat Marwick's report claimed, obsolescent. To modernize completely would have required heavy capital investment owing to the increasingly interrelated nature of modern foundry technology, and to this extent Kenricks' limited cash resources partly account for the firm's continuing poor performance lasting for many years, particularly because of the low profitability of all the associated companies, none of whom had sufficiently high sales to offset overheads, lower unit costs, and raise profits. However, we have seen that foundry experts recommended thorough-going modernization only where a level of sales could be relied upon to support mass production. Moreover, in the foundry trades at any rate, the concept of interrelatedness when discussing firms is useful only to a degree, for it was possible, as contemporaries made clear, to replace components separately, with the degree of mechanization determined by the product market. Liquidity, then, while it increased Kenricks' difficulties, was not fundamental to the company's problems. Thorough-going modernization ultimately depended on the level of sales, and to this extent Kenricks' commercial policy becomes the major internal factor in explaining the company's history during the inter-war years. Here blame can be apportioned largely to the failure of Sir George, though his successor, Byng, cannot escape criticism for perpetuating the broad commercial strategy adopted by his cousin.

Throughout the early decades of the twentieth century until his voluntary but long-awaited retirement in 1934 Sir George remained at the apex of the hierarchical managerial structure, ruling the company in a thoroughly autocratic fashion. The lines of communication to the Chairman, who remained aloof from his subordinates, did not permit the movement of ideas, and even Byng, whom Sir George patronized as the company's crown prince, for a long time deferred to the views of his elder cousin whenever a difference of opinion arose. Not until some time in the 1920s did Byng begin discreetly to countermand some of his more preposterous instructions, and on occasion, after lengthy argument with Byng, Sir George would even admit to having been in error. In the closing decades of the nineteenth century Sir George's efforts in the technical and commercial fields had contributed to the company's success, but his energies were channelled increasingly into commercial policy. In this connection the formative years of his career at West Bromwich were years of growth and expansion; but this was due in no small measure to a favourable secular demand for cast-iron products, and a continued preference on the part of consumers for the high-quality articles made by Kenricks, whose reputation in this field was built on the company's achievements since the middle of the century. Judging from the sales and pricing policies of the inter-war years, with the elimination of all quantity discounts except on those lines sold by association agreements, it seems that—especially in the traditional lines—Sir George took the view that Kenrick's products were unequalled, and that price-cuts were symptomatic of weakness. Moreover, his apparent disregard for turnover, as reflected in his readiness to raise the price of an article as soon as it began to sell well, was particularly frustrating for his salesmen and managers (none of whom possessed authority to make quotations under any circumstances), while at the same time it reduced the possibility of establishing an unchallengeable position within the market. Such a sales policy, which has been described by the manager of the London office at that time as 'rigid and unimaginative', has been attributed to his lack of contact with customers. Coupled with his apparent insensitivity to customers' wishes, Sir George's unapproachability helps to explain why the suggestions advanced by his salesmen, not to mention the company's customers, received scant attention.

Such complacency on the sales side, which Sir George and subsequently Byng determined, was matched by the attitude of Clive, whose power in the works increased from the 1920s. Though apparently sharing the perversity of the ageing Chairman, Clive differed from his Unitarian cousins in many respects. Either of these factors, or both, may have contributed to the apparent lack of harmony on the Board, though this never became overt. His eccentricities may also help to explain why, like the Commercial Directors (though it is difficult to distinguish between the attitudes of Sir George and Byng), Clive was intolerant of customers' complaints and unsympathetic towards suggestions for product improvements not related to technical processes. As an engineer, he showed concern for the technical aspects of manufacturing, but made no concessions to consumers' tastes if by so doing 'unnecessary adjustments' to a product would be required; for him an article's use was all-important, its appearance and detail seemed to him to have little significance. In the absence of persons responsible for design and quality control, such attitudes were especially unfortunate, but as the resources of the company dwindled, the likelihood of such staff appointments diminished; indeed, in 1932 the Works Chemist was given notice owing to the company's financial difficulties.

While Clive apparently failed to recognize the importance of control and organization in contributing to efficient management, nevertheless he proved to be responsive to broad changes in consumer demand, and showed a professional interest in changing technology and manufacturing processes. This explained the development of numerous new lines at the foundry from the mid-1920s onwards—a policy, if it can be so described, of haphazard diversification which from the standpoint of selling proved to be unsatisfactory, even though one or two particular items (gas cookers and gas fires) were of a price and quality comparable with other brands making a much greater impact in the market at that time. Gas irons sold moderately well, mainly because the typical distribution channel was the retail ironmonger, with whom the Kenricks had well-established links. Gas and electric fires, however, were handled chiefly by wholesalers dealing in general domestic appliances, and by a few large department stores. Moreover, the trade in fires typically introduced new models each year and this involved using new sets of patterns. This the Kenricks refused to do; neither would they compete by varying the colour of their fires.

In the case of new lines of household appliances, sales efforts were spread over too many different articles and salesmen were offering to the same customer hollow-ware, builders' ironmongery, hinges, and sundry articles such as potato-mashers and smoothing-irons of various kinds. Though there was some attempt to sell through builders' merchants to meet the needs of that trade, apart from the articles sold direct to local authorities on contract, nearly all Kenricks' products in the home market found outlets through retail ironmongers, for the company did not offer quantity discounts to attract the larger wholesalers. This policy was predicated on the assumption that wholesaling was on the decline. Notwithstanding a few connections with major department and retail stores, this situation remained unaltered. At a time when specialist retailers were emerging, particularly in the field of gas appliances and in electrical goods, Kenricks was at a disadvantage with respect to the sale of these articles, but in order to obtain such outlets it was necessary to manufacture and supply them in large numbers. Moreover, specialist retailers, who were being deserted by many manufacturers in favour of wholesalers, showed a preference for stocking whole ranges of articles sold by brand, a policy which helps to explain why the half-hearted venture in the production of aluminium hollow-ware proved such a failure.

(D) PUBLIC HONOUR AND BUSINESS FAILURE

Throughout the inter-war years Kenricks was renowned still as the major British maker of cast-iron hollow-ware, while in markets for its other numerous products the company was no more than one of a number of medium-sized foundries struggling to compete with the established specialists in the various lines of manufacture. The company's dwindling financial resources (handsomely supplemented by Lloyds) were spread too thinly over too wide an area, and as a result the company failed to establish for itself a national reputation in the growing market for domestic appliances (which, in retrospect, appears to have been its most promising section at that time)—or in any other new lines. One implication of this was the failure of the firm's sales force (unable to offer rebates to retailers on many goods and too small for direct distribution through retail outlets) to capture a share of the market large enough in any instance to support mass production. The conclusion which suggests itself is that the complacency to be found on the sales side, together with the waywardness on the production side, proved to be a disastrous combination on the board.

The question then arises, how was Clive able to influence so strongly the course of the company's development when the Chairman and Byng, who shared the direction of major policy with Sir George, were themselves forceful individuals? The answer probably lies partly in the public careers of these two men, and partly in the character of the family firm. Continuing a family tradition, Sir George's public career revolved around education. He became a member of the Birmingham School Board in 1880 and was elected to the Council of the Birmingham and Midland Institute in 1885. His service on the Birmingham City Council began in 1902, and he was Chairman of the Education Committee from 1903 (the year in which he received the freedom of West Bromwich) until 1921. His knighthood was conferred during his year as Lord Mayor of Birmingham in 1909, when King Edward VII opened new buildings of the University of Birmingham—to which Sir George (and the company) had donated several thousand pounds, and in which he had taken great personal interest. Not until 1935 did he finally retire from the Council, after having received the freedom of the city of Birmingham in 1923.

Byng, a staunch Unitarian, likewise enjoyed a lengthy and active public life, from the time he was elected to the City Council in 1914 until his retirement from that body thirty-five years later. For a long time he was Chairman of Edgbaston Divisional Unionist Association, Honorary Treasurer of Birmingham Unionist Association, and Chairman of the Unionist group on the City Council. From the beginning, he was a member of the Public Health and Education committees, and was Chairman of the latter from the time Sir George, 'owing to infirmity and deafness', relinquished the chairmanship in 1922 until 1928, and from 1931 to 1943. During that time he acted on several *ad hoc* committees, both of the Birmingham City Council and of the Association of Municipal Corporations, and also represented the Council on many outside bodies. He was Lord Mayor of Birmingham in 1928–9. In 1938 he was awarded the freedom of the city, and from 1939 to 1957 acted as Deputy Pro-Chancellor of the University of Birmingham. Meanwhile, Byng continued to serve as a co-opted member of the Education Committee after his retirement from the Council in 1949 until his death in 1962.

Such a brief, bare outline of their activities cannot convey the amount of time and effort spent upon public duties, but newspaper comments from time to time stressed this aspect of the lives of the Kenricks. In 1908 a report in the *Birmingham Daily Post* referred to Sir George's 'personal services in the cause of all branches of education' which were said to have been 'as devoted and self-denying as his munificence has been open-handed and unsparing'. Twenty years later the same newspaper referred to Byng's 'long record of unselfish public work', a record to which he was to add for many more years. In such activities, of course, these two men were emulating their forebears. An article in the *Birmingham Mail* in 1928 referred to the Kenrick family as 'one of a small group which for more than a century—but especially during the last fifty or sixty years—has influenced the social, civic, and religious life of Birmingham as probably no other group has done in any other town in the same period'.

It is true that the predecessors of these twentieth-century Kenricks had also combined public service with business affairs without evident detriment to the firm's success. However, the external pressures facing the company prior to 1890 (coupled with its virtually unrivalled reputation in the production of quality cast-iron hollow-ware) were less intractable than those which, especially after World War I, faced the Chairman and his cousins. As Sir George advanced in years he became increasingly out of touch with the needs and style of business enterprise in a period of widespread reorganization and rationalization in the foundry trades, while at the same time Byng was spending more and more time on public affairs. Sir George's proposals for amalgamating firms in the cast-iron hollow-ware trade in order to raise efficiency seem strangely in contrast to his lack of ideas for reviving the fortunes of his own company. Meanwhile, throughout the inter-war years Byng attended the office on most days, but rarely did he spend the whole day at West Bromwich.

However, absence from the general office cannot, by itself, explain why Clive, without formal discussion among the Directors, was able virtually to determine the scope of the company's production. One important factor enabling him to influence major policy was the lack of technical knowledge of his fellow Directors, none of whom was equipped to challenge Clive's judgement of matters of costs and production—especially in the absence of adequate statistical data. Furthermore, contentious points were omitted from discussion if they seemed likely to produce family disagreements, and, in any case, long-term aims were never discussed. Even the decisions taken in the late 1920s, when the company entered the bath trade, were not accompanied by an assessment of the wider implications of such a policy, and neither were the subsequent movements into the field of domestic gas and electric appliances.

The distribution of power among the Directors corresponded roughly to the age structure of the family, and this made it imperative, if the company was to succeed, that the senior Kenrick holding the greatest power should use it effectively. However, although well suited by nature to such a dictatorial role, during his later years following World War I Sir George seemed to be incapable of contemplating radical measures to reorganize the company to meet altered economic circumstances. Had the temperament of Byng been more forceful he might, as in minor matters, have done more to offset the failing of his cousin who clung on to power. But there was no question of a take-over of power by the younger men. Byng was the heir apparent and by temperament he was no revolutionary. Indeed, he must shoulder much of the blame for the lack of firm leadership from the middle years between the wars. As secretary of the Cast Iron Hollow-ware Manufacturers' Association he excelled, presenting evidence, preparing memoranda, and working out solutions of compromise based on consensus to accommodate different interests. But while in this capacity he influenced policy, he was not called upon to the same extent to take risky decisions independently. Similarly, as the tireless Chairman of the City of Birmingham Education Committee he proved to have no peer, and again his influence on policy was considerable. As Chairman and Managing Director of Kenricks his personal responsibility was greater than in either of his other two major roles to which we have referred, and he found it very difficult to make business policy decisions—a temperamental difficulty exacerbated by his complete lack of knowledge of management accounting. Thus throughout the inter-war years the company lacked firm, full-time, informed, and vigorous leadership.

(E) WAR AND POST-WAR STRATEGY

World War II was an interlude which gave rise to circumstances allowing Kenricks to expand its labour-force, increase production and turnover, and to secure handsome profits. This had the effect of vastly improving the company's financial position. Most of the capital expenditure incurred between 1939 and 1945 was not spent on machinery and equipment which could be applied directly to the manufacture of products for civilian use, but the introduction into the factory of the die-casting process, using zinc alloy to produce grenade centre-pieces and mortar-bomb tails, had the effect of enlarging the firm's scope of production, and this process subsequently formed the technical basis for the company's revival in the 1950s. Before that occurred, however, Kenricks, like so many other firms in similar circumstances, was to experience for the second time the acute difficulties of a period of post-war reconstruction.

When peacetime production was resumed, the company's affairs were managed by the same persons who had been responsible for the conduct of affairs prior to 1939. However, from 1945 Byng, then aged 73, while retaining his position as Chairman, withdrew from day-to-day business affairs, and William Kenrick assumed complete control of sales policy. Clive continued to be Managing Director of the works until 1950, during which time his influence on the company's policy reached its height; and at Stourport on 1 January 1949 Gerald handed over the duties of Managing Director of Baldwins and Anglo to Clive's son, Cecil John Kenrick. Hugh Kenrick assisted his brother William in sales management.

Before describing the process of reconstruction at Kenricks, it seems relevant to draw attention to an alternative policy which the company might have followed with greater success than that which was actually adopted. First, the stamped-steel side of the Kenricks' interests might have been developed. Although urged by William in a memorandum on post-war planning for Anglo in 1944, this possibility was not exploited. Second, we have seen that in the late 1920s and early 1930s the company had succeeded in selling gas and electric irons, and, to a lesser extent, fires, and that these smaller types of domestic appliances could be produced economically and sold successfully by the medium-sized unit. Kenricks had virtually abandoned these lines in 1933, but in view of the sanguine P.E.P. *Report on the Market for Household Appliances* published in 1945 the possibility of reviving these lines, and other solid-fuel-burning appliances, might well have recommended itself to the Kenricks, who at that time possessed ample financial resources for capital expenditure. The report forecast a substantially greater demand for household appliances in each of the first ten post-war years than in any prior to 1939. In fact, the Directors showed no inclination to challenge the established steel (or aluminium) hollow-ware makers, neither did they attempt to develop the field of gas and electric household appliances, where certain brand-names were already well entrenched.

Indeed, as in the critical period in the inter-war period, post-war strategy 'emerged': Clive's memorandum on capital expenditure and re-equipment presented in September 1945 formed the 'plan' for future development. Its adoption seems to have been a formality in the absence of any discussion of alternative proposals (which, in any case, were not forthcoming), and the only questions to receive serious consideration were those relating to the amount of capital to be channelled into Clive's projects, rather than the direction in which it was possible and desirable for the company to develop in its long-term interest. The result was a decision to re-equip the works for bath and cistern production, at a cost of £50,000.

After recovering from the low point in 1946, sales rose slowly and remained steady, at slightly more than £248,000 in 1948 and 1949. Over half Kenricks' sales were concentrated in three items: cast-iron hollow-ware, mincers, and builders' ironmongery, the relative importance of the first of these owing in part to a continued hold on colonial markets. Although the respective values were low, because of the fall in total output compared with pre-war records, the company's export trade was high in proportion to output. However, apart from Anglo's stamped steel hollow-ware, the long-term export prospects looked unpromising, partly because some lines were facing a decline in over-all demand and partly because of growing competition, both from British and European firms.

The profits of the war years had enabled much of the capital expenditure, approaching £100,000 between 1945 and 1951, to be met from internal reserves, but in 1948 it was found necessary to ask Lloyds to agree to an overdraft of up to £25,000 without security. This was raised to £40,000 in

1950, as the company's financial position worsened. The bath trade offered little hope for the immediate future, and the British Bath Manufacturers' Association found that anticipated output of its members exceeded probable demand by far. In March 1950 William represented the company at a meeting of the British Bath Manufacturers' Association at which it was reported that the anticipated output of the members was greatly in excess of the probable demand, and for this reason all members were urged to accept a quota scheme. It seemed plain to William that this would be prejudicial to the interests of his company, heavily committed as it was to the large-scale production of baths, and the Chairman and his fellow Directors supported him. Such a stand against the limitation of possible sales was especially necessary in view of the poor trading results produced by the West Bromwich works in the late 1940s.

A. W. Baldwin may not have been the only member of the Board to recognize the signals, but he it was who resolved to stir the Kenricks into radical action of some kind. He wrote a personal letter to the Chairman, a quotation from a letter from Kingsley to Newman appearing on the copy: 'There are occasions on which courtesy or reticence is a crime, and this is one of them.' Baldwin expressed his lack of confidence in the post-war capital investment programme then nearing completion. 'I am still convinced that unless we very soon inject a supply of vigorous new blood from outside, we shall fade right out of business.' He made it clear that if a majority on the Board opposed, on principle, the appointment of someone from outside the two families to one of the highest managerial posts, he would resign:

With my considerable experience of other Boards, and with evidence by hearsay and by figures of how our company compares with others in similar trades, I should be dull indeed if I did not know that we need a drastic regeneration in order to regain our place in the ranks of successful manufacturers . . . There is a lack of accomplishment, of real professionalism in our work, which in older and easier days may have had its merits . . . but it is dangerous . . . to continue these proud traditions of family management which any competent businessman would pronounce in our case to be below the standard required for survival.

As Baldwin had hoped, the ageing Chairman behaved in characteristically magnanimous fashion, acting promptly on the basis of the discussions which had taken place. It appears that, judging from his subsequent actions, Byng had misunderstood the point which Baldwin had tried to make at their meeting, interpreting his criticism as indicative of a lack of confidence in him, both as a Chairman and Managing Director. In fact, after criticizing the combination of the roles of Chairman and Managing Director into one, on the ground that such a double role gave needlessly large powers to the person filling that position, Baldwin had urged the appointment of a Managing Director who would act under Byng's chairmanship and receive the strength of his support. However, after discussing the company's future with Clive, Byng requested

W. L. Barrows, of Smith, Howard, Thompson & Co., to look for a suitable person to assume the roles he himself had filled hitherto.

The description of his meeting with Clive, outlined in a letter from Byng to Baldwin, suggests that personal relationships had hampered the process of management:

I began by pointing out that we were running for control by the Bank and asking whether he had any plan for action. He was of the opinion that what was wrong was the low level of sales. But he really had no clear plan or indeed any plan for increasing them. We both were trying to avoid recrimination, but I had to say that no profit was being shown in that branch, hollow-ware, where sales had materially increased. After some talk I told him that I thought that there was not complete agreement between the commercial side and the production side and my plan was that he and I should retire from the daily management and that we should bring in someone from outside who would command in both departments. He at once said that if the Board wished him to go he was quite ready to do so. I told him that I wanted him to agree because I had converted him to the view that it was the proper course; but there was an alternative, namely that I should clear out and he should take charge of the whole show, but that I could not go on as at present. He did not jump at my offer and obviously was partly convinced. He said that no doubt we were getting old and a bit stuck in ways. It was agreed that I should ask W. L. Barrows if he could help us in finding a man preferably in the forties and with engineering training or experience.

Baldwin expressed firm opposition to the possibility that Clive might become Chairman on Byng's retirement, saying that he 'dreaded Clive's management'. After discussions with some of the foremen and senior members of the staff, William agreed that the primary problem was one of management and 'human relations'.

In March 1950 Clive announced his retirement, whereupon William took over as temporary Managing Director at West Bromwich. John Donkin, an engineer formerly with G.E.C., was appointed joint General Manager with William, although Donkin was not given a seat on the Board. The same year saw the first set of Shepherd's patent castors produced at West Bromwich, utilizing the pressure die-casting process initially introduced for munitions manufacture and since then used to make zinc-alloy hardware for the building trade. Owing to the combination of those factors the year 1950 proved to be an important turning-point in the history of Archibald Kenrick Ltd.

(F) ENTERPRISE, MANAGEMENT, AND THE FAMILY FIRM

Faced from the end of the nineteenth century with problems of a secular decline in demand for cast-iron hardware, the Kenricks chose restrictive agreements and diversification. The Kenricks were moving spirits in the formation of trade associations whose object was to regulate the prices and output of certain products. Plainly, in the case of the Cast Iron Hollow-ware Manufacturers' Association restrictive practices had as their purpose the provision of insurance for its member manufacturers against a sudden change of circumstances. To the extent that it was successful, the association and its policies placed a brake on change at a time when the country's long-term interest would have been served by a fundamental transformation of its economy—in particular a more rapid decline in the traditional industries (like cast-iron hollow-ware) and a redistribution of resources into the new industries with some of which the older industries were in competition. By spreading output thinly, and by fixing prices to cover the costs of the least efficient firms such associations retarded the transference of business to the more efficient firms, thereby delaying the extinction of surplus capacity, and retarding the redirection of resources to the rising growth sectors. However, so long as entry to the finished-metal trades remained relatively easy, and as competing technologies were forthcoming, the importance of restrictive agreements in this section of industry should not be exaggerated.

Kenricks' strategy of expansion and diversification, and perhaps by implication the policies of other hardware firms, can be better understood when placed in the context of Professor Penrose's theoretical discussion of these aspects of the growth of firms, at the same time throwing some light on the problem of the mobility of capital and enterprise between declining and rising industries. The direction of expansion adopted by the West Bromwich firm in this period underlines the importance of its emphasis on the fact that because resources (including managerial services) are not non-specific, the relevant 'market demand' for any particular firm does not encompass the entire range of goods and services sold and purchased. Professor Penrose points out that each firm is concerned with only a brief range of products and focuses its attention on particular product-markets selected from the total market: 'The selection of the relevant product-markets is necessarily determined by the "inherited" resources of the firm—the productive services it already has.'[6]

The diversification of Kenricks' product structure grew out of the company's basic area of specialization, the production of light castings for domestic and building uses, and it is interesting to note that that part of diversification which was due, virtually by accident, to earlier acquisition (particularly of Anglo through Baldwins) did not proceed very far, even though the changing composition of consumer demand for hollow-ware favoured the growth of stamped-steel hollow-ware. There was little serious attempt to achieve growth from this technological base which differed from that with which the Kenricks had traditionally been associated, and investment was channelled into the process rather than into the line of product on which the company's reputation had initially been established. Thus rather than choosing to expand in the same market with new products based on different technology, the bias of hardware manufacturers tended to favour diversification within the same area of specialization, making more products based on the same technology and sold either in the firm's existing markets or in new ones.

In pursuing the latter policy, specifically by supplying a variety of engineering (including electrical) castings, Cannon, Clarks, Holcrofts, Siddons, and Izons were notably successful in terms of survival as profit-making firms. After pursuing a policy of producing more items based on the same basic technology and sold in the firm's existing markets—in particular builders' ironmongery—during the 1920s Kenricks belatedly adopted the mode of diversification favoured by some other medium-sized firms making cast-iron hollow-ware. As a result, for several years the company's over-all success depended on its performance in the bath trade, and to a lesser extent on ranges and flushing cisterns. Not surprisingly, the company achieved little success in this trade, characterized as it was by the sale of homogeneous products, which could be manufactured more cheaply by using technology suited to large-scale production, and where even the vestiges of Kenricks' goodwill built up in the nineteenth century were irrelevant. It is noticeable that, with the notable exception of Cannon, the cast-iron hollow-ware makers who turned to the industrial markets and shunned the production of finished consumer goods seem to have fared better in the long run than their erstwhile competitors. Ultimately, Kenricks' change in fortune occurred on the basis of expansion in old and new markets with a modified version of a traditional product (castors) based on a new technology (pressure die-casting in zinc). This course of development, and in particular Kenricks' failure to achieve greater success with stamped-steel or aluminium hollow-ware, may be explained partly by the factors alluded to by Penrose, partly by the unwillingness of the Kenricks to embark upon aggressive commercial policies to create markets, and partly, perhaps, by the customary convention that the Stourport companies' activities were subordinate to those of the parent company.

While it would be absurd to discuss Kenricks' managerial problems mainly in terms of organization theory, it is clear that no adjustment was made in the hierarchical-cum-functional system of organization throughout the company's history. Specialists, who included a works chemist, engineer, and subsequently accountant, were appointed, but such expert personnel appear to have had minimal influence on the Managing Directors to whom each was directly responsible. The new strategy of diversification since the late nineteenth century created fresh administrative needs, but no attention was paid to the classification of relationships between those making different kinds of decisions and at different levels. Indeed, custom and convention were important influences on the conduct of the company's affairs; the relationships between, and responsibilities of, those making different kinds of decisions were ill-defined and no distinction was made between strategic and tactical decisions. Furthermore, as we have noted elsewhere, and as the report of Peat Marwick made clear, the Kenricks paid scant attention to providing the information necessary for creating the basis for informed decisions by the Directors. The younger Kenricks remained completely in the dark as to their precise responsibilities and functions. Reflecting upon the inter-war years William E. Kenrick later declared: 'My father never made it clear what he wanted from me.' Neither was there any move to introduce professional managers into the firm before 1950. This tends to underline Professor Penrose's dictum that 'the managerial competence of a firm is to a large extent a function of the quality of the entrepreneurial services available to it'. Professor Chandler has already drawn attention to the resistance to change exhibited by family firms.[7] In such circumstances, even supposing they saw the need for change, the younger generation would typically be inhibited from pressing for changes contrary to the wishes of the older generation who, owing to their senior position in the family, necessarily reserved the ultimate authority in business affairs too. This fact underlines the peculiar character of the family firm, which offered to its owner-managers a way of life in addition to a source of income, twin 'returns' from their investment of time, effort, and money, which were inseparable—as the Kenricks' decisions of 1937 and 1952 showed. The firm was an institution to which the family felt obligations and from which it expected rewards; the family was likewise an organization the members of which acknowledged certain obligations in the sphere of religion, politics, and public service. That these sometimes conflicted with the requirements of business becomes evident in the history of Kenricks in the twentieth century. Generalizing about family firms, Professor Penrose refers to characteristics often to be found associated with them: contentment with a comfortable profit, the absence of a pecuniary maximizing approach to business, and an unwillingness to raise capital by means which would reduce the owner's control of the family firm.

This observation appears to have some bearing on the conduct of Kenricks's affairs since the turn of the century, during which period the firm clearly lacked 'enterprise' as she has defined it: 'a psychological predisposition on the part of individuals to take a chance in the hope of gain, and, in particular, to commit effort and resources to speculative activity.' Not until the company's profits were subject to heavy pressures did the systematic investigation of possible avenues for profitable expansion (a feature of 'enterprise') begin. From about the 1890s until 1939—and later—the firm lacked that 'general entrepreneurial bias in favour of growth' which Professor Penrose sees as a characteristic feature of enterprise. Furthermore, the priorities of the Managing Directors were such that they were unwilling to act upon expert recommendations that the company should acquire the entrepreneurial services of professionals at director level. This would have allowed the senior Kenricks, first Sir George, and subsequently Byng, to have delegated executive tasks, to have concentrated on determining strategic policy, and to have fulfilled their public obligations as outstanding Birmingham citizens—or it would have allowed Byng to turn away completely from business affairs with which, as he acknowledged privately, he had always felt out of tune.

Kenricks' history between 1926 and 1950 shows, dramatically, just how determined a family firm can be in resisting the most extreme pressures for change, either with respect to the recruitment of managerial talent or external finance, or in adopting modern methods. Prior to 1950 Kenricks' sole manager to enter from outside the family was, in fact, related by marriage. Finance for development was forthcoming when required, whether from the family or from the bank, with whom the family had long-standing connections. Even down to the 1950s it seems that the Kenricks' social position weighed the balance in favour when the bank was asked to extend credit. These factors provide additional support for the view advanced by Professor Landes that among other factors 'the availability of local resources within and without the enterprise go far to account for the persistence of traditional patterns of business organization and behaviour into the twentieth century'.[8] In their 1957 study Carter and Williams found large tracts of British industry where parochialism, frequently linked with family control, still prevailed—especially in those industries where the small and medium-sized firms continued to predominate.[9] The fortunes of such industries, and, indeed, in former times, a substantial part of the economy, depended to a considerable degree upon innumerable small-scale decisions and tiny but cumulative adjustment in technology which occurred in the local world of quite small family firms.[10]

The potential weaknesses inherent in family enterprise are not in doubt, but it is necessary to inquire as to the extent of family control over various business sectors at different times. Even when such an investigation has been carried out, however, it will not be possible to assess the actual significance of family enterprise—or lack of it—until we possess more studies of individual business. For the mere existence of family control—even of family management—does not mean that the conduct of business in any particular case was necessarily inefficient and unenterprising. While providing a textbook example of the weaknesses of the parochial family-type of organization for much of the first half of the twentieth century, the reversal in fortunes beginning at Kenricks in the early 1950s warns us against making sweeping generalizations.[11] A further point which deserves emphasis is that with regard to Kenricks' history neither of the two basic propositions underpinning the assumption of rationality in received economic theory—that firms seek to maximize profits, and that they operate with perfect knowledge—hold good. If this were true for a substantial part of the business sector, it would have serious implications for our interpretation of historical change, for unlike the theorist who concerns himself with notional time, the historian must place the time dimension at the centre of his analysis.

Clearly, in Kenricks' case certain alternative actions—those which would alter the character of the firm—were fundamental to any decisions that were taken. The existing structure and organization were taken as parameters rather than variables, and it is striking how economic security, in the sense of indefinite survival, though perhaps without complete control and management, was subordinated to the first parameter. For the Kenricks, survival meant complete independence. The profit goal appears to have been less important than independence or security—in prosperity or depression—and personal relationships meant that certain alternatives were ruled out on political grounds, even though from an efficiency standpoint certain policies might have been desired and desirable.

The difficulty of assessing the relative importance of the entrepreneurial factor in the business process has long been stressed by one historian after another, but while general disagreement on this matter prevails, all historians are nevertheless agreed that speculation can only give way to firmer conclusions after much more historical spadework has been carried out.[12] We do not suggest that in looking on this particular plot the empirical basis has been broadened substantially in this respect. Nevertheless, the results of a recent field-study survey of sixty-four firms conducted between 1969 and 1971[13] largely corroborated the findings of our case-study, which suggests that our detailed analysis of the economics of a small business, firmly embedded in a social, institutional, and family context, has produced a realistic paradigm relevant to any discussion of the dynamics of family enterprise, longevity of firms, and business failure.

NOTES

1 This essay is based upon Chapters 3, 4, and 6 of Roy Church, *Kenrick's in Hardware: A Family Business, 1791–1966* (David & Charles, Newton Abbot, 1969).
2 *Report of the Committee of Inquiry on Small Firms* (Ind. 4811, H.M.S.O., 1971).
3 Jonathan Boswell, *The Rise and Decline of Small Firms* (London, 1973), pp. 15–16.
4 P. Sargent Florence, *The Logic of British and American Industry* (London, 1953), p. 320; Richard E. Caves et al., *Britain's Economic Prospects* (London, 1968), pp. 304–5.
5 The exception was the acquisition, almost accidentally through the take over of Baldwins, of the Anglo-American Tin Stamping Company of Stourport, which produced hardware by the stamping process.
6 E. T. Penrose, *The Theory of the Growth of the Firm* (Oxford, 1960), p. 82.
7 Alfred D. Chandler, *Strategy and Structure: Chapters in the History of Industrial Enterprise* (Cambridge, Mass., 1962), pp. 320, 380.
8 David S. Landes, 'The Structure of Enterprise in the Nineteenth Century: the Case of Britain and Germany', *Extrait des rapports de XIᵉ Congrès International des Sciences Historiques* (Stockholm, 1966), v, 114.
9 C. F. Carter and B. R. Williams, *Industry and Technical Progress* (Oxford, 1957), pp. 24, 89.
10 In the Report of the Committee of Inquiry on Small Firms in 1971 the Bolton Committee revealed that even then owner-managed businesses, like Kenricks, employed approximately 6 m. (25 per cent) of the U.K. working population, and accounted for nearly 20 per cent of G.N.P. When agriculture, fisheries, etc. and all professional businesses were excluded the figures were 4·25 m. (18 per cent) and 14 per cent of G.N.P.
11 In 1977 Kenricks is still 'alive and kicking' under the fifth-generation Chairman Martin Kenrick.
12 See, e.g., T. C. Barker, 'The Significance of Small Firms: A Review Article,' *Business Archives*, N.S. ii, 2 (June 1972).
13 Boswell, op. cit.

7

Management and Policy in Large-scale enterprise: Lever Brothers and Unilever, 1918-1938[1]

CHARLES WILSON

(A) BUSINESS GROWTH AND BUSINESS MANAGERS

IT has become a commonplace amongst economic historians that significant changes in economic behaviour and institutions in the past have frequently been the product of economic crisis. In the business microcosm the same may be said to have been true of the 'managerial revolution', certainly in the oils and fats industries of Britain (and of the Continent too). In Lever Brothers, which by 1918 controlled the largest part of those industries in Britain, the separation of ownership and management dates from the first half of the 1920s—years when business was struck by a crisis of unprecedented magnitude and complexity.

Its severity was slackening by the time the creator of Lever Brothers, William Lever, First Viscount Leverhulme, died in May 1925. Yet the events of the crisis itself ensured that his mantle fell not upon his son (whom he himself had groomed for the succession) but upon a professional accountant, Francis D'Arcy Cooper. Cooper was to be the first of a series of professional executives under whose leadership Lever Brothers were to grow into an Anglo–Dutch concern of world stature.[2] In a sense, therefore, the future of one of the world's largest business concerns turned on the events of the early 1920s and upon the solution which was found to the problem of the succession to the leadership when its founder died. The essay that follows shows that the change in management of Lever Brothers—from owner-manager to professional, non-owner manager—was closely related to changes in *policy* and, more gradually, to changes in the *organization* of the business, initially in headquarters administration, later in the productive mechanism itself.

Until 1918 William Lever had steadily raised his business to a position of undisputed leadership in the soap trade. Starting—it was a characteristically audacious touch—in the middle of the 'Great Depression' of the 1880s, he had expanded his output at a spanking pace; he had created Port Sunlight as a model of enlightened, welfare capitalism; he had smashed to pieces the Soap Makers' Association, that comfortable trade club which had divided up the United Kingdom into a heptarchy of local monopolies, by launching his new type of free-lathering soap on the basis of a national market; and to do all this he had recruited every available device of advertising, salesmanship, and commercial technology which he deemed appropriate to business expansion. During the First World War he had invaded, with similar boldness, the margarine trade thus far the virtual monopoly of Dutch and Danish manufacturers. A few days before the Armistice of 1918 he had opened a vast new margarine plant at Bromborough on the Mersey. Equipped with seed-crushing, oil-refining, and fat-splitting plant, it had a production capacity of 2,000 tons of margarine a week. Consumption was running at about 240,000 tons per annum. Plainly, Lever was set to lead the edible side of the oils and fats industry as he already had the non-edible side.

But development in Britain was by no means the whole story. Even before the home market was saturated, Lever's boundless energies had sent him off round the world in search of new markets and new ideas. He had found them, in abundance, in the United States, where he had set up a soap business, an oil mill, and a factory. Other enterprises had been set up in Europe and the Dominions—France, Belgium, Germany, Denmark, Sweden, Holland, Switzerland, Canada, Australia, New Zealand were all familiar with Lever's products and advertisements. His adventures in Africa and the Solomons in search of raw materials for his factories will be touched on later. It is enough to say that even by 1914 Lever had created a world concern that was a perfect prototype of the 'multinational' that was to form the centre of controversy in the 1960s and 1970s. Lever too came in for his share of Labour and radical criticisms for his overseas adventures. He rejected them with contempt. Were English workmen robbed of work? 'There is not a word of truth in it,' he thundered to the shareholders in 1912. 'If we had not these works abroad we should not have this trade. . . . in 1895 we employed at Port Sunlight less than 1,500. In 1911 . . . we employed . . . in the United Kingdom . . . over 6,000 . . . so that this policy, instead of making less work in the United Kingdom, is making more.'

The immediate post-war economic climate could not have been more favourable to Lever. Prices were high and still rising, capital for acquisitions, mergers, and new investment in urgent demand. Popular optimism was unrestrained. Lever shared to the full in the prevailing euphoria. Was not butter short? Were not all his products, edible and non-edible, in apparently insatiable demand? Brushing aside the cautious pessimism of his advisers, he raised the limit of Lever Brothers' authorized capital from £40 m. to £100 m. by mid-1919. His immediate aim was to enlarge his share of the British soap trade once again—this time by acquiring his old rivals, Crosfields and Gossages in the north, John Knight's in the south. There was also room for more margarine plant to supply the west of England, Scotland, and Ireland. Overseas his plans had scarcely begun.

All these projects went forward. They gave him control of about 60 per cent of British soap output, raising doubts on the part of the Standing Committee on Trusts whose Chairman (Sir William Beveridge) called him to account for the level of his prices. He did so with all his customary vigour, breathing defiance and unrepentance. His prices (he declared) were fair; the manufacturer had to have regard to the price at which he had bought his stocks of raw materials, not the market price at the moment of the sale of his final product. He would be a fool (he declared) to aim at monopoly, because monopoly would, in a simple process of technology like soap making, bring its own nemesis as new competitors would rush to set up new industries. The Committee listened respectfully, if unconvinced.

Perhaps Lever was not strictly a 'monopolist': but he was near enough to it to live to see his prediction come true. The inquiry on prices had come at a critical moment: raw material prices had turned down, competition was on the march. The first cloud on the horizon came from the direction of the oil-milling industry. The combine within that industry, known as the British Oil and Cake Mills (B.O.C.M.), was the creation of J. W. Pearson, himself a Lever in miniature and a skilled tactician in commercial warfare. In 1921 he decided to enter the soap market. He did so with a flourish of advertising attractions and a product called New-Pin Soap. It did not last long because Lever was compelled to buy it out—on terms very favourable to Pearson. Levers acquired B.O.C.M. in return for the demise of New-Pin. But the affair was ominous: it heralded the rise of highly effective competition in soap from the Cooperative Wholesale Society and, later on, from Lever's great U.S. rival, Procter & Gamble, now poised to enter the British market. Since the largest part of Lever's profits still came from the British soap market, which carried a score of less profitable (and some apparently hopelessly unprofitable) ventures, the situation was not promising. That it turned into acute crisis was due to two developments which occurred virtually simultaneously in the first half of 1920.

(B) BUBBLES

The first was Lever's decision to purchase, in most extraordinary circumstances, the control of the Niger Company; the second was the collapse, between February and July of that year, of the prices of all raw materials used by the soap and margarine industries, especially those tropical products handled by the Niger Company itself. Palm-kernel oil fell from £115 a ton to £55; palm oil from £98 to £53. Lever's at this time were themselves holding raw-material stocks which had cost them £18 m.: they did not yet know that the Niger Company was also not only holding large stocks but actually buying more in speculative hopes that the market would rise. The details of the Niger Company purchase by Lever are recorded elsewhere.

Three points only need be mentioned here. First, on 21 January 1920 the Lever directors agreed to buy the Niger ordinary share capital for a sum of rather more than £8 m. Second, and remarkable even in that phase of feverish optimism, no investigation of the Niger accounts took place. Third, the management of the Niger Company was to remain in the hands of the Niger Company for another five months.

Lever sent an approving telegram to the Director in charge of the purchase: 'Congratulations. Price high but suicidal if we had let opportunity lapse.' Such was the general euphoria that the manager of Lloyds Bank joined in the rejoicings, offering 'every consideration' to Lever in the necessary arrangements.

By the spring the outlook had changed, and much for the worse. Starting with the collapse of a silk speculation in Japan, the storm moved westwards to Europe. One bubble after another burst. Consumption, government spending, bank credit were slashed one after the other. Prices fell rapidly until about a year later, when a floor some 50 per cent above pre-war levels was reached. Meanwhile, a number of other unwelcome chickens had come home to roost. The Niger Company, it transpired, was due to pay off an overdraft to the banks of another £2 m. in July.

The acquisitive mania had landed Lever in other doubtful purchases. There was the Philippine Refining Corporation, an oil-refining business built up by Carl W. Hamilton, an American described by Lever as a man of 'nerve and agility . . . a man of resource'. There was a large investment in Thames Board Mills, bought 'to secure our supplies' of paper; the Sanitas Disinfectant Company; the Trufood Company, a Welsh limestone quarry; Lever himself bought the greater part of the islands of Lewis and Harris in the Outer Hebrides; to handle their produce he also bought a chain of retail fish shops— the Mac Fisheries—which in turn owned their own trawling companies and the Helford River Oysterage, to say nothing of Walls' Sausages, bought to provide the product which was the other half of a fishmonger's trade. To the same end he took a share in the business of Angus Watson of Newcastle (a former employee of Lever Brothers) whose Skipper sardines had become almost as much a household word as Sunlight soap. Not content with all this, Lever toyed with other proposals—to buy a palm-oil plantation in Sumatra, a sawmill in Plymouth, a colliery in the north of England, a toilet preparations factory which owned a well in the deserts of Algeria (said to yield water of particularly valuable quality but condemned by a later investigator as 'an incubus to the Company'). Most dangerous of all, Lever did not hesitate to enter into serious negotiations to buy the Niger Company's greatest rival in the West Africa trade, the African and Eastern Trade Corporation; only the appalling state of affairs revealed by the scrutiny of the Niger Company accounts saved him from consummating the purchase.

In spite of the pressure on his cash resources created by these purchases and by the fall in sales—margarine sales especially slumped to less than a half by weight and a quarter in value compared with 1919—Lever managed to pay in this *annus mirabilis* of 1920 all his preference dividends. This represented a colossal burden of over £3 m., a figure that resulted from Lever's insistence on retaining the ownership of every ordinary share in his own hands. He also managed to pay himself, as sole ordinary shareholder, a dividend of 20 per cent. His address to the shareholders continued to express utmost confidence in the future, utmost defiance of the forces of gloom and stagnation.

Yet in reality the great days were over. The old magic had gone and the magician could no longer wave his wand to command City opinion at will. The *Investors' Chronicle* struck the new note, at once sour and sceptical. 'Read in cold print [it wrote of his speech] we confess that his remarks leave us with a feeling of emptiness.'

It was not alone in this view. The bankers who were invited to help him discharge the Niger Company's debts in August were polite but chilly. The first to be consulted replied: 'May I say that I do not think anybody feels that your great Company is not perfectly good, but that you have gone ahead too quickly in view of a difficult financial situation. The truth is that there is not enough money to go round and it has to be strictly rationed, as, say, sugar or any other commodity.' Others, less metaphorically disposed, did not beat about the bush: they bluntly declared that the only way to restore Lever Brothers to health was for them to get rid of the Niger Company. By the end of the year (1920) the cash situation was acute. The bankers no longer made it any secret that they were thoroughly alarmed by what seemed to them Lever's reckless improvidence. He himself was now aware of the fact. It is also likely that it was the banks who suggested the nature of the rescue operation which Lever (from the U.S.A.) proposed to his Directors in a cable: 'Suggest you call in D'Arcy Cooper for assistance if he can help.'

Before considering the consequences of that cable, we need to consider, in greater depth, the nature of the crisis of 1920 which occasioned it. Why had Lever, tough and experienced business man that he was, chosen to plunge so deeply into West Africa and its trade? For it was the magnitude of the Niger catastrophe that lay at the heart of the Lever Brothers' crisis. To understand this it is necessary to examine the structure of the soap industry and to a lesser extent that of the margarine industry.

Even before Lever's appearance on the scene with his 'new soap' in the 1880s, it was a truism of the soap trade that its profitability depended primarily on the relation which raw material costs bore to the market price for soap. Raw material supplies had occupied much of the time and attention of the Soap Makers' Association in the 1880s and 1890s. The very *raison d'être* of the Association came increasingly to turn on price agreements because, in their absence, raw material fluctuations produced alarming instability of soap prices. The justification for price-fixing was apparent—at least to the members of the Association. 'Now [declared the Chairman of the Association at the Annual Meeting of 1905] whether the market letter [for tallow] moves up or down, the price of soap pursues the even tenor of its way.'

But the violence of the raw-material fluctuations of 1906 was such that they could not be contained by the normal manipulations of the Association. New technology had created new uses for oils and fats. Tallow, coconut oil, cottonseed oil were now in demand not only by soap makers but by manufacturers of margarine and other forms of edible fat. Hence the epic attempt by Lever to create the famous 'Soap Trust' which brought upon him the attack by the *Daily Mail*. His triumph in the great libel case which followed was nevertheless a setback to his schemes for the soap trade, which was left in disarray. This did not prevent him from edging forward on other fronts. The new strategy consisted, first and foremost, of forays into the raw material production and trade itself.

From the 1906 crisis onwards Lever retained a neurosis about raw material supplies. He was probably correct in asserting that the raw material market was in permanent danger of being cornered by speculative 'rings'. The fear of being squeezed on prices by merchants and brokers became almost an obsession and remained with him in some degree for the rest of his life. This, and the fact that raw material prices were still high in the second decade of the century, took him to the Solomon Islands and to West Africa in search of supplies of tropical oil-bearing seeds produced under his own control. Since the British Government took too strict a view of its duty to native land to suit his taste, Africa, so far as plantations were concerned, meant the Belgian Congo. Firmly rejecting the views of those of his colleagues who thought his theories misguided, Lever built up a massive investment in raw materials with the object of increasing output. For, even in face of much scepticism, his conviction never slackened that such increase lay within his power. 'It is all a question of whether the supply should be ten per cent below the requirement or five per cent above . . . if below, prices will rule high. If . . . above, prices will rule reasonably and in our favour.'

It was as simple as that; and on that basis (and in spite of a frequent absence of evidence that his theories really worked and a total absence of profit on, for example, the Congo venture) his tropical enterprises grew and multiplied. By the time the Niger purchase occurred, Lever had acquired no less than seven West African trading companies (in addition to his plantation companies) mostly looked after by a headquarters in the Royal Liver Building at Liverpool. Forays into French Equatorial Africa continued.

The complexities of the raw material business need not detain us.[3] It is enough to remark that Lever's revolution of the soap trade rested on marketing a type of soap which required an unprecedented proportion of lauric oils, derived from coconut and palm-kernel oil coming mainly from West Africa.

The advent of the margarine makers (including Lever himself) enormously increased the demand for African oil-bearing seeds, especially because the discovery of fat-hardening processes (hydrogenation) round about 1910–11 vastly increased the utility of such oils to manufacturers of both soap and margarine.[4]

Such was the background to the Niger purchase. The driving forces behind Lever's acquisitive mania of the immediate post-war years—in so far as they had a rational basis—were: first, the intensification of competition in the soap trade in conditions of deepening depression; second, the increasing dependence of Lever on soap profits at a time when these were becoming more difficult to make; third, Lever's continuing conviction that the safest (and perhaps the only) way to control the price of raw materials, crucial as ever to his manufacturing profits, was to control their *source*. The notion of Lever Brothers as a 'vertical combine', often contested by his colleagues, and sometimes modified and infringed in practice with his approval, nevertheless remained basic to Lever's thought and policy.[5]

The presence of a rational argument for the raw material investments, controversial though it was, may help to explain the zeal with which the Niger purchase was pursued and concluded. It could neither explain nor excuse the feckless haste and nonchalance of the transaction itself, which contradicted all those principles of meticulous accuracy and responsibility which Lever had so often in earlier days demanded from his colleagues and subordinates. Baffled and discomfited, he turned on his supposed advisers with demands that they should answer why things were as they were. Of the purchase of Jacksons, an engineering firm, he wrote: 'I have never myself understood why this business was purchased. I have never seen that it could possibly be of any interest to Lever Brothers'. Of the Director who had carried on the Niger negotiations he demanded angrily: 'What I should like you to do is to write myself . . .what answer I must make . . . when I am challenged by shareholders (and I am almost certain to be) as to why Lever Brothers did not give instructions to the Company's Auditors . . . to make a full investigation of the Niger Company's books before completing the deal.' To which his colleagues might have replied (if they had been able to muster up the nerve) that they had never been encouraged to contradict what they knew to be the Chairman's wishes.[6] The chain of command had simply broken down.

To meet the crisis, Lever flung into the battle all his business acumen and intellectual and nervous energy. It was impressive, yet nothing could alter the frightening facts as others saw them. This great conglomeration of assorted enterprises, in scope and dimensions what would be described today without cavil as a world multinational concern, was as much a personal autocracy in organization and ethos as it had been thirty years earlier, when it had been a small soap company at Port Sunlight beginning its long battle for the English soap market. Then Lever had been a man of 40 at the height of his powers.

Now he was 70, and his enterprises and markets were scattered over vast areas of Europe, North America, West Africa, and the Pacific. Significantly, when the crisis broke, he was in North America. (He was still to make a number of journeys abroad including an exhausting tour of the African enterprises in 1924 when he was 73.) His achievements had been extraordinary: even now he could still labour with black energy to reform, to economize, and to innovate, driven (as he himself wrote in a cool, analytical letter in 1923) by 'fear', not for himself but for the business he had created. Yet none of this could hide the truth. The crisis had severely tried the business and its creator: both had been found wanting. The most important single fact in the Lever history was that at this point it proved possible to find a successor capable of rescuing, reforming, and re-creating the Lever empire; most remarkable of all, of doing it in collaboration with Lever himself. The old man's fundamental magnanimity and wisdom were never seen in a better light.

(C) RESCUE AND REFORM: THE ROLE OF D'ARCY COOPER

When he told his Directors (in the cable quoted earlier) to consult D'Arcy Cooper, he could not know, of course, what the future had in store. On the face of it, the scope for their co-operation seemed very limited—limited, in fact, to Cooper's ability to find enough cash to help Lever out of his predicament over the Niger acquisition. The personalities of the two men could hardly have been more different. Where Lever was (superficially at least) extrovert, ebullient, optimistic, autocratic, Cooper was a somewhat shy man, reserved, unaffected. He was (in 1920) little more than half Lever's age, and he was an accountant—a partner in Cooper Brothers who had for many years been Lever's auditors: a member of a tribe, in fact, for whom (as for the whole tribe of bankers) Lever had all the dislike of the Victorian radical which at heart he remained. Hardly a promising augury for the future. Yet from early in 1921 Francis D'Arcy Cooper was regularly consulted on all major matters of policy as if he were already a Director (though he did not join the Board officially until 1923). It was about that time that Lever remarked to Angus Watson that Cooper was 'one of the type of men that I consider most resemble a warm fire and people naturally seem to come up to him for warmth.'

The tribute is all the more remarkable when one recalls that Cooper had done two things which Lever might have been expected to resent (and at first almost certainly did resent). First, he had intervened in the management of Lever's company, a prerogative which Lever had jealously guarded as his most precious possession for a quarter of a century by allowing no one else any share whatever in the equity of his company. Second, in order to provide collateral security for the loan which he obtained from Barclays Bank, Cooper had been compelled to agree to the bankers' insistence that Lever's should issue equivalent value in the form of £8 m. of debentures. The management of the Niger Company, whose policies and motives were both open to suspicion, was also to be reformed and strengthened. Thus Lever might have felt himself and his policies pilloried; his company in fee to creditors who (unlike mere shareholders) could sue at law if Lever failed in discharging his obligations. That Lever could be brought to swallow these indispensable but still unpalatable medicines was due to Cooper's personality and to the unlikely mutual sympathy which developed between the two men. Lever proved, even at the age of 70, sufficiently adaptable and generous to recognize Cooper's total integrity, and shrewd enough to respect the habit of command that lay behind his unaffectedly modest manner. Cooper in his turn was wise enough to respect the genius of the man who had created this great, though temporarily ailing, business and allow full scope to his expertise and energies. He also enjoyed excellent relations with Lever's son and heir, Hulme Lever, who was doing valuable work in the company.

On this basis, the reorganization began and the old autocracy was slowly put into commission by a series of reforms which were undoubtedly Cooper's work. A so-called 'Policy Council' had existed for many years but its excessive size and mediocre membership had ensured its impotence. It was now replaced by an 'Inner Cabinet'—a Special Committee consisting of Lever, his son, and two Directors. They took power 'to co-opt any professional gentleman not being a Director of the Company to assist and advise them'—a formula which spelt Cooper as clearly as the letters of his name.

Below the Special Committee which was responsible for high policy were other, more specialized, committees—one to supervise the operations of the manufacturing companies, another for Lever's West African interests, another specifically to co-ordinate matters of capital and finance and handle the delicate and continuing relationship with the banks. A special Committee of Enquiry left for Nigeria in the summer of 1921 to look into affairs in that area. It did not take long to find out that the prevailing chaos resulted largely from the almost total absence of effective communications between Liverpool, London, and West Africa, where the agents did much as they liked, clerks inserted imaginary figures to balance their books, and nothing in the way of a coherent pricing system existed. It was to be a long time before the raw material businesses were restored to health. The Congo enterprises, heavily loaded by the Congo Government with charges for providing transport, housing, hospitals, schools, etc., paid no dividends until 1926.

The export trade, where Lever's held a very large share of the market, was nevertheless judged also to be in need of attention, largely because of the ancient but still virulent rivalries between the three companies which conducted it—Levers, Crosfields, and Gossages. The instructions given to the new single head in charge of exports included a command 'to obviate any undue competition between companies, to facilitate the working of the Export business and increase the Export trade'. This was the first intimation that Lever's own traditional policy of encouraging his operating subsidiaries to 'compete' to the utmost was to be modified.

Another group much in need of attention was the overseas manufacturing and trading companies in Europe and the Commonwealth (not, as we shall see, the U.S.A.). The Foreign Associated Companies Control Board was given a modest brief only: to provide opportunities for 'periodical discussion of the affairs of the various Overseas Companies'. Behind this diplomatic vagueness lay the knowledge that these 'children' of Port Sunlight (as Lever had once described them) were not growing more amenable with age. His promise that they were there to serve the public of the countries in which they operated was taken seriously and slowly being redeemed by the appointment of local managers. But nationalism remained a powerful force. Cooper moved gingerly.

Not so Lever himself. The domestic soap market remained his home ground. No one knew it better than he, and its centre, Port Sunlight, was his personal creation. The existence of the whole Lever business now depended upon the profits made by soap, and the level of soap profits in turn upon costs. Hence the axe of economy was wielded by Lever and by no one else. There were (he wrote) 'too many inefficient men, too many highly paid men, too many elderly men, and men past their work'. The measures Lever took were draconic but not indiscriminate: mostly they took the form of pensioning the elderly and giving the younger three months' notice. By 1925 the work-force at Port Sunlight had fallen from 8,000 to 5,000: in 1927 production at the 1921 level was achieved with 4,000 less workers. The number of man-hours needed to produce a ton of soap fell from 115 to 61. More efficient technology combined with the fall in raw material prices to reduce costs per ton from £10 to £3·2 by 1923. Yet soap prices were also falling and unit profits with them. In the midst of the struggle for corporate survival Lever died, in May 1925, soon after his return from the Congo. Within a week Cooper was appointed to succeed him. It was providential that no one had a higher regard for Cooper's capacities than Lever's son and heir who might well have expected to succeed his father. It was not least due to his good sense that a dispute over inheritance was avoided and the fortunes of the company placed firmly in the hands of a man whose sole claim to authority rested on professional ability.

The change was to condition the entire future of the company. It signified nothing less than the complete metamorphosis of Lever Brothers from a private empire owned and controlled by one man into a public company administered by a professional management. It might be argued that this change had started four years earlier. Cooper's immediate task, nevertheless, was to complete the restoration and reorganization of central control which he had already brought a long way.

One of his first steps was easier for him to take than it would have been for his predecessor. With his eye on the size of the bill for preference and debenture dividends. Cooper decided that there was to be no Ordinary dividend for 1925 or 1926. He also sold off every bit of surplus company property he could identify, from Plymouth to New York, from Tokyo to Toronto. And to such measures of first aid he added a continuing reform of the mechanism of central control designed to concentrate the energies of managers on productive and selling efficiency. One *ad hoc* committee urgently investigated research programmes 'directed to commercially profitable results.' Another looked into levels of advertisting expenditure—especially by the soap firms. Not surprisingly, they recommended reductions and a stiff degree of central vigilance over advertising costs for the future.

Once again, the new administration was questioning the traditional policy of 'internal competition between companies' by which Lever had salved his *laissez-faire* conscience—but at high cost. A new Sales Executive Committee had as its object to manage soap sales policy so that the producer companies 'could concentrate as little as possible on fighting each other and as much as possible on fighting outsiders'. The same treatment was applied to the export trade. Thus the fundamental structure of the whole concern was gradually simplified, to some extent centralized, and—but to a small extent only—production rationalized. At management level, measures were added to men; men were chosen from a wider catchment area; internal competition was reduced; the idea of 'vertical' relations between firms within the concern, slowly gave way to the doctrine that each firm should stand on its own feet justifying itself by its competitive efficiency and profitability in the market place.

By 1929 Levers' profits (over £5½ m.) showed that the new regime and its measures were having results. No geographical area recorded a loss. The salient features of the accounts were three: first, although the United Kingdom soap trade accounted, as ever, for the largest volume of turnover and profits, over £250,000 came from Mac Fisheries, which the company had rescued from the wreckage of Lever's personal enterprise in the Hebrides,[7] along with Walls' Sausages and Angus Watson's canneries: 'diversification under distress' it might be called, but diversification none the less, and a foreshadowing of future development policy.

Second, only one firm made a large loss—the unhappy position of Planters margarine reflected the current overcrowding in that market and especially the pressure of Dutch competition from the newly forged alliance of Jurgens, Van den Berghs, and others known as the Margarine Unie. They were already engaged in discussions with Cooper about the future. Finally, the largest single profit-spinner outside Britain was Lever Brothers, Boston, U.S.A. (£620,000). Throughout the long crisis since 1920 this American company, under the brilliant direction of Francis Countway, a business genius comparable with Lever himself, had been the one bright star in the Lever constellation. Between 1920 and 1925 Countway had increased his sales from $12·5 m.

to $19 m. and his profits from $763,000 to $1·6 m. From 1925 to 1929 the volume of his soap sales rose from 40,000 to 91,000 tons; his profits to over $3 m.

Countway was also responsible for major changes in his products. He had made Lux soapflakes a household word in the United States and they in turn reflected the rising standards of life in a society which was now using even more delicate fabrics on a national scale. Henceforth Boston was to become a model for the rest of the Lever organization.

(D) UNILEVER AND THE ERA OF RATIONALIZATION

The merger with the Dutch Margarine Unie was accomplished by an agreement signed on 2 September 1929. The negotiations were not the result of the world depression, which only became apparent as the agreement was being implemented. The alarming events of the autumn doubtless comforted the two sides that they had been wise to arrange their merger. But the problems facing the negotiators would have been even greater than they were if the policy of both British and Dutch concerns had not been influenced to a growing extent by professional managers whose activities were entirely separated from share ownership. They were correspondingly less influenced by the personal and family feuds which had for decades divided the older generations of owner-managers of the major firms involved.[8]

In the long run, changes in managerial objectives involved changes in managerial style and background. Yet even though the new men appreciated, for example, the advantages of a university education, management still had a long way to go before it made radical changes in traditional moulds. Thus the members of the management team of the new Unilever concern of 1929 were not as yet drawn to any large extent from the ranks of University graduates. A few were—for example, Ernest Walls, an Oxford graduate (who was a Chairman of a number of Cooper's new headquarters committees between 1922 and 1929); Herbert Davis (a Cambridge economics graduate who came in with Jurgens in 1929), Luke Fildes (a Cambridge graduate and barrister who became Secretary of Lever Brothers soon after the end of the First World War). But neither Cooper nor his first and most trusted junior, Geoffrey Heyworth, was a graduate of anything but what William Lever once called 'the University of Hard Knocks'. Many others were similarly men of (mostly) middle-class origins who would in an earlier generation probably have gone into the army, the Church, or the law. There was still a large number of north-countrymen, friends or acquaintances of the Lever family or simply local boys who had found a job with Levers or Crosfields or Gossages or one of the other Lever subsidiaries. The move to London (in 1921) had loosened the grip of the north on Lever's, widening the area for their recruitment while depriving them of some of their northern flavour. The management was therefore a varied group, certainly not yet dominated by graduate talent. Nevertheless, it was

significant that Cooper himself felt the need for university connections strongly enough to join the Cambridge University Appointments Board as early as
1929: Geoffrey Heyworth later followed in his wake. The nature of managerial
training and objectives certainly changed significantly in these crucial years.

For the new, as for the old management, the economic foundations of the
concern remained largely unchanged. The British soap trade was more than
ever its basis, for it now carried not only itself, as it were, but also the dubious
fortunes of the raw material enterprises. Its condition was therefore crucial:
but so far little radical attention had been devoted to it. The reason was not
far to seek. Lever's strong belief in 'internal competition' had its counterpart
in an equally strong disbelief in any form of 'rationalization' as a means of
dealing with overproduction or excessive costs. When his South African
Chairman, Schlesinger, had proposed to close down works in his territory,
Lever flatly refused to listen: such policies, he declared, 'always led to the loss
of trade'.

When Cooper joined Levers, this was the prevailing doctrine; and coming
from Lever himself it commanded Cooper's respect. He might improve on
Lever's ideas on finance and administrative organization: he would defer to
him in strictly commercial and industrial matters in which he was still a tiro.
Even after he became Chairman he made haste slowly. The New-Pin factory
could be allowed to die: it was only, after all, as new as its name and merely a
pawn in a tactical business game now concluded. Five very small factories in
the south of England came under the hammer. That was all—for the moment
at least. Cooper saw his first task as the reform of the high command; operations in the field would have to wait a little longer. He nevertheless recognized
that the soap factories were badly in need of reorganization. They produced
too many brands which cost unnecessarily large sums to produce and sell:
the ideal policy (he admitted) would be 'to concentrate our energies on about
five soaps and four powders.' Some of his colleagues pressed him to achieve
this by rationalization: 'If [they urged] . . . the manufacture of all articles were
pooled and carried on at three or four centres, as was the case in the Tobacco
Industry, savings of £2 a ton would be made on distribution costs alone.'
Cooper still hesitated. 'The great objection to the wholesale closing down of
smaller factories was the fear that the goodwill of the products of associated
companies would be lost.' The argument gained force from certain obstinate
facts of the soap trade: only one firm—Lever's own at Port Sunlight—possessed an indisputably national market for its products. Four others—Crosfields, Watsons, Gossages (in the north), and John Knights (in the south)—
had strong regional markets and a foothold in the national market. Christo-
pher Thomas, of Bristol, held the west of England. Otherwise goodwill was a
local matter. The regional patterns of the Victorian soap market were still
plainly visible.

That views changed was due to three factors. First, Cooper, like many other knowledgeable men in the soap trade in Britain and Europe, came to be convinced by 1929 that the soap trade had reached (as he put it) 'a fixed state'. For this there was weighty evidence: consumption statistics changed little between 1924 and 1930. Total production actually fell (from 469,000 to 453,000 tons). Within this stagnant market, however, one encouraging fact emerged: while the older 'hard soaps' were in decline, the newer flakes and powders (like Lux and Rinso) were on the increase (11 per cent between 1924 and 1930). This suggested that the industry was undergoing changes which could no longer simply be ignored. Third, the contact with the Dutch margarine industry after 1929 brought new and more positive attitudes to rationalization, which in turn supported the views of those who had for several years pointed to North American experience as favouring rationalization of production in Britain also.

Among these was Geoffrey Heyworth, a young executive who had gained wide experience of the North American market from his service in the Lever business in Canada, where the influence of Countway (and his vigorous rivals Procter & Gamble) was strong. In 1929 Heyworth became a member of the three-man Home Soap Executive. In 1931 he read a remarkable paper to a conference of managers on the urgent need to rationalize the Lever soap industry in the United Kingdom. In it he pointed out that there were in Unilever in Britain no less then forty-nine manufacturing companies and forty-eight separate sales organizations. Armies of salesmen fought endless battles with each other to sell (mainly) household soap. The whole system cried out to be simplified, modernized. But how? By finding out (as Lever would himself have done) what the housewife wanted and ensuring that she got it by means of a system of production and distribution which gave her reasonable choice at reduced cost. Heyworth identified seven principal 'fields of use' for soap: they were served by household soap, carbolic soap, powders, flakes, scourers, dish washers, and toilet soaps.

His plan involved concentrating sales in the five largest firms while gradually reducing the number of smaller ones. Brands were to be examined, assessed, retained, or phased out. It was to take the next twenty years to implement the plan in full but Cooper, now convinced that at last he had a master plan and an organizer capable of realizing it, accepted at once. The first results were remarkable. In a single year (1932) in the west of England the sales force was cut from 220 to 154, the number of packs from 852 to 294, both without any loss of total sales in the area. Rationalization of production followed. Gossages of Widnes, Hudson's at Bank Hall and West Bromwich, three London factories, Mill Bay at Plymouth, J. L. Thomas at Exeter—all went, with large savings as their production was moved respectively to Port Sunlight, Crosfields of Warrington, and John Knights.

By the time these schemes matured, the views of the experts on the 'fixed state' of the soap market were being proved wanting. Economic depression might persist, but as living costs dropped, the value of the real wages of the employed population in Britain rose. So did soap consumption: from 16·53 lb *per capita* in 1930 to 19·79 in 1938. Yet the average price per lb fell along with other prices. Moreover, the types of soap made, sold, and used changed, along lines similar to those experienced in the U.S. in the 1920s. Flakes and powders of detergent power higher than that of the old hard soap, and much easier to use, were 18 per cent of total sales in the United Kingdom in 1924: by 1938 the proportion had nearly doubled. In terms of tonnage the increase was from 85,000 to 176,000. (Total production, after falling between 1924 and 1930, then rose gently to reach 524,000 by 1937.)

The details of the Heyworth plan need not detain us.[9] But it is not too much to say that if Cooper's medicine of the 1920s saved the company from extinction, Heyworth's heart surgery of the 1930s gave it a new lease of more vigorous life. Even more than Cooper, Heyworth spanned the worlds of owner-management and professional management.

He and his two brothers had come into Lever's through a family connection. All three reached the Board strictly on merit. Like Cooper, Heyworth was an accountant who had stayed in Canada with the Lever business there after being demobilized from service with the Canadian Army. On his return to Port Sunlight he had come to see what was wrong (as well as what was right) with the company as Lever ran it. At Crosfields (whose Chairman he became) he learned the importance of science and technology to the oils and fats industry, for Crosfields were leaders in research and development. From Cooper he learned that genius at the summit was not enough. The structure of this vast business had to be reorganized so that its problems could be identified and defined, plans for meeting them contrived, understood, and communicated to the whole body of managers. To make this possible, human relations within the business and with the world outside must be improved. A continuing flow into the business of a carefully selected body of potential managers and specialists from universities and other institutions of higher education and training was necessary to ensure the future through a continuity of principles and policies.

Inevitably, Heyworth was to be Cooper's successor as Chairman. Under him the second phase of managerial revolution achieved the first major rationalization of production and distribution and a third phase—of technological revolution and diversification—was initiated. The 1920s and 1930s thus saw a fundamental reconstruction of Lever Brothers' organization which covered every aspect of the business from the manufacture and selling of its products to the control of high policy-making, finance, and top managerial appointments. Its success was to be based on more systematic policies, especially on prices and raw-material buying, on organizational flexibility deriving in turn from empirical use of managerial experience, and on a chain of communications which encouraged the devolution of authority and the development of confidence in the middle ranges of management. A degree of central authority would remain, essential as ever: its scope would be adjusted to circumstances.

The development of systems of management less dependent on individual authority unquestionably owed much to the changing context in which business operated—the growing complexity of technology, of market organization, of the volume of capital recruited and employed. Nothing in the business's history between the 1920s and the 1970s suggests that these revised forms of management were to be in any way infallible: on the contrary, like personal management, they can easily be shown to be compatible with torpor, stagnation, egregious error, and total failure. Sometimes they have even owed their rescue to that individual genius which they are commonly supposed to have replaced and improved upon. Yet in general it must be accepted that while individual enterprise continued to play a role in business growth (especially where new invention or innovation is a dominant factor of an industrial process), systematized, collectivized, professionalized management was made increasingly necessary by business circumstances from the 1920s onwards.

Unilever was a case-history, early in Europe but swiftly to be followed by others. Here, the retrieval of the near catastrophe of the early 1920s led to a reformation of the whole mode and system of management, at once continuous and irreversible.

NOTES

1 The sources used in this chapter are to a major extent those on which the author's *History of Unilever* (2 vols., Cassell, London, 1954) was based. Additional evidence and occasional variations in interpretation are marked by footnotes. The author gratefully acknowledges the generosity of Unilever Ltd. in granting him full use of the *History* of which it owns the copyright and in checking a number of factual points. Also the kindness of the Third Viscount Leverhulme in supplying information relating to his father's and grandfather's roles in the events of the 1920s.

2 Total capital employed by Lever Brothers Ltd. rose from less than £2 m. in the early 1890s to just over £12 m. in 1914, £47·3 m. in 1920, and some £65 m. in 1929. The Lever Group's share of total soap consumption in the U.K. and Eire rose from about 17 per cent in 1900 to 42 per cent in 1918 and 51 per cent in 1938.

3 They are fully described and analysed by Frederick Pedler in *The Lion and the Unicorn in Africa: the United Africa Company, 1787–1931* (London, 1974). The author was himself a Director of the U.A.C. and an expert on the economics of the African trade. See esp. Chs. 9–20.

4 See *History of Unilever*, vol. i for the complex diplomacy surrounding the development of the various competing patents, in which Lever and the margarine makers played a leading role.

5 This is a modification of the view I expressed in the *History of Unilever*, i, 186. The suggestion that the years of the First World War saw the effective demise of the idea is, I have come to believe, premature. It was not abandoned until after Lever's death and continued to play a larger role in his ideas and actions, especially over the Niger affair, than I at one time supposed. (The phrases 'vertical combine', 'vertical integration', 'backward integration', etc. are of course jargon of a later day.)

6 There was a significant legend that upon appointment, each Director was required to sign, along with his contract of service, his undated resignation too, just in case the Chairman should at any time find it necessary.

7 His philanthropic plans to improve the lot of the islanders having been defeated by the crofteis and the Board of Agriculture in combination, Lever had departed for ever with a remarkable address to the islanders which ended thus: 'I am like Othello, with my occupation gone, and I could only be like the ghost of Hamlet's father, haunting the place as a shadow.'

8 See *History of Unilever*, esp. vol. ii *passim*.

9 They are set out in vol. ii of *History of Unilever*, esp. pp. 345–7, and in Ch. III ('The Soap Industry', by Ruth Cohen) of P. Lesley Cook and Ruth Cohen, *Effects of Mergers* (Cambridge, 1958).

8

Manufacturers and Retailing in the Food Trades: The Struggle over Margarine[1]

PETER MATHIAS

(A) THE RIVALS EMERGE

THE fortunes of the individual firms which subsequently came together as Allied Suppliers began to converge through their developing relations with margarine manufacturers early in the twentieth century. The crux of the matter was that they got caught up in a progressively more intense struggle for dominance in the British margarine market being waged by Jurgens and Van den Berghs, two rival Dutch dynastics, against the Maypole Dairy Company, once it became involved in the industry itself, and against William Lever.

From the beginning of the margarine industry as a mass production and mass consumption business in Europe the British market, and particularly the multiple shop companies in that market, was of prime interest to manufacturers. It was the most rapidly expanding food market, in point of numbers and income, that existed. The free-trade system made it very much the largest available market to be exploited by imports. There was, in any case, virtually no native 'butter interest' to protect, and as yet no major British manufacturers in their own national market. On the side of demand, the labouring masses in the new urban industrial society showed no qualms, such as were usual elsewhere in the late nineteenth century, about eating margarine on bread. Bread, jam, and margarine became a new staple of diet.

Special problems existed, however, if this potentially important market was to be efficiently managed, most of them springing from the fact that margarine was perishable. Speed in getting the product from factories to shops, rapid turnover in the shops, efficient stock control were therefore prerequisites for effective trade, quite apart from the other requirements of efficient merchanting. Without this, deterioration gave the product a bad reputation, cut sales, and increased losses on returned or abandoned stock. A national wholesaling and distributing organization, involving a shop inspectorate also, was a costly and complicated organization for a manufacturing firm to sustain in order to gain the custom of a large number of small, independent shopkeepers, some of meagre turnover and uncertain credit.

Contracts with multiple shop companies had great attractions in these circumstances. Their turnovers were much greater per shop, in general, than the independent grocers. They were mainly specialist traders handling only a few lines, with their whole organization geared to keeping down their overheads by rapid deployment of stocks. Quality in standard products, no less than minimum prices, had been the foundation for their success. An efficient system of shop-inspectors, keeping branch managers up to the mark, already existed. In addition, the basis of their trade lay firmly in the working-class market, without those pretensions to gentility which would prejudice margarine custom. The multiples were thus technically and commercially—even socially—strategically placed for success in the margarine trade. The sheer profitability in terms of turnover offered to the manufacturer by the scale of contracts offered by the largest shop companies enhanced their attractiveness still more. Running factories as close as possible to capacity, being able to predict throughputs and organize raw material markets (in equally perishable commodities at this stage) upon definite assumptions about demand, lay at the roots of low-cost production in the industry.

Large multiple-shop contracts remained wholly advantageous only as long as they stayed put. Short-run contracts on this scale increased uncertainties. At worst they encouraged an extension of capacity which could become redundant if the contract were then lost. Multiple-shop patronage thus raised in much more acute form the question of stability of demand. Being shrewd and powerful in the markets, the instinct of most large retailing firms was to keep as much freedom as possible, always testing price and quality in alternative sources of supply and making a virtue of their independence to keep all their actual suppliers alert by the threat of changing to new ones. If successful, trading with the independent retailers thus implied that the manufacturers needed to set up their own distributing organization: developing custom with the multiples led them into attempts to secure longer contracts or some other means of control. Van den Berghs had moved more quickly along this path than Jurgens but conscious rivalry between the two firms soon brought incentives of its own for hastening the pace.

Home and Colonial Stores became a customer of Van den Berghs for the first time in 1906. Being one of the largest distributors of margarine, with a steady trade of about 70 tons per week at this time, Van den Berghs made efforts to secure their custom. The move of Home and Colonial away from Albers Creameries was consolidated by Van den Berghs taking over £25,000 in debentures subscribed by Home and Colonial and agreeing to advance up to £25,000 (a credit policy which had helped to confirm the loyalty of many wholesalers in Britain). In return Van den Berghs obtained the exclusive contract for all Home and Colonial margarine sales (i.e. they agreed not to divide their custom) for two and a half years at £3 per ton rebate—on a quantity guessed at 8,333 tons. Home and Colonial did not at once become the enthusiastic advertiser of Van den Berghs' margarine and Van den Berghs conspicuously failed to confine their special favour to the Stores. In the event, Home and Colonial remained content, as Van den Berghs' largest customer, for only four years.

Van den Berghs' primary interest, as in the case of Jurgens but not of the Maypole Dairy Company, was to maintain margarine prices at a level where the individual grocer would find it profitable to consider stocking it. Their own interests were too much divided to find tolerable a Maypole policy of prices decided wholly in terms of the very small margins, low unit costs, and high turnover of the most efficient multiple shop companies. Indeed, the desire to impose what controls they could on retail prices proved the strongest single incentive for buying their way into the shop companies. In any case Van den Berghs were accepting too many commitments with rival companies to please such a powerful customer as the Stores.

Apart from these dealings with independent companies operating on the largest scale, Van den Berghs thought connections with multiple shop firms important enough to involve direct investment on their part, which they realized would raise certain problems with their other customers.

In the years after 1896 Van den Berghs took financial stakes in various small dairy companies to secure margarine sales. However, the main base that they were seeking upon which to consolidate their retailing interests did not turn up until 1906. George Beale needed capital for the Meadow Dairy Company after five years of struggle to get resources for expansion. Although his business was as yet puny in relation to the giants of the trade it enjoyed a very high local reputation. Van den Berghs were investing in a man and the future possibilities of his business. Their sponsorship of the Meadow Dairy as a public company in 1906 thus went far beyond a normal loan to a customer. From the beginning Van den Berghs looked to George Beale as the main organizing centre for their own retailing interests (that they had evidently decided to build up), their main source of expert advice for shop company trade. This was reflected in the scale and nature of their investment. Van den Berghs appear to have organized the public incorporation of Meadow, putting in over £20,000 of capital (but leaving Beale in control). This investment was a considerable act of faith in a company then boasting only 16 shops, taking not much more than 1 per cent of Van den Berghs' sales.

From 1906, with the reconstruction of the Meadow Dairy Company Ltd., Van den Berghs began a systematic policy of encouraging George Beale to extend his operations as rapidly as proved possible, gradually feeding the other associated companies to Meadow to concentrate and improve the efficiency of the whole. By April 1910 margarine sales to these companies had advanced to 130 tons per week and almost a quarter of total sales, as against

220 tons per week being sold by independent multiple shop companies, such as Liptons and Sainsburys. Meadow's expansion to some 70 shops in the first four years of the new regime explains the bulk of the increase. They were now taking about 50 tons per week. In 1912 the various small companies (except for Pearks dairies) were absorbed by Meadow, and Van den Berghs took financial control.

Throughout these years Van den Berghs had been plunging heavily with investments to secure turnover and keep their large Rotterdam plant running economically at something close to full capacity. They were proving much less successful than either Jurgens or Maypole in the race for tonnage and profits between 1906 and 1914, and one may interpret their policy of integrating forwards into the control of retailing companies largely in the light of a desperate search for turnover in increasingly adverse competitive conditions. The policy they encouraged upon the companies they influenced reflected this same pressure: fast expansion of outlets as close to the wind as possible financially, at the expense of profits, leaving the members of the family to pacify the preference shareholders and their nominees on the Board as best they could. As a safety-valve there was always the recourse of switching some corporate indebtedness on to the personal accounts of members of the family. Pricing policy followed in the same footsteps, designed for turnover rather than adequate returns. They were out to pin a mortgage on the future. Little success attended all these efforts until after 1914. Maypole increased its lead greatly, tripling production between 1906 and 1914 from 330 to 1,000 tons per week. Jurgens tripled theirs from 150 to 480 tons per week. Van den Berghs increased only from 480 to 680 tons per week—and that increase was confined to the years 1912–13.

The structure of their trade also might have proved impolitic if these peace-time conditions had continued. Their 'associated company' trade was now a little over a quarter of their total English turnover, with independent companies taking a little short of a half, and the small grocers (either by wholesale or direct retail distribution) the remaining fraction. Direct control over just a quarter of total turnover would not do very much to keep the factories in full production (even if it could provide a core of trade and the most fruitful base for expanding trade). But this might serve to prejudice independent shop companies, of which the Home and Colonial and Lipton contracts were the most valuable and the least secure, and even rouse the enmity of the small retailers and the wholesalers who owed their existence to this custom. From the point of view of the associated companies themselves an equivalent balance of advantage and liability lay in these links with powerful manufacturers. Finance for expansion—by way of contribution to capital and elastic trading credit—proved the great advantage, in circumstances where a fairly small, fairly new, scarcely respectable (in City terms) provincial business was hard put to get long-term finance from any other source on any scale, be it the local bank manager or the Stock Exchange. Van den Berghs and Jurgens were large enough to enjoy access to much capital, from English or continental sources. They were bold enough to take big risks with their own and other people's money, and skilled enough, in the result, to make them pay. On the debit side, for the family dynasty or the entrepreneur who wished to remain fully master of his fate, lay the possible loss of control if things no longer went well under their management. The whole structure of the multiple shop movement changed as these equations of advantage and liability worked themselves out in the decisions of so many owners of independent retailing companies to throw in their lot with manufacturers who offered investment capital with their margarine.

Jurgens had been closely watching Van den Berghs' progress in developing financial links with rising shop companies to secure permanent margarine contracts and then expand turnover. Their own failure to come to terms with Maypole now revealed potentially dangerous consequences of isolation in the English market, given the way in which margarine sales were moving. Jurgens customers were mostly small retailers, exactly the class of shop which was being driven out of the market by the large multiple shop companies, particularly the Maypole Dairy Company whose custom they had clearly lost for good. With their production less than a half that of Maypole (and rapidly sinking year by year) and less than a third that of Van den Berghs in 1906, drastic improvement had to come on all sides of their business—manufacture and sales—if they were to meet the challenge of the times. New factories and some co-operation with Van den Berghs in Holland brought much improvement to Jurgens' margarine between 1906 and 1908. Their selling organization in England was shaken out, and upon the better quality, more active advertising of new brands, and tighter control of distribution they began to forge ahead. To complete their new effectiveness in the British market—particularly to have greater influence in steadying retail prices—some control of shop companies was necessary to complement the other changes.

Anton Jurgens was always the man for imaginative organization schemes. He instinctively wanted to strike a bargain with a competitor by devising some grand joint scheme rather than to battle to the death over prices. His interest in shop companies, from the first, was significantly different from Van den Berghs', whom he observed losing money on their investments and reducing the general profitability of the margarine trade by going all out to expand their sales—'the policy of getting turnover', as he called it, 'regardless of whether there is any profit at the price or not, and even at good prices they give far too good quality'. This mistaken strategy, in his view, induced a contagion of competition from other retailing interests and from small manufacturers, 'who simply upset matters against our interests and make matters so complicated that we can't work them properly'. This played into the hands of the retailers against the interests of all manufacturers. To cope with the tide now running in favour of the multiples in England and to attempt to stabilize retail prices as much as to extend turnover, Jurgens now set out to emulate Van den Berghs in gaining control of retail companies, though for these rather different motives. If they had failed with a very large retailing company—the Maypole—they had to succeed first with small ones and then look for openings as opportunity arose.

The difficulty was that they were not gaining the custom of the large shop companies, who were also not offering the opportunities for a manufacturing concern such as Jurgens to buy their way into control. Jurgens' first successful stroke lay in an agreement for the exclusive margarine contract for Shepherds Dairies, as long as the £10,000 which they agreed to advance was still outstanding. By the autumn of 1910 Shepherds Dairies comprised some 35 shops selling 35 tons of margarine weekly. Losses continued throughout 1911, always with the expectation in Jurgens that they were about to turn the corner. Not until they had gained a firmer hold in the retail trade did Jurgens command the necessary expertise to straighten out this unprofitable investment.

Jurgens' other ventures into retailing proved no more auspicious. Indeed, this experience may well have convinced them that to get involved in retailing at all was only worth while if it could lead to an association with a major firm, of the highest status in the business, upon whose managerial efficiency the 'outsider', primarily a manufacturing concern, could capitalize. In 1912, new horizons opened at last, with the chance of a really massive contract— potentially the largest available in the land—and conversion into a permanent consolidated venture such as Gerard Jurgens had been itching to do since the Maypole venture fell through. Jurgens had at last found Home and Colonial Stores uncommitted to Van den Berghs.

When it appeared that the long reign of Van den Berghs with Home and Colonial was coming to an end Jurgens took immediate steps to pay court. Their prospects were good, for Maypole's Southall factory was not to be considered as a possible supplier, that company being a chief rival of Home and Colonial. Levers' margarine factory (Planters) had not yet really come into the market as a competitor commanding major manufacturing capacity and it seemed problematical whether Home and Colonial would really want to build up a relatively small foreign supplier like Albers into their client manufacturer. At the time Home and Colonial were much more firmly established in the cheap butter market than in margarine but this did not mask the great potential.

In June 1912 Jurgens succeeded in securing a major order for supplying over 60 tons of margarine per week to Home and Colonial for the rest of the year (leaving 40–53 tons per week to be shared between Van den Berghs and the Cheshire factory). Towards the end of the year this was extended. Gerard was told by a Director of Home and Colonial that in the course of this year

Pearks alone had opened 38 new shops immediately in their vicinity; and he said: 'now fancy the check of Fenchurch [i.e. Van den Berghs] coming along . . . asking for further contracts in view of such action'.

Special efforts were made to improve quality in order to impress this powerful client. So important was the potential contract for both parties that Anton Jurgens and William Capel Slaughter at once began negotiations for a long-term agreement carrying with it the exclusive supply of margarine for the Stores. Neither could afford the normal temporary contracts struck by the multiple stores, who wished to keep their freedom of action to switch suppliers at short notice as greater opportunity offered elsewhere and to split their custom. Jurgens might well be involved with extensive capital investment to create enough capacity to supply their new giant customer. The new relationship might prejudice some of their other relationships in the market. Some assurance of continuity was vital, looking at the project in the narrowest terms. Given their larger objectives, the more secure the links they could establish with a major retailing company the better pleased they would be. Home and Colonial, too, could not buy margarine as they did most of their other lines. No other commodity had such powerful, or so few, manufacturing interests behind it, jockeying for supremacy in the British market. Alternative sources of supply (even on the Continent) outside the committed parties were virtually non-existent—at least those operating on the largest scale. To set up one's own plant involved formidable investment and continuing overhead expenses, quite apart from the problems of finding the necessary skills. And in the shops margarine was enhancing its status year by year as a commodity of the very first importance in tonnage and in strategic value to draw custom towards other lines. Maypole had fully demonstrated this centripetal pull exercised by a first-class margarine trade and, in addition, it was a weapon of very great influence in pricing strategy by the opportunities it offered as a 'loss leader'.

Thus both sides felt in need of each other to an extent which eventually overcame the natural antagonisms engaged in a close relationship. Negotiations consisted in a struggle between William Capel Slaughter, who was striving to secure Home and Colonial's commercial strength in the margarine trade at the same time as warding off Jurgens' control and influence in retailing, and Anton Jurgens, equally determined to use his firm's assets as a supplier and Home and Colonial's need for an assured supply as a lever to win as much power as he could from their connection. The compromise reached proved in retrospect to be a turning-point in the fortunes of both firms. Both Anton Jurgens and William Capel Slaughter knew, from the outset of their discussions, that the stakes were high.

Jurgens' first proposals were far reaching, linking the two businesses into a joint venture in the margarine market, short of the point where each formally shed any of its sovereignty. Anton proposed that Jurgens obtain the monopoly for the exclusive supply of Home and Colonial's margarine requirements for ten years.

Anton further proposed, in principle, that Jurgens should agree to forgo their rights of extending interests in the retail trade against Home and Colonial if, in return, the Stores renounced their intention of building a margarine factory of their own—for which they had already acquired the freehold site. This was not all. Anton Jurgens hoped to merge all the aspects of the two firms which related to the role of margarine in their joint fortunes. He had plans for a special 'margarine board' to be established by them jointly, to concentrate in one policy-making centre responsibility for buying, manufacture, selling, advertising, and 'the interchange of ideas'.

Such a body, it was clear, would bring Jurgens' representatives directly to the seat of control in Home and Colonial business. Slaughter felt attracted by much of Anton's plan but demurred at swallowing it completely. He was taken aback by learning that Van den Berghs would have to be let into the secret (under their 1908 pool-agreement with Jurgens) for he feared the prospect of reprisal by his late allies. His own counter-proposal was that Jurgens, Van den Berghs, and their shop companies should pool their interests with Home and Colonial in one way or another, to establish a common front against the main enemy, Maypole. Jurgens were not slow to see the implications that this might well prove an instrument for allowing their shop companies to fall under Home and Colonial influence, but Anton Jurgens' imagination responded instinctively to such grand designs and he immediately stated that 'no scheme was too big for Jurgens'. Gerard Jurgens demanded greater caution and Slaughter was asked to reconsider his proposals (which were based on a highly optimistic assumption about Van den Berghs' reactions). Gerard Jurgens put the case that Van den Berghs could not possibly agree to suffer any restrictions on their own retail trade if Liptons (who were taking 200 tons of margarine weekly) were not included. He also thought that their hand would be strengthened if they made a joint approach to Van den Berghs, with their own relationship a *fait accompli*. (Slaughter replied that he did not appreciate a strategy of 'approaching with the stick plainly visible behind the olive branch'.)

The real point was that Jurgens considered Van den Berghs as much of an enemy as Maypole—despite all the contracts and limited agreements between them. The link with Home and Colonial was as much an anti-Van den Bergh move as an anti-Maypole move in Jurgens' view and to let Van den Berghs in (without some great compensation) would rob the whole project of its point. Slaughter yielded to these arguments, but not to the implications of Jurgens' control of retailing. The final agreement, signed on 18 December 1914, allowed Home and Colonial Stores half the capital of the consolidated retail interests of Jurgens, now called Shepherds Dairies. There was also joint responsibility for management—half the members of the management committee were Home and Colonial nominees, half Jurgens' nominees. Jurgens supplied all the margarine required by the new Shepherds, and Home and Colonial all other provisions at cost price. But Jurgens had got a foot in the door on a joint retailing venture with Home and Colonial.

The major margarine agreement between the two firms followed the main lines of Anton Jurgens' original proposition (apart from the fusing of responsibilities in a joint 'margarine board'). Profits were agreed for Jurgens at 1s. per cwt of margarine supplied, plus 50 per cent of the net profits made by Home and Colonial on the resale of all margarine up to 300 tons per week, and 40 per cent on the resale of all margarine in excess of that target (or 1s. per cwt, whichever yielded the higher total). This proved, as Jurgens had intended, the main support upon which their offensive against Maypole and Van den Berghs could be mounted in the years ahead, and a foundation for further development in the control of the retail trade. The consequences proved equally profound for Home and Colonial Stores.

Home and Colonial Directors were probably as anxious about Van den Berghs' relations with Liptons, operating on a sale equivalent to themselves, as with their more formally controlled, but much smaller, competitors Pearks and Meadow. Liptons were taking some 5 per cent of Van den Berghs' total sales in England in 1906. To lose a single customer on this scale might cause damage and Jurgens were making every effort to secure this trade. Liptons remained surprisingly faithful to Van den Berghs, considering there were no financial ties between them. This incident apart, dealings between the two firms remained mutually satisfactory and Liptons' share of Van den Berghs' trade with shop companies gradually increased. Then, in 1912, Van den Berghs succeeded in striking a longer-term bargain with Liptons. They agreed to supply all their margarine until the end of 1914, when the agreement was to be extended until the end of 1918. Van den Berghs also contracted to provide Liptons with £15,000 for margarine advertising in that year. This contract had gone one step further than the 1906 agreement with Home and Colonial Stores. Instead of rebates for the large customer came a modest fixed profit for the manufacturer. Liptons remained financially quite independent, but there was the beginning of functional interdependence, between manufacturer and retailer, with the former assuming some responsibility for advertising. And it was certainly not within the normal contractual conventions of the large multiple shop companies to tie up their custom to a single supplier, at a fixed profit, for five and a half years. Jurgens, however, had also been advancing advertising revenue to some of their clients without any such implications.

(B) MAYPOLE'S CHALLENGE, 1914–1924

Home and Colonial thus emerged as the first main rival to Sir George Watson of Maypole. After the link with Jurgens in 1912 a major backer with manufacturing capacity in Holland (but not yet in England) could wield commercial influence on a scale and with an efficiency fully commensurate with Maypole. Van den Berghs, on the other hand, were not as yet in such a threatening position through their contracts with other multiple shop companies, although these were more widespread. Liptons, despite great size, were already beginning their time of troubles, a much less sure foundation for mounting a major margarine offensive. With about half the national margarine trade in the hands of multiple shop companies, Maypole with one-third of it thus faced their major challenge from Home and Colonial backed by Jurgens. Both groups were competing in the cheapest end of the trade, marketing mainly one brand at the lowest prices in the range existing for the product—a strategy fully in accord with the nature of the margarine market in pre-war England.

The 1914–18 War dramatically changed the terms on which the post-war struggle was to be waged. With the increase in butter prices margarine sales increased by over 60 per cent, with much of the incremental demand being for higher-quality pre-wrapped brands. This initially favoured Jurgens and Van den Berghs more than Maypole. Moreover, Maypole, not selling sugar, was prejudiced for some months in 1916 by sugar rationing, because other shops used sugar sales as a means of tying custom for margarine. But thereafter Maypole gained greatly over its Dutch rivals. Raw-material and shipping shortages prejudiced margarine imports from Holland during 1917 and in March 1918 the Dutch Government prohibited exports. The two Dutch firms were caught without much manufacturing capacity installed in Britain, and Maypole recouped from a nearly monopoly position. In the longer term, however, the war years brought dangerous consequences for Maypole. The company had not appreciated the implications of the trend towards a higher-quality margarine, while the wartime shortages eventually brought too much manufacturing capacity into existence to support peace-time levels of demand —output could have been double the annual demand of 250,000 tons in 1918 and 350,000 tons in 1920. By virtue of its great wartime bonanza Maypole had extensive plant and high overhead costs in crushing mills, refinery capacity, and a West African palm-oil business, all of which needed to be run at capacity if unit costs were to be kept low. The business was dangerously committed to success in selling margarine and its wartime expansion had pushed the stakes higher.

The years after 1920 saw a war of attrition in the margarine trade in Britain: there was overcapacity, overproduction, falling prices, and unprofitable trade on trend for all those jockeying for the leadership in it. In the last analysis victory went to the company with the greatest resources able to stand the strain longer than its rivals: the irony was that the policy of the victim in the struggle rather than of the victor set the pace.

The position was the more serious for Maypole because independent retailers had increased their share of the national market to above 60 per cent during the war from a mere 25 per cent and Maypole would have great problems in re-establishing an independent trade which it had relinquished in 1914. Maypole, the party in the struggle with most to gain by such a policy of amalgamation (for Jurgens, Van den Berghs, and Levers were selling the bulk of their supplies to independents), pursued it least actively. Jurgens and Van den Berghs, who had least to gain from the multiples' standard policy of pushing margarine with as narrow margins and as low prices as possible, bought their way into shop companies most aggressively. Although still much smaller than the giants of Maypole, Liptons, and Home and Colonial, the Meadow Dairy Company enjoyed profit rates almost twice that of the latter firm (to the benefit of Van den Berghs who held most of the ordinary shares) and were to continue to do so for some years.

Home and Colonial resisted Jurgens' attempt to jockey them into buying smaller companies and, after Lever had declined the offer of a controlling interest, Jurgens bought their way in in December 1919 for just over £1 m. This at last gave Jurgens direct control of a major shop company, the essential instrument for crippling Maypole. At this time, however, the direct motive had been the need to control retail prices. As far as Jurgens were concerned, the Home and Colonial Directors had always proved much too reluctant to increase prices and go for the quality trade. They followed Maypole, and would have followed it to disaster, according to Anton Jurgens, since anyone at that time 'competing with the Maypole on their own lines would almost certainly go to the wall'. With a casting vote in the Home and Colonial boardroom in their pocket Jurgens could at last 'avoid the Home and Colonial dragging down the prices when it does not suit our interests for them to do so'. In the event, the decision to take control of Home and Colonial proved more effective as an offensive than a defensive weapon in the next four years. It was also a threat on a much larger scale than Van den Berghs' control of Meadow. Finally, it meant that three major parties in the struggle for the British margarine market wielded direct power of controlling decisions at all stages in the fight—refining, manufacture, and retail sale. Formal confrontation was complete.

Even before the end of price control of raw materials, quota allocations, and the registration scheme in May 1919 Maypole went back to its old policy of undercutting rivals, but prices quickly rose under pressure of demand on raw-material markets. Meanwhile, Jurgens were extending their hold on manufacturing capacity, despite unpropitious conditions, which enabled them to increase the weight of their attack. But Maypole's costs were probably 12s. per cwt. for the cheap grades as against 20s. per cwt for Jurgens (largely selling to wholesalers and independent retailers who needed wider margins). Fighting Maypole thus involved them in very heavy loss in the short run as long as Maypole maintained its efficiencies in costs and quality.

Van den Berghs, meanwhile, had not attempted to emulate Jurgens' expansion or Maypole's efforts to cut prices and lead the market. Their sales had risen from 860 tons per week in 1918 to 1,250 per week in 1920 (whereas Jurgens had passed them, going from 720 tons to 1,480 tons in the two years). Almost half of Van den Berghs' output had been made in Holland, where manufacturing costs were lower, and they maintained their policy of concentrating on the better-quality end of the market. Shop company sales rose to absorb 30 per cent of their output in 1920; Meadow, the most successful profit-maker, taking about 20 per cent and Liptons coming back to Van den Berghs for their margarine contract after severing connections with Southall supplies in 1918. A Jurgens' spokesman could comment wryly of Van den Berghs in March 1920, 'They are in business to make profits.'

Market trends changed during this same year. Raw material prices took a steep plunge, taking retail prices and profits with them, particularly as consumption proved to have reached its peak. Maypole led the price-cutting in April and December. Prices of the cheapest quality went down from 1s. 1d. per lb in early 1920 to 8d. in May 1921, and eventually reached 7d. (their pre-war level) in January 1922. Blue Band and the quality grades fell from 1s. 6d. to 1s. per lb. Even such a dramatic response as this did not stem the tide of falling demand. Consumption fell between 80,000 and 100,000 tons in 1921, partly occasioned by strikes and unemployment, but more by the return of cheap butter to working-class tables.

Butter consumption rose from 146,000 tons in 1920 to 239,000 tons in 1921 (and lard, margarine's competitor in the kitchen, from 84,000 tons to 126,000 tons). De-control of butter prices in April 1921 coincided with increased imports and much release of stocks, so that butter prices fell by 50 per cent in the course of 1921, the most important single explanation for the complementary fall in margarine. Once more it was proved that the average Englishman would not eat much margarine if he could get butter at only twopence more per pound. And the multiples had undoubtedly regained their pre-war position of selling more than half the nation's margarine.

Maypole did not share in this success. Its output had fallen by nearly 300 tons per week reducing margarine profit to zero for much of the year. Clearly the time was opportune for a policy other than more price cuts. By the end of December Sir George had admitted to Sydney Van den Bergh that he was prepared in principle to sell the Watson interests in Maypole.

Negotiations ran out into the sand without decision, however, largely on Van den Berghs' less sanguine view of Maypole's profitability than Sir George Watson's—but then Sir George himself had been to a large extent responsible for the failure by leading the price-cutting campaigns so aggressively (against Jurgens' and Van den Berghs' wishes). This had harmed everyone in the trade and suggested, even to Maypole's Board (who learned of one rash price cut in their evening paper), that erratic and spasmodic moods were replacing a settled commercial policy in the firm. Liptons had long been subject to similar hazards and the diagnosis was the same: the onset of rattled and capricious management at the head of the firm.

All hopes of an agreement on prices collapsed when Van den Berghs failed to buy out the Watsons, bring in Lipton, and organize a profit-pooling arrangement. Margarine was now selling at a lower price than soap. Arthur Wall of Jurgens was uneasy: 'It seems to me', he wrote, 'that the Maypole have set their minds on making the pace such as no other manufacturer can live, if they decide to serve people with an article to retail at the same price as Maypole's, and at the same time to allow these people a margin of profit.' Until the end of the year not only did profits on tea and butter disappear but the cheese, milk, sugar, and jam markets were also difficult.

Danger signals were now flying for all to see. With only four articles in its shops—margarine, butter, condensed milk, and tea—Maypole was in a vulnerable position compared with other multiples offering a very much larger number of lines (and now extending them in new ranges such as tinned products, biscuits, etc., where profit margins were wider than in the traditional staples of the multiple-shop trade). Maypole spread a little canvas to catch the wind in new markets, but enjoyed no real freedom in sales policy. In May 1921 it had acknowledged Van den Berghs' good sense by introducing a 'superior' quality margarine of its own at 1s. per lb, Mayco. But this proved more difficult than it seemed for there was no tradition of price discrimination in the upper bracket of the margarine market in Maypole and its manufacturing plant was not geared to this line of business. Compromise also came in the other traditional Maypole product, butter. Again moving with the tide, the Watsons sought to gain in the cheap butter market some fraction of what they were losing in margarine by importing cheap New Zealand butter for sale at 1d. below their fresh-made Danish butter. During 1922 they introduced dried milk and beef suet; a year later they added sugar and lard to the list. Before the link with Jurgens allowed reorganization of Maypole's commitments in processing oil and making margarine there was not so much room for manœuvre. In a given number of shops with given accommodation (they were mostly shops of very limited frontage) the introduction of each additional article was likely to be at the expense of the turnover in the staple commodities.

Although the problems had begun with falling margarine sales, extending the number of lines compounded the difficulties of restoring them. The fact of the matter was, however, that Maypole *had* to specialize in margarine, without very drastic surgery, for they had over £2 m. invested in refining and manufacturing capacity to produce it. The burden of mounting overheads there could produce as much of a drag on profits as unremunerative selling in its shops. And this was an expense which could not be shaken off. For all Sir

George Watson's threats to sell his factories and buy abroad (or set up refining capacity abroad) there was not much chance of this way out at the time.

Through 1923 the same trends, and the same main response—price-cutting —continued, particularly with the cheaper grades of margarine. Jurgens, as usual, were hit more than Van den Berghs by this. Liptons (having returned to Van den Berghs on this occasion from Planters) now acted as the rogue elephant over prices. Maypole turnover was down to 800 tons per week by July 1923 and both Home and Colonial and Meadow showed a similar decline in margarine turnover. Again, both major parties attempted to hold the position steady on the main front by seeking a general price agreement and then moving along a flank with new gambits. Once more the fate of the independent multiple shop companies came into the argument. Van den Berghs pressed forward to build up their numbers of shops to 1,000, aiming to rival the commercial weight of Maypole, Home and Colonial, and Liptons. By the end of 1921 Meadow and its associated companies possessed some 550 shops, 650 by the end of 1922, and 750 by the end of 1923.

Anton Jurgens's reactions to this build-up was to hold on all the more firmly to Home and Colonial no matter how tempting the offers. 'I have more fear than I can express,' he wrote, 'that once control of the Home and Colonial has gone from us we shall not have sufficient say in the fixing of the retail prices in England, which our position warrants over here.' Anton turned again to work on Sir George Watson. It was the story of 1921 once more. Watson was holding out for a higher price than Jurgens were willing to entertain, while his own margarine pricing policy was driving his profits and share prices further down. At the annual general meeting on 20 May a considerable volume of criticism was let loose, with more losses to be written down in the Gambia and still falling production and profits of margarine. Complaints were registered about the quality of Maypole brands, and suggestions made for more new lines. The ordinary dividend of 3*d*. came as a further shock, and another £250,000 had to be found from reserves to provide it. City commentators hinted at the need for 'new blood' on the Board.

This proved to be the end of the road for Sir George Watson. Profits had fallen relentlessly year by year from the £1 m. of 1919 to £205,000 of 1924. Margarine sales were falling equally relentlessly, despite all his sacrifices in price, from the 82,000 tons produced in 1920 to under 40,000 tons in 1924. Lever remarked acutely that 'Sir George Watson is very reluctant to learn the lesson that low price, even coupled with excellent quality, is not the last word in food products'. The point was simply that, with the marketing conditions of the 1920s and its intimate relationship with the state of the butter market, there was no longer any price-elasticity left in margarine. A lower price (implying a cheaper quality) proved much more likely to lead to a decline in sales. The only buoyancy left was for the higher-quality product selling at a higher price. Lever still thought that all the Watsons' manœuvring was designed to make Maypole more attractive for a take-over bid, but the more likely explanation appears that he was hoping to stick out the struggle longer than Jurgens (who were also losing money on margarine), unwilling to accept defeat and waiting for something to change radically in the market, which might save him. But the clouds still gathered without a break in the summer of 1924, and on 18 July he signed a contract selling his holdings—some 16 per cent of the voting power of Maypole—to the Home and Colonial Stores. Another dynasty had failed.

The pressures of the business context in which the Watsons found themselves in 1924 were probably too powerful to overcome. In a sense the whole heritage of their developing commitments in the margarine industry since the turn of the century now told against them. It is doubtful how long they could have survived at the head of the firm, even had they been determined on all counts not to sell. Lipton was himself to prove a little more obstinate and, being so, a greater threat to the ultimate fate of his creation. Perhaps one of the main considerations in the last analysis was the absence of a second generation in the Watson family waiting to take over the succession. It was not that old age itself dictated the problem: Sir George Watson was 63 at the time of the sale. But the generations had taken their toll in a more subtle way. He had been in business since before 1880, his methods fashioned, his experience tried, his instincts and judgement formed in the pioneering generation of multiple stores. The other two brothers, Charles and Alfred, who had been such energetic wrangling partners on the Board in the early days, were born within four years of George. The younger brothers who came in afterwards never seem to have become powers in their own right. In all the correspondence that the struggle occasioned after 1914 always George is the decision-taker, the spokesman, the strategist. There was a failure in purely dynastic terms. Before 1914 they had never failed. Thereafter the brothers had tired as they aged. They had also become very rich and acquired the non-business interests and way of life of those getting accustomed to wealth for its own sake rather than wealth as a means of doing more business.[3] And there was always the consideration that their stake in the business had to be looked on as an investment needing protection—or a switch into more profitable or less insecure assets. When it came to the last fight they needed to protect their wealth rather than their business—long though it was that these two had appeared identical. Some might have said that these considerations encouraged a failure of nerve. The brothers were also in the position of seeing themselves as the last of the line. Not one son wanted to take over the reins of power. Two brothers had no sons, two remained bachelors. Neither of Sir George's sons followed their father. Only a son of Alfred remained in the business in 1924, as Assistant Secretary. Here was the absence of another motive which might have given them more appetite for battle. Successors in top management and power were absent after 1914 who could have spoken to their fathers and uncles from other seats in the boardroom in their own terms, with the intimacy and confidence that only kinship would give—and the weight that only a substantial shareholding provided. Capriciousness and obstinacy might have been checked before difficulties became too extreme. Greater flexibility in policy, a greater willingness to move with the times might have come in with the missing second generation. For all these reasons, too, it is right to speak of a dynastic failure.

(C) CRISIS AND CONSOLIDATION

General repercussions from Jurgens' move in the provision trade were favourable on the whole, for Sir George Watson's adamant policy over price-cutting had made him many enemies. For Van den Berghs, however, the purchase came as a great shock: they had remained quite in the dark about it. Their first reaction was to seek countervailing power at once to block the increased leverage they believed the Maypole purchase would give to Jurgens. A whole range of multiple store companies were sounded, including Liptons, but for the moment no more was heard of these wild-cat schemes.

Jurgens' intervention came too late in 1924 to save Maypole profits in that year. Even with Sir George Watson out of the way attempts at agreement between firms still enjoying their own sovereignty proved ephemeral. A hope of improved profits induced firms to break away; a downward movement of raw-material prices, an attempt to take avoiding action by dropping the price of some other article, was always likely to lead to one group of stores cutting margarine prices.

These continuing circumstances of uncertain demand through to 1927, a continuing threat of oversupply and falling prices, put increasing pressure on the shop companies and led eventually to the fall of Liptons. The whole trade had been watching carefully the recent misfortunes of the great firm, blundering about, it seemed, in an increasingly competitive world, with an ageing autocrat at its head. It was apparent to all that Liptons, despite their large number of shops (about 600 in the British Isles), the independent tea business, and wide international ramifications, had never been a particularly profitable concern; this dated from the initial overcapitalization at incorporation in 1898. Here was one reason for caution, in addition to its great size which made any amalgamation difficult to absorb as well as expensive to accomplish. The record since 1924 also contained cautionary tales. In that year profits were insufficient to provide any dividend on ordinary shares, and even part of the preference share dividend came from accruing surpluses in 1923.

Sir Thomas Lipton blamed everything except his own management—unemployment, taxation, falling markets—and was known to have said that not even £10 per share would tempt him to sell: 'this business was his life and he would hang on to the last'. Events now moved quickly to a crisis. Profits announced for the year in 1925 proved to be a mere £30,000. Anton Jurgens reflected the general opinion when he bluntly diagnosed that the failure 'was solely due to management—practically always a decisive factor'.

At the annual general meeting in July 1926 the announcement that the preference dividend was to be passed brought angrier criticism than ever before, with demands that Sir Thomas retire. But with legal control still vested in his own hands they had reached an impasse. Anton thought that 'unless some radical improvement is soon made, this company looks like going to the wall completely'.

Sir Thomas's one legal weakness lay in the debenture and preference shares. Failure to cover the debenture interest, in particular, would invoke immediate reaction by his powerful creditors, seeking the opportunity of blocking further interference in their efforts to save the business. Emergency action could not save the dividends, however, and £50,000 interest on debenture capital came from reserves rather than trading profits. At this point Van den Berghs decided that they would bid for Sir Thomas's shares, despite all the management reorganization problems this would involve.

Margarine sales in Lipton shops at 75 tons per week would give them an extra profit of £500 per week (or $3\frac{1}{2}$ per cent interest on an investment of £750,000 in buying the shares). Discreet inquiry had also convinced them that it would not be an impossible task to pull the business back into shape. Information was that the overseas and export trade (mainly a tea business) remained in good heart returning a net profit of £130,000–140,000 per year. The Lipton business in the United States and Canada remained highly profitable also but, as it belonged personally to Sir Thomas rather than to Lipton Ltd. (the English company), it had to remain outside the calculations of liability and asset in Van den Berghs' estimate. Liptons possessed more manufacturing capacity (in lines other than margarine) than other shop companies. The six factories were also reported to be paying their way on a competitive basis. This left the responsibility for trouble with Sir Thomas's erratic and arbitrary personal autocracy at the head of the business and with the actual management of the shops at the grass roots. About half the English shops made losses but on the whole Liptons' trade in the better-class districts remained satisfactory. Only in lower-class areas had the shops lost customers on a large scale to other multiples and co-operative stores. There had been serious decline here ever since 1923 and in 1927 twenty shops had been closed down because their turnover was so low. General standards of buying, on the other hand, remained competitive. Indeed, skills in merchanting in Mincing Lane were rumoured to have provided most of the profits in some recent years.

With this private diagnosis of Liptons' troubles the next steps became clear, should Van den Berghs take the plunge. Strong leadership had to be imposed at the Board level but the roots of the trouble lay too deep for change at this level to be effective (as it had been, for example, in the case of Jurgens' move into Maypole). An infusion of management skill and strength also had to come at shop-inspector level. George Beale and his Meadow Dairy Company were the only main allies and assets which Van den Berghs enjoyed for this task. It was really up to Beale. Any decision to take control of Liptons was really a vote of confidence by Van den Berghs in George Beale and the team he had assembled in Meadow. He thought that by closing down the worst shops he could cut away the waste timber in the company and write off the capital loss within the year. He would then need a free hand to move some of his lieutenants over to Liptons to set about the difficult (and unpopular) business of imposing higher standards of efficiency and control all down the line from head office to the assistants behind the counter. Things, he knew, would have to get worse before they could get better. There were losses to be written down. Closures, the public hue and cry over absent profits, and the changes in control would forfeit goodwill in the short run.

Eventually, Van den Berghs were offered Sir Thomas Lipton's holding (in the English company only) for a sum of £600,000. This represented about one-quarter of the issued share capital, but brought with it overwhelming control because the balance was known to be distributed amongst over 21,000 share-holders, with a maximum holding of £7,000. The Board accepted the offer on 8 September 1927. On the same day a working arrangement between the Meadow Dairy Company and Liptons was announced whereby senior executives of Meadow took over positions in Lipton. With this strong bridge established at the head of the two firms the transfusion of new energy into Liptons could begin. This could not show in the accounts for two years. In 1929 Liptons' capital had to be written down from £3,250,000 to £1,422,250. But from here improvement set in, after yet another original dynasty had failed.

(D) RETROSPECT ON THE MARGARINE WAR

With the acquisition of Liptons by Van den Berghs the four principal shop companies in the British provision trade had finally come under the aegis of the two rival Dutch margarine manufacturers. Each now had its two main client companies—Jurgens with Home and Colonial and Maypole; Van den Berghs first in the field with Meadow (which they promoted and built up rather than took over as a giant) and now completing the circle with Liptons. The game had been played with point and counterpoint. There remained only the final coupling of the two rival manufacturers themselves, each with its tributary retailers, to bring to birth the heir—almost, it might be said, the residuary legatee—of the long-drawn struggle: Allied Suppliers. When Jurgens and Van den Berghs announced their agreement to come together as the Margarine Union in 1927 the logical basis had been established.

Looking back from 1927 there is some paradox in the great determination of Jurgens and Van den Berghs to buy their way into multiple stores in Britain during the 1920s. Indeed, their motives changed over the years in accordance with the changing logic of events rather than the simple logic of most assumptions about the advantages of vertical integration. Originally Van den Berghs held that boosting turnover was the overriding argument. This was why they were so anxious to promote lively young firms such as the Meadow Dairy Company in pre-war years. In the commercial context of the margarine industry at that time—one might say in the technological specifications of the product—the multiple companies were the only retailers with sufficient expertise to sell it efficiently, which meant selling it rapidly. From headquarters their chiefs could impose the necessary standards upon a large number of outlets without any bother to the margarine manufacturers. We have seen that as much as 50 per cent of the nation's consumption of margarine in 1913 passed over the counters of these four multiple shop companies (one-third of it over Maypole counters alone).

This overriding motive of having to orientate sales (and hence control) towards the multiple shops to secure outlets did not, however, continue in quite the same form after 1914. At the end of the war the share of the market of the four companies had dropped to perhaps a quarter of total national consumption (itself much larger). In the immediate post-war phase they recovered to take up 40 per cent of total sales in 1921, a period which saw the investment of Jurgens in Home and Colonial. But thereafter the percentage dropped, as did total consumption. In the course of six years their turnover had been halved and the percentage of the diminishing national market reduced to about 20 per cent. In some cases turnover and profit fell for other reasons, as well as falling margarine sales; but margarine suffered most severely. At first sight, therefore, this is not the anticipated context for massive investment by margarine manufacturers in shop companies: when their sales are decreasing steeply, their importance relative to other outlets diminishing, and their profitability as general investments on the wane.

There were particular explanations for some of these phenomena which could be thought temporary—Lipton's mismanagement, Sir George Watson's price-cutting, the decline in purchasing power—and it may be that this was the belief in Jurgens and Van den Berghs. But if the central cause for the decline in total sales of margarine was the challenge of cheap butter and other fats, the central cause for the *relative* decline in the market being experienced by the multiple shop companies was a further change in the nature of the product. As the use of hardened oils increased, so the dangers of quick deterioration of margarine declined. Small corner-shop grocers could handle it as safely as shops with rapid turnover and efficient stock control.[4] Thus one of the great pre-war advantages of the multiple-shop companies in margarine sales depreciated. Pricing policy revealed a further aspect of the market—and another paradox. The multiples offered the advantage of cheap prices and standard quality, prospering on the mass market of working-class incomes. Yet the decline and fall of the Maypole Dairy Company on this policy between 1921 and 1924—hit more severely by falling markets than the others as an integrated concern manufacturing almost exclusively for its own shops—marked the end of a phase.

The Dutch manufacturers feared and fought Maypole, not because they wished to take advantage of its profit-margins by integrating forwards to control it, but because they wanted to put a stop to unremitting price-competition and enable the many thousands of small retailers up and down the country to sell at a profit. This was also exactly the reason for Jurgens' move to control Home and Colonial. Once established in control of their multiple shop companies, conflicting interests emerged. Much more than half their market, as manufacturers, lay beyond the retail outlets they controlled. Pricing policy needed to be fashioned in the light of the general interest and undoubtedly this implied less vigorous price-cutting by the multiples than previously. But, where national consumption was stationary or falling, this meant robbing their custom in favour of the non-specialist grocer. There were still, of course, some actual and many potential independent manufacturers and distributors waiting to come in if this policy was pushed beyond the limit —and that limit was narrow in the inter-war period. All the pooling agreements proved ephemeral in practice, evidence of the underlying strength of spontaneous reactions to the slightest swell of market forces. The co-operative societies were outside the group. There was the immediate threat of imports until the tariff of the 1930s or of invasion from the Continent or the United States. Small independent producers would mushroom if margins remained wide for any length of time, while the wholesaling and retailing interests themselves would erupt into price-cutting in these circumstances.

Given this context, it remained true that, with Maypole brought into line after 1924, the price-cutting which had brought losses to every manufacturer in the trade disappeared, and margins improved enough to make margarine a line worth stocking again for the small independent grocer. He now also had the advantages of a wartime experience which introduced margarine to the middle class—his main customers—and made it respectable. No premium remained on anonymity when buying it. Moreover, the new 'quality' packet trade aided this class of trade. The experience of the first half of the 1920s had proved conclusively that, taking the market as a whole, demand for margarine was too inelastic to profit from any further price-reduction in a standard article.

Given the context of the inter-war period and the pricing policy which the Dutch manufacturers wished to impose on their own multiple shop companies, it was clear that their profitability and turnover in margarine would decline (and with it perhaps their general profitability and attractiveness as investments where margarine held a central place in their fortunes and linkages existed between sales of this line and others, such as sugar). But *ex ante* the pressures to gain control of such firms were irresistible. They were enemies whose influence in the trade could render sales everywhere else unprofitable unless checked. And on a falling market, even if their share of the trade was declining, gaining control of a large multiple firm was the quickest way of becoming assured of a large weekly margarine contract. As individual units, if not as a category of retailers, they still possessed much the most attractive contracts available to margarine manufacturers. And, as markets shrank, so the pressure for turnover increased and the need to appropriate sections of the trade as available. Direct competition between Jurgens and Van den Berghs added a momentum of its own to the race. Each feared the consequences of the other extending control in retailing and sought opportunities for going one better. Such apprehension could prove a more potent force in motivating policy than any review of the disadvantages of such investment seen before the event. Indeed, had all the negotiations and attempts at purchase been successful in the 1920s scarcely a multiple shop company would have remained independent.

Once established, investment in shops did bring serious conflicts of principle to manufacturers interested in basically one foodstuff, of which their own outlets did not absorb most of the trade. Keeping such a large amount of resources tied up in this way could only be justified if the investment remained profitable—directly in terms of retailing profits and dividends to the companies, or indirectly through margarine contracts. We have seen the incompatibilities these double objectives involved if driven to the limit. Reactions from associations of independent retailers or wholesalers might also prejudice sales severely, if there were thought to be hidden advantages by way of rebates —if not lower prices in the shops—given to their own shop companies. Managing a large provision business demanded a range of skills which the margarine manufacturers did not themselves possess. Such a business had to have a life of its own, a capacity and initiative to respond to available opportunities, an ability to grow and struggle for efficiency amongst its competitors on its own terms, if there was to be any hope of keeping able and ambitious men at its head.

The margarine contracts remained, of course, the umbilical cord which tied the shop companies to the manufacturers who had become their masters. This—and ultimate control—apart, the group of shop companies brought together by the struggles between rival margarine makers in the 1920s thereafter evolved with a history of their own.

NOTES

1 Allied Suppliers was formed in 1929, in the wake of the merger which created Unilever, in order to group together the main national retailing companies which Van den Berghs and Jurgens had acquired in the preceding years. These multiple shop companies were the Meadow Dairy Company, the Maypole Diary Company, the Home and Colonial Stores, and Lipton Ltd. This chapter analyses the moves by which the margarine manufacturers took control of these retailing firms. It is taken from Peter Mathias, *Retailing Revolution*,

A History of Multiple Retailing in the Food Trades based upon the Allied Suppliers Group of Companies (Longmans, London, 1967), pt. 2, sect. 1 ('The Struggle over Margarine'), pp. 195–258. See also C. H. Wilson, *The History of Unilever* (2 vols., London, 1954) for the wider context.

2 Sir George Watson's estate totalled over £2 m. at his death.

3 Margarine in the early twentieth century, being made predominantly from vegetable fat, probably did not keep as well as the margarine of 1890 and before, made from animal fats.

9

The Big Three:
Competition, Management, and Marketing
in the British Motor Industry, 1922-1939[1]

ROY CHURCH and MICHAEL MILLER

(A) EMERGENCE OF OLIGOPOLY

THE rapid growth of the British motor industry between the wars has been widely recognized as a crucial aspect of the structural renovation of the economy during a period dominated in the popular mind, and indeed until comparatively recently in the eyes of historians, by mass unemployment and economic waste. Both major sectors of the automotive industry—the production of private cars and of commercial vehicles—participated in this growth, which, if striking over-all, was intermittent and more notable in terms of the volume than the value of output. On the eve of the Great War, Britain produced about 34,000 units of both classes; by 1924 some 117,000 cars and 30,000 commercial types were produced, and in this year the manufacturing branch of the motor and cycle trades was responsible for one-fifth of the total net output and employment generated by the British engineering industries.[2] In 1929 output reached 179,000 cars and 59,000 commercial vehicles; the Slump caused only a brief recession in this industry, and by 1935, when 325,000 cars and 92,000 buses and lorries came off British production lines, motor and cycle manufacturing accounted for 22 per cent of the net output of the whole engineering sector.[3] The peak year of the period was 1937, with an output of 379,000 cars and 114,000 commercial vehicles.

For cars, the stimuli to growth are well defined. The average value of new cars sold fell by one-half from 1924 to 1938,[4] a result of the interaction of a shift towards the purchase of smaller cars over time and of rapid improvements in the efficiency of production, especially after 1930 when flow-, or mass-production methods first became firmly established in the British automotive industry.[5] Especially after the Slump, the growing real incomes of the middle class overcame a certain stability in new car prices, and carried home sales to successive record levels. At the same time, private car exports began to assume a quantitative importance for the first time, owing to a combination of the depreciation in the pound sterling and the desire by Dominion customers for more economic motoring than could be offered by the American car preferred hitherto. If the home market was marginally restricted by the levels of vehicle and petrol taxation, government intervention did have a more positive side: except in 1924–5, when the McKenna duty of 33⅓ per cent ceased to operate, imports made little headway under normal conditions of trade.

The purpose of this chapter will be to define and assess entrepreneurial responses to the conditions and opportunities outlined above. Progress in the car sector was accompanied by, and largely conditional upon, a profound evolution in the organization of the industry. In the 1920s British car production was based on a large number of small firms, with a high mortality rate. By the end of the 1930s a clear triparite structure had evolved comprising three large firms, three smaller ones on the periphery of mass production, but

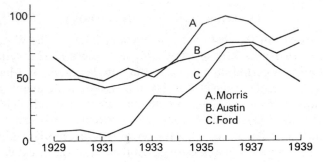

GRAPH 1. Pt. 1. Output of Private Cars by the Three Largest Producers (000s)

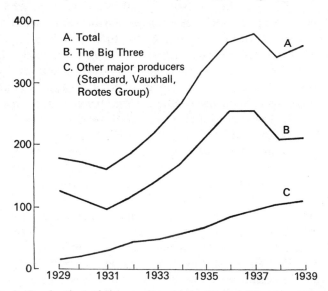

Pt. 2. Production of Private Cars in the United Kingdom (000s)

growing, and an unstable fringe of firms competing on those aspects of performance or comfort which the larger companies gradually subordinated to price. The question with which we are here concerned, therefore, is the changing competitive positions of the three firms which emerged as the dominant car-making trio during this period: Morris, Austin, and Ford (see Graph 1). Maxcy and Silberston's study explains these shifting positions mainly in terms of external factors—the changing structure of demand, rapid model changes and diversification, and the penetration of the British market by American firms.[6] By contrast, we shall concentrate on those internal factor which influenced the ranking of particular firms, although external factors will, as their importance in explaining structural change warrants, provide the context for our analysis.

(B) THE AUSTIN STRATEGY

The reasons for the rise of Morris to pre-eminence in the 1920s are well known as a result of the analysis of the company's history by Andrews and Brunner:[7] forceful but imaginative control and management by W. R. Morris (later to become Sir William, and then Lord Nuffield); conservative finance combined with aggressive pricing policies; and efficient standardized quantity production of the popular Cowley and Oxford motor cars under the guidance of able and dedicated designers and engineers, notably Frank Woollard and A. A. Rowse (both with experience of munitions production). The success of Austin, dependent largely on the creative engineering ability of Sir Herbert Austin (later to become Lord Austin of Longbridge) and the production and organization skills of C. R. F. Engelbach, was less spectacular, hampered as the company was by crippling financial burdens which effectively prevented a comparably rapid post-war development. Much of the capital raised to finance the immediate post-war programme was for the purpose of the large-scale production of a single 20-hp model, a car which proved to be too expensive to achieve a large market penetration, and in 1921, in response to the insistence by agents handling Austin cars for a smaller, cheaper model, such a policy was agreed to by the Directors.[8] Sir Herbert Austin's own proposal for a very small car designed to supersede the motor-cycle sidecar combination and tap a new market was dismissed in favour of a 12-hp model to compete with the Morris Cowley. In that same year the Official Receiver refused permission to proceed further with manufacturing operations pending a complete review of the company's affairs, while Austin cars were banned from the Motor Show at Olympia. Subsequently, a Creditors Committee nominated C. R. F. Engelbach, a former Armstrong Whitworth apprentice with experience of managing the Coventry Ordnance Works, to be Austin's Production Manager.[9]

Undaunted by what might have been interpreted as a slight to his own contribution to the company's development, Austin proceeded to transform his household into a workshop and without support or encouragement from his colleagues designed the baby utility car which his co-Directors had rejected. Their attitudes altered after the interest which the prototype Seven attracted at Olympia in November 1922, and production began in 1923. Thus the company's post-war revival began on the basis of Austin's own engineering and creative design skills. Without his persistence and determination to secure the implementation of his personal manufacturing strategy the company's colossal financial difficulties would almost certainly have engulfed the Longbridge enterprise. It was, indeed, this prospect which almost led to the sale of the company to General Motors Corporation—a venture initiated by Sir Herbert Austin himself, but frustrated by a dispute over the value of the firm's assets, and by the opposition of his co-Directors.[10] Engelbach later recalled how a perpetual shortage of working capital at this time hindered development, but how rigid economies, together with the remarkable commercial successes of the Austin Twelve and Seven, reflected in a rising turnover, raised morale inside Longbridge. Simultaneously, raw material suppliers and the banks gained renewed confidence in the company, extending credit for the modernization programme, completed in 1927, which marked the advent of continuous large-scale production. A sharp rise in labour productivity and a marked fall in unit overhead costs[11] at last brought profitability to the company.[12]

Austin's production experienced a sustained and rapid increase: from 2,600 units in 1922 to an estimated 25,000 in 1926, 38,000 in 1927, and 50,470 in 1929.[13] Already by 1927 the Seven accounted for over 50 per cent of car output; in 1929 the figure was 64 per cent, and this despite the riposte to the Seven from Cowley by the introduction of the Morris Minor. Austin met the Slump with a range of only four models, and this narrowness of appeal makes all the more interesting the fact that models designed nearly a decade before, although extensively improved and revised thereafter, provided the firm not merely with survival but with remarkable prosperity during the Depression years. The contrast with experience at Cowley is very marked, as we shall see.

There were two recurrent themes in the history of the British motor industry between the wars. On the one hand, there had to be a continuous stream of responses to competitors' attempts to create new markets and to invade existing ones; on the other—and especially in the case of indigenous firms—it was necessary to replace ageing and often highly individualist founders by second-generation management. The Austin enterprise largely avoided both difficulties: there was a tradition of successful engineering, as we should expect from a man of Sir Herbert Austin's training and experience, and, moreover, 'One of the recipes of [his] success was that for all his conservatism, he invariably kept a best-seller in his catalogues'[14]—even if the brilliant idiosyncrasy of the Seven was never repeated, and the sense of purpose sometimes diminished. As the rest of the industry began to recover, Austin began rapidly to increase the number of models and variants offered—the typical response to disappointed expectations, but closer scrutiny of Austin's model ranges reveals a concentration upon a range of about half a dozen cars throughout the 1930s, additions being produced by the simple expedient of combining basic components in various ways.

Permutations apart, the most successful new Austin model of the mid-1930s was the Ten-Four of 1932, which was aimed at the £150 to £175 price bracket. With the Morris Ten of 1933, the Standard Ten of 1934, and perhaps the rather cheaper Ford Ten of 1935, we can observe a sequence of convergence on the price-power combination pioneered by the Hillman Minx. The Minx, a 9·8-hp model selling at £159 in saloon form, was the progenitor of a line typical of the 1930s—the Family Ten; but the Austin model was in full production before the Minx itself, or the Morris reply.[15] As a result, Austin sales during the middle years of the 1930s were heavily dominated by the Seven and the Ten. From 1932 to 1937 Austin car output increased from 46,000 to 80,000 units,[16] and in 1933 Austin was—if briefly—the largest British manufacturer of private cars. During the dynamic years from 1932 to 1936 the company produced a round total of a quarter of a million cars. In 1937, on the eve of yet another short recession in the motor trade, Austin Motors Ltd. achieved its highest gross profit of the decade, but this was the last season in which the Seven sold well.[17] Austin output and profits were hit hard in 1937–8. In the following year the company was urgently engaged in revitalizing its product range and the results for 1938–9 show a marked recovery in the firm's finances. Austin car production recovered almost to peak levels, at a time when Ford, its erstwhile rival for second place in the British car industry, was suffering a continuing loss of its market share.

In general, then, the history of the Austin concern after 1927 is one of substantial progress, followed by a phase of sustained profitability but lagging design—a situation parallel to the earlier experience of Morris, and only really remedied in 1939. Austin never enjoyed the breadth of market appeal of the Nuffield conglomerate, but neither did it suffer the prolonged crisis of that concern. Within this limit, it was a progressive and investment-conscious enterprise which spent over £1 m. on new investment during the financial years 1936–7 and 1937–8 alone, besides demonstrating a degree of sales stability which eluded its two main rivals for pre-eminence, Nuffield and Ford. In part this seems to reflect the differences in managerial performance in each of the companies, which were, to some extent, influenced by the structure of the firms themselves. Thus the Nuffield empire and the international Ford enterprise contrast sharply with the Longbridge factory complex which comprised the Austin Motor Company. Because expansion, impressive though it was at Longbridge, occurred through internal growth rather than through integration in either vertical or horizontal form, the problems of managerial control appear to have been less challenging than for Ford and Morris Motors and it proved possible at Longbridge for the pyramidal structure of management to survive without unduly jeopardizing the exercise of managerial control and continuity. Sir Herbert Austin remained at the apex of one of the three giants of the British motor industry, presiding personally over an ageing Board of Directors, deliberate in decision-making, phlegmatic in his dealings with others,[18] though essentially seeking to safeguard the company's solid commercial achievements. The success of the lesser car makers from the mid-1930s, Rootes, Standard, and Vauxhall, in addition to Ford, brought about a decline in Austin's share of the market (as it did for that of Morris), and the resignation of Engelbach in 1938 to make way for Leonard Lord marked the beginning of another critical phase in the battle between Austin and Morris.[19]

(C) FORD: FAILURE AND CHALLENGE

It is interesting to ask why Ford, the biggest seller in Britain in 1923, failed to generate an energetic response to Morris's leap forward in the 1920s, given the availability to Ford of advanced American technology, unequalled commercial experience, and unparalleled production know-how even before World War I. Hitherto, historians of the British motor industry have concentrated on the success of Morris, but Ford's failure to loom large in Britain in the 1920s is equally relevant to any attempt to explain the changing distribution of sales between motor manufacturers between the wars. The history of Ford's international development[20] demonstrates clearly that at the time when Morris, and to a lesser extent Austin, was most effectively managed, Ford's managerial performance was lethargic at worst and at best unimaginative. Percival Perry (later to become Sir Percival and then Lord Perry of Stock Harvard), whose association with Ford began in 1905 and who since 1911 had been Managing Director of the American Ford assembly plant at Manchester, was replaced at the end of World War I. The reason for his replacement was the conviction among Ford managers in Detroit, including Henry Ford himself, that Perry's involvement in government affairs during the war had been excessive, to the detriment of Ford's business in Britain. Owing partly to the division of loyalties but also to sheer physical exhaustion, Perry had, it seemed, allowed the administration of Ford to be shared among a coterie whose composition depended upon interrelated business connections, political association, and personal relationships.

From 1919 three American managers had conducted Ford's British affairs, but in 1922 falling sales of the Model-T Ford once again prompted Detroit to send a small team to investigate and report on the state of the British outpost and to modify the Ford in order to offset the effects of the 1920 Finance Act, which had included the tax of £1 per unit of horsepower so damaging to the typically high-powered American cars. The modifications amounted to nothing more than the introduction of right-hand drive, and Ford continued to offer to British car buyers a vehicle more suited to American roads, fuel prices, and taxation conditions. As British manufacturers, notably Morris and Austin, began to compete against Ford the unsuitability of the American Model-T to British conditions led to Ford's decline. Furthermore, the policy of abolishing wholesale distribution of Ford cars, substituting agreements with exclusive Ford agents, proved to be unpopular among distributors. Ford agents had been antagonized by the practice of trying to force sales by dumping cars upon dealers who had not requested them, accompanied by threats of cancellation of their agencies if they resisted. One result had been the defection of many Ford agents to Morris.[21] The report on the Ford enterprise in Britain was written by two Detroit managers, Klann and Gehl, who informed head office in December 1923 that 'the more we analyse the organisation and their methods, the more we are convinced that organisation and quality have been sadly neglected and it is going to take a considerable time to rebuild it'.[22] Indeed, management and morale at Manchester were abysmal,[23] but the responsibility for Ford's policies in Britain was as much that of the central management in Detroit which provided the guidelines for subsidiary operations, and was to continue to do so.[24] In 1924 Ford slipped into second place among car producers in Britain, and although managers were replaced at Manchester, Henry Ford still refused to allow any substantial modifications of the Model-T to meet the needs of British buyers, concentrating on persuading the British public that Ford cars assembled in Manchester were, indeed, almost entirely British-made.[25] The original plan for the Dagenham plant, which was intended to treble production capacity, indicated a commitment to the British industry strongly out of tune with the commercial ineptitude of pushing an unchanged Model-T in the face of opposition from his new managers at Manchester. When Gehl returned to Detroit from Manchester in 1924 he argued strongly for a model with a high-speed, small-bore engine to compete with British cars of low horsepower rating, but Ford refused to listen, his unbounded confidence in the model remaining unshaken. The Dagenham project, too, was left in abeyance. Of all Ford's international operations Kanzler, one of Ford's Detroit generals, reckoned that England represented the low point in Ford accomplishment: 'we have been defeated and licked in England', he remarked in 1926.

Ironically, in 1926 Jenkins, American Managing Director of Ford in Britain from 1924, had suggested to Ford that he should purchase and send to the U.S. a 7-hp Peugeot and two Austin Sevens for careful examination, a proposal which Henry Ford dismissed. In the same year Sir Herbert Austin, ever in search of relief from financial difficulties, wrote to Ford underlining the decline in sales of Ford cars, and reopened the question of collaboration between the two companies in the British market. But Ford was preoccupied with the discontinuation of the Model-T in 1927 and its replacement by the Model-A, which appeared in Britain later in that year. The new car was available with an engine with a smaller bore than the regular American model and a taxable horsepower of 15 instead of the 24 for the regular American engine. With the exception of the right-hand drive introduced in 1923 this was the first *factory* change designed to cater for the specific demands of the British market. In fact, the American character of the new Ford cars remained, and the Model-A failed to compete with the lower-horsepower cars of Morris, Austin, Singer, or Standard, whether on account of design, running costs, or price. In 1928, when aggregate British motor-car production reached a record level, Ford sold fewer cars in Britain than in any year since 1913. Nevertheless, Henry Ford was confident that the Model-A would restore the company's fortunes in Europe, and the plans for Dagenham, which was to be Ford's major manufacturing centre to supply the whole of Europe—a European Detroit—were refurbished. In 1928 Jenkins was replaced by Perry, whose resourcefulness and vision in having advocated, even before his eclipse in 1918, the establishment of precisely the kind of British Ford company now envisaged, was thus eventually recognized by Henry Ford. Once more Ford's British operations were reorganized, together with important managerial changes, and this was the origin of Ford's forward momentum in the 1930s.[26]

The planning of Dagenham was predicated upon an output of 200,000 vehicles per annum, these comprising American-type models for sale throughout Europe. By 1931 the great design was in ruins, and in late 1932 this massive works was staggering under the weight of a continuing sequence of financial crises, owing in part to the Slump and the associated efflorescence of economic nationalism in vehicle-producing countries.[27] Hence the determined defence of its manufacturing rights by the British company in the face of French and German attempts to appropriate production for their own markets: hence the powerful Ford invasion of the British commercial vehicle market.[28] The total number of vehicles produced at Dagenham from 1931 to 1939 was a fraction over 600,000; of this, 65 per cent were cars, 23 per cent commercial vehicles, and no less than 12 per cent were tractors. In fact, and despite this range of products, the Dagenham works (upon which, it might be recalled, £2 m. had already been spent by early 1931 without the slightest return) even in 1934 was producing at less than one-half of its down-graded capacity of 120,000 units. In early 1932 *The Economist*, noting that 'Dagenham is on the threshold of its career as the European exemplar of Ford ideals of efficiency', added that its capabilities far exceeded the absorptive capacity of the British market.[29] This was to remain the situation for many years.[30]

Why this huge plant, embodying as it did American know-how, and a lot of imported equipment, fared so badly is a major issue. For most of the 1930s Dagenham, although hardly suffering threats to its very survival, was far from yielding lucrative returns to its owners. The central issue for Ford managers in England before the Second World War was volume, and at almost any cost. Only large-scale operations could justify the investment, for only large volume could spread overheads sufficiently for Ford to compete at all. It was for this reason, and it is a simple and obvious one, that Ford was unique amongst the more important British producers in choosing to compete primarily in terms of prices, instead of designing for a known or suspected market class. Equally it was for this reason that the English company did not offer a 'range' of models, but—if we ignore the various V-8 models—concentrated its efforts entirely at the cheapest end of the market. Here, even if the interchangeability of parts between the commercial and private lines had to be sacrificed, and even if competition was at its most severe, there was always the possibility that the vagaries of competition would be vented in changing shares of what was, after all, the most rapidly growing sector of the home market. Dagenham demanded long runs, and these were most easily accessible in the 8 hp to 10-hp categories. This was not a policy which British manufacturers, or even the General Motors' subsidiary, Vauxhall, felt inclined to emulate; and, as we shall see, there are clear signs that by the later 1930s the Ford strategy was being quickly eroded by quality competition. Nevertheless, Ford used an appropriate policy—appropriate, that is, to the singular needs imposed by its cost-structure. Only in later years, when the lag in Ford design was no longer regarded by potential customers as being more than offset by the price-differential, did Dagenham face a renewed crisis in its fortunes, caused by its dangerous and ultimately debilitating strategy.

As we have noted, the idea of a small Ford for export markets was first mooted in the 1920s and the designs for such a model were in existence in 1928. The project was discussed again in 1930. However, Sir Percival Perry was initially unconvinced that Dagenham could carry the costs of a small car and simultaneously finance the large drafts necessary to complete construction. He was therefore prepared to rely upon the small-bore version of the Model-A, the so-called Model-AF, as the main product for the European market. But by mid-1931 the self-evident could no longer be ignored, and Perry found himself confronted with stark alternatives—to court bankruptcy by continuing to produce a car neither Britain nor Europe wanted, or to find another line suitable at least for the home market, and hope for export sales. For a charge of $535,360,[31] Dearborn studied 15 European cars which were shipped across the Atlantic, and 'pretty darn quick'[32] produced 14 prototypes of a new light car which was to prove the salvation of the English subsidiary. Perry had asked for the car in October 1931. It was ready for exhibition in England in February 1932, and was in volume production by that September. The Ford Model-Y, with a 933-cc engine rated at 7·96 hp, sold as a two-door saloon for £120 in 1933. It thus competed directly with the Morris Minor and the Austin Seven, since Rootes, Standard, and Vauxhall had no cars in this class. Dearborn designed the new car, but it was left to Dagenham to arrange for its production during 1932, and output was only slowly augmented. Then from 1932 to 1933 car production increased from 12,000 to 36,500 units, and of these figures respectively 8,000 and 33,000 were Model-Y cars. In the twelve months ending 30 September 1934 the 8-hp Ford captured 56 per cent of U.K. sales of that class. The great success of the venture casts a somewhat gloomy sidelight on the abilities of experienced British firms to satisfy the requirements of their own market. The Model-Y was available as a roomy four-door saloon, with a synchromesh gearbox a year ahead of Austin, Morris, and Standard,[33] and at a price lower than comparable British cars. Ford became the third largest producer of cars virtually overnight,[34] and with an output twice the level which Rootes, Standard, or Vauxhall could achieve.

British hopes that the Model-Y might succeed abroad as well, thus providing a solution to the vital problem of output, were dashed. Sales in the protected markets of France and Italy were poor, and in 1933 the local purchase of parts in Germany began. Nor did sales of American-type cars, including the V-8 of 1932, which were produced at Dagenham, provide much relief. Much more important was Dearborn's next essay in European design, the Model-C of October 1934. This had a bigger engine, of 10 hp compared to the 8 hp of the Model-Y Popular, and in its cheapest form sold for £15 more than the Popular model. It could perhaps be seen as a response to the decline in Ford production in 1934, though since the problem in that year was firmly located in export markets this appears to be unlikely. Rather it appears as a normal process of broadening out the range to tap the enormous growth of the 10-hp class unleashed by the Hillman Minx and its Austin and Morris imitators, but at a price well below these other cars. Ford was to continue to rely on its 8-hp and 10-hp products until the war, duplicating the changes in design and specification adopted by its competitors. A four-door De Luxe saloon cost £145, but this car never seems to have sold as well as did the 8-hp Popular.

Two points of considerable interest remain to be discussed—the dramatic gesture of the £100 Popular, and the erosion of Ford car production in 1938 and 1939. The price reduction of 17 October 1935 by which Ford offered a full four-seater saloon for £100 has been examined in some depth by the historians of Ford activities outside the United States. The total cuts involved were 20 per cent. It is clear that one important cause of the cuts was the introduction of the Morris Eight at the 1934 Motor Show: this was the car which sold more units than any other produced in Britain before the Second World War.[35] As a result, total Ford sales in the U.K. during the 1934–5 season, though higher than the previous year, were only marginally so. Another cause of some significance is that between 1933–4 and 1934–5 the addition of the Model-C Ten, instead of increasing Ford's total sales, partly diverted sales from the 8-hp car. 'Dagenham, the best integrated automobile plant in Europe, needed volume if its size were to be an advantage, and now the sales of its most promising product were falling off'; its 'financial obligations could be met only by big volume production, and that production was needed at once', and without the two-year delay required to bring an entirely new model into full-scale production. By the diligence of small economies, the adoption of American purchasing techniques including detailed investigation of costs and advice to suppliers, and finally by cutting dealers' margins,[36] the price of the Popular was reduced by £5 in January 1935, by £5 in September, and at last by £10 to £100. From 1934–5 to 1935–6 Ford domestic car sales rose from 31,000 to 53,000 units:[37] of this increase, the 8-hp provided two-thirds, and although new registration statistics suggest that V-8 sales improved after the transfer of production from Canada in 1935 there is no evidence that sales of the 10-hp car fell. Again from 1935–6 to 1936–7 the increase in Model-Y sales accounted for two-thirds of the over-all increase in Ford domestic sales. It cannot be denied that the £100 saloon attained a substantial market impact, but the policy of price-cutting did not produce satisfactory profits: no vast new market had been created, contrary to the expectation which the myths of the Model-T and the Morris Cowley seemed to warrant. The cheap Ford cars were being outsold by dearer cars which offered more comfort, performance, and sometimes even individuality. As Sir Miles Thomas observed with respect to the £100 Minor, 'No one wants to keep down with the Joneses'.[38]

The Ford experience is deservedly the best-known example in our period of the pitfalls of pricing a design, rather than designing for a price. Ford car output fell by 23 per cent from 1937 to 1938, and by a further 20 per cent in 1939, a year in which four of the other five large British producers were recovering from the 1937–8 recession. [39] It may be that the dislocative effects of the war were important in the latter year, and, to be sure, a decline in export business does seem to have occurred; still, the Ford share of the total output of the Big Six fell from its peak of 22 per cent in 1937 to 19 per cent in 1938 and to 15 per cent in 1939, so that at the very least a loss of home-market dynamism must be claimed. Here we can suspect that a factor already important in the recent failure of price-competition was now to be seen in isolated operation. The improvement in competitors' cars, dating from the Morris Eight of 1934, and carrying on through the Series-E Eight of 1939, the Austin Ten of 1937 and the Eight of 1939, the Standard Eight of 1938, and the Vauxhall Ten-Four of 1938, simply presented a challenge with which Ford prices and redesign could not cope.

(D) CHANGING STRUCTURE OF DEMAND AND ENTREPRENEURIAL INITIATIVES

Simultaneous with Ford's resurrection was the relative decline of Morris and Austin which Maxcy and Silberston attribute to several causes: the shift in demand to small-horsepower models, in part the result of a fall in real incomes during the Slump, and concurrent increases in taxation; increased competition, especially from the American-owned companies of Ford and Vauxhall; an emphasis on rapid model change and a wide range of models; and finally, management difficulties.[40] It seems extremely unrealistic to consider the shift in consumer preference for cars up to 10 hp, which was in part due to the Slump, as independent of the policies of competing firms.[41]

Amongst the largest firms, Austin, which suffered less than Morris from the changing structure of demand, was not the only large firm to have been offering a small car when the change occurred. Singer, one of the three biggest producers in 1929, had pioneered the small economy car before 1914, but despite aspirations to mass production failed to exploit this advantage. Similarly, Standard had been one of the first to manufacture this kind of car, but had long since discontinued production when the character of the market began to change. Then came the decision of Standard's managers to re-enter the small-car market, which meant, in effect, the introduction of a new car to accord with motor-car design and technology of the late 1920s. Hillman had also produced a light car, of 9 hp, before World War I and immediately following the war had specialized in the 9-hp and 11-hp models, but these had been discontinued in favour of the 14-hp car on which Hillman's post-war reputation was established.[42] Introduced after the acquisition of the Hillman-Humber combine by the Rootes brothers, the Minx was an entirely new car designed to appeal to economy-minded buyers in the new 10-hp class. There was thus little 'accidental' about the emergence of Standard and Hillman among the Big Six at this time.[43]

The shift in demand to small-horsepower models benefited those firms which recognized or anticipated the trend towards cars of this type even before the Slump intensified the trend so strongly that it became clear to all. The vehicle registration data show that the average horsepower of newly registered cars was falling from 1926–7 and the evidence of the tax returns for earlier years shows this to have been a continuation of a trend dating from 1922 at the latest.[44]

The significance of the success of the small popular economy car, and the roles of Singer and Standard as well as Austin in its commercial development, become clear when we recognize that the growth in the sales of very small cars during the Slump was a response to lower incomes, which gave impetus to the desire for motoring economy. Total sales to new owners fell violently during the Slump, and not until the continuing fall in car prices and real motoring costs began to interact with the well-known rise in real incomes of the 1930s was a new phase of market expansion unleashed. In trying to develop their lower-powered models in the later 1920s Singer and Standard were seeking to overcome two serious discontinuities in the growth of the home market. First, from 1925 till 1932, total domestic sales showed no sustained expansion, although they proved stable in the face of depression. Secondly, within this over-all stagnation, the only sector of the market which proved to be expansible was that of cars up to 10 hp. Sales of such models increased from 38,000 units in 1926–7 to 60,000 in 1928–9 and to 69,000 in 1931–2.[45] The policies of

Singer, Standard, and later Hillman, were not simply responses to this movement: they helped to create it, and were rather reactions against a market situation which in 1929 elicited a prediction from the author of the yearbook of the Society of Motor Manufacturers and Traders that home-market saturation (the point at which new-owner sales fall to zero, so that new cars are sold only to maintain the existing stock) was imminent.[46] Although it was in a sense accidental that the Austin Seven preserved that company from a fall in sales as large as that faced by Morris Motors Ltd. during the Slump, it was not fortuitous that Standard and Hillman gained most during this period. It is important to recognize this fact for a fuller understanding of the dynamics of the British motor industry between the wars.

Clearly, increased competition from the American companies was important, but it is also relevant to emphasize the relative failure of Ford's management policies in the British market before 1931 and the reasons for them, for although that company had access to the vast financial and technical resources and production experience of the American parent company it was not until after managerial reorganization that Ford made a marked impact. The context of developing world depression was conducive to radical policy changes by both Ford and General Motors, but no simple superiority of American methods and resources can explain the timing and intensity of competition between the British firms and the American subsidiaries. Constraints on its financial resources, despite eventual profitability, were the major brake upon Austin's response to Ford's competition. Nevertheless, the Austin Ten, introduced in 1932, enabled the company to withstand competition better than Morris, until the latter's recovery in 1935. That recovery had much to do with the resolution of internal strife produced by 'some uncertainty in management' to which Lord Nuffield's biographers tactfully refer,[47] but which since then has been amplified by Sir Miles Thomas in his autobiography.[48] His account, together with remarks made by other contemporaries, suggests that management problems and policies were probably more important than other factors (for examples, the ill luck in not producing a viable baby car when the shift in demand occurred)[49] in explaining Morris's relative decline during the early 1930s.

(E) THE NUFFIELD RESPONSE: EROSION OF LEADERSHIP

By 1929 Morris was apparently firmly established as the biggest British car producer, although the output at Cowley in that year was little better than the level of two years before. In fact, the company was on the threshold of a sustained production and managerial crisis which would have broken a less well-established and financially robust enterprise. The root of the problem is not difficult to identify: the evolution of the home market demanded—for the first time in its history—that the core of Morris' empire, the Cowley works, face up to the prospect of creating a second generation of volume-selling models from scratch. And, as Lord Nuffield's biographers admit, Cowley was ill equipped to perform this task. Certainly the prospect was made more daunting by two complicating factors: the misreading, in the later 1920s, of the development of the home-market structure and a series of executive conflicts triggered off by the company's dismal performance during the Slump. Between 1926 and 1929 Morris Motors developed five new models. Morris himself was anxious to build up the export side of his business, and this required the production of larger engines than were appropriate to the changing domestic market. Although Thomas, Morris' Sales Manager, had pressed for the introduction of a small car to compete with the thriving Austin Seven it was two years before the rapid recuperation of Austin convinced Morris that such a car was needed. The result was the Morris Minor in 1928, which was priced identically with the Seven. Moreover, in the light of subsequent developments at Cowley, it is instructive to note that the Minor engine was designed, and initially produced, at the Wolseley plant in Birmingham— which had also produced the unsuccessful 15·9-hp Empire car of 1927.[50] But the 11·9 h.p. Cowley was still Morris Motors' bread and butter line, and the sales of this car collapsed during the early 1930s as powerful competition from cars of a lower taxable capacity commenced. From 1929 to 1932 Morris Motors introduced four more new (or revised) models, but in 1933 Cowley produced a mere 44,000 units, one-third fewer than 1929, and very little better than the Slump year of 1931—yet from 1932 to 1933 U.K. production of private cars increased by 20 per cent. Worse, Morris Motors' trading profit crashed from £1·167 m. in 1929 to £0·343 m. in 1933—a drop of 71 per cent.

After the formation of the public company, Morris Motors Ltd., in 1926, and the acquisition of Wolseley in 1927, William Morris had become increasingly preoccupied with minor technical details, besides showing a tendency to shun Board meetings, exhibiting a predilection for taking decisions without consultation, and apparently embarking on an undeclared policy of pitting the constituent companies within the organization in competition against each other.[51] Such behaviour intensified as the external pressures on the firm increased, and several key managers—men who had greatly contributed to the expansion of the 1920s—such as F. G. Woollard, A. A. Rowse, and E. H. Blake left in disillusion.[52]

The Morris group responded to these crises in four ways, of which only one —the bewildering array of new models—was clearly unproductive. Much more important were the policies associated with the career of L. P. Lord as Managing Director from 1933 to 1936. Lord was an able production engineer who had remained in Coventry with Hotchkiss when it became Morris Engines Ltd., and had since thoroughly reorganized Wolseley for the production of the 847-cc power unit for the Minor. Impressed both with the effectiveness and with the rapidity of Lord's work at Wolseley, and at last alarmed by the decay in the vitality of his creation, Nuffield conceded to Lord complete control at Cowley. There, the appearance of the forceful outsider, who undertook to stay until Morris once more outsold Austin, did prove to be the turning-point.[53] During Lord's tenure at Cowley progress was made in three directions: the reorganization amongst companies in the group; the generation of the capacity to create and—vitally—to go on creating new models with a clear market orientation; and the adoption of a new, rationalized, and complementary marketing strategy for the group as a whole. In comparison to these, the proliferation of short-lived models, which was after all a common response to disappointing sales in the motor industry in the 1930s, merits summary treatment. In the case of Morris Motors, it mostly involved small-selling six-cylinder models. Worse, the explosion of models and variants infected the *other* members of the group. Table 9.1 demonstrates the problem, and its eventual resolution; the comparative data for Austin and Ford show a similar movement, but one much more restricted in scope.

TABLE 9.1

The Big Three: Number of Different Models and Engine Capacities Produced (Model Years)

	1929	*1931*	*1933*	*1935*	*1937*	*1939*
Nuffield:						
1 Basic Models	13	16	23	22	15	17
2 Engines	10	8	12	18	8	10
Austin:						
1 Basic Models	4	4	7	7	7	8
2 Engines	4	4	7	9	6	7
Ford:						
1 Basic Models*	2	2	4	3	4	4
2 Engines	2	2	4	3	4	4
(* Different Models[1]	1	1	3	3	3	3)

[1] i.e. different chassis, by disregarding of different engine options (e.g. the A and AF models) or utility models.
Source: Fletcher & Son Ltd., *Motor Car Index, 1928–1939* (reprinted Brighton, 1964).

New models were not enough:[54] although during 1934, partly as a result of this frantic model-floating, the output and profits of Morris Motors Ltd. began to recover, already Lord's second line of attack was developing. Production reorganization and integration were long overdue. The haphazard structure produced by internal expansion and undigested acquisition in the 1920s was extensively reformed. At Cowley in 1933–4 layout and equipment were completely reconstructed, with £300,000 being spent in 1934 alone. Central to the productive strategy were assembly-line techniques, with a moving track and the supply of components by supplementary conveyor systems. Of course, this required the redesign of some models to fit them to the new technique and, cognate to this, specialization in component supply within the group was extended.

In late 1934 the first important product of the new regime was introduced; the Morris Eight was to prove Cowley's first best seller since the heyday of the Morris-Cowley.[55] But after the initial decision to market such a car, Nuffield himself took no part either in its design or in the organization of its production.[56] In the following year Morris Motors developed its range of Series II models, including a number of short-lived six-cylinder cars. The introduction of the Series III two years later did not prevent the group suffering a severe set-back in the recession of 1937–8, but 1939 resulted in a record profit, and record levels of output were being attained before the war. For this the continued emergence of new models, with carefully gauged design and price targets, was crucial—for example, the redesigned Series-E Eight and the new unitary construction Ten of the summer of 1939.

Yet the revival of Nuffield's fortunes lay not only in the obvious facts of new models and a new productive integration; for the group also went over to a novel sales strategy aiming at the common use of components by the different marques within the group,[57] the presentation of complementary lines by these marques, and a superficially radical attempt to break away from the dislocative syndrome of supplying new models (or variations on a basic theme) for successive seasons. Here the idea was simple: to stabilize production over the year as a whole by publicizing a policy of 'continuous improvement', coupled with infrequent changes involving total redesign. This policy, known as 'Series production', was introduced during 1935, as reference to the models mentioned above will indicate. For 1936 and 1937 the whole Morris range, except for the Series I-Eight, were termed Series II. For 1938, when the Eight was relabelled Series II, the rest of the range, comprising only four models, were called Series-III models. Nuffield himself regarded the scheme as a success, as in a seasonal sense it may have been; but the barely unabated flux of models in the very late 1930s casts doubts on its value as a mechanism for embodying continuous improvement.[58] Equally instructive were the methods used to secure long runs of production of components, by sharing them amongst the several marques, as had always been the case so far as the use of Morris components for M.G. cars was concerned.

It has not been our intention to imply that the Nuffield group was even close to foundering. Even in its worst years, the 1930s, it was only overtaken as the leading car producer in one year, and after the rigours of the Lord administration the company achieved production levels only Opel could rival in Europe. But the history of Morris Motors Ltd. does raise in acute form questions about the determinants of long-term viability in the motor industry —for, in a meaningful sense, a modern production unit was only created in the 1930s, not during the burgeoning years of the previous decade. To historians the problem of succession looms large in this company. On the one hand, there was a need to replace an ageing best seller with a sequence of accurately targeted products. Not until 1934 was Morris Motors capable of fully replacing the pre-war model, and no other general vehicle producer of the period shared the extent of this group's output instability. On the other hand, there was the question of replacing a still-dominating founder, whose energies were more and more diverted to eleemosynary and leisure pursuits and later still to rearmament. Indeed, the revival of the firm, which by 1939 offers the historian an image of commercial and financial health, technological modernity, and market acumen, was largely achieved with Lord Nuffield *in absentio* by L. P. Lord and Oliver Boden.[59] After creating the original management team responsible for the striking success of the Morris-Cowley, he proved incapable of retaining his best men, and especially of fostering managerial cohesion in the face of rapid growth and of the complex problems of a large organization.[60] Such failures were crucial, for in an industrial context which offered less and less scope for the luck of the gambler, his own talents were narrow and increasingly suspect and therefore it was upon the effectiveness of his administration and his willingness to concede managerial control while retaining personal ownership that his own continued prestige within the industry depended. Sir Miles Thomas recalled that Nuffield's interests grew 'at a rate faster than his personal capacity to handle that type of business. He remained a mechanic, whereas [the firm] demanded engineering ability and directorship'.[61]

There is ample evidence of a situation almost approaching managerial anarchy which developed after the acquisition of Wolseley. From 1927 Nuffield allowed his apparent antipathy towards Cowley to generate resentment and intrigue among managers which his own personal relations, amounting in some cases to jealousy, did nothing to improve.[62] One result was that some began to take independent action, for example in the design and building of the prototype 1932 Morris 10-hp car. Intersubsidiary rivalry was intensified further by Nuffield's inability to give clear orders, and when he did make decisions they were typically without forethought, by hunch, and often arbitrary.[63] These failings were not helped at all by his geographical isolation in Oxford away from the main manufacturing centre of the industry, which in the opinion of one senior manager helped to explain his insular approach to the business and his preference for internal promotion.[64] There is little evidence of such managerial disarray either at Longbridge, ruled continuously since 1922 by a long-established triumvirate of mutually respectful professional men with a fully participating, albeit conservative, Chairman at its head, or at Dagenham where the problems of the corporate structure had been tackled and, to some extent, solved. Thus, even by the Slump Nuffield's entrepreneurial flair, the classic combination of a sense of market potential and the knack for its effective exploitation, proved insufficient to sustain his reputation as one of Britain's most effective business leaders.

(F) PRODUCT DIFFERENTIATION, PRICING, AND THE ROLE OF INDIVISIBILITIES

One of the factors cited by Maxcy and Silberston to explain the changing fortunes of the motor manufacturers is the growing emphasis in this period upon rapid model changes and a widening range of models. Reflecting a trend away from standardization, a corollary of product differentiation was the presence of diseconomies due to the expense of retooling for model changes and short production runs. This, we have suggested, was a response to the difficulties of car makers in search of new sales leaders. It applied to each of the Big Six firms, though clearly, owing to the sheer size of Morris and Austin for most of the period, it would seem reasonable to suppose that long production runs of a single popular model—the Cowley and the Seven—could have offered those economies of large-scale production which resulted from the existence of indivisibilities. Given the limited size of the British market one might have expected production of the Cowley or the Seven to have provided Morris or Austin with the economic basis for securing and retaining an even greater degree of dominance in the popular car market than they did; and yet the Big Three of Austin, Ford, and the Nuffield group were always under pressure from a number of unstable yet active secondary producers. Thus Singer and Clyno in the 1920s and Standard, Vauxhall, and Rootes from the early 1930s succeeded in sharing the popular market with them at the expense of the smaller producers in the late 1920s and early 1930s and later to the cost of the Big Three themselves (Table 9.2).

TABLE 9.2

Percentages of British Production of Private Cars

	1929	*1932*	*1935*	*1938*
Austin	25	27	23	21
Ford	4	6	17	18
Nuffield	35	33	31	23
Big Three Total	64	67	71	62
Rootes, Standard, and Vauxhall	8	23	23	31
All Others	28	10	6	8

Sources: These estimates have been obtained by applying the individual percentage shares in Big Six production (G. Maxcy and A. Silberston, *The Motor Industry*, London, 1959, Table 2, p. 107) to Maxcy's earlier estimates for the shares of 'Austin and Morris' and 'Ford and Vauxhall' in total British production (P. L. Cook and R. Cohen (eds.), *Effects of Mergers*, London, 1958, Table IV, p. 380). The results are very close to our own estimates, which were used in the preparation of Graph 1.

Our evidence, which warns against exaggeration of the extent of indivisibilities in the British motor industry before the mid-1930s, is consistent with what we know of the organization of production on the part of the major firms.[65] Firstly, the advanced deployment of machinery on a line system to achieve a high degree of continuity in production was possible for annual output levels of 10,000 cars in the late 1920s, and moving assembly lines were exceptional in the British industry.[66] In 1931 G. S. Davidson stressed that the Morris system of quantity flow production differed from mass production in that it involved many separate operations needing time for efficient completion rather than providing maximum output at the greatest speed.[67] The technical indivisibilities in motor manufacturing before the mid-1930s were, in all probability, considerably less than in subsequent years.[68] Secondly, the general and heavy use of bought-out supplies of component parts gave access to the productive economies generated by external, specialist producers. The absolute extent of dependence on such specialists is far from clear. The evidence of the Censuses of Production, as used by Barna,[69] does not distinguish *internal* transfers of parts between different establishments in common ownership from purchases from independent firms, whether in the same or a different trade. Thus Barna estimated that in 1935 56 per cent of the home-produced value of the motor and cycle industry was accounted for by purchases of components and materials, but of the total value involved (£91 m.), after deduction of imports and unallocated expenditures, over £36 m. came from other establishments in the motor and cycle trades,[70] which quite often could be separate departments of the same company. Firmer evidence is provided by the P.E.P. report on the motor industry, which gives two examples of the costs of production of typical cars made by different firms in 1938.[71] For one, bought-out components were responsible for 58 per cent of such costs, and 74 per cent if materials were included. For the other, these items together absorbed 63 per cent of production costs: a somewhat lower level, to be sure, but still high in itself. Variations in the degree of integration between major producers were important, and so too were the opportunities to tap the external economies available; but a further implication of the P.E.P. report is that such externalities were large by the mid-1930s.[72] The enhanced flexibility of organization permitted to all firms by the structure of the industry thus made the specific performance of the main competitors more a function of individual financial resources, design, and business policies.

There is some validity in the stress placed by Maxcy and Silberston upon external factors to explain the changing relative importance of the car producers, but the implication of our research is that the dynamics of the car trade were such that internal factors played much more than a subsidiary role. Examination of the profitability of the major producers[73] reveals little more than that Ford, the mass producer *par excellence*, experienced markedly lower earnings than either of the other two big producers, whilst the market shares obtained by the Big Three separately (Table 9.2) demonstrate no consistent pattern save the diminution in their total share of production, and indeed of their ootput volume, in the later 1930s. This trend itself casts further doubt on the significance of internal economies of scale as a guarantee of dominance over time. What they could do was to provide low-cost production, but as Ford's sales and profit experience showed, low-cost production and price competition only ensured survival with unstable sales and low profitability. The success of Austin and Morris, though marred, like Ford, by instability, is explicable in entrepreneurial terms. For despite their respective shortcomings, Lord Nuffield, Sir Herbert Austin, and L. P. Lord understood the British car market in which non-price competition was the key both to buoyant, if erratic, sales and high profitability owing to scale economies. On the side of demand, the income-elasticity for the output of all producers taken together was high, and in addition the average price elasticities for the products of individual companies were similarly high, so that individual growth appears to have been narrowly based in terms of profitable models, and the obvious instability of profits was the by-product of any lag in evolving a new sales leader. Hence the emphasis on model specification comfort, performance, and even limited individuality, which was sedulously cultivated by big and small firms alike, in order to protect sales by the deliberate creation of market imperfections—to minimize price-elasticity and to maximize goodwill and the brand image of over-all value.

On the supply side, the effects of indivisibilities in creating cost barriers to new entry appear to have posed much less of a problem to aspirants in the inter-war years than is commonly supposed. This claim receives support not only from the companies' profit figures, but also from the small discrepancy which existed between the prices of popular cars produced by the Big Three and their smaller competitors.[74] Furthermore, we have argued that the volume threshold at which economies of scale began to operate was relatively low, and that the structure of motor-car production was such as to make all car manufacturers similarly dependent on external parts. This, together with the imperfections in the competitive market for cars, combined to produce a climate in which the access to the top table was always a possibility, even at the expense of the Big Three. Clyno and Singer in the 1920s made such a bid but failed to sustain their momentum. In the 1930s Standard, Vauxhall, and Rootes intensified their efforts and achieved much more, as the doubling of their combined share of Big Six car production from 17 per cent in 1930 to 34 per cent in 1939 shows.[75] Both internal and external factors explain why the opportunity for the secondary producers to join the Big Three continued to exist. For central to the dynamics of the motor industry was the process of competition by design, by which mechanism those improvements in product convenience and reliability, so decisive to the creation of the mass market, were generalized. None of the larger enterprises was capable of dominating all sectors of the market simultaneously, and experienced discontinuous progress based upon a few best sellers. The solution to the problem of retaining a continuously successful model, let alone of a composite range of market leaders, eluded them all.

NOTES

1 This chapter forms a part of the results of our research into the motor industry financed partly by the Houblon Norman Trust, the Nuffield Foundation, and the Research Fund of the University of Birmingham. We are grateful for the co-operation extended by those in the motor industry who made available to us the archives of the Austin and Ford Motor companies; to Elizabeth Brunner of the University of Lancaster, who allowed us to consult notes assembled in preparation for her joint publication with the late P. W. S. Andrews, *The Life of Lord Nuffield* (Oxford, 1955); and to Lord Thomas of Remenham, formerly Sales Manager at Morris Motors and the Nuffield organization, who in addition to allowing us to interview him, commented on the final draft.

2 Including the engineering, shipbuilding, and vehicle trades.

3 The net output of the motor and cycle trades (defined as firms employing more than 10 persons on average) increased substantially, from £40·6 m. in 1924 to £45·0 m. in 1930 and to £55·5 m. in 1935. The net output of all other sectors of the engineering group, excluding motors, cycles, and repairing, increased only from £153·7 m. in 1924 to £176·3 m. in 1930 and to £184·9 m. in 1935.

4 R. Stone and D. A. Rowe, *The Measurement of Consumers' Expenditure and Behaviour in the United Kingdom, 1920–1938* (Cambridge, 1966), ii, Table 24, p. 58.

5 L. Rostas, in his *Comparative Productivity in British and American Industry* (Cambridge, 1948), Table 97(a), p. 171, estimated that the annual output of motor vehicles per operative increased by 25·5 per cent from 1924 to 1930, but by 56·3 per cent in the shorter period from 1930 to 1935.

6 G. Maxcy and A. Silberston, *The Motor Industry* (London, 1959), p. 107.

7 *The Life of Lord Nuffield.*

8 The following brief account of the Austin Motor Company is based on the Minute Books of that company and the biography written by Z. E. Lambert and R. J. Wyatt, *Lord Austin the Man* (London, 1968).

9 *Who's Who in the Motor Trade* (1934), p. 44.

10 *The Times*, 19 Sept. 1925. G.M.C. went on to purchase Vauxhall Motors Ltd. instead.

11 C. R. F. Engelbach, 'Some Notes on Reorganizing a Works to Increase Production', *Proceedings of the Institute of Automobile Engineers*, xxiii (1927–8), 498.

12 *The Times*, 21 Aug. 1926, 8 Jan. 1927, 9 July 1927. A total of £727,000 had to be written off assets in 1926.

13 Austin Motor Co., *Austin Through the Years* (n.p., n.d.); *Autocar*, 3 Feb. 1928; Austin Minute Book (The Austin Motor Company Ltd., Longbridge, Birmingham), 28 Aug. 1929.

14 M. Sedgwick, *Passenger Cars, 1924–1942* (London, 1975), p. 137. The conservatism referred to is not Sir Herbert's well-known political affiliation, but the tardiness of the company in accepting advanced design features, in contrast with Morris.

15 Loc. cit.

16 Our estimates, but equal to that implied for 1932 by Maxcy, 'The Motor Industry', in Cook and Cohen (eds.), op. cit., Table IV, p. 380.

17 This model is discussed in considerable detail by R. J. Wyatt, *The Motor for the Million: The Austin Seven, 1922–1939* (London, 1968).

18 Sir Miles Thomas's foreword in Lambert and Wyatt, op. cit., pp. 8–12, and by interview.

19 Lord told Sir Miles Thomas, at that time a senior executive with Nuffield, that with Longbridge as his base his intention was to take Cowley apart 'brick by bloody brick', as he had, of course, earlier done from the inside, though then as a constructive rather than a destructive exercise.

20 Mira Wilkins and Frank Ernest Hill, *American Business Abroad. Ford on Six Continents* (Detroit, 1964).

21 Ford Archives (Ford Motor Company, Detroit), ACC. 6B260.

22 Ford Archives, ACC. 572, Box 18, 13 Dec. 1923.

23 When Klann arrived in Manchester, Gould, the manager in charge, avoided him. 'After waiting three weeks for an interview I busted the door open and here he was with his feet on top of the desk drinking tea and reading the morning paper.' Klann also discovered that Gould and the other main manager, Davis, were not on speaking terms. The under-manager in charge of body-building, an Englishman called Tom Gorst, objected to Klann's suggestions that he wear overalls instead of red flannel shirt, dickey, and cuffs, explaining that he was a carriage-builder by trade. Klann's reply was 'tomorrow you are going to build *cars*'. (Ford Archives, Oral History Section, Sept. 1955. Reminiscences of W. C. Klann, vol. 2, pp. 172–3.)

24 This responsibility was not acknowledged by Kanzler and Sorenson to whom Klann and Gehl reported back and Kanzler dismissed the American managers in Manchester as 'a bunch of clowns'. Wilkins and Hill, op. cit., p. 141.

25 *Autocar*, 7 Mar. 1924; *Motor Trader*, 16 July 1924; *Ford Times*, 19 Dec. 1924. The McKenna duty pushed Ford in the same direction.

26 A handful of key managers who had been with Perry at Ford before 1918 were re-appointed by Perry. (*Ford Times*, Nov. 1933, p. 630.)

27 Against which Perry railed at the 1933 company meeting. He noted that the original conception was that Dagenham should export four-fifths of its private and commercial vehicle output, as well as 90 per cent of the tractor output recently transferred from Cork. (*The Economist*, 24 June 1933.)

28 This pattern had emerged in the previous decade, as the Model-T was squeezed out of the car market, so that sales of commercial variants preponderated. (*The Economist*, 16 Apr. 1932.)

29 *The Economist*, 9 Apr. 1932.

30 In Ford's best pre-war year, 1937, only 113,000 units of all types were produced. On its books, the company had land, buildings, and plant valued at £5 m. in 1931, and at over £9 m. in the peak year of 1937. On the operations of this gigantic complex of factories, to which associated works were added by Briggs Motor Bodies Ltd. and the Kelsey-Hayes Wheel Co., Ford earned £2·75 m. gross in 1939, but for no other years was the profit much over £1·5 m. With respect to net profits, the best year of the 1930s (excluding 1939 because of distortion caused by the war) was as early as 1933, when net profits stood at £0·756 m. Of this, £0·444 m. was provided by profits on foreign exchange transactions, and otherwise net profits remained low in the face of a rapid accretion of charges for depreciation.

31 Reduced to $210,000 as an emergency measure to help stem the haemorrhage of Dagenham finances in late 1932. Wilkins and Hill, p. 245.

32 The Chief Engineer at Dearborn, quoted ibid., p. 239.

33 Sedgwick, op. cit., p. 279.

34 Even in 1932–3 the Model-Y was produced in larger numbers than any other comparable British model. (*Ford Times*, Nov. 1933, p. 630.)

35 And this was why it became a price-leader, the target of an optimal combination of design and price upon which other producers attempted to converge (see Maxcy and Silberston, op. cit., p. 106). But whether other manufacturers could have competed on Dagenham's own terms, by price, remains open to question; and we remain unconvinced that they could, at least in the mid-1930s.

36 Only a slight reduction was involved, although dealers complained of even this (Wilkins and Hill, p. 302), but this aspect still invites comparison with the equally famous Morris price-reduction of February 1921, which was similarly an attempt to grow out of trouble. On that occasion, roughly one-quarter of the price-cuts for the Cowley two- and four-seater, and as much as 70 per cent of the much smaller reductions for the Oxford two- and four-seater, were obtained by the device of a reduction in distributors' margins from 17½ to 15 per cent. These figures have been computed from Andrews and Brunner, op. cit., pp. 100–1.

37 Achieving U.K. market shares of 11·5 per cent and 17·5 per cent respectively. Data from the Ford Motor Co.

38 Sir Miles Thomas, *Out on a Wing* (London, 1964), p. 168.

39 There seems to be little need to invoke in explanation, as do Wilkins and Hill, p. 304, the recession of 1937–8 (which itself did not seriously reduce the Ford percentage share of the home market), the flood of dumped German cars (which reached a peak in 1937 and ebbed quickly thereafter), or even the grave political uncertainty of these years—let alone the adverse publicity of Henry Ford's acceptance of a medal from Hitler's Germany in 1938 (cf. ibid., pp. 282 and 308).

40 Maxcy and Silberston, p. 107.

41 A convenient source for the changing structure of the home market is the table provided by Andrews and Brunner, p. 187, of the percentage distribution of new registrations by taxable horsepower.

42 *Automobiles of the World* (1921), pp. 149–50; Pollitt Papers 263/21 (in the possession of Mr. D. C. Feild, for whose assistance the authors are most grateful); G. S. Davison, *At the Wheel* (London, 1931), p. 103.

43 'Whether by accident or design' Hillman and Standard 'probably owed their success to the shift in demand'. (Maxcy and Silberston, p. 108.)

44 E. J. B. Sieve, 'British Motor Vehicle Exports' (unpub. Univ. of London Ph.D thesis, 1950), ii, Table 14.

45 These developments are discussed at greater length in our unpublished article, The Growth and Instability of the Motor Industry in Britain between the Wars, to appear in N. K. Buxton and D. H. Aldcroft (eds.), *Instability and Industrial Development, 1919–1939*

46 Society of Motor Manufacturers and Trades, *The Motor Industry of Great Britain* (London, 1929), p. 45.

47 Andrews and Brunner, p. 195.

48 Thomas, *op. cit.*

49 Maxcy and Silberston consider Austin to have been 'more fortunate' in this particular respect: 'Probably it was this more than anything else that was responsible for the smaller decline in Austin's share as compared with that of Morris' (pp. 107–8).

50 Thomas, p. 157, and Andrews and Brunner, Notes.

51 Cf. Thomas, p. 142. Morris 'liked to spur people to bigger efforts by telling them of the shortcomings of one of their colleagues. It was a peculiar technique.'

52 Ibid., p. 179, and by interview. Andrews and Brunner, pp. 195–6.

53 One senior manager recalled that Lord Nuffield had walked into Lord's office at Wolseley and said: 'I want you at Cowley. Things are in a mess there'. Andrews and Brunner, Notes.

54 Nor was price-cutting. It is obvious that the Morris policy noted by *The Economist* of 2 Apr. 1932, of meeting competition by reducing prices to the limits imposed by the dictates of prudence, implied a degree of living off fat which even a firm so flushed with reserves as Morris Motors could not indefinitely sustain. The best-known example of price-cutting by the group is the £100 Minor two-seater of 1931. Of this, Morris himself commented that it was 'the first commercially successfully British car to sell at the round figure of £100' (*The Economist*, 25 Apr. 1931, p. 910). This is valid only in the restricted sense that the antecedent Minor was a success: it is not correct in its implication that the £100 variant sold well. Thomas comments that 'actual buyers wanted something that showed that they had *not* bought the cheapest product offered' (p. 168).

55 In its first eleven months, 50,000 units were sold; in under two years, 100,000; by spring 1938, over 200,000, and by July of that year, 250,000. The Eight came to dominate a market which others had already cultivated.

56 Though Nuffield was worried about the development of the Eight, according to one senior manager responsible for its production, his precise contribution to its creation and development was limited to a general insistence that it had to be right when it was put on the market, and making available, without question, all the money Lord required. (Andrews and Brunner, Notes.)

57 A good example of this is provided by the number of engines used by the three car marques in the group before the acquisition of Riley in 1938. Together these sold models with eighteen different cubic capacities in 1935. By 1938 there were only eight different sizes.

All engines used by M.G. were shared with other members of the group, Morris listed only one unique size, and Wolseley only two. And see Table 9,1

58 We have referred to the Series-production idea as 'superficially radical' because it had been a part of Austin policy for many years. See *Motor*, 18 Sept. 1928: 'The Austin policy has been, at least during recent years, to incorporate refinements in the standard products of the company as soon as they appear desirable, and not to wait until the Olympia Show, to bring out what are popularly known as "yearly models".'

59 This is particularly ironic in view of Nuffield's later criticism of absentee managers of whom he said 'nothing is more pernicious to sound business'. (W. R. Morris, 'Policies that Built the Morris Motor Business', *Journal of Industrial Economics*, i (1954), 205.)

60 Cf. Thomas, p. 159. 'After the early nineteen thirties it is fair to say that insofar as the actual business of designing and making motor cars and trucks was concerned Sir William Morris . . . played little or no creative part. He would give vent to a considerable amount of negative criticism. But that was all.' Sir Miles considered the formation of Morris Motors (1926) Ltd. and the acquisition of Wolseley in 1927 to be important turning-points in Morris's life (ibid., p. 157).

61 Referring to the years from 1927 to 1939, Sir Miles added that Nuffield 'began to get a sort of psychological conflict with himself, because he knew the business was slipping out of his control, and he made rather desperate efforts to call the thing back into his own control, every now and then'.

62 Andrews and Brunner, Notes.

63 Sir Miles Thomas recalled that Morris 'had the idea that he had a god-given gift of indicating his wishes by so much as a smile and a nod. And his organization would put it into effect and implement it in the way he wanted. It did not work.'

64 Andrews and Brunner, Notes.

65 Morris had always been basically an assembly firm, but even Austin, usually considered to have been essentially a manufacturing enterprise, bought in 55 per cent of the net sales value of Longbridge production in 1931 (Austin Minute Book, 12 Oct. 1931). By that time the proportion of bought-in components by Morris was in all probability not dissimilar, given Barna's national estimates (see below n. 69).

66 In 1928 Longbridge became the first British factory with a 'mechanically driven' track for the assembly of chassis and car bodies. Engelbach, *op.cit.*, p. 517; *The Times, British Motor Supplement*, 12 March 1929.

67 Davison, op. cit., p. 85. Similarly, a report on 'the Automobile Situation in the World and Europe in 1927', by Carl Hicks and G. D. Babcock to the President of the Dodge Motor Corporation, after fulsome praise of the factories and machinery of Citroën and Opel, was ambiguous in its comments on the Cowley plant where the machinery was 'more complicated' than anywhere else ever visited either in Europe or the U.S. (Mss. Detroit Public Library).

68 R. Wild, 'The Origins and Development of Flowline Production', *Industrial Archaeology*, xi, 1 (1974).

69 T. Barna, 'The Interdependence of the British Economy', *Journal of the Royal Statistical Society*, cxv, Pt. 1 (1952).

70 Ibid., Table 7, pp. 52–3.

71 *Political and Economic Planning*, Engineering Reports, ii, Motor Vehicles (1950), Table 35, p. 132.

72 Ibid., p. 133, where the evidence of Rostas, op. cit. is interpreted to mean that the British industry was much further behind in assembly work than in the actual production of the parts assembled. 'In 1935 physical output per operative in components manufacture appears to have been almost half the American level, compared with about a fifth in assembly' (P.E.P., op. cit., p. 133). Rostas estimated the number of vehicles assembled per operative per annum for 1935 to be 6 in the U.K. and 30 in the U.S.A. (Table 100, p. 173), a ratio of 1:5 compared with a ratio of 1:3 for aggregate output per operative (Table 98, p. 171). By deduction of assembly workers from the total number of operatives employed, an estimate of the number of cars (i.e. sets of parts) produced by non-assembly workers can be reached.   73 Maxcy and Silberston, Table 6, p. 160.

74 See Charts I and II in Maxcy and Silberston, pp. 101 and 104.

75 Ibid., Table 2, p. 107.

10

Business Implications of Technical Developments in the Glass Industry, 1945-1965: A Case-Study

T. C. BARKER

ECONOMIC historians have long appreciated the importance of technical invention. Indeed, the original approach to industrialization was largely in terms of new machines and processes rather than via investment and organization. Historians have not, however, gone on to use business records to study these inventions in further detail in order to see how they were financed and over what period, when they began to make money—and how much. For the most part, detailed writing about technical matters has been left to scientists and technologists, who have usually been concerned with development up to the point where new machines and processes worked but not necessarily to the stage where they produced a satisfactory return on capital. Papers on these matters appear in learned scientific journals, written in language which non-specialists often find hard to follow. There they languish, largely unconsulted by historians and unrelated to the economic events which were their *raison d'être*. Economists, in particular, do not venture much into this field for, as Jewkes, Sawers, and Stillerman put it in their standard work on the subject, *The Sources of Invention* (p. 19), 'the subject is not one to which economic analysis is easily applied; it may yet prove impossible to apply it so. And the descriptive economist finds his way blocked by the complexity of the subject'. Even they pay little attention to the development of inventions though the second edition of their book (1969) contains a revealing table (pp. 214–16) showing the time and cost involved in developing a number of major inventions; but development as such was not their main concern.

Here is clearly an important area for the attention of the business historian, with access to the relevant records. What light can be shed on the element of serendipity in technical advance? Or upon the coincidence of the development period with years of prosperity in the company concerned? Or the need, in the case of major inventions, of massive research facilities? Is it possible for a historian to master the mass of scientific and technical data anyway? This chapter seeks to investigate one such invention, the Pilkington Float process, in an attempt to indicate answers to some of these questions. Now licensed the world over, because of its lower costs it is rapidly replacing existing methods of making plate and window glass not only in Britain but also elsewhere. In 1975–6 it contributed the major part of Pilkington's £20m. licensing income. It is certainly one of the major inventions of the post-war period. The time has not yet arrived to publish the full story with customary detail and annotation; but even an abbreviated and abridged version may indicate some of the possibilities of this branch of business history.

(A) PILKINGTON BACKS RESEARCH AND IDENTIFIES A MOST PROMISING AREA OF TECHNICAL DEVELOPMENT

At the end of the Second World War Pilkington Brothers of St. Helens, Lancashire, was still a private limited company controlled by family directors. It was sole producer of all the flat-made glass in Britain, having reached an agreement in 1936 for the purchase, over the following years, of Chance Brothers of Spon Lane, Smethwick, its solitary British competitor. If any major development was to be made in the glass industry in Britain, therefore, it would have to be made by someone either working for Pilkington or supported by it, for it alone possessed the expertise and technical resources to bring a costly and sophisticated new process to fruition. The company had long employed scientists, as well as engineers, in its works. In the later 1930s it brought some of them together, and supplemented them, in new central research and analytical laboratories. At the end of the war 57 people, 14 of them graduates and most of the rest analysts, worked there; by 1950 the research staff itself numbered 52, including 24 graduates. A new Head of Research, W. J. R. Merren, had been appointed after the war. An Oxford physicist, he had worked for some years for the Admiralty and was Chief Scientist at its Mine Design Department when he came to St. Helens in 1946. 'My own experience is wide rather than specialised', he wrote in support of his application, 'and if I had to make any claim it would be the possession of a practical outlook and the ability to adopt the scientific approach to problems.'

Pilkington had also during the 1930s formed a Technical Committee, composed of production directors, works managers, and, in due course, the Head of Research. Ten group committees, on which less senior people also sat, reported regularly to it on specific technical functions, the idea being that anyone, no matter how junior, who had a bright idea would be encouraged by other specialists in that field to go away and make something of it. Although the groups had no spending powers, it was hoped that these promising suggestions would be subsequently reported to the Technical Committee, carefully monitored, and, if appropriate, supported financially. Such technical efforts as these were, however, tended to focus upon comparatively trivial matters. Shortly after the war, at a special meeting in September 1946, attended by the newly appointed Head of Research, the Committee drew attention to the need 'to cultivate a sense of proportion which had sometimes been lacking and which had resulted in insufficient attention to matters of the first order of importance'. The Committee was in future to be known as the Manufacturing Conference and the first item on the agenda at every meeting was to be Programme of Future Development Work. Top priority was to be given to innovations which would be really worth while and not just of interest to backroom boffins.

The Manufacturing Conference had little difficulty in identifying the process which would yield the best commercial return to research and development. The company's window glass and rolled plate glass processes were already mechanized and continuous; but the manufacture of polished plate glass, the quality product, was not yet quite continuous and was certainly still very costly. Pilkington had made great strides in this branch of the industry between the wars and had a world lead in it; the need to keep ahead was a further reason for concentration in this area. Technical momentum had been achieved which the company did not want to lose.

Between the wars Pilkington, first in collaboration with the Ford Motor Co. at Detroit in the early 1920s and then on its own, had transformed what had been an intermittent process—the molten glass had to be poured out of pots on to a casting table, and each plate of glass had to be ground, and then polished, one at a time, and one side at a time—into a process that was almost continuous: the molten glass was flowed from a tank furnace, annealed, and then passed through a twin grinder, a long series of grinding heads above and below the moving ribbon of glass which ground both sides simultaneously. The machine produced glass with more perfect parallel surfaces than before, though the grinding, of course, removed the lustrous fire finish which the cheaper sheet or ordinary window glass possessed, for sheet was drawn upwards straight out of the tank without any subsequent processing. Nevertheless, the new machine was a great improvement upon existing methods of making plate glass. It was licensed in 1937 to the leading continental manufacturer, the St Gobain Co., for non-exclusive use in France and its territories, and for exclusive use in Germany, Italy, and Spain where St Gobain also had factories. Pilkington's twin grinder was a great international achievement which gave the company considerable influence in its negotiations with glass manufacturers abroad.

But it had two drawbacks. It had not proved possible to develop a commercially satisfactory twin polisher at the end of the production line—there was no water to disperse the heat caused by friction when this final part of the machine was run at speed—and polishing had to be done by a series of heads, one side at a time. The process was therefore not entirely continuous. Secondly, the whole plant was enormously big and costly to run. The tank furnace, annealing lehr, grinders, and polishers stretched out in a line no less than 1,400 ft long, which, as contemporaries used proudly to note, was 70 ft longer than the *Queen Mary*, the largest ship afloat. It took 1,500 kW of electricity to run. This long line of machinery, feat of engineering though it was, required to be cut down to size; or some alternative to grinding and polishing needed to be found.

In 1931 the company had created two non-family directorships for outstanding members of its staff, and it fell to the holder of one of these, James Meikle, in his capacity of chairman of the Manufacturing Conference, to lead the search for a substitute for grinding and polishing. Born in 1890 and educated at Allan Glen's School and the Glasgow Royal Technical College, he had trained as an electrical engineer in Glasgow before coming to St. Helens in 1914 to help manage Pilkington's electric power plant. Lord Cozens-Hardy, himself an electrical engineer who had married into the Pilkington family and had emerged in 1931 as chairman of the company's newly formed Executive Committee, took the view that electrical engineers were the salt of the earth and, other things being equal, deserved every encouragement. Meikle, a man of considerable administrative, as well as technical, ability, became interested in plate glass-making, in 1931 was appointed manager of Pilkington's plate glassworks at St. Helens, in 1936 became a member of the Board, and in 1939 the main production director. At the end of the war he instituted a careful search for well-qualified engineers and scientists which led to the building-up of the technical staff which has already been noticed. By one of those remarkable coincidences which change the course of events, attention came to be drawn to someone with the name of Pilkington who happened to fall into this category.

(B) DISCOVERY OF AN INVENTOR AND THAT OF AN EXPERIMENTAL ENGINEERING DEPARTMENT

Lionel Alexander Bethune (Alastair) Pilkington (b. 1920; educ. Sherborne School), who was to be not only the inventor of the Float process but also the dominating personality who drove, argued, and cajoled it through all its development difficulties and ultimately became Chairman of the company and F.R.S., was then reading for a Mechanical Sciences degree at Trinity College, Cambridge. He had started his degree course in 1938–9, and, after being away in the war, was, in 1945, one of that splendid band of ex-servicemen who made British universities such mature and lively places for a few brief years. Round about the end of the war Alastair's father, Col. Lionel Pilkington, the managing director of an engineering company in Reading, happened to be brought in touch with the St. Helens Pilkingtons through an interest in genealogy. (Sir) Richard Pilkington, M.P., a member of the glass-making family and a shareholder but not a member of the Board, had acquired from another keen genealogist a family tree which he took great pains to extend during the latter years of the war and, at leisure, after it. (He lost his seat in Parliament, like many others, in July 1945.) He got into touch with Col.

Lionel, and having made contact through this interest in their ancestors—an interest which showed beyond any doubt that there was no traceable link between the two branches—they also came to discuss the living generations.

The rising stars at St. Helens at this time were W. H. (Harry) Pilkington (b. 1905; educ. Rugby and Magdalene College, Cambridge) and D. V. (Douglas) Phelps (b. 1904; educ. Harrow and Magdalen College, Oxford), a Pilkington descended by the female line. Both had joined the company in 1927 and both had been put through the mill for a full seven years before becoming directors, Harry Pilkington on the commercial side and Douglas Phelps on the manufacturing. The former was to become chairman of the company from 1949; the latter became chairman of its Executive Committee of directors from 1947. Both of them, at Richard Pilkington's suggestion, met Lionel Pilkington to talk about Alastair. A Board minute of 29 November 1945 takes up the story. It is of particular interest not least for its rather ungrateful reprimand of Richard Pilkington and for the way it sees the family as something which spread outwards from St. Helens. It nevertheless reached the ineluctable conclusion that no true Pilkington, however remote, could enter the company as anything but a family trainee:

The Directors considered a report furnished by Col. Phelps of an interview which he and Mr. W. H. Pilkington had had with Col. Lionel G. Pilkington on the subject of the possibility of his second son, Alastair, joining the P.B. Organisation after completing his studies at University. The matter had arisen from an almost casual introduction by Mr. Richard Pilkington. The Directors felt that it should be pointed out to Mr. Richard Pilkington that the method of introduction was very irregular. Mr. L. G. Pilkington's branch of the Family broke away at least 15 generations ago [i.e. as far back as Richard Pilkington's researches had been able to take him]. It was agreed, however, that a member of the Pilkington Family, however remote, could be accepted only as a potential Family Director. After considerable discussion, the Board agreed that, in principle, they were prepared to open the door wider to really promising candidates . . .
With regard to the particular case under discussion, it was considered that before any action in respect of Alastair Pilkington was taken, we should take steps to learn more about Col. L. G. Pilkington—in particular his business and Family background. He is the Managing Director of Pulsometer Engineering Co., Reading, which Lord Cozens-Hardy pointed out was a small but old and well established company, he believed of Quaker origin.

These inquiries evidently proved reassuring. Harry Pilkington saw Alastair, Lionel Pilkington told the company that there would be no difficulty in finding £20,000 or so in due course to buy the requisite number of shares to qualify his son as a director if he made the grade, and works managers and technical directors reported favourably upon the prospective family trainee after he had been subjected to a three-day scrutiny at St. Helens. So Alastair Pilkington started work with the company on 12 August 1947. His first job as technical assistant ('an unusual status for an ex-officer') was on brick gas producers, where pokers six feet long were needed to clear the clinker ('quite rugged'). It did not take him long to learn that there was much that was still little understood about glass-making. His inquiring, analytical mind started pondering over some of these problems, particularly the actual process of glass-melting within tanks, a subject that was then occupying the attention of the Manufacturing Conference. The Research Department carried out experiments on it, information was collected from the various works, and Alastair Pilkington and a colleague produced two reports during 1949 before he was posted, in October of that year, to the company's other plate glassworks, near Doncaster, as production manager. There he continued these investigations into melting using a small tank with half an inch of molten tin at the bottom of it.

In the meantime the engineering team which was being assembled in the works at St. Helens was pursuing the search for a substitute for grinding and polishing. An American, Urban Emmett Bowes, Director of Research of the Owens-Illinois Glass Co., the world's leading glass bottle-making concern, had patented the idea of passing a ribbon of glass, already formed by a rolling machine, between rapidly vibrating platens or plates, the aim being to produce, without grinding or polishing, glass that was flat (like plate glass) and fire-finished (like sheet). The American plate glass manufacturers showed no interest in this idea, so Bowes approached Pilkington who began to experiment with it on a laboratory scale in the Research Department by the end of 1947. These experiments gave ground for hope and in March 1948 the Manufacturing Conference gave the work high priority. By June of the following year the Research Department was able to report that, while the quality of polish was not up to plate glass standards, relatively little grinding and polishing would be needed to reach those standards. Trials on a pilot plant in one of the works were decided upon. This decision was of importance not because the Bowes process ever came to anything but because it led, in September 1950, on the instructions of the Manufacturing Conference and without any formal reference to the company's Executive Committee, to the creation of a separate Experimental Engineering Department composed initially of engineers alone and operating in one of the works, remote from the Central Research Department and its scientists. The Bowes process had been taken away from Central Research: a rival and unrelated organization was set up to exploit it further. The scientists and engineers, who had everything to gain from close collaboration, now worked more and more apart.

The Bowes process had a bearing upon Float in another way. It also led to the use of molten tin, though at a lower temperature than it had been used for the furnace experiments at Doncaster. A method of handling the still soft ribbon of glass as it emerged from the platens was needed, and tin, at just above 600 °C., could be used to convey it until it was cool enough to be passed over rollers without marking. Kenneth Bickerstaff (b. 1925; educ. Cowley

School, St. Helens) had joined Pilkington in 1941, studied at the local technical college, and gone on to take a First in Mechanical Engineering at the Manchester College of Technology (now UMIST) in 1949. After a short spell with Armstrong Whitworth, he returned to Pilkington in 1950 and was soon experimenting with tin as a conveyor using a simple piece of laboratory equipment. (At this point the rift between scientists and engineers had not reached the point at which an engineer did not come to the Central Research Laboratories to use facilities made available to him by one of the senior physicists there.) Small strips of ordinary sheet glass were heated above 600 °C. for the purpose, and tin was used because this metal was readily available, comparatively inexpensive, and, apart from lead, the obvious choice.

Pure tin is uniquely and ideally suited for floating glass, for its specific gravity is much greater than that of it. It also has a low melting-point, 232 °C., far below the 600 °C. at which glass is sufficiently viscous for its lower surface to pass unmarked over rollers, and a high boiling-point, 2,623 °C., well above the 1,500 °C. at which glass was melted and refined. This boiling-point was also sufficiently high to ensure a low vapour pressure even at 1,050 °C., the top end of the temperature range at which the molten glass was at a working consistency.

Alastair Pilkington, having learned about the practical side of glass-making and of management at works level, was brought back to St. Helens in the middle of 1951. Very soon after his arrival, Meikle, who had become increasingly affected by deafness, announced unexpectedly that he had decided to retire from active management on 9 October 1951, his sixty-first birthday. Alastair Pilkington then found himself suddenly promoted to the post of assistant to Meikle's successor, J. B. Watt, another non-family works manager—this time on the sheet glass-making side—who, like Meikle, had been promoted to the Board. With J. B. Watt's main interest being in sheet glass, Alastair Pilkington continued to be mainly concerned with plate, including the installation of twin grinders in factories of licensees abroad. The existing machines had been improved and speeded up in the later 1940s, and a high-speed continuous (single-side) polisher had been brought into operation. (Development work on the twin polisher was then stopped.) The twin grinder was licenced to Glaver in Belgium in May 1950 and, after protracted negotiations, to Libbey-Owens-Ford in the United States at the end of March 1951. The Research and Development of the 1920s and 1930s were now producing economic advantages which were to be of help in producing increasing amounts of plate glass, and from these profits Float was also to be financed, as we shall see.

(C) THE ACT OF INVENTION AND EARLY EXPERIMENTAL WORK

Soon after his return to St. Helens, Alastair Pilkington was made a member of the Manufacturing Conference. At one of its meetings at which the Bowes experiments were discussed, he came up with the idea which was to lead to the first Float process experiments. As the minutes of the meeting record:

Mr. Barradell-Smith [in charge of the Experimental Engineering team] thought that there is a possibility of producing by the Bowes Process a glass better than the best Sheet for distortion . . . Rolling appears to be another promising method if the ribbon can be subsequently fire-finished without marring its bottom surface. Mr. L. A. B. Pilkington suggested that this might be done by floating the ribbon on a bath of molten tin in a neutral atmosphere. It was decided that it is worth trying this to find out whether it gives a fire-finished effect.

That particular meeting gave rise to much more than a further investigation of the use of tin as a conveyor. It started off what originally came to be called, after the inventor (but also providing a useful code name), the L.A.B. project. This also included the idea of fire-finishing at higher temperatures. Here, in fact, was the act of invention. Alastair Pilkington later recalled that the idea of re-heating the glass over tin and then floating it down through a temperature gradient to the point at which the tin could be used as a conveyor, came to him suddenly one evening as he was helping his wife to wash the dishes. All of a sudden, ideas which had been assembling themselves in his mind over the previous months, but were still out of focus, fell into place and made sense. He saw Barradell-Smith the next day and a special meeting was held to discuss the whole matter soon afterwards; but neither the Director of Research nor any of his staff attended it. Their absence was singularly unfortunate for this marked the real beginnings of the new L.A.B. project.

After some larger-scale experiments on tin as a conveyor, following up Bickerstaff's work, and some static tests, the first small pilot plant began to be used for experimenting between the end of 1952 and April 1953. The bath, divided into two parts, was 25 ft long and the ribbon of glass 12 in wide. The whole thing cost only £8,000, including £1,500 for 1·7 tons of tin. The hot end of the bath (at about 1,000 °C.) would receive glass which had been melted in the usual way in a tank furnace and formed into a ribbon using water-cooled rollers as in the existing plate glass process. The ribbon would pass directly down from the rollers to the surface of the tin where it would be re-heated so as to remove all surface imperfections caused both by the rollers and by its journey between them and the bath. The surface of the tin being dead level, the lighter ribbon of glass, it was hoped, would acquire strictly parallel surfaces as it floated upon it. This ribbon would then float frictionless to the cooler end of the bath (600 °C.) at which temperature, as the Bowes conveyor experiments had shown, it could be safely removed without danger of marking. In this way the whole costly grinding and polishing process could be completely eliminated and, since it was already known that small pieces of glass which had been floated upon molten tin emerged with a fire finish on their lower surfaces—and heaters above the bath could give such a finish to the upper surfaces—there was a reasonable hope that the resulting ribbon would not only have good parallel surfaces but also be fire-finished as well.

This was the aim at the end of 1952 when experiments began. In fact, at this stage problems were of the simplest sort. Not the least of them was merely to maintain the sealed casting round the bath. The apparatus was, Alastair Pilkington recalls, 'a leaking box of molten tin'. All sorts of difficulties arose but none was permanently insoluble. Although no glass of saleable quality was produced. the results were considered 'very promising'. The process was basically stable, a continuous run of 85 hours had been achieved on one occasion and $\frac{1}{4}$-in. glass had been made at the rate of 160 in. per minute. There was no doubt about both surfaces being fire-finished. Such faults as the glass had all seemed capable of eventual correction.

By this time Alastair Pilkington had been made a subdirector (he became a full director two years later). There was, therefore, the closest communication between the top management and those who were actively involved in the development of the new process, most of them engineers and their helpers in their late twenties or (like Alastair Pilkington himself) early thirties. This was to be very important not only for receiving the necessary support from the highest quarters but also for maintaining morale among the development team. Far from thinking that they were ever forgotten men, every member of the team knew that (as one of them put it later) 'Alastair has a direct line to Sir Harry'. Accelerated promotion right to the top, possible only for a family trainee, was beginning to produce remarkable results after the inventor had been only six years with the company.

A provisional application for a British Patent was filed in December 1953 in the names of Alastair Pilkington and (much to his surprise) Kenneth Bickerstaff (in respect of his work on tin as a conveyor). The complete specification followed in November 1954 for 47 countries. Pilkington's rivals would soon know that it had an interest in floating molten glass on an unspecified molten liquid, though they would not know how seriously Pilkington was pursuing the idea. They might, however, be put on the scent and be tempted to follow it themselves and, if they could, to devise a better means of manufacture by this route without falling within the scope of the Pilkington patent. From now on the sooner Pilkington could develop the process and produce saleable glass, the better.

Two more pilot plants were built before the company embarked upon a full-scale production model. The second pilot, of the same order of magnitude as the first, costing £9,500 (including £3,500 for tin) and also flowing a 12-in. ribbon, was used for further experiments in March, July, and September 1954. The third, a larger prototype, flowing a 30-in. ribbon and costing £30,000, came into operation in February 1955. By this time the Research Department was standing more aloof, refusing to second scientists to work alongside the engineers, seeing its role as being confined to undertaking specific investigations referred to it. The scientists, only too aware of the formidable problems involved, did not share the optimism of the Experimental Engineering Department which, at the end of 1954, reported that 'the basic problems of handling glass on molten tin appear to have been solved'.

(D) BUSINESS PROSPERITY ENCOURAGES MAJOR INVESTMENT AND CARRIES THE EXPERIMENTERS THROUGH MISFORTUNE

The advocates of Float were fortunate in the fact that the application for a production unit came before the Group Executive in the spring of 1955. The British economy was then doing well and the world demand for glass, for use both in the rapidly growing motor industry and in building, had reached famine proportions. In May 1955, for instance, jobbers as far inland as Chicago were offering Pilkington long-term contracts if it could only meet their immediate needs. In Britain building controls had been removed in the previous year and an enormous pent-up demand for office accommodation had been added to the already high rate of house-building. Pilkington was making good profits and plate glass was making its full contribution to them.

TABLE 10.1
Pilkington Group Total Sales and Plate Glass Sales,
and Profit on these, 1952–7 to 1955–6
(£000)

Year to 31 March	Total sales	Profit	Plate glass sales	Profit
1951–2	29 192	3187	5835	898
1952–3	27 098	1453	4785	291
1953–4	33 449	4584	6302	1156
1954–5	37 231	5760	7422	1775
1955–6	42 571	5180	9153	2061

The two twin grinders, one at Cowley Hill and the other at Doncaster, were further speeded up with consequent economies of operation. The ribbon speed of 95 in. per minute in 1948 had been increased to over 140 in. per minute by November 1951, and 160 in. per minute were being mentioned in the middle of 1955. But this pre-war machinery—now growing a little elderly—could not be speeded up indefinitely and future projections suggested further large increases in demand for plate glass.

When Alastair Pilkington presented his report to the Group Executive in support of an immediate start on a Float production plant, everything was in his favour. Business was very good and additional capacity would soon be needed. Why not back Float development as an economical alternative to some of the additional grinding and polishing capacity that would shortly be needed anyway? It was an attractive proposition. If progress on the pilot plant went on at its existing rate, a production unit could be started up, it was thought, in a little over eight months. The costings suggested that ¼-in. Float glass could be made at 10*d*. per sq. ft ,compared to 21·28*d*. per sq. ft by existing plate glass methods. It was estimated that the Float plant would cost £65,000 to build and a further £140,000 to operate during further development trials before saleable glass could be made, but this was very much less than the millions which another plate glass production unit would cost. The Group Executive was impressed by these arguments and gave its approval to the Float plant, though it was not so sure of early success: 'After discussion it was felt that the introduction of the new glass, even if successful, might be quite a few years off yet, and that in the meantime plans for future expansion in both plate and sheet glass should go ahead unchanged.'

While the production unit was being designed and built, experimental work continued at the third pilot plant, for the enlargement of which the Group Executive voted a further sum of £16,425. There the engineers' confident expectations were soon shattered by two unexpected technical difficulties; and a third serious problem also arose. These blows came in quick succession during the summer and autumn of 1955, only a few months after the major investment decision had been taken:

1. It was discovered that the process could make glass of only one thickness (or substance as it is called in the industry). Try as they might, the experimenters could only produce glass ¼-in. thick. The Research Department was able to show that this equilibrium substance, as it came to be known, was caused by the relative surface tensions of the glass and the molten tin. Here Pilkington was lucky, however, for most of its plate glass sales were of ¼-in; but it meant that the process would not, without further development, be able to make ⅛-in. substance, needed for the manufacture of laminated safety glass. This development, however, was postponed because of a second, and more pressing, defect which revealed itself at that time.
2. When Float glass was toughened, a bloom —technically described as 'a slight obscuration of the surface by a greyish film'—appeared on the lower side. This ruled out the new product for toughened safety glass, too. The Research Department, having been asked to do so, showed this to be caused by a high concentration of tin ions which had penetrated the surface of the glass and was caused by oxidation of the tin. Great efforts, therefore, needed to be made to remove all traces of oxygen from the atmosphere.
3. The citation by the U.S. Patent Office of two old U.S. patents dating from 1902 and 1905, both of which disclosed commercially unworked processes for making a glass ribbon, using molten tin to support it. Fortunately, in the end it proved possible to distinguish the Pilkington processes from these early ones, and after four years an American patent was eventually granted to Pilkington.

Far from causing the company to lose faith in the new process, these revelations strengthened its determination to make it work. Additional resources were set aside for development. Sir Harry Pilkington, the chairman, by nature an optimist who already enjoyed a considerable reputation among his fellow directors as a decision-taker and leader, never wavered in his support. This was to be as vital as Alastair Pilkington's unflagging confidence and powers of persuasion.

As the engineering team struggled on at the pilot plant to remove traces of oxygen from the atmosphere, to improve the steering of the ribbon, and to put more heat into the tin—special heaters had eventually to be imported from Germany—the Executive was busy working out a sales policy for the new product. The plan was to offer Float at the same price as plate and to introduce it, via Pilkington's associate Triplex, to the motor trade for a use which could be controlled in the early stages so that the two products would be interchangeble. The car makers were not so concerned with quality as many other buyers; and in any case the safety-glass manufacturers had to re-heat the glass in order to toughen it, and they often had to bend it as well.

The production unit was ready for starting by the spring of 1957. It had taken nearly two years to build, not the eight months that had been forecast, and the cost was now estimated not at £55,000 but at £676,000 (and was to rise higher). Yet even this was very much less than the millions required by a new plate glass line; and all was met out of current earnings, the sums charged against trading revenue for depreciation and replacement in the company as a whole rising from about £2 m. in each of the years 1953–4 and 1954–5 to £2·7 m. in 1955–6 and to over £3 m. in 1956–7. On 25 April 1957, before the production unit was started, Alastair Pilkington sounded a timely note of caution:

Before the final decision was taken to light up the tank at Cowley Hill [Pilkington's St. Helens plate glassworks] a most careful examination of the glass was carried out, and it was only after a long series of tests in which we are able to relate the cause and effect, that we felt in a position to recommend going into production. However, past experiences makes us approach the whole venture with great humility as we are beginning to be aware of how many new problems we are likely to meet.

The suspense at this point must have been quite considerable. But nobody in the know, except perhaps some in the Research Department, envisaged anything but ultimate success. The Directors were busily at work on a public announcement of the company's great achievement which they believed to be imminent.

Sir Harry Pilkington inaugurated the Cowley Hill Float production unit at a small ceremony on the morning of 6 May 1957 in the presence of some other Directors, the Cowley Hill Works Manager, and members of the development team. He noted in his diary: 'Lit Float. Is it the day of the Century? Then to office for two hours, Stockport for good Chamber of Commerce luncheon speech—drove fast to Heathrow with Alastair then plane held up by Strike but reached Frankfurt at 12.30 and to bed.' Glass began to flow from the tank on 8 May. Four days later Alastair Pilkington reported that all seemed to be going well at that stage, and at the end of the month the Group

Executive, having heard that the unit was 'fairly close to producing saleable glass', fixed 10 July for the London Press conference should the process prove successful. In fact, no saleable glass was made for fourteen months and the Press conference had to wait for another year and a half.

(E) THE CLIFF-HANGER AND THE BEGINNINGS OF TECHNICAL SUCCESS

The production unit soon revealed that even higher standards of purity were needed in both the tin and the atmosphere above it if the chief imperfections of the process were to be removed. Oxidation was the real enemy and the final attacks upon the means whereby the smallest trace of oxygen could penetrate the Float unit were numerous and difficult. In the first four months the plant worked only 74 out of 124 days and cost £287,000 to operate. The frequent shut-downs were often caused by the rolling machine which formed the ribbon before it passed into the bath. Iron scale was falling on the top surface from the roller shield or from the mild steel pipe carrying the atmosphere to the roller enclosure, and possibly also from the top roller itself. Condensation on these water-cooled rollers was another cause of trouble, for this caused specks. It was therefore decided to pour the molten glass direct from the furnace into the tin and let it form its own ribbon there. (This had been tried out on the third pilot plant.) It had the obvious advantage of saving heat, but it produced new problems of bubble and devitrification. Nevertheless, in this second phase it was possible to run the plant for 74 out of 79 days. Then the tank was damaged and tin got into the casing. The repair took a month.

Now, within measurable reach of technical success, as the development team confidently believed, the going became particularly hard. Argument and advocacy—making the most of every step forward and minimizing the importance of defects by indicating that none of them was present all the time—were proving less and less persuasive. The only real argument at this stage of development was the production of some saleable glass, however little or intermittent. The Group Executive began to show signs of disenchantment, though its concern was also caused by the more difficult trading circumstances which the company was then encountering. Group profits were falling annually: £5,180,000 (1955–6), £4,371,000 (1956–7), and £4,190,000 (1957–8). The sum charged against trading for depreciation and replacement, on the other hand, was rising, to £3,044,000 (1956–7) to £3,654,000 (1957–8). And other calls on capital were known to be imminent, among them heavy expenditure upon a new and relatively vast head office and upon new and extensive research and development laboratories. The fixed capital cost of the Float unit had now reached £800,000. More serious, the operating costs were running at the rate of over £900,000 a year, approaching a quarter of the Group's pre-tax profits in that particularly bad year, and it was this which was the main source of anxiety. 'We are bleeding to death', Barradel-Smith is reported to have said in an uncharacteristically pessimistic moment. The drain on resources was bad enough, though it could still be met out of income; but worse in a way was the fact that Pilkington had been depending upon Float to supply its growing market for quality glass, particularly to the motor trade, and had no alternative to turn to. In February 1958 the company felt obliged to take out a costly insurance policy in the shape of a modern high-speed plate glass grinder and polisher. This was to be installed at Doncaster at an estimated cost of £3 m. These were anxious—and indeed rather cliff-hanging—months. The company had taken a calculated risk on Float when its foreign rivals were busily installing grinders and polishers of improved type. Float *had* to work. The future of the British flat glass industry was at stake.

From January 1958 the Float bath was used for a time at lower temperature as a conveyor to build up a stock of thin rough plate glass for subsequent grinding and polishing by the continuous process. This done, the plant was converted back for the manufacture of Float glass, even more stringent efforts being made to reduce the oxygen content in the atmosphere. This new chapter of activity, however, was again dogged by disappointment. The plant was never out of trouble. It was again switched to the manufacture of thin rough plate glass.

It was the next spell of production which eventually, and at long last, reached the point at which small amounts of glass were regularly produced of a quality acceptable to the warehouse for sale to the motor trade. There were six production runs in this series, and it was on the twelfth day of the fifth of these that saleable quality began to be produced. There was a deterioration during the night—it was like watching a patient—but the following day the distortion level improved again and remained acceptable until the end of that particular run. A certain amount of glass of similar quality was again produced for a week during the next run, and the Group Executive learned that those in charge of the process were confident that they had at last overcome the majority of the known problems.

A fortunate accident played its part in this achievement. As the man who at that time was assistant works manager at Cowley Hill later recalled:—

After a particularly frustrating day, a very tired operator succeeded in cracking part of the apparatus. Many other parts of the plant were in a pretty poor state too. Suddenly, to our surprise, we succeeded in manufacturing good, saleable glass and, without enquiring too deeply into the reasons for this sudden change of fortune, we continued successfully for several months.

The real turning-point in this natal period, however, came with the realization that it was the depth of the tin level, critical to as little as one-eighth of an inch, which played the major part in controlling distortion.

The Executive decided that the time had arrived to let Sir Graham Cunningham, the chairman and managing director of Triplex, into the Float secret and to seek his help with the testing of the new product. Sample wrap-round windscreens were made from Float at the Triplex factory at Willesden.

The support of Triplex became vital at this stage, and here Pilkington had the advantage of being not only its main supplier of glass but also its major shareholder, owning 33 per cent of the Triplex share capital. Pilkington's Flat Glass Management Committee soon learned that the full co-operation of Triplex had been obtained and on the following day the first consignment of Float glass for regular processing was sent to its Kings Norton works. It was invoiced 2*d.* per sq. ft less than plate. All the marketing plans so carefully laid during the earlier months when the process was giving nothing but trouble were now proving their worth.

Sir Harry Pilkington announced Float to the world at a Press conference in London on 20 January 1959. The basic principle, that of floating 'a continuous ribbon of glass . . . on an unspecified molten metal in a controlled atmosphere', was divulged, the economic advantage of cutting out the costly grinding and polishing processes was stressed, and the various phases of experimental work were outlined. The quantity of the new glass being produced was said to be 'quite considerable but not yet enough for it to be offered freely.' It was admitted that 'years of development work still lie ahead before the full commercial advantage of the Float process can be realised.' But from all this, few of those listening (or, presumably, competitors abroad) would be able to deduce the extremely fragile and unprofitable state of things at Cowley Hill. The proportion of saleable glass had to be increased beyond 40 per cent of the ribbon before production became profitable at existing glass prices; and these higher proportions needed to be sustained over long runs without awkward stopages which would turn profit into loss. There was, in fact, a huge loss on Float of £931,000 in the year ended 31 March 1959. Fortunately the company's trading results were better again; despite this loss its pre-tax profits reached nearly £5·6 m.

(F) THE FINAL HAUL TO PROFITABILITY

The engineers kept on beavering away to increase the saleable proportion of the ribbon and to produce this consistently week in and week out. But there were still to be more serious set-backs. Having sold 500,000 sq. ft of Float by later February 1959 and got production up to 100,000 sq. ft per week—the break-even point was about 200,000 sq. ft—the plant ran into more trouble when the damaged part of the apparatus was replaced. The directors became alarmed to receive a paper showing a budgeted deficit on Float of £357,000 for the half year. In August 1959 Pilkington, without stocks of Float and short of twin-smoothed plate, had to import 2 m sq. ft of glass from the Continent in order to supply its customers. Once again the complicated process had disappointed its advocates. Some of its critics, bearing in mind not only its name but also the Press conference reference to the occasion on which Alastair Pilkington had had his brainwave, called it the Sink process.

Not until November 1959, when more than 200,000 sq. ft of Float glass was being packed in the warehouse each week, did the new product start to be sold for general glazing in the home market. Production below the cost of $\frac{1}{4}$-in plate was first achieved in January 1960. But these gains came towards the end of the financial year ended 31 March and for that year as a whole the process again returned a loss of £525,000. Fortunately, the glass business continued to flourish; and despite this Float glass loss the company returned an impressive pre-tax profit of £8·6 m. The decision was taken to build a second Float unit, even though the first had still to prove itself fully. A small profit (£350,000) was at last made by the process in 1960–1, but the costly development for non-equilibrium substances again turned this into a loss of £103,000 in the following year. Only since 1962–3, when it returned a profit of just over £1 m., has Float been uninterruptedly profitable.

In that financial year, with the second Float line, which had a larger capacity than the first, in production and a third being built, foreign manufacturers realized that they could not hold back any longer from manufacturing themselves under licence lest Pilkington, with lower production costs, should get too far ahead of them in world markets. The first licence was issued to the Pittsburgh Plate Glass Co. in July 1962 and the second to Glaces de Boussois in the following December. There was then a rush of would-be licensees. Even at that stage, however, ten years after experimenting had started, the production and Research and Development men were still grappling with outstanding problems such as distortion in thin glass and toughening bloom (a certain, though smaller, amount of underpolishing was then still needed). At this juncture even Sir Harry was showing signs of losing patience. The minutes of the General Board on 25 July 1963 capture his mood: 'Sir Harry stated that the Group Executive had been disappointed that the last few months had not seen a solution to the main troubles, such as bloom, undercleaning, and the production of some of the thin substances. Our position as the only manufacturer of Float in the world, and the resultant freedom from competition in sales of Float, was fast drawing to a close, and we really had not grasped our opportunity.' Float profit fell to about £250,000 in that financial year (1963–4); but the summer of 1963 saw the last of the technical development crises. Pilkington phased out its plate glass production and stopped making plate glass altogether in 1967. By 1970 there were already 28 Float glass units operating abroad, including two of Pilkington's in Canada. In 1972 the number of plate glassworks in the non-Communist world had fallen (from 37 in 1961) to 20, and some of these had been taken out of service but not demolished. Within ten years of the first licence being granted Float glass had become universally accepted.

(G) SOME POSSIBLE CONCLUSIONS AND FUTURE LINES OF INQUIRY

How did Pilkington come to succeed and lead the world? Why did none of its international rivals, equally skilled and experienced glass manufacturers and backed by large Research and Development organizations, make the discovery and bring it to a successful conclusion?

Perhaps the first point to emphasize is that this was an extremely radical innovation, quite removed from anything previously attempted in glassmaking, although, as has been seen, American inventors had the idea of using tin years before the state of technology made it feasible to do so. Pilkington's rivals preferred edging forward from the known, not leaping into the unknown. One of them, for instance, devoted its Research and Development resources to the acid-polishing of plate glass.

Pilkington did not stumble on to this discovery just by accident. The arrival of Alastair Pilkington at St. Helens was, of course, a quite extraordinary, indeed eccentric, accident. But the series of events which led to experiments with molten tin at higher and lower temperatures were part of a very conscious attempt after the war to identify and improve the part of the company's manufacturing operations which was likely to yield the best financial returns. Yet although Pilkington knew as much as anybody about glass, it knew nothing about tin or the problems created by the interaction of molten tin and molten glass at 1,000 °C. The engineers, all enthusiastic young men—age may have been important—pressed on in ignorance. 'If we had known all these horrors at the beginning', Sir Alastair later commented, 'we would certainly not have gone ahead'. The scientists, all too aware of the theoretical difficulties of what was being attempted, would not have set off in the first place and were generally discouraging when difficulties began to reveal themselves. The engineers, for their part, believed that in a process so complicated and involved the Research Department could make little contribution except in answering specific queries. The main results could emerge only through trial and error. Provided no single difficulty proved intractable there was a case for pressing on.

The coincidence of periods of heavy expenditure, or of decisions to invest, with prosperous and profitable years was of great importance. Thus 1955 was an ideal year to secure commitment to a production unit in the first place, the good profits of the later 1950s carried the heavy costs of production-scale development, and the particularly large profit in 1959–60 made it easier to authorize the second production unit. If these investment decisions had been required to be taken at a later period—at the end of the 1960s, for instance—it seems much less likely that approval would have been so readily given. Also of great importance was the faith which the Group Executive showed in the process even when it seemed to be so prone to trouble, faith that was maintained not just in the exciting early days but also during the hard slog to maturity when the by then seasoned engineers were still being surprised by totally unexpected setbacks. Here Alastair Pilkington's logical and clear advocacy was most important, and it was the accelerated promotion he gained as a family trainee which placed him in a position to display it so successfully.

Pilkington's status as a private family company was also probably an important ingredient in ultimate success. Here the personality and support of the future Lord Pilkington, the chairman, need to be brought out, and the fact that he was not accountable to a large number of anonymous shareholders. The secrecy of the process was such that it might have been very difficult indeed to have divulged the problems of development even to a handful of major outside shareholders in order to win their support. But perhaps it may be argued that, given the prosperity of the business during the development period, this would not have been necessary.

How many features of this particular invention and its development are unique to Float and how many common to other such ventures? One may point to various stages at which it might have been stopped and would then be deemed by posterity to have failed. How many other inventions, which did fail, given the good fortune of timing and personality—probably much more important than the intricacies of science or technology—might have succeeded? There is clearly a fruitful area here for investigation and comparison. But this will be possible only if the relevant business records are made available and if historians are prepared to make more use of them for this purpose.

III

11

A Pioneer of Public Enterprise: The Central Electricity Board and the National Grid, 1927-1940[1]

LESLIE HANNAH

(A) THE STATE AND ELECTRICITY

THE nationalized industries form an important and growing sector of the British economy, and the electricity supply industry, in particular, has had a significant part to play both in the evolution of the public corporation and in Britain's economic development in the twentieth century. The historical reasons for state ownership and control vary from case to case, but in many industries, including electricity supply, their special economic and technical characteristics meant that some form of public supervision was considered necessary from the beginning.

In the early electric lighting legislation of the 1880s, for example, maximum prices were set and provision was made for the ownership of electricity supply undertakings by local authorities. This solution was sponsored not only by Fabians and Liberals—enthusiasts for 'gas and water' socialism in the abstract—but also by Conservatives, who were proud of their municipal enterprises and anxious to extend them in order to relieve the rates. Although private companies had often been the innovators in the supply industry, the statutory right of municipalities to the first option on the local supply franchise soon bore fruit, and by the turn of the century municipalities controlled twice as much of the industry's capacity as private enterprise.

However, by this time changes in the technology of the industry—in particular, improvements in transmission and steam-turbine technology—made large-scale units more economic, and meant that the local supply areas originally designated were no longer appropriate. In some parts of the country, power companies were established to produce on a larger and more efficient scale, but since the existing undertakings had statutory monopoly powers in their local area it was not easy for newcomers to obtain outlets. The existing municipal and company undertakings opposed their new rivals and successfully lobbied Parliament to restrict their supply powers. Some of the larger undertakings—such as N.E.S.C.O. on the north-east coast—were none the less able to gain bulk supply powers over wide areas, but many others were simply too small to function efficiently. In London, for example, there were as many as 70 undertakings, each with separate power-stations, whereas London would really only have required four stations if they had been built at the optimum scale dictated by technological development. The changing technology and economies of scale (which became the hallmark of the electricity supply industry) had produced similar problems in other industrial countries. However, parochialism, entrenched vested interests, and a penchant for ideological commitments to municipal or private enterprise—which prevented co-operation to achieve optimally sized undertakings—proved more divisive and resilient in Britain than elsewhere.

The First World War highlighted the industry's shortcomings, and in 1918 the Williamson Committee went so far as to recommend that District Electricity Boards should be established in 16 areas of Britain to control generation and transmission, taking over these rights from existing undertakings. Again, however, this solution was rejected by Parliament, which feared the extension of state control and remained divided by interest groups representing the monopoly power of municipalities and companies. In its turn, that monopoly power protected the undertakings from the forces of competition, so that there was little pressure—either economic or political—for them to adopt the optimal scale of production. Instead of providing that pressure, Parliament established the Electricity Commission in 1919 with the duty of encouraging voluntary interconnection and bulk supply agreements. In the absence of compulsory powers, however, progress remained slow. Within a few years the Commissioners themselves were convinced that more positive government initiatives were needed.

When the Conservatives returned to office in 1924, they found that the minority Labour Government which they replaced had been planning substantial reforms in the industry, and the political significance of promises of cheap electricity was not lost on Baldwin and his Cabinet. Sir Philip Cunliffe-Lister, the President of the Board of Trade, expressed the disturbing truth: '[Electricity] is so inefficient today that it has been amazing to me that the Labour Government did not attempt to nationalise it.' The obvious course was to appoint a Minister of Transport (the department then responsible for electricity) capable of pushing through an ambitious measure. Baldwin offered the post to Lord Weir, the wealthy Chairman of a Scottish engineering company who had been a business recruit to the wartime government, rising to become Director General of Aircraft Production and, finally, Secretary of State for Air. However, Weir was now disillusioned with politics—at least the front-line politics of Parliament—and he refused the post.

Although Wilfred Ashley, Baldwin's second choice, took the ministerial post, Baldwin still wanted Weir's advice and, after a few weeks, he agreed to become Chairman of a committee to investigate the national problem of electrical energy. As an industrialist, he was already concerned about the inefficiency of the British supply industry, and he made it clear to the Prime Minister that he did not intend to chair a committee with public hearings: it was to be small, private, speedy, and to the point. The stipulation was accepted and he was joined on the Committee by Sir Hardman Lever, formerly Financial Secretary to the Treasury, and Lord Forres who (as Sir Archibald Williamson) had earlier chaired the most influential wartime committee on electricity supply and had made it clear that he felt the rejection of his proposals in 1919 had been a mistake. There could be little doubt, then, that they would recommend a new political initiative and, even before the Committee began its sittings, Weir had warned Baldwin that: 'he was not to expect a report which would merely adjust the existing difficulties of the Commissioners and make progress along existing lines easier, and that he must expect to be presented with a new electrical energy policy involving in its application courage and possibly a considerable financial investment.'

From the start, the Committee felt that Britain had fallen seriously behind other countries and that the absence of cheap electric power was delaying the post-war industrial revival. The primary indictment had to be of Parliament itself for wrongly rejecting the advice of earlier expert committees. If this advice had been acted upon, it reported,

Electricity would have been cheaper and our task would have been infinitely easier and probably unnecessary . . . Five years of patient and capable effort [by the Electricity Commissioners] have been unavailing . . . The policy of suasion can only be written down as a failure. . . . Of the 438 generating stations owned by authorised undertakings, not more than about 50 can be regarded as being of really suitable size and efficiency . . . The percentage of standby plant is high and the load factor is unreasonably low . . . The resultant loss to the country has been heavy, and becomes daily heavier.[2]

This indictment was no more sweeping than those offered by earlier committees, but in one respect Weir's Committee went further by recommending that interconnection on a national, rather than merely regional, scale was both technically feasible and commercially justifiable.

On the basis of the technical advice received, the Committee produced a projection of the size and shape of a national system of generation and transmission as it might appear in 1940, by which time it was expected that consumption in Britain would have quadrupled to 500 units per head. Instead of the existing average price of just over 2*d.* per unit, and a likely future price, under existing conditions, of 1·5*d.* per unit, electricity could be sold by a nationally planned, interconnected network at 1*d.* or less per unit: by 1940 the savings to consumers would amount to more than £44 m. annually. Against these potential benefits, the cost seemed small. Frequency standardization—a necessary prerequisite to interconnection—would cost £10½ m. over three or four years and the construction of a national 'gridiron' of transmission lines some £25 m. over five years. Overall, however, this expenditure would save capital since, in the absence of a national transmission scheme, even more capital would have to be wastefully expended in the supply industry on inefficiently small power-stations.

This sketch of an alternative future for the industry presented the central issues with stark clarity. The crucial problem which remained was not technical but political. A national transmission network was unlikely to be accepted if it meant nationalization or the alienation of the vested interests of existing undertakings to new authorities, and it was on this question that the Weir Committee produced the real breakthrough. Its key proposal was that the existing undertakers should retain control not only of distribution but also of the construction and operation of power-stations. However, the co-ordination of new power-station planning and the control of power-station operation within the framework of a newly constructed national gridiron of high-tension transmission lines was to be the responsibility of a new state-financed body, to be called the Central Electricity Board. The Board would buy electricity from selected stations and would plan the installation of new power-station capacity in conjunction with existing undertakings; it would resell electricity to undertakings wholesale and at cost price (after allowing for the cost of consrtucting and operating the gridiron). The Electricity Commissioners would have powers to close down inefficient stations but, in most cases, the Committee expected that the obvious benefits of cheap electricity would induce undertakings to take a supply from the Central Board. The compromise was pleaded with ingenuity and diplomacy: 'We propose not a change in ownership, but the partial subordination of vested interests in generation to that of a new authority for the benefit of all, and this only under proper safeguards, and in a manner which will preserve the value of the incentive of private enterprise.'

However necessary change was, it remained to be seen whether a Conservative Government would have the necessary political will and parliamentary strength to establish such an ambitious scheme of state enterprise. By December the Cabinet had resolved on action and drafted a Bill, Baldwin having unexpectedly and ardently placed his weight behind the Weir Committee's proposals. When the Government's decisions were announced early in 1926, the municipal and company undertakings, though somewhat relieved that they were to retain some of their independence under the scheme, nonetheless reacted with acerbity. A strong group of Conservative back-benchers also opposed the Bill fiercely, arguing that it was the thin end of the wedge of nationalization. Yet the Federation of British Industry—conscious of the need for cheap electricity in industry—overruled some members' objections and supported the Bill, and the Cabinet could also rely in Parliament on the support of the Opposition.

Although the 1926 Act was thus passed with Liberal and Labour support, the Conservative Cabinet was quite clear that state intervention in the industry was to have its own stamp on it. The C.E.B. would construct, own, and operate the grid on behalf of the state, and would exercise direct control over the operations of the best privately and municipally owned power-stations. But it was a vital part of the thinking of Baldwin and his colleagues that the Board should be a commercially minded and efficient arm of the executive, as distinct as possible from the alleged bureaucratic red tape of the civil service. As Baldwin had said earlier in the year, 'When I speak of a Board I do not mean a nationalised authority. I do not mean a government department. What we have in mind is a Board managed by practical men closely in touch with the industry.'

This conception as it emerged in the 1926 Act was a new one—though the idea of using business men to carry out government policies efficiently within *ad hoc* state organizations had gained some currency in the First World War—and it was eventually to lead to the modern conception of the public corporation of which the C.E.B. became a prototype. The Board was an authorized electricity undertaking and, like other undertakings, had no power to make regulations or orders of the kind made by a government department. By the same token, it was not subject to direct Treasury control on questions of finance and staffing. The members were appointed for terms of five or ten years and, as an extraordinary guarantee of their independence, government had no power to dismiss them, even for incompetence, unless they had been absent from their duties for six months or more. Parliament could, of course, discuss their affairs—as indeed it could discuss anyone's affairs—but it was not permissible to raise C.E.B. questions in the Ministry's annual vote and within a few years the tradition was established that the Ministry only rarely intervened in the affairs of the Board, except on those matters strictly specified by statute.

For all these attempts by the Conservative Government to distinguish it from state enterprise in general, however, the Central Electricity Board was, under the Act, to be appointed by the Minister of Transport. Despite attempts to secure parliamentary control of the Board's salaries during the passage of the Bill, the Government had successfully insisted that the salaries should be at the discretion of the Minister and it was announced that the full-time Chairman would be paid £7,000 per annum, a sum considerably in excess of normal government salaries—a Permanent Secretary was paid only £1,800— and clearly designed to compete with the private sector. The appointment was a crucial one. The Chairman would, in effect, be the Managing Director with over-all responsibility for the Board's efficiency. Although the choice was not easy, by mid-January the Government had determined on Sir Andrew Duncan, and, when the Shipbuilding Employers' Federation hesitated to release him from his position with them, the Prime Minister intervened to stress the national importance of the Board's work. The S.E.F. yielded and Duncan's appointment was announced on 21 January 1927.

Sir Andrew Duncan,[3] like Lord Weir, was an Ayrshire Scot. Unlike Weir, who was a second-generation capitalist, he came from a humble background in Irvine and Glasgow and was essentially self-made. He was a reserved man of proverbial Celtic charm. He first came to prominence as Coal Controller in 1919–20, when, as the government negotiator, he succeeded in reconciling the hostile parties in the coal dispute of 1920. It was the qualities of charm, tact, and patience then displayed which no doubt recommended him as the potential Chairman of a Board which would have to operate in collaboration with the diverse and conflicting vested interests of the electricity supply industry. To assist him there were six part-time members: three industrialists, a municipal man, a Director of the Bank of England representing the Treasury, and, as a token labour representative, Frank Hodges.

While the Board members fulfilled a useful overseeing role and, in the early years especially, were involved in day-to-day decision-making, the major work of planning and administration would necessarily fall on their full-time chief officers, and expense was not spared to attract the right men. John Brooke, who as Permanent Secretary at the Ministry of Transport had been the senior civil servant in charge of the 1926 legislation, moved to become Secretary of the C.E.B., but for the senior financial post the Board thought it important to get a practising accountant who had been in touch with business and industrial concerns. It appointed David Coates, who was to retain responsibility for the financial side of the Board's operations until nationalization. However, it was the engineering staff who would play the crucial role in the planning and execution of C.E.B. policy for developing a national grid and, after considering several highly qualified candidates, Duncan appointed Archibald Page, at a salary close to his own, to be Chief Engineer and General Manager. Page had been one of the first Electricity Commissioners, although in 1925 he had left to become Director and General Manager of the County of London Company, a pioneer of large-scale power-stations in London. By origin yet another Ayrshire Scot, his earlier experience with Glasgow Corporation and the Clyde Valley Company was to be invaluable in preparing the first grid scheme—that for Central Scotland. To assist him two other senior engineers were appointed: Harold Hobson came with Page from the County of London Company to the post of Supply Engineer, and Johnstone Wright, Chief Engineer and Manager to Belfast Corporation, joined as Deputy Chief Engineer. This triumvirate was to remain at the head of the C.E.B. for the next twenty years.

Both the Board and its chief officers were determined to set a distinctive stamp on the C.E.B. from its inception, to confound the critics on the right, and to resemble the civil service as little as possible. Their image of themselves was as a down-to-earth business-like organization seeking progress by co-operation rather than by the state dictation implied in the 1926 Act. When in later years C.E.B. men were referred to as having been working for a national-ized industry, they reacted angrily, pointing out that they had a 'business' Board which was no more subject to dismissal by the Minister than company directors were by shareholders. In the C.E.B., as in private industry generally,[4] the inter-war period was the golden age of directorial power and management autonomy. The Board also underlined its independence in its financial policy, raising all capital (in the form of non-voting fixed-interest securities) by private placings and public issues on the London market without Treasury guarantee. Above all, it was anxious to take the supply industry's future 'out of politics' and felt that it now had the necessary legislative framework within which to attain this.

(B) BUILDING THE NATIONAL GRID

It was not until March of 1927 that the C.E.B. had its first formal Board meeting—some twenty-two months after the presentation of the Weir Report to the Conservative Government. In the intervening period, the Electricity Commission had retained Sir John Kennedy and Charles Merz as consulting engineers to prepare an economic and engineering appraisal of a practical scheme for the construction of a national grid and the selection of efficient generating stations. Although there were many subsequent alterations to grid routes and station selection, the basic engineering outlines of their suggested schemes were accepted by the Commissioners and the Board. After reviewing the experience of the U.S.A., Australia, and South Africa in transmission technology, they recommended that the grid should operate at a primary voltage of 132 kV, significantly higher than that generally in use in Britain at that time. They also agreed on the major priorities in building the grid: that the industrial areas in which most electricity was generated—South Wales, central Scotland, the Midlands, and the north—together with the metropolis— should be treated first; that in those areas the grid should be completed by 1932 to stifle further uneconomic separate development, and that the whole system should be planned to have a capacity sufficient to meet needs as far ahead as 1940.

Although the target completion date of 1932 might have seemed difficult to meet because of the parliamentary delays in establishing the Central Electricity Board, the Electricity Commissioners were able to do much preparatory work on the required grid schemes during 1926 and early 1927. The burden on the new and untried C.E.B. organization was also alleviated because both the Board and the Commissioners continued to employ the leading electrical engineering consultants—Merz and McLellan, Kennedy and Donkin, Highfield and Roger Smith—to provide the technical and financial informa-tion required for evaluation of the regional schemes. Whilst the Board relied on outside experts for the evaluation of schemes, in the last resort they were prepared to back the judgement of their engineers and would sometimes modify technical recommendations where it was important to do so in the interest of good business relations. Duncan expressed his policy to representatives of the municipal electricity supply undertakings in these terms:

it would be the height of folly for the Central Electricity Board to pretend that it could make the Grid the success it could, and should, be without the fullest co-operation of the supply industry. The Board never had thought that. He wished to assure the industry that the Central Electricity Board would not be a heart-breaking bureaucracy, but that it intended to do its job by seeking the utmost collaboration and co-operation with the industry.

This was essential for, it will be recalled, the C.E.B. was not, in Weir's scheme, to own or operate power-stations, but merely had power to direct their operation. These powers would obviously be more effective if a good co-operative relationship could be built up than if the C.E.B. had to rely on legislative compulsion. However, the industry itself had opposed the creation of the C.E.B., and, even after the legislative battle was lost, local engineers continued to resist the idea of taking a bulk supply, whether from the Board or elsewhere. The Board thus met continuing friction and coolness.

Although these omens were hardly favourable, it was the statutory duty of the Board to consult the local undertakings about the regional schemes and it required all the tact and diplomacy of Duncan and Page—who shouldered the main burden of these discussions—to bring them to a constructive conclusion. They tried to meet all criticisms in personal consultations rather than in time-consuming and refractory public hearings, and were willing to make timely concessions to secure co-operation rather than to seek confrontation by relying on their legal powers.

The crucial decisions concerned the routes of interconnecting lines and the building of new stations. In these cases the Board was prepared to act decisively, though not always along the lines foreshadowed by the Weir Committee. Careful economic assessment of each case on its merits was the Board's major aim in policy development, but it was sometimes compromised by expediency, for its desire to placate individual undertakings seems to have led to the deliberate selection of an excessive number of stations. The Weir Committee had recommended a target figure of 60 stations to serve the whole country, although it had recognized that the current fashion for concentrating generation in 'superpower' stations could be uneconomic because of the additional costs of transmission. The Commissioners implicitly accepted this qualification in their draft schemes by selecting as many as 118 stations and by the time the C.E.B. had made further modifications this number was increased to more than double the number envisaged in the Weir Report. A major factor in their decisions seems to have been the Board's recognition that prestige attached to an undertaking having its stations 'selected' and they bestowed the favour freely, erring on the side of generosity to win the willing co-operation of undertakings, and gain effective control of their power stations.

The obstacles to speedy agreement on questions of grid planning naturally delayed work, but it is perhaps not surprising—in view of the Ayrshire origins of the Board's leading personnel—that they were overcome first in central Scotland. This was the first area scheme to be approved, and the first contracts for the grid in Scotland were placed in December 1927. The other area schemes soon followed: south-east England, central England, and north-west England and North Wales in 1928, mid-east England in 1929, followed in 1930 by south-west England and South Wales, north-east England and eastern England, and in 1931 by south Scotland.

Among the various problems encountered in the construction of the grid, the non-co-operation of landowners occasioned a vast amount of painstaking work, sometimes by Board members on a personal basis, while aesthetic objections to the steel towers (pylons) on which transmission lines were to be carried were at least equally severe. It is easy to understand that their strident novelty created a *frisson* among country-lovers akin to that which Wordsworth had felt a century earlier when the Kendal & Windermere Railway was being constructed. The Board strove hard to gain public acceptance and in parts of the Lake District, the Sussex Downs, and the New Forest it resorted to expensive re-routing and undergrounding to preserve areas of natural beauty. Fortunately for the grid, the environmentalist lobby's dislike of the pylons was balanced by a strong popular desire to promote the electrification of country areas and isolated towns. In the Lake District, Workington Corporation was not slow to assure the Board that an electricity supply was required in west Cumberland, despite the distant complaints of city-dwelling nature-lovers writing in the London Press; and politicians, similarly conscious of the benefits, shared the local authority's view. Even apart from the long-term benefit of cheap electricity which the grid promised, it was welcomed for the employment opportunities it could offer. In the Depression of 1929-33 (when the bulk of grid construction was undertaken) the C.E.B. provided an immediate increase in jobs, many of them in the most depressed industrial areas. At a time when the rest of British industry was cutting back investment in response to the stock-market crisis of 1929 and the international collapse of 1931, the C.E.B. and the electricity undertakings were engaged on a large bout of spending; and in 1931-2, the two years of deepest depression (with up to 23 per cent of the work-force unemployed), capital expenditure by the industry was higher than ever before. The downturn in the economy was thus less sharp, and the recovery earlier and stronger, than it would have been in the absence of the C.E.B.'s investment programme.

The concentration of the work of constructing the grid in the depression years—when there was surplus labour and ample manufacturing capacity—was a happy accident, but, combined with the efficiency of the C.E.B.'s own organization and management, it did enable it to complete the grid ahead of schedule and within the original cost estimates.Some individual sections of the grid began operating under temporary trading arrangements in 1930, and by the end of 1932 some 1,360 miles of primary lines, 596 miles of secondary lines, and 94 miles of underground cable had been energized. Most of the rest followed in the course of 1933, and on 5 September of that year the last grid pylon was erected in the New Forest. Initial estimates of grid construction costs had varied from £24 m. to £29 m.; and despite additional undergrounding, re-routing, and the construction of some additional secondary lines, expenditure in each of the areas had been kept broadly within these initial estimates.[5] Full grid trading under the terms of the 1926 Act—with the C.E.B. directing the operation of selected stations and buying and selling electricity to and from electricity undertakings—could therefore begin in central Scotland and mid-east England in January 1933 and in south-east England, eastern England, central England, and north-west England in the following year. By the end of 1934 the grid was operating in most[6] of the country.

(c) OPERATIONS: REFORMING POWER GENERATION

The advent of the grid transformed the operational control of major power-stations throughout the country. As soon as trading began, the Board sent formal notice to the owners of all the selected stations; from that moment on the Board took over the direction of the operation of these stations which from that time forward worked for the grid and not solely for the undertakings (which, however, continued to own and run them). In return, the Board accepted responsibility for all costs, including capital charges (depreciation and interest) and overheads, irrespective of whether it used the station or not. The Board thus became responsible for both the security of supply and the economical generation of most of the electricity sold by public supply undertakings in Britain,[7] and it now had clear executive authority to use the grid to achieve by compulsory means what the industry had in a desultory fashion been groping towards under the voluntary provision of the 1919 Act. As in the preparation of schemes, however, there was something to be said for tempering compulsory powers with a co-operative approach, and district consultative committees were established by the Board in each grid area. A National Consultative Committee was also established to discuss broader policy questions, but all these committees were advisory, not executive. It was the C.E.B. itself which, subject to the provisions of the 1926 Act, took the major policy initiatives and devised the operating procedures.

The change in the character of the Board's work from that of planning and construction to that of operating and managing the grid system of national power generation and transmission was reflected in an increase in the number of staff directly employed and in changing internal organization. By 1934, when most grid areas were operating, the Board's work-force had risen to

1,248 (of whom less than half were manual workers) from an initial level in the grid construction stage of 300–500, and, in view of the complex trading relationships with electricity undertakings, the commercial side of the Board became as important as its technical side. The Board's increased scope was also reflected in the change in the title of the head of each district from District Engineer to District Manager in 1931. In 1932–3 Archibald Page's duties were divided and he became General Manager whilst the more technical duties of the post became the prerogative of Johnstone Wright as Chief Engineer. At the same time Harold Hobson, previously known as the Supply Engineer, received the title Commercial Manager to reflect the new and wider scope of his duties when trading began. This separation of engineering and commercial functions remained and when in 1935 Sir Andrew Duncan resigned the chairmanship, the structure was firmly established: he was succeeded as Chairman by Archibald Page, Harold Hobson became General Manager, and Johnstone Wright remained Chief Engineer.

The grid was designed to be operated in seven self-sufficient areas with grid control centres at Glasgow, Newcastle, Manchester, Leeds, Birmingham, Bristol, and London.[8] Inter-area tie-lines were provided for use in emergency and to facilitate maintenance. The regional grid control centres were able to plan generating programmes so as to concentrate production on the more efficient stations much more effectively than had previously been possible under voluntary agreements for bulk supply and joint working. In each area the stations with the lowest operating costs were singled out to supply the base load by working non-stop, three shifts a day, for most of the year. There were also two-shift stations—also of high efficiency—which closed down at night and, sometimes, during the summer and at weekends; in addition, these stations were held in readiness in the event of interruption of supply from the base-load stations. Finally, there were peak-load or one-shift stations which were operated for only a few hours in winter to meet the peak. The retention of some of the less efficient stations for short periods of operation did not seriously increase fuel consumption and had the merit of deferring the need to invest in large, new capital stations to meet the growth in peak demand. There were also some 300 non-selected generating stations outside the grid system, but most of the undertakings operating them found it more economic to take a grid supply at least for their base load, using their own stations for peaks only. There was clearly room for negotiation here and the Board agreed to pay such undertakings a rental for the use of their station at peak times in return for agreement to take their supplies from the Board, thus bringing their stations under the control of the regional grid control centres.

The upshot of these arrangements for the centralized control of selected and non-selected stations was the concentration of generation on the more efficient stations. The efficient base-load stations operated at high-load factors—thus increasing their efficiency further by eliminating start-up and shut-down costs—and soon supplied the bulk of the nation's power needs. By 1935, when there were 148 generating stations operating under the direction of the Board, only 28 of these were base-load stations and more than half of the system's requirements were generated by only 15 stations. In 1935 operating costs were 11 per cent less than the costs of the same stations under independent operation in 1932, and by 1938, with the new stations on stream and average efficiency even further improved, the C.E.B. estimated that its power costs under interconnected operation were £32 m.—£3¼ m. less than under independent operation.

The grid also opened up the way to reducing costs by the development of new, efficient power-stations, achieving scale economies on a level unattainable by the smaller, independent undertakings. However, the immediate impact of the grid was to slow down the building of extensions and new stations: for with interconnection it was possible to supply national electricity requirements with a much lower level of spare plant than had been necessary under independent operation. In 1925 as much as 43 per cent of the plant installed in power-stations was for reserve purposes, but by 1938 interconnected operation under C.E.B. direction made possible a lower target safety margin of around 10 per cent. By that year the Board estimated that it had saved undertakings some £33 m. of capital expenditure on the spare plant which would otherwise have been necessary. However, when new extensions and new power-stations were planned, the C.E.B. was now able to consider the likely growth in demand for the whole grid region rather than a single undertaking, and it was therefore possible to plan for larger units. Given the economies of scale in the industry, this meant lower operating costs and cheaper capital costs. The skill with which the C.E.B. planned the system could therefore have a fundamental long-term impact on its efficiency.

What did the C.E.B. and power-station designers actually achieve? In the period 1920–9 there had been net additions to generating capacity of some 4,291 MW, and by 1937 there was a further net addition of 2,313 MW, bringing the total British public supply capacity to 8,913 MW. The majority of these inter-war plant additions became selected stations in the grid schemes and it was on their design and operation that the efficiency of power generation fundamentally depended. The C.E.B. supported those engineers wanting to increase the capacity of sets in their new plant programmes, and also hoped to be able to minimize capital costs by standardizing on a limited range of sizes. Of the 172 new sets whose installation it authorized between 1927 and 1942, more than half were in the two standard sizes of 30 MW and 50 MW. The Board's new plant programmes also allowed for some experimentation with larger sets, though only in south-eastern England was demand felt to be growing sufficiently rapidly to justify sets above 60 MW: two 75-MW sets were sanctioned at Barking 'B' in 1930 and another in 1937; at Battersea a 105-MW set was sanctioned in 1933 for the 'A' station and a 100-MW set in

1936 for Battersea 'B'. Despite some criticism that it was too conservative in its policy, the Board therefore chose not to risk going beyond the sizes at which it was confident that economies of scale were not merely theoretically attainable, but were likely to be attained in practice. Even with this cautious policy, it was able to reverse Britain's earlier technical backwardness relative to her competitors. In the 1920s sets in Germany, for example, had been consistently larger than those installed in Britain, but by the 1930s Battersea's 105-MW set was the largest operating in Europe, and the only others above 60 MW were 2 x 85 MW and 3 x 80 MW sets in the German Zschornewitz and Klingenberg stations.

The new power-station construction programme, coupled with the C.E.B.'s policy of concentrating base-load generation on the newer, more efficient stations, led to a substantial and sustained improvement in the over-all efficiency of British power generation. Figure 11.1 shows the thermal efficiency achieved by all British stations; the performance of the best station in each year is also shown for comparison. As can be seen, not only did larger sets and design improvements yield a continuing advance of the technological frontier but, more significantly, the average performance showed an even stronger upward tendency, as the Board was able to concentrate demand on the more efficient stations. More concretely, these figures meant that each ton of coal produced more electricity: from only 443 units per ton in 1914 and 631 units in 1920, output rose to 1,566 units per ton by 1939. The gap between British and American power-station efficiency—which had been wide in the 1920s—had been virtually eliminated by the later 1930s. The consumer did

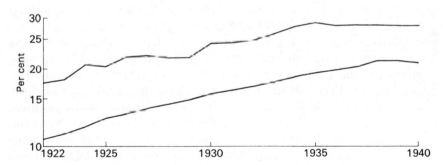

FIG. 11.1. Thermal Efficiency of British Steam-Generating Stations, 1922–1940
(log scale: slopes indicate rates of growth)

not benefit from this technical efficiency as much as had been hoped, for the government-backed coal-owners' cartel used its market power effectively in the economic upswing to raise power-station coal prices by 50 per cent between 1932 and 1938, but increasing efficiency did enable the supply industry to withstand these rises without raising its own prices and discouraging consumption.

In discussing the future organization of power generation from the viewpoint of the mid-1920s, the Weir Committee had laid some stress on the need to maintain diversity and rivalry in the process of innovation, and used this to rationalize the (essentially political) decision to leave power-stations in the hands of the existing undertakings. In general, the C.E.B. respected the undertakings' views on design, for its members were not themselves experts on the generation side, and the senior engineering staff of the undertakings were, in their turn, happy to co-operate with the C.E.B. when it might mean that they would be accorded the challenge and prestige of building a new selected station for the grid system.

Over the question of the siting of station extensions or of new power-stations, however, the C.E.B. had the last word and was able to plan the growth of generating capacity in relation to the needs of the system as a whole. Rather than authorizing entirely new stations, the Board at first favoured expanding on the major sites sanctioned and developed in the 1920s: usually a more economical expedient than an entirely new site, since it required less outlay on civil engineering works. By the mid-1930s, however, many stations were nearing their limit for extensions and the Board devoted more attention to the planning of new stations. It usually favoured sites near the main load centres rather than on coalfields or on the coast, for although sites distant from the load centres often had lower running costs than urban sites, their extra transmission costs to reach the load centres usually told against them.

The Board also resisted political pressure to site new stations in the depressed regions. It was a fact of life that electricity was sold where both industry and people were prosperous and increasingly this meant the south-east and Midlands. Thus when Lord Weir, with Ministry of Transport backing, proposed that new stations totalling 2,000-MW capacity should be erected in the distressed mining areas of South Wales to attract industry and to export surplus supplies to central and southern England, the Board reacted angrily. It doubted whether Weir's scheme for Wales would really enable electricity to be cheapened and it threatened that the required transmission lines would cost £20 m., a grossly absurd overestimate. It is a measure of the C.E.B.'s independent status that the Government, after first threatening to withhold authorization for a station in south-east England, gave way to the C.E.B. opinion, a fact which seems all the more remarkable in the light of the contemporary experience of the steel industry in which a *privately* owned steel company *was* persuaded by the Bank of England and by political hints to invest in South Wales against its own better judgement.[9] On environmental questions, however, the Board and the undertakings had to give way to parliamentary pressure and stations like London's Battersea were forced to install flue-gas washing plant in order to reduce the smoke hazard.

These increasingly stringent environmental requirements, together with the divided responsibility for power-station planning and design, and the growing complexity and size of new power-stations, also made themselves felt in construction delays. Already in the 1920s (when large new power-stations were built in only two years from inception of a scheme to commercial operation) there were complaints that construction was long drawn out compared with large stations in the United States. By the 1930s, when the C.E.B. became responsible for planning, longer periods of three or four years were sometimes necessary. Since the C.E.B. carried the capital charges of all selected stations, the correct planning of grid generation extensions was a condition of its financial success: if too little plant were installed. the Board would be forced to interrupt supplies and would lose load, if it installed too much it bore the whole commercial risk of the capital charges on the plant installed, even if the loads forecast by undertakings did not materialize. The three- and four-year load forecasts for each region therefore became a vital tool of C.E.B. planners and they devoted somewhat more attention to the problems of forecasting than had been common in individual undertakings.

They had little chance to develop successful forecasting methods in the changed conditions of national operation, however, and when pessimistic load forecasts and over-optimistic plant completion targets coincided, the grid system could find itself stretched. In 1938 the Board found itself in this position for the first time as load forecasts were falsified by rearmament (which boosted industrial demand) and by an abnormally cold week which coincided with the annual peak demand just before Christmas. At the same time shortages of skilled labour and of materials slowed down power-station construction, and output capacity was some 4·7 per cent below expectations. The situation was particularly acute in the south-east which had been less seriously hit by the Depression, and in the west where armament factories were being developed out of range of potential bombing attacks. Thus at the time of peak demand in December 1938, although there was a 181-MW surplus in Scotland and the north, there was a 208-MW deficit in the central and southern parts of the country. The deficit could be covered partly by bringing older plant into service and by reducing the margin of spare plant, but the Board recognized that the problem would be a long-term one and started to plan farther ahead and to allow a wider margin of spare plant for such contingencies—a wise precaution since in the event little more than half the plant it programmed could, in fact, be commissioned in the year for which it was planned. The immediate crisis of 1938 was overcome by the exploitation of the hitherto dormant possibilities of the grid as a national, rather than merely regional, network. During 1937 the north and south of the country were regularly run as two main systems, and in the following year a national grid control centre was established at Bankside, London. Thus during the winter months late in 1938 when there was a deficit of capacity in the south, it proved possible to run the whole system in parallel for lengthy periods, providing much needed relief to southern power-stations by exporting electricity from the northern areas in the peak periods. The grid thus proved its value in a crisis and, if the measure of efficient spare capacity planning is that when everything seems to be going wrong supplies can still be maintained, the Board had passed the crucial test.

Whatever its technical and operating merits, however, the C.E.B. knew that in the last resort it would be judged on its financial viability. The Government had set the C.E.B. the objective of covering its costs without being a burden on the taxpayer, or on the supply undertakings, but had recognized that losses would be made in the early years of development before full trading had begin. The Board therefore set its prices for the wholesale supply of electricity to undertakings with the aim of breaking even over a ten-year period from the inception of trading. This posed considerable problems for if it made a loss it would face serious political criticism; if, on the other hand, it set prices too high, independent generation would continue to be economic and it would fail to win the load necessary to break even. Its pricing policy successfully enabled it to negotiate this tightrope and in fact it reported an accumulated surplus of £2¾ m. by 1939 and £7 m. by 1945. Moreover, like many private companies in this period, the Board created secret reserves, and real levels of profit were somewhat higher than these published accounts provided to ministers suggested. Thus the C.E.B. did rather more than break even, and since the contingencies (against which these surpluses were a safety net) never materialized, it in fact turned over an accumulated surplus of £16 m. on nationalization in 1948. This implies, of course, that the Board had been wholesaling electricity for some years at somewhat above the average cost of production.[10]

(D) TARGETS AND PERFORMANCE

Although it had never been the intention of Parliament that it should make a surplus, the Board could not suppress its delight at having made a profit. While management might derive legitimate pleasure from financial success, however, it would be misleading for us to judge the Board's work on this basis: it was, after all, a legislatively privileged organization selling to statutory monopolies and was not subject to the discipline of competition in the market place in the normal sense of that phrase: any 'profit' could represent the fruits of monopoly power rather than a reward for efficiency. The real savings of the grid, moreover, accrued—and were intended by Parliament to accrue—not to the Board, but to the electricity supply undertakings, and ultimately, to the electricity consumers themselves.

These potential savings had been sketched out in great detail by the Weir Committee in 1925, and the national grid can claim a first place in the annals of government initiatives in industrial affairs for the extraordinary accuracy of these forecasts on which the major investment was based. The Weir Committee had assumed a growth in electricity sales of 19 per cent per annum, and on this basis it expected 1940 sales to reach 500 units per head of population—21,385 m. units in all—at an average retail price, if the grid were successfully completed, of 1*d*. or less per unit. It was thus some credit to the Board that by 1940 this output was in fact slightly exceeded—with sales of 518 units per head being achieved—and a price to the final consumer only slightly higher than expected—1·061*d*. per unit—was attained. The proportion of this price over which the C.E.B. had some control was that which related to generation rather than to distribution, and here also the forecasts of 1925 proved remarkably accurate. The cost of energy 'at the busbars' (i.e. at the point where energy is fed into the transmission or distribution system) had been 1·098*d*. per unit in 1923, and the Weir Committee set a target of 0·36*d*. for 1940: the actual price paid by the C.E.B. for the power it brought from stations generating under its direction averaged 0·34*d*. per unit in 1939 and 0·39d. per unit in 1940. If we look behind these over-all figures, it is true we can discern substantial divergences between the Weir Committee's plan and the actual outcome: standardization proved more expensive than anticipated, the cost of coal rose rapidly, the operating costs of the grid system and the capital costs of new generating plant exceeded expectations. But these effects, which might have prejudiced the scheme's success, were cancelled out by other factors: power-station efficiency improved to a higher level than had initially seemed feasible, it proved possible to run the grid system with better load factors and a lower level of spare plant than had been envisaged, and interest rates fell, an important benefit in a capital-intensive industry like that of electricity supply. Good luck therefore played its part in bringing the plans of 1925 to fruition, but by the standards of other projects,[11] the achievement of the industry seems none the less impressive. The Board had its share of good fortune: it was a happy coincidence that it constructed the grid during the Slump (when men and materials were in plentiful supply) and that its main trading occurred in the easier conditions of the recovery of the 1930s (when the growth of load made possible the rapid realization of savings). The management of the Board—and of the power-stations which worked in concert with it—also deserves credit for maintaining production schedules and containing over-all costs; for while the efficiency increases (which partly cancelled out unexpected increases in general costs) were not expected, they were worked for, and all this was achieved despite the extremely difficult relations which persisted as a legacy of the political battles behind the 1926 Act.

Yet beyond the immediate sphere of influence of the Board's own engineers and managers, there was also a more fundamental reason for the uncanny accuracy of the basic forecasts made in 1925. That reason can be found in the Weir Committee's dominating motive in making its recommendations. It is simply that in 1925 Britain's electrical development lagged seriously behind that of other industrial nations and the creation of an interconnected power-station system by the C.E.B., far from being a technological leap in the dark, was rather a process of catching up along a path already well trodden by foreign electricity supply systems. The main features of the technology—and of the conditions for its economic application—were well known and the C.E.B. was a technical follower, not a pioneer; introducing the best of (largely foreign) practice into the chaotic British inheritance of costly local power generating systems. The Board made great play with the claim that its was the first truly 'national' grid, but, whilst this might have some patriotic appeal, it was not a matter of technical novelty. There were several more extensive interconnected power systems abroad at the time the British grid was being built, and the 132-kV transmission system was well tried when it was adopted by the Board, and by 1940 was looking positively outdated.

To point this out is, of course, no more to condemn the Board than an injunction to use L-plates would be a condemnation of a would-be driver's desire to learn. The capabilities of the British electricity supply industry, in which most engineers had been cut off from more advanced transmission practice, were necessarily limited, and British consulting engineers, with their extensive experience on overseas contracts, reasonably chose for their inexperienced compatriots a well-tested transmission voltage. Furthermore, the needs of the British economy—which was fortunate in having plentiful coal supplies near most of the major load centres—were not such as to require pioneering on the frontiers of transmission technology. In contrast to countries in which electricity had to be transmitted for long distances between hydro or brown coal production centres and distant consuming areas, Britain required not high voltage transmission, but rather interconnection on a regional basis in order to economize on spare plant and operating costs; for this purpose a 132-kV system was perfectly adequate. To say that the Board was not in any important sense a technological pioneer is not, then, to detract from its essential achievement of increasing the efficiency of British power generation, nor indeed is it to deny that the grid presented challenging opportunities to management and engineering staff for creative problem-solving, for high-voltage transmission technology needed to be adapted to British conditions. But such adaptations were made within the confines of a technology whose fundamental parameters were already known.[12]

In recent discussions of Britain's economic performance, there are two related doctrines which constantly recur: that the British are good at inventing new techniques but not at applying them, and that Britain has a low rate of economic growth because she has borne the costs of path-breaking and other countries are catching up. In the electricity supply industry between the wars the picture was assuredly the reverse, with foreign countries as the early innovators and Britain reaping the benefits as the late-comer. It was, on the whole, a happy experience and one with which the industry could be well pleased.[13]

In the space of fifteen years between 1925 and 1940 the national grid system enabled the British supply undertakings to overcome their previous lag in development and inaugurate a vigorous expansion of sales based on low prices for the consumer.[14] By the late 1930s Britain's electricity consumption per head of population equalled that in countries with similar income levels. It was only when the process of catching-up was complete that technical pioneering could safety be allowed to come into its own, and the next stage of the C.E.B.'s development was to present problems not merely of working out an existing technology but of developing a new one appropriate to an unknown technical and economic future. But that story belongs to a later part of the growth of public enterprise in the electricity supply industry, a story which must be told elsewhere.[15]

NOTES

1 This chapter is a condensed version of parts of the author's forthcoming history of the British electricity supply industry between 1882 and 1948 to be publshed by Macmillan in 1978. Full acknowledgements, disclaimers, and citations of sources are made there.

2 *Report of the [Weir] Committee appointed to review the National Problem of the Supply of Electrical Energy* (H.M.S.O., 1926), paras 7, 22, 17.

3 Sir Andrew Rae Duncan (1884–1952), knighted 1921, G.B.E. 1938. He remained Chairman until 1935 and a member until 1940, leaving to become Chairman of the Executive of the British Iron and Steel Federation (1935–40, 1945–52), President of the Board of Trade (1940–1), Minister of Supply (1940–1, 1942–5), and National (i.e. Conservative) M.P. for the City of London (1940–50). At the time of his appointment he was Chairman of the advisory committee at the Mines Department (1920–9); he became a Director of I.C.I., Royal Exchange Assurance, North British Locomotive Co., Dunlop, and the Bank of England.

4 In private industry, ownership was increasingly divorced from control, and the formal rights of shareholders had little effect; before the development of take-over bids in the 1950s there were few effective disciplines on Directors to maximize their shareholders' returns.

5 The standardization on the 50-H_z frequency of non-standard local systems cost an additional £17·3 m., £6·8 m. above estimates, but this was largely due to factors beyond the Board's control.

6 Two areas did not start C.E.B. trading until 1937: south Scotland, where hydro-electric schemes were not yet complete, and north-east England, where standardization was a protracted business.

7 Selected stations accounted for 82 per cent of public electricity supply in 1934–5, 93·6 per cent in 1938–9, and 96 per cent in 1946–7. Because of special agreements with non-selected station owners the proportions generated under the direction of the Board were somewhat higher than these figures suggest.

8 The two small districts—south Scotland and eastern England—were amalgamated for operational purposes with their larger neighbours—central Scotland and south-east England. North-east England and mid-east England were amalgamated in 1943, reducing the number of districts to six.

9 Richard Thomas & Co. located its new steel strip mill at Ebbw Vale, rather than on the Lincolnshire iron ore fields which Stewart & Lloyds, for example, had chosen for their Corby plant.

10 'Average cost' includes here the 'normal' rate of profit, as represented by the interest rate paid on the Board's capital. It goes without saying that the modern conventional wisdom that the correct price to charge is not historic average cost but long-run marginal cost (see e.g. M. V. Posner, *Fuel Policy: A Study in Applied Economics*, London, 1973) would not have been acceptable since the Board's long-run marginal costs were considerably lower than historic average costs, given the inheritance of bad investment decisions from the

early 1920s, which the C.E.B. bore. A subsidy would thus have been required: a solution which would have been as repugnant to the C.E.B. as it was to the Government.

11 Cf. I.C.I.'s decision in the later 1920s to build a large new high-pressure chemical plant at Billingham: cost and sales estimates were wildly optimistic and much of the capital at Billingham had to be written off in the 1930s. (W. J. Reader, *Imperial Chemical Industries: A History*, ii (Oxford, 1975), 111, 120–9, 171–8.)

12 The national responsibility of the C.E.B. did, however, result in the gradual development of a coherent design philosophy and an integrated operating philosophy which were to become a major strength of the British system, compared with the more fragmented and voluntary schemes of interconnection abroad.

13 The C.E.B.'s experience in the 1930s was not exceptional: other science-based and mass-production industries, in which Britain had fallen behind in the period 1900–30, also experienced rapid growth in the 1930s and the growth rate of the economy over all was in that period one of the highest achieved by industrial nations (see H. W. Richardson, 'The New Industries between the Wars', *Oxford Economic Papers*, xiii (1961), and his *Economic Recovery in Britain, 1932–39* (London, 1967).

14 D. A. Wilson, 'The Strategy of Sales Expansion in the British Electricity Supply Industry between the Wars', in L. Hannah (ed.), *Management Strategy and Business Development* (London, 1976).

15 In the present author's forthcoming history of the nationalized electricity supply industry since 1948.

12

Imperial Chemical Industries and the State, 1926-1945[1]

W. J. READER

(A) PUBLIC POLICY AND PRIVATE PROFIT: THE I.C.I. MERGER, 1926

IN December 1926 the founders of I.C.I. announced

> The Company has, of deliberate purpose, been given the title of 'IMPERIAL CHEMICAL INDUSTRIES LIMITED'. The British Empire is the greatest single economic unit in the world, one in which every patriotic member of the great British Commonwealth has a personal interest. By linking the title of the new Company to that unit, it is intended to lay emphasis upon the fact that the promotion of Imperial trading interests will command the special consideration and thought of those who will be responsible for directing this new Company.

The economics and the sentiments of this confident statement are out of date, but there is still no doubt about the truth of the central implication: that I.C.I. was and is closely associated with wide aspects of public policy. During the period covered by this chapter, I.C.I.'s relations with the state were continuous and close, though never formalized by state shareholding or direct government representation on the Board.

One of the original impulses towards the foundation of I.C.I. came from the direction of public policy, via that network of semi-official channels, straddling the frontier between business and politics, through which so much influence flowed in Great Britain between the wars. The impulse arose, as these things often do, from a conversation at lunch-time. The lunch was held in January 1926 and the lunchers were Sir Harry McGowan and Reginald McKenna. McGowan (1874–1961), son of a Glasgow brass-fitter, was Chairman and Managing Director of Nobel Industries Limited: an amalgamation, which he had been instrumental in forming, of the principal explosives firms in Great Britain and their associates and subsidiaries in non-ferrous metals, ammunition, and motor components. He was a professional manager, of strong views and dictatorial temperament. McKenna (1863–1943) was a representative figure of the ruling upper middle class of late Victorian England. A scholar of

Trinity Hall, he had read for the Mathematical Tripos and rowed for Cambridge University. Then he had practised at the Bar until he went into Parliament in 1895, and under Campbell-Bannerman and Asquith he held steadily more important positions until from May 1915 to December 1916 he was Chancellor of the Exchequer. The fall of Asquith put an end to his formal political career, but he remained close to the centre of affairs as Chairman of the Midland Bank from 1919 to 1943, preferring to exercise influence from that appointment rather than power from ministerial office. The proposition he put to McGowan was that Nobel Industries, for reasons of national policy rather than commercial profit, should take over British Dyestuffs Corporation and, with it, responsibility for the British dyestuffs industry: an industry of prime importance if the country went to war.

McKenna and McGowan both knew the British dyestuffs industry only too well. After a promising start in the 1850s it fell far behind German competitors, and in 1914 it was totally inadequate to supply not only dyestuffs but a large range of related chemical products—drugs, photographic chemicals, rubber chemicals, ingredients for explosives, and poison gases— without which the war could not be carried on.[2] A peculiarly inept sally by Government into company promotion, in 1915, produced British Dyes Limited which was supposed to be, but never was, an amalgamation of the principal British dyestuffs makers. In fact, most of its activity was concentrated on the manufacture of dimethylaniline for explosives, not dyestuffs at all.

In 1918–19 the Government tried again, this time getting the two main British dyestuffs businesses into common ownership under a holding company, British Dyestuffs Corporation Limited. The driving force came from the President of the Board of Trade, Sir Albert Stanley (1874–1948), another man of two worlds, business and politics. He became Lord Ashfield in 1920 and built a great reputation on his work for London Transport (as well as being a Director of I.C.I.), but B.D.C., despite the benefit of plentiful advice from McGowan, who for a time had a seat on the Board, was not a happy venture. The Corporation had the misfortune to be formed on an ambitious scale in the hectic optimism of the brief post-war boom and then to be plunged, burdened with too much capital, too much productive capacity, and two quarrelling Managing Directors, into what was perhaps the biggest economic disaster in modern British history: the Slump of 1920–1. B.D.C.'s constitution gave the Government a 17 per cent holding, the right to appoint two Directors with wide powers of veto, and, in the last resort, complete control over the Company's activities, though the control was chiefly negative: a matter of finding out what B.D.C. intended to do and telling it to stop. On top of everything else, B.D.C. was disliked and despised by most of its important customers, who far preferred to buy dyestuffs from the Germans as they had done before the war. The Government, however, prevented that—after a great deal of damage had been done by German imports in 1920—by the Dyestuffs (Import Regulations) Act 1921: a measure which did nothing to endear B.D.C. to cotton manufacturers struggling against ferocious Japanese competition.

From this unpromising, indeed hopeless, situation B.D.C. sought to escape by coming to terms with the Germans, exchanging access to the British market for German technical knowledge. The Germans were very keen to get into Great Britain but they had no opinion at all of B.D.C.'s competitive strength and as a consequence the terms they offered were extremely unattractive, including a fifty-year profit-sharing agreement. A draft was eventually worked out, after two years' negotiating, in December 1923, which B.D.C. was prepared to sign. The minority Labour Government of the day, however, advised by a committee of which Reginald McKenna was Chairman, refused its consent, and the agreement died. After that, with the backing of Sir Philip Cunliffe-Lister (formerly Lloyd-Graeme and later Lord Swinton), President of the Board of Trade in Baldwin's Government which came to power in October 1924, B.D.C. was comprehensively reconstructed. The Chairman, Sir William Alexander (1879–1954), withdrew to the Conservative back benches, where he had had a seat since 1923 and where he remained until 1945. Lord Ashfield, who did not like him (nor did McKenna), succeeded him. The Government abandoned its veto powers and accepted £600,000 for a share-holding which had cost £1,700,000. The capital was written down from £9·2 m. to £4·8 m.

This was the business, with an unhappy history of official intervention, which the Government, through McKenna, offered to McGowan. He found the offer most unattractive, and said so. 'I told Mr. McKenna', he said in 1946, 'that I could not contemplate surplus earnings of Nobels being used to bolster up British Dyes.' Then he passed on to the wider question which lay behind McKenna's proposal—how to reconstruct the British chemical industry to meet increasingly formidable foreign competition.

What was in the minds of both men was the formation, in the autumn of 1925, of I.G. Farbenindustrie, a very large merger of German chemical businesses with an outstanding record of technical and commercial success stretching back half a century and more. In the United States also the trend of the early 1920s was towards large, diversified chemical businesses. The competitive threat was obvious, and McGowan had his answer ready: 'If we had a combination of, say, Nobels, Brunner, Mond and British Dyestuffs Corporation, and possibly the United Alkali Co., we would be in a much more powerful position in which to negotiate with the IG.' McGowan, in other words, was proposing to amalgamate every important firm in the British chemical industry, just as, in 1918, he had amalgamated every important firm in the British explosives industry. McKenna, according to McGowan, 'heartily approved the idea' and wanted to take it straight to the Prime Minister. This was the genesis of I.C.I., and it will be seen that the Government was in it from the start. Its concern was chiefly with warlike supply. Like every other combatant Government, except the German, at the outbreak of the Great War, the British Government had been badly frightened by the inadequacy of its own country's dyestuffs industry, and it was determined not to be caught again. Hence its concern for the welfare of B.D.C. Beyond that, it could see the need for strengthening the British chemical industry generally, and thus the idea of what was at first called 'a British IG' began to take shape, not quite on government initiative, but certainly with government blessing.

We are not here concerned with the set of curious chances by which I.C.I. was actually brought into being, in R.M.S. *Aquitania* in mid-Atlantic on passage from New York to Southampton, nor need we examine Sir Alfred Mond's scheme for a gigantic alliance between British, German, and American chemical interests. That was defeated in New York, by the opposition of the proposed American partner, before the *Aquitania* put to sea. Sir Harry Mc-Gowan appeared in New York, rather like the Demon King through a stage trapdoor, just as the American blow was delivered and Mond fell in with McGowan's ideas instead of his own. Their agreement led to the merger of the four largest British chemical businesses of the day: Brunner, Mond; Nobel Industries; British Dyestuffs Corporation; United Alkali Company. Imperial Chemical Industries, thus formed, was impressively large by most standards of measurement.

It was large in capital employed—£73 m. It was large in the number of people employed—47,000 in the United Kingdom alone. It was large in its geographical spread—factories, jointly owned with Du Pont, De Beers, and other partners, in Canada, South Africa, Australasia, South America, as well as a substantial and varied export trade. It was large in the breadth of its activities, which covered heavy chemicals, explosives, dyestuffs, and fertilizers. Comparisons in matters of industrial size are notoriously difficult to make, but I.C.I., in the 1920s and 1930s, was generally held to be the largest manufacturing enterprise in the United Kingdom, far ahead of any but three or four others, and in the chemical industry of the world there were certainly no more than two or three larger businesses. The balance of I.C.I.'s activities differed a good deal from those of other businesses in the same class, and on the organic side, at the time of the merger I.C.I. was underdeveloped on the organic side. By 1939 it was catching up fast, and there is no doubt that the merger succeeded in its major objective: to make sure that the British chemical industry could stand up for itself, or alongside, the American and German heavyweights.

Sir Alfred Mond (1868–1930), raised to the peerage in 1928 as Lord Melchett, became the first Chairman of I.C.I., with McGowan as President and the two of them as joint Managing Directors. Mond was a frustrated politician. From Brunner, Mond's business (founded by his father, Ludwig Mond, in partnership with John Brunner) he had gone into Parliament as a Liberal in 1906, and from 1916 to 1922 he held office as First Commissioner of Works and then (1921–2) as Minister of Health. Lloyd George's fall ruined his political career and he moved back, as a second-best, into business, though not at first into the family firm, except as a non-executive Director. The discovery of dishonest dealings in which he was in no way involved, by Brunner, Mond with Lever Brothers obliged him to take a more active part, and it was as full-time Chairman of Brunner, Mond that he participated in the negotiations leading up to the founding of I.C.I.

Mond, who remained an M.P. until he was ennobled, thus occupied the same middle ground between business and politics as Ashfield and McKenna, and the I.C.I. Board included other figures from that part of the landscape. Among the early Directors, as well as Ashfield himself, there were Lord Reading, who had been Lord Chief Justice and Viceroy of India; Lord Weir, who had been Secretary of State for Air; Lord Birkenhead, who had been Lord Chancellor. The tradition continued into the 1950s and beyond. Directors of this stamp might, perhaps, be considered informal trustees for the public interest, and they certainly ensured a close connection between I.C.I. and the world of government and politics. It was ensured in other ways as well: it was not by chance that Imperial Chemical House was built only a few hundred yards along the Embankment from the Houses of Parliament.

Mond's own view of I.C.I.'s affairs, as might be expected from his earlier career, had a political slant to it: that is to say, as well as seeing them from an ordinary commercial point of view he saw them also from the point of view of the national interest as understood by a Liberal Imperialist (after 1926, a Conservative) who claimed to have invented the word 'rationalization' and prided himself on being, as he put it, 'the Head of the Chemical Industry in this country'. As an ex-Minister of the Crown, Mond held a public position which McGowan deeply respected and did not attempt to challenge. As a far more experienced business man, and as the author of a design for I.C.I. which had been preferred to Mond's own, McGowan might have been expected to resent seeing Mond in the Chair, but he did not lack magnanimity and he seems to have been perfectly content. Moreover, all the evidence suggests that in matters of policy he was usually prepared to defer to Mond's judgement. Certainly the first major investment decision taken by the Board of I.C.I. came straight from Brunner, Mond, with Alfred Mond's enthusiastic endorsement. He did not foresee that within a year or two of his own death it would bring I.C.I. to the point of seeking government assistance, and assistance from a Labour Government at that.

(B) AMMONIA, PETROL, AND POLITICS, 1926–1939

To Mond's mind, when I.C.I. was formed, the most promising technical development which any of the founder firms brought into the merger was a process for synthesizing ammonia which Brunner, Mond had brought very close to the point of commercial production. The project, based on Billingham near the mouth of the Tees, was very large, and it was straining Brunner, Mond's unaided resources, which was one reason why Brunners had no objection to being absorbed into I.C.I., with its command of very considerable reserves, in cash and investments, belonging to Nobel Industries.

Ammonia was needed chiefly, in peacetime, as a source of nitrogen for fertilizers, particularly ammonium sulphate. One of the periodical messages of doom about world food supplies had set off a search, early in the century, for practical means of adding to the world's production of ammonia, and a process developed by the Badische Anilin und Soda Fabrik was in production in Germany by 1913. Ammonia could also be oxidized to nitric acid for explosives, and consequently a process for synthesizing ammonia might be of great importance in war. The Haber-Bosch process, as developed in B.A.S.F., had in fact been of very great importance in Germany between 1914 and 1918, being used almost entirely for explosives, not fertilizers.[3] As a consequence, governments everywhere, including the British Government, were anxious to encourage the development of synthetic ammonia processes, though preferably by private enterprise rather than at public expense. Brunner, Mond in 1919 were ready enough to oblige, having immense self-confidence and being eager to diversify. A piratical descent upon B.A.S.F.'s works at Oppau, in the heady atmosphere of victory and 'Make Germany Pay', produced a certain amount of stolen information which the Germans promptly stole back again, and after that a process was developed, chiefly by Brunner's own staff, which came into I.C.I. in 1926. The process worked by combining hydrogen with nitrogen from the air to form ammonia (NH_3) under severe and, at the time, unfamiliar conditions of heat and pressure. The engineering problems were formidable, the more so because the object was to develop a large-scale process capable in the end of supplying nitrogen for the production of fertilizers in quantities measured in hundreds of thousands, perhaps millions, of tons. Development costs were bound to be high and capital investment very large: hence Brunner, Mond's straitened circumstances in 1926.

Mond was not deterred by considerations like these, nor by the information that enough ammonia was being supplied in Great Britain, as a by-product of coke ovens, to make all the nitrogenous fertilizers that farmers in the home market could be persuaded to buy. What Mond foresaw was a plant, owned by I.C.I., large enough to supply the entire nitrogen requirements of the British Empire, with a supporting service of agricultural advisers under the direction of Sir Frederick Keeble, F.R.S. (1870–1952), who gave up the Sherardian Chair of Botany at Oxford to devote himself to the enterprise. Again there were trifling difficulties, such as Keeble's own opinion that 'unfortunately most of the British Empire thinks it needs phosphorus much more than nitrogen', and the fact that the entire demand from the British Empire was not so large as might be imagined, being no greater than the demand from Germany, the home market of I.C.I.'s chief rival, the I.G., Mond and his advisers and McGowan, who in this matter was easily persuadable, brushed these inconveniences aside and in the autumn of 1927 I.C.I. was committed to the investment of some £20 m. in fertilizer plant at Billingham.

Given the received opinion of the day (implied in the founders' statement about I.C.I.) that Great Britain would find economic salvation in the markets of the British Empire, the fertilizer project had obvious political attractions for Alfred Mond. But behind this vast project loomed another, no less vast, which had the same sort of attraction even more strongly, being related both to Imperial defence and to the social problem of unemployment in coal-mining. Of the two, the matter of unemployment was the more prominent at first; the matter of defence, later. The project was for the production of motor fuel from coal. The technology was closely related to the technology of synthetic ammonia, since the motor fuel was to be produced by treating coal with hydrogen in very similar vessels and under very similar conditions to those required in the ammonia process. The engineering knowledge gathered for the one could largely be applied to the other, and both processes required hydrogen in large quantities. The political importance of the process, if it could be made to work economically on a large scale, needed no emphasizing. It would do something to make good the lack of home-produced petroleum, not only in Great Britain but elsewhere in the Empire, and that might be very important in war. It would do something, also, to provide work in the coal-fields, which was of immediate importance in the conditions of the late 1920s and early 1930s. Beyond even these two considerations there was the point that the world's sources of petroleum were very imperfectly known, and expert opinion held that they might very well run dry by about the middle of the century. In that case the prospects before an alternative supply of motor fuel—and other oils—might be enormous.

The project, like most new projects in the chemical industry of the 1920s, had its technical home in Germany, with the I.G. Even before I.C.I. was formed, and no less energetically afterwards, Mond was trying to get access to I.G.'s technical knowledge of the petrol process, perhaps in return for access to the British market for dyestuffs. In these negotiations the I.G.'s spokesmen did nothing to play down their technical competence, of which the chemical industry of the rest of the world stood in awe, and Mond was certainly led to believe that they had taken the petrol process further than in fact they had. Long and expensive development work turned out to be necessary, both in England and Germany, and the first commercial plant in Great Britain was not put up until the mid-1930s.

The worst difficulty, however, was not technical: it was economic. Petrol produced in the orthodox way in the 1920s and 1930s was very cheap indeed. One of I.C.I.'s men, in 1932, put the 'normal and proper price' of petrol in ship at London at 5–6*d*. (say 2–2½p) a gallon, and when he spoke it had just been selling at 3*d*. (a little over 1p). Marketing costs, profit, and taxation

barely brought the retail price as high as 2s. (10p) for the best petrol, and in
1928 it was under 1s. 2d. (less than 6p). To compete, petrol would have to be
produced from coal very cheaply indeed. This it never could be. The estimated
cost of large-scale production in I.C.I. moved downward from 11·8d. (4·9p) a
gallon in 1929 to 7·93d. (3·30p) about four years later, but the reduction was
by no means great enough. Coal-based petrol was never at any time a commercial proposition which could stand on its own feet, yet it was of great
importance to I.C.I. that it should stand. Mond and his colleagues very
quickly realized that it was only likely to do so with government support, and
they set out to seek it.

Mond's own line of approach, early in the proceedings, was towards supplies for the armed services. The way was opened for him, early in 1928, by
Sir Maurice Hankey,[4] who asked for confidential information on I.C.I.'s
progress with the petrol project. Mond, with characteristic confidence, told
Hankey 'there was no technical difficulty: it was merely a matter of money.'
Within a few years, he thought, the Germans would make themselves independent of imported liquid fuel, and he asked for government help, nature
unspecified, for putting up plant for some 200 tons of petrol a day. He did not
get it. The year of the Kellogg Pact, 1928, was no year to talk to the Cabinet
about spending money on warlike supply, especially with the 'ten-year rule' in
force and the author of it, Winston Churchill, at the Exchequer. The First
Lord of the Admiralty might have been an ally, but he was not. What the
Navy wanted was fuel oil, not petrol. There were conversations at the Admiralty, but all that came of them was the information, interesting but not
useful, that the United States, from which most of the Navy's oil came, was
'to be regarded as unfriendly' and might even be actively hostile.

By the beginning of 1930 the petrol project had reached that all too familiar
stage of development when a lot of money has been spent without coming in
sight of commercial production and if more is not spent all that has been
spent will be lost. In January 1930 a Chairman's Conference in I.C.I., guided
by McGowan (where Mond was is not clear), agreed with considerable mis-
giving 'that if we did not go on with the process we should have wasted what
we had already spent'. Over the months and years to come the same argument,
the sums in question ever mounting, was more than once repeated.

At the same time another motive for keeping the petrol project alive was
emerging. The world agricultural depression hit I.C.I.'s fertilizer programme
in the latter part of 1929, and by December it was becoming hideously clear
that far more plant had been built than was ever likely to be put to profitable
use. While the closings and the sackings went on, the Board's mind began to
turn to the idea of using plant originally intended for fertilizers on the petrol
project instead. That could certainly be done with the hydrogen plant, which
could serve either purpose indifferently, and perhaps also some of the ammonia plant could be turned over to making methanol (CH_3OH—methyl

alcohol or wood spirit) for blending with petrol. Something would thereby be saved from the ruinous collapse of the fertilizer business, and as time went on this became a leading motive in I.C.I.'s negotiations with the Government for help with the petrol project.

The case which I.C.I. put to Ramsay MacDonald's minority Labour Government in November 1930 was based on economic nationalism, at that time very fashionable. Petrol made from coal at home, although 'at too early a stage of its life to be a good commercial risk', would replace petrol imported from abroad, which would help the balance of payments (I.C.I. called it 'the equation of exchange between Great Britain and foreign countries'). But I.C.I. would need protection against competition from the oil companies, 'probably the wealthiest industrial groups in the world'. Let the Government, therefore, compel importers and refiners of petroleum to buy a quota, proportionate to their imports, of home-produced fuel. The Government, advised chiefly, it seems, by Sir John Anderson (1882–1958), turned aside the proposal for a quota and asked I.C.I. to submit proposals for large-scale plant, indicating, through Anderson, that it 'might consider taking a large financial interest'. The request probably surprised I.C.I., who had been very chary of raising the question of putting public money into the scheme. But it did as it was asked, and in March 1931 presented its proposals to the President of the Board of Trade, the Air Minister, and a distinguished band of civil servants, led once again by Sir John Anderson. Sir John, to the surprise and fury of the I.C.I. delegation, did a thorough job of demolition. He attacked especially the return which I.C.I. was looking for on the £1¼ m. which it had spent on development. 'This is scarcely a helpful attitude', one of I.C.I.'s senior Directors wrote later, 'to the advancement of industrial research.' Yet after all the Government which Sir John was advising was a left-wing Government, not over-friendly to the notion of profit, and I.C.I. was approaching it somewhat in the posture of a lame duck. In I.C.I. they evidently considered that his ability outweighed his hostility, for in 1938 he was elected to the Board.

I.C.I. did not look for state help again until the Labour Government had been overwhelmed by a sterling crisis and flung far from office by the result of the General Election of October 1931. In the meanwhile, I.C.I. carried on its own private international diplomacy which in April 1931 led to four inter-related agreements sometimes known, collectively, as the Hydrogenation Cartel, regulating relations between I.C.I., the I.G., and the oil companies and setting up an arrangement for pooling patents which gave I.C.I. access to the long-coveted German technical knowledge of the petrol process.

Meanwhile, in December 1930, Alfred Mond—Lord Melchett—had died at a bleak moment in I.C.I.'s history. He was succeeded as Chairman by Sir Harry McGowan, who remained Managing Director, but no new colleague was appointed to the office to replace Mond, so that sole power rested with McGowan, who was not one of the least dictatorial figures of the 1930s.

McGowan had none of Mond's standing in public affairs but he had good connections towards the right-hand side of British politics which he knew well
enough how to use. The incoming President of the Board of Trade, in the
autumn of 1931, was an old friend, Walter Runciman (1870–1949). By mid-
November 1932 a new I.C.I. plan for producing petrol, 100,000 gallons of it a
year, was on Runciman's desk. There was no suggestion, this time, that the
Government should put up capital, but it was asked to guarantee to I.C.I., for
ten years, a works realization figure of 13·5d. (5·6p) a gallon, which implied a
contingent promise to support petrol prices in some manner unspecified if
they fell below 13·5d. That was not a proposition which the Government was
prepared to accept. On the other hand, with unemployment running between
$2\frac{1}{2}$ m. and 3 m. the Government could hardly afford to turn down out of hand
a scheme which would preserve jobs, otherwise at risk, in Billingham and
eventually increase employment there by 1,000 men or so, as well as relieving
matters slightly in the coalfields. I.C.I., for its part, was unwilling to give up
its search for government help, and in the spring of 1933 McGowan was back
at the Board of Trade, bargaining.

I.C.I.'s principal negotiator was the Finance Director, W. H. Coates, once
a civil servant at the Board of Inland Revenue. Perhaps because he had been a
civil servant he quickly got on terms with Sir Horace Wilson, Chief Industrial
Adviser to the Government and particularly influential with Neville Chamberlain, in 1933 Chancellor of the Exchequer. These two, who must have been
men of like mind, worked out an agreement on lines which had been slowly
emerging since the Government imposed an import tax of 8d. (3·3p) a gallon on
petrol in 1928. The central idea was that if the Government could be persuaded to refrain from taxing home-made petrol equally, and to retain the
protection against imports, it might just be possible to make the Billingham
plant pay. Petrol from Billingham, it must be pointed out, was very good petrol.
There was no question of protecting an inferior article, but simply a matter of
protecting home-produced goods against goods from abroad: a line of thought
attractive to every government in the world in the early 1930s. By 23 June 1933
the bargaining was over. McGowan led an impressive I.C.I. delegation,
including an ex-Viceroy and an ex-Secretary of State for Air, to meet the
Chancellor of the Exchequer. It was almost like a diplomatic interchange
between two sovereign states. The Chancellor 'intimated the willingness of
H.M. Government to provide a margin of preference in relation to duties of
Customs and Excise in respect of light hydro-carbon oils produced directly
or indirectly from British coal.'

What that turned out to mean was explained by McGowan in a passage
which no doubt many of his audience (the I.C.I. Board) found no less mysti-
fying. There would be, he said, 'a preference of 36 pence-years . . . in the fiscal
years following the 1st April 1935' (that being the earliest years in which petrol
plant was likely to be in production). By this formula the Government

remained free to manipulate the rate of customs duty, to introduce an excise duty, or to do both, so long as there was a preference in favour of home-made petrol. I.C.I., assuming that the period and rate of preference would lie between $4\frac{1}{2}$ years at 8*d*. and 9 years at 4*d*., prepared to put up plant. Ramsay MacDonald assured the House of Commons, 'that, although the statement [announcing the preference and the method of granting it] is rather long and complicated, when it is down in print it will be very simple', and the House must have believed him, for the whole matter passed into law as the British Hydrocarbon Oils Production Act 1934. I.C.I. had not waited for the Act, and already by January 1934 10,400 men were at work in one way or another on hydrogenation plant, for making petrol, at Billingham. On 15 October 1935 the Prime Minister attended the opening ceremonies, and on 7 February 1936 the first petrol began to flow.

(C) WARLIKE SUPPLY, 1935–1945

In the early 1930s I.C.I. needed help from the state. From about 1934 onward, with war becoming every day more likely, the state needed help from I.C.I.

Such an emergency had been foreseen from I.C.I.'s earliest days, and Baldwin's Government had the military importance of a strong chemical industry well in mind when it put its weight behind the merger of 1926. Nearly ten years later Lord Weir, giving secret advice to the Committee of Imperial Defence, referred to I.C.I. as part of what he called the 'professional armaments industry', along with Vickers, Woolwich Arsenal, the Royal Dockyards, and the Royal Ordnance Factories.[5] Trade in war materials, when Weir wrote, amounted to less than 2 per cent of I.C.I.'s turnover, as McGowan virtuously—and quite truthfully—pointed out, a few days later, to that fine flower of the inter-war liberal conscience, the Royal Commission on the Private Manufacture of and Trading in Arms.[6] This, however, was only because the drive for rearmament had scarcely, as yet, got under way. When it did, the true warlike importance of I.C.I. would emerge.

Merely by carrying on its normal activities of supplying materials to other industries, I.C.I. would contribute indispensably to war production, but there would be far more direct applications of chemical technology than that. Ammonia synthesis would supply the basis of nitric acid for explosives; dyestuffs know-how would be applied to explosives, war gases, pharmaceuticals; petrol would be produced by hydrogenation; many products required in peacetime industry—chlorine and cyanide, for instance —would become chemical weapons or ingredients of them. Almost any branch of the chemical industry could be applied to war. Some, such as the production of war gases, had no peaceful application at all. These activities, all within the conventional boundaries of the chemical industry, might be considered to provide a wide enough field for any single business or group of businesses, however large, but I.C.I.'s importance to the war effort of Great Britain

ran wider still. No other organization, industrial or academic, privately
owned or owned by the state, could match I.C.I.'s combined command of
scientific talent, industrial technology, and managerial skill. More and
more problems were found to require precisely that array of resources,
particularly for the development of new weapons, and for the development of
the atomic bomb most of all.[7]

For all these reasons, during the period of rearmament and war—say, from
1935 until 1945—I.C.I. came to occupy a central position in the war-making
machinery of the state, and its activities, as time went on, were directed ever
more exclusively towards strategic purposes. By the time war broke out the
preparations for it were already claiming most of the management's attention,
and as the impact of war deepened and spread, the ruling considerations of
ordinary business—considerations of profit and loss, of meeting market
demand in the present and preparing to meet it in the future, of salesmanship
—ceased to matter. Everything was swallowed up in one overriding purpose:
victory. In an economy centrally directed towards this one aim, which is the
nearest approach to socialist planning that this country has so far experienced,
I.C.I. became a government agency, on a very large scale, for investment,
construction, research, development, and production. It is instructive, nearly
forty years on, to watch these wartime wheels go round, to contrast the wartime situation with the situation in the 1930s, and to consider what reflections
suggest themselves.

Work as a government agent, strictly speaking, was work undertaken, outside the normal run of I.C.I. operations, because the Government required it,
found the capital for it, and remained the owner of all the assets employed in
it. I.C.I., as manager, received fees which, over all, amounted to about 1·2 per
cent of the capital invested on behalf of the Government[8]—in no sense a
commercial proposition. Work done by I.C.I. in its own factories was nominally done under more or less normal commercial conditions, but by 1941 it
was all either for government account, directly or indirectly, or undertaken
only with government consent. The value of sales rose 114 per cent, by 1944,
over the 1934 figure, and profits by 92 per cent, but the suggestion of prosperity
is an illusion. All the books were open to government inspection and taxation
was designed with great care (after experience between 1914 and 1918) to make
sure that extra wartime profits were forfeit to the Inland Revenue. It is fair to
look upon all I.C.I.'s wartime work as being done for the state, under state
control, for rewards determined by the state, and not as normal profit-making
enterprise at all.

Many firms acted as government agents during the war, but I.C.I. was the
largest agent of all, responsible before the end of the war for the building and
management of 25 factories.[9] Wartime construction reached its peak during
1941 and 1942, when projects representing some £36 m. capital expenditure
were due to come into production, and by the autumn of 1943, when activity

was levelling off, about £58 m. expenditure on I.C.I. 'agency factories' had been authorized since 1937 or before. The investment was divided among I.C.I. manufacturing groups roughly as follows:

General Chemicals Group	£19·2 m.	Alkali Group	£2·8 m.
Fertilizer Group	16·8	Dyestuffs Group	0·3
Explosives Group	11·8	Plastics Group	0·2
Metals Group	5·6	Leathercloth Group	0·014
	Special Weapons Group	£1·4 m.	

The largest 'agency factory', costing £6·2 m., was for a joint project with Shell, at Heysham, to produce petrol by hydrogenation. Even in wartime the petrol process turned out to be uneconomic, and the plant was partly converted to ammonia synthesis. The biggest share—some £16·8 m.—of the total investment went to General Chemicals for poison gas and its ingredients. The gas was never used. In explosives I.C.I., in its own and agency factories, produced about 25 per cent of the total British wartime output of cordite, about 15 per cent of the output of T.N.T., and 16 per cent of the output of tetryl. Some thirty years later a good deal of the cordite was lying inside Welsh mountains. The Special Weapons Group designed and produced such lethal gadgetry as the Blacker Bombard, a 29 mm spigot mortar, and a gun known as the P.I.A.T. (Projector Infantry Anti-Tank) which was designed to be fired from the shoulder at oncoming enemy tanks.

The atom bomb was eventually born in the U.S.A. but it was conceived in Britain of Anglo–German parentage. In July 1941 the Maud Committee of eminent scientists, working on theoretical considerations advanced by O. R. Frisch and R. Peierls, reported that a bomb could probably be made in time to be used during the war. In September Churchill, advised by the Chiefs of Staff, somewhat sceptically decided to let the work go ahead.[10] This was precisely the kind of project which I.C.I., among British firms, was uniquely equipped to tackle, because it required scientific knowledge allied to the technology of heavy industry, and the managerial skill required to put them both to work. From the first, therefore, the Maud Committee called I.C.I. into consultation, and McGowan and half a dozen others became parties to the greatest state secret of the war. As time went on, others in I.C.I. joined the project, but very few were allowed to know the full significance of its code name, Tube Alloys. This is no place for an account, with all its bitter implications, of the frustrated attempt to make a British bomb and the subordinate British part in the eventual American success. All that is necessary for our purpose is to observe that I.C.I., a government agent, put very considerable resources, human and technical, at the disposal of the state and that by June 1944 the state had spent some £870,000 through I.C.I. on research, as well as sums spent by I.C.I. which were never fully charged to government account. Far more was spent on research for Tube Alloys than on any other war project and some of the ablest men in I.C.I. were diverted to it. One of them,

(Sir) Wallace Akers, became a temporary civil servant and the working head, under the Minister, of Tube Alloys as a whole.

Akers's appointment illustrates an important point, perhaps the most important of all, in the story of I.C.I.'s wartime relationship with the state: namely that the state, although in control of I.C.I.'s entire business (and, indeed, of the entire business of the nation), was obliged to rely on I.C.I. to make its control effective, rather than merely nominal. As a consequence, there were men from I.C.I. (as from other large companies) in high positions throughout the administrative machinery of the British war effort. In 1942 the I.C.I. Secretary reported that two members of the main Board, five Chairmen and Directors of manufacturing groups, and thirty-three other staff had been 'seconded to Ministries'. Moreover, those who remained at the head of I.C.I., such as McGowan himself and other Directors and Group Managers, were scarcely less officials of Government than their colleagues who were formally transmogrified into temporary civil servants. I.C.I., as a result, was far from being a passive tool in Government hands. Powerful influence, at very high levels, could be brought to bear on the formation of policy, as McGowan was well aware. In October 1941, when the industrial necessities of the development of atomic energy were very imperfectly understood, he tried to get the whole project, so far as it related to industrial rather than military purposes, handed over to I.C.I. Fortunately for I.C.I., he failed—but only just. In matters of agricultural policy I.C.I. had more success. Men from I.C.I., acknowledged experts with strong views, were well placed in the Ministry of Agriculture, where they worked hard to get their views adopted. They were not universally popular, but they had their way; so much so that in certain matters connected with wartime farming I.C.I. came close to directing the policy of H.M. Government.

Two non-executive Directors of I.C.I., Sir John Anderson and Sir Andrew Duncan, left the Board to join the Government, Anderson at the end of 1938 and Duncan in 1940. Anderson, as Lord President of the Council, was responsible for Tube Alloys and for the Agricultural Research Council. Both responsibilities brought him closely in touch with I.C.I. and in each he showed himself quite as austere in dealing with them as he had been, in the 1930s, as a senior civil servant.[11] Nevertheless, after the war he came back to the Board (where he became known as Jehovah) and so did Duncan.

In sum, then, the connecting tissue between I.C.I. and Government, both at the political and the official level, was already strong when war broke out. Methods of wartime administration fortified it still further, and indeed it may be said that the war consolidated I.C.I.'s position within the state. Let us stand back from the narrative and consider its implications.

(D) REFLECTIONS

Except for some forms of fundamentalist religion, including Marxism, there can be few doctrines which have been held with greater emotional force and mental rigidity than Free Trade and *laissez-faire* doctrines in Victorian England. Right up to 1914 the idea of state intervention in the running of private business was abhorrent, even immoral, to most of those in any position to influence public policy, and the attitude persisted throughout the first months of the Great War. Then, under the pressure of the shell shortage and other crises of supply, there was an abrupt change. The Munitions of War Act 1915 brought overt and far-reaching state intervention, and by the time the war ended a powerful organization existed to control industry. After the war there was a rush to dismantle it, and a good deal of demolition was accomplished, but the state and business, once joined together, were never afterwards entirely put asunder. The theory, no doubt, still was that the politicians and the civil servants, on the one hand, and the business men, on the other, would in normal times keep out of each other's way, so that private enterprise, unhampered by the state's dead hand, would remain both private and enterprising. The practice was somewhat different. For one thing, when the men of the 1920s talked of 'normal times' what they really meant was 'before the war', and in that sense times were never normal again. Then, whether times were 'normal' or not, those at the head of affairs in politics, administration, and business had grown used, during the war, to working together, and they never again retired into separate compartments. Men like McGowan and Mond in business; like Baldwin, Runciman, and Cunliffe-Lister in politics; like Warren Fisher and John Anderson in the civil service; like McKenna, Weir, and Ashfield in positions overlapping all the rest—all had easy access to each other and continued the wartime habit of consultation and co-operation. Nor was the process confined to the right-hand side of politics. Herbert Morrison, Ernest Bevin, and Walter Citrine were perfectly prepared to join in and Bevin once went so far as to include himself in the phrase 'we industrialists'.

It was in this early dawn of the modern era of state intervention in business affairs that I.C.I. was born. It had at all times a strong infusion of public purpose and it was never a private institution, if by that is meant an institution which should be run in the interest of a narrow group of owners. I.C.I. was very large straightaway and its shares were so widely distributed as to make it inconceivable that any individual shareholder, or even any likely group of shareholders, would dispose of enough voting power to dictate policy to the Board. I.C.I., in fact, was formed at a time when nationalization was not a public possibility, but experiments were nevertheless being made to find suitable forms of organization for large enterprises of outstanding national importance, with results which were nationalization in nature if not in name. The B.B.C. and the Central Electricity Board, both set up in the same year as the I.C.I. merger—1926—were two important examples. The London Passenger Transport Board, set up in 1933, was a third. In I.C.I. there was no tincture of public ownership, but the public purpose was there, and it is significant that Lord Weir, who was Chairman of the Committee which proposed setting up the C.E.B. as a state-owned monopoly, and Lord Ashfield, the first Chairman of the L.P.T.B., were both on the Board of I.C.I.—Weir from 1928 to 1953 and Ashfield from 1926 until his death in 1948. With the possible exception of the Anglo–Iranian Oil Company (later B.P.), in which nearly half the shares were owned by the Government, no other large enterprise, nominally privately owned, approached nearly so closely to the character of a public corporation as I.C.I., but without the disadvantages of overclose political scrutiny which outright public ownership has later been found to bring.

Questions of ownership apart, the idea that government should take a part in the organization and direction of business and should even offer financial help in cases of distress was gradually easing its way into the general body of commonplace ideas during the years between the wars. This was exemplified, among many other measures, by the Trade Facilities scheme of the 1920s, the Coal Mines Act 1930, and the scheme of 1934 to assist four 'special' (i.e. depressed) areas, to say nothing of the wholesale abandonment of the Old Religion—Free Trade—in protectionist policies from 1931 onward.

I.C.I. was set up as a direct result of interaction between matters of state and matters of commerce. The British Government wanted the merger to safeguard the nation's war potential. Mond and McGowan wanted it to give them standing in the world's chemical industry, though there were present in their minds also, especially in Mond's, notions of national policy. These two lines of thought converged to produce I.C.I.

When all allowances have been made for the disastrous decision to overbuild at Billingham, the result remains impressive. In a matter of ten or twelve years, between 1926 and the late 1930s, four large businesses, each with a strong sense of its own identity, were welded into a whole that was more than the sum of the parts, and by the time war broke out the British chemical industry—that large part of it, at least, which was represented in I.C.I.—was rationally organized, technically powerful, inventive, and well able to look after itself in international trade. Moreover, it had reserves of managerial skill which under the stress of war turned out to be almost infinitely adaptable. I.C.I.'s foundations were laid both in public policy and in sound business practice, and in this aspect of I.C.I.'s history, perhaps, we may find a good deal that is relevant today to the practice, if not the theory, of handling economic affairs.

NOTES

1 This chapter is largely based on material in W. J. Reader, *Imperial Chemical Industries: A History* (2 vols., Oxford U.P., Oxford, 1970, 1975).

2 L. F. Haber, *The Chemical Industry during the Nineteenth Century* (Oxford, 1958) and *The Chemical Industry, 1900–1930* (Oxford, 1971); J. J. Beer, *The Emergence of the German Dye Industry* (Urbana, Ill., 1959).

3 Haber, *1900–1930*, pp. 198–204, 207–8.

4 Later Lord Hankey, Secretary of the Committee of Imperial Defence, 1912–38, and of the Cabinet, 1919–38. Born 1877, died 1963.

5 Committee of Imperial Defence, Sub-Committee on Defence Policy and Requirements, 'Industrial Production', a memorandum by Lord Weir, 27 Jan. 1936, among the Weir Papers at Churchill College, Cambridge.

6 Minutes of Evidence taken before the Royal Commission on the Private Manufacture of and Trading in Arms, Fifteenth Day, Wednesday, 5 Feb. 1936 (H.M.S.O., 1936), pp. 439, 443.

7 See Margaret Gowing, *Britain and Atomic Energy, 1939–1945* (London, 1964), generally.

8 W. Ashworth, *Contracts and Finance* (London, 1953), p. 156.

9 W. Hornby, *Factories and Plant* (London, 1958), p. 449.

10 Gowing, op. cit., p. 106.

11 See above, p. 235.

13

Management and Men:
Aspects of British Industrial Relations
in the Inter-War Period[1]

W. R. GARSIDE

BUSINESS historians on the whole have sorely neglected the industrial relations activities of employers, especially within individual firms. The trade union viewpoint has dominated the history of collective bargaining[2] and with entrepreneurial theory virtually devoid of a body of unifying concepts with which to analyse the employer's role in such bargaining,[3] there has been little incentive to correct the imbalance in the conceptual treatment of this important aspect of business growth and development. To some extent the inaccessibility of relevant records, for whatever reason, and the preponderant bias of existing sources towards strictly 'business' themes will help perpetuate the gaps in our knowledge. But those gaps could be narrowed if something of the sophisticated, rigorous, and thoughtful attention already devoted to entrepreneurial behaviour in its diverse forms was directed towards identifying the determinants and nature of such behaviour in relation to labour.

The chequered history of British industrial relations between the wars provides an appropriate background against which to conduct such an inquiry. The period up to 1933, in particular, was one of painful economic transition, during which both sides of industry sought to protect their vested interests. A conflict soon developed between those employers who tried to establish, and to provide means for interpreting, collective agreements with labour on the basis of a mutual recognition of the legitimate rights of each party and those who were alien to co-operative bargaining with the unions and apparently anxious to contain their effective power.

The tension which ultimately developed between the tendencies towards confrontation and co-operation was heightened by the 'negative voluntarism' of the state, by which collective bargaining was encouraged but left to take its own course, free from government interference. In the absence of policies specifically designed to provide adequate minimum standards of life or the security of full employment there was no sound economic basis on which collective bargaining could develop its potential to the full. The attitude of the individual employer within industry was therefore of critical importance. Some business men were willing and able to take a long-term, progressive view of prevailing economic conditions and to modify their relations with labour accordingly; others were traditionally suspicious of their work-force and reluctant to compromise, even in the short run. Neither group was necessarily confined to particular industries—whether 'new' or 'old'—nor were such extremes of attitude atypical.

However, because of the limitations of the available sources, it is difficult to do full justice to the employers' role in the development of industrial relations in this period. The material which exists concentrates on the 1920s in particular, relates more to industry-wide than to firm-based activity, is biased towards the basic rather than the 'new' industries, and offers little indication of the implications for collective bargaining of changes in the scale and corporate structure of industry. But there is a view amongst students of industrial relations that it was the reluctance of British employers' organizations to act purposefully after the First World War in order to develop a common policy of nation-wide collective bargaining that led to the victory of the autocratic, class-conscious employer over his more progressive, collaborative counterpart in the period between 1920 and 1933. Since the essentially passive role of British employers is claimed furthermore to have coloured the subsequent development of the regulation of industrial relations, at least up to the 1960s, it is worth investigating, albeit on a modest scale, how far the evidence of employer activity in selected industries substantiates this characterization of the inter-war period. Such a survey may also prompt others to engage in the necessary primary research and empirical investigations on which a more composite and analytical approach to the entire problem of the industrial relations activities of employers can be built.

(A) POST-WAR ADJUSTMENT

The trade union movement which employers faced at the end of the First World War had undergone a radical transformation and appeared to pose a serious threat not only to the well-being, but to the very future, of the existing capitalist order. During the war trade unions gained new status and power. Their collective bargaining rights were extended; national wage agreements became standard rather than exceptional and both government and employers constantly found themselves having to seek the consent of the labour-force in order to execute their plans. Other developments made industrialists fearful of the terms and conditions under which peacetime negotiations with labour would be conducted. Traditional wage differentials were seriously undermined during the war and despite labour's advances there emerged a distinct feeling of unequal sacrifice in the face of substantial wartime industrial profits. The formation of the Triple Industrial Alliance in 1913 between the miners, railwaymen, and transport workers for the purpose of joint industrial action in support of each other's demands provided, in theory at least, the means by which they could bring important sectors of the industrial economy to a virtual standstill. The war had added to this potential threat by increasing substantially total trade union membership and prompting close co-operation between unions in the same industry, encouraging them to act in concert in the presentation of industrial claims. By 1918 the major unions had elevated this trend to a conscious policy of formulating national programmes, which members of the Triple Alliance sought to submit simultaneously to employers and the government at the end of hostilities.

To the threat of combined trade union pressure was added the problem of local negotiation with the rebellious shop stewards' movement. Unofficial action to press home labour's enhanced bargaining strength had found its most powerful expression in the engineering and shipbuilding industries where an effort was made to redress the balance in favour of employers which had resulted from labour dilution (the use of semi-skilled and unskilled labour in skilled jobs). The government's insistence that shop stewards should be formally recognized and consulted over dilution angered many employers. In addition, the activities of the shop stewards and the extension of government control to coal-mining and railways had popularized the grand ideal of workers' control or, at the very least, state ownership of industry and had encouraged the belief that political, but especially industrial, action could effectively dismantle the capitalist control of the means of production. The echoes of the Russian Revolution merely added substance to the fears and hopes on both sides of industry.

Acceptance of trade unions as equals in the affairs of industry had become so much a part of the wartime industrial consciousness that employers had begun to consider seriously their own strategic position in the post-war world.[4] The several attempts made before 1914 to provide a central organization among employers had all failed. But war-time conditions provided an effective catalyst. By striving for national collective bargaining and by itself becoming directly involved in private industry, the government played an important part in encouraging the growth and development of national employers' organizations. The fragmentation of industrial and commercial representation which existed in 1914 was, if anything, accelerated by the war, and Chambers of Commerce, trade associations, and employers' organizations within individual industries gained in strength and authority. But a formal structure did emerge to provide for the consideration of labour matters at national level and was to prove of some significance in later years. In 1915 the British Manufacturers' Association was created from 200 leading industrial firms to represent manufacturing as distinct from commercial interests. This was followed in the next year by the establishment of the Federation of British Industries to co-ordinate and represent the views of industrialists on general policy issues. The National Confederation of Employers' Organizations which developed out of the employers' side of the National Industrial Conference called by the government in 1919, restricted its membership to associations only, to the exclusion of individual firms. (It was also necessary to provide a central organization for industries such as inland transport, shipping, and building which had been excluded from the F.B.I., the watchdog of manufacturing interests.) The British Manufacturers' Association seceded from the F.B.I. to launch the National Union of Manufacturers in 1917 in defence of the interests of small firms. The N.C.E.O. eventually emerged as the employer equivalent of the T.U.C. and sought to achieve the fullest co-operation of its constituent federations in dealing with the more important issues of industrial relations.[5]

The wartime government had not left the uncertain development of peace-time labour relations entirely to fate. By 1916 reconstruction was in the air and employers welcomed the appointment of a committee under the chairmanship of J. Whitley:

1. To make and consider suggestions for securing a permanent improvement in the relations between employers and workmen.
2. To recommend means for securing that industrial conditions affecting the relations between employers and workmen shall be systematically reviewed by those concerned with a view to improving conditions in the future.[6]

The results of 'Whitleyism' are well known[7] and need not be recounted in detail. What is interesting from our point of view is that action to improve matters was centred firmly upon exploiting the long-established traditions of the British industrial relations system. This meant that effort was concentrated on improving the machinery of collective bargaining and disputes procedure, in order to give more practical expression to labour's demands for higher living standards and a greater degree of control and influence over the decision-making machinery in industry, without fundamentally modifying either the existing practice of industrial negotiation or the balance of power between employer and employed.

The assumption implicit in the deliberations was, in essence, that the wage-earner's claim for a better standard of living would be met from the increased prosperity resulting from his co-operation in the reconstruction of industry. Joint Industrial Councils were to be established in each industry where the two sides were organized on an industry-wide basis. This was to be followed by a network of district joint councils and works committees. Not surprisingly, organized employers in 1917 generally welcomed such initiatives[8] since, having carefully rooted itself in the wartime spirit of equality within industry, the Whitley Report had emphasized contractual co-operation and not class conflict as the basis upon which reconstruction was to be carried out, without committing anyone to anything. The establishment of Joint Industrial Councils was popularly regarded as a concession of industrial self-government to the workers but, as the post-war years were to show, recalcitrant employers were under no effective compulsion to concede the official wish that 'the work people should have a greater opportunity of participating in the discussion about the adjustment of those parts of industry by which they are most affected.'[9]

Where employers refused to co-operate and accept joint consultation on the basis of mutual trust and respect nothing could be done. In industries such as building, pottery, and printing, in which similar experiments in co-operation had already developed, and in others such as cement manufacture, flour-milling, and electricity supply, where there was evidence of more enlightened attitudes among employers, some progress was made. But in many other industries where the Whitley proposals were adopted, such as soap and candle manufacture, paint and varnish, heavy chemicals, and electrical cable-making, it was soon apparent that employers had never been under any illusion as to who would effectively determine the pattern of post-war industrial relations.[10] The majority of others remained openly apathetic towards the entire spirit of the Whitley scheme, fearing that it might be used 'to claim control of management, to force disclosure of business secrets and to give practical power to labour extremists'.[11]

As it was, the immediate industrial relations problems of the post-war period occurred in those industries which had cold-shouldered the Whitley Report from the start. The miners and engineers were less concerned with improving the existing industrial system than with replacing it. The official wartime resolve to lay the foundations for industrial peace had not countenanced the vehemence with which important sections of the trade union movement were to claim their share of 'the brave new world' so glibly promised by politicians.

Faced with a sudden outburst of industrial unrest in 1919–20, many employers felt that their earlier fears about the worst consequences of trade union militancy were uncomfortably close to being realized. The year 1919 began with unofficial strike action amongst engineers on the Clyde led by shop stewards. The government, in its wartime role as employer in the mines and railways, faced national strike threats from both industries. Lloyd George strategically outmanœuvred the miners, fobbing them off with the appointment of a Royal Commission to investigate their industry's problems, but succeeded only in deepening distrust and anger within the industry by promptly rejecting the majority recommendation of nationalization of the mines, despite previous assurances that the findings would be accepted 'in the spirit and the letter'. Successive administrations and private employers were to pay dearly for this distinct breach of faith. Nor were employers any more comforted by the handling of the railway dispute. The unions successfully called a national strike, won public support for their cause, portrayed the government as a bad employer, and forced it to settle under duress.

Employers were keenly aware that certain sections of the trade union movement were bent on achieving their aims through direct industrial action and were angered by the government's handling of the post-war labour problem. The emergence of a Parliament of 'hard faced men who look as if they have done well out of the war' only appeared to strengthen the attractiveness of open conflict. Prices were rising, profiteering was rife. Important groups of workers had already come to feel that although they had secured some wage advances through the operation of conciliation and arbitration they were less than might otherwise have been obtained through militant action.[12] The trend towards wage settlement on a basis of bargaining strength rather than custom, important in only the relatively few industries that were strongly unionized in 1913, was now greatly enhanced. Moreover, there was, amongst the miners and railwaymen, a strident call for a fundamental change in the ownership and control of their industries. Support for the workers' control movement had been minimal in 1914 but the shift in emphasis of trade union activities from political to industrial action and the wider recognition and strength obtained by the movement during the war had led to the most important labour and union organizations embracing the ideal in one form or another. The fact that few agreed over the form and content of such workers' control was neither here nor there. To workers' representatives it was a powerful unifying concept. To employers it was an ideological flower that needed to be firmly nipped in the bud.

Industrialists who were determined in the immediate post-war period to reassert their authority over labour found a useful ally in the government. In 1919 it seized the opportunity to exploit the gullibility of those workers' representatives whom Lloyd George saw as intent on fostering co-operation and reconciliation, and called a tripartite conference to seek a remedy for industrial conflict. Employers at first appeared equally anxious to establish a more responsible and reasonable working relationship with labour. The F.B.I. had resolved in February 1919 that it should take 'immediate action in conjunction if possible with the Engineering Employers' Federation and the National Organizations representing labour with a view to summoning a joint Conference of employers and employed for the formation of proposals for dealing with the present grave conditions of industrial unrest'.[13] Unfortunately, the F.B.I.'s enthusiasm did not reflect the attitude of the general body of British employers. The Federation's approval of the Whitley Report and its implicit acquiescence in the view that labour had a right to participate in the determination of working conditions had not, for example, found parallel expression in the individual employer's response to Joint Industrial Councils. The refusal of miners, railwaymen, transport workers, and engineers to support the National Industrial Conference soon after its inception in February 1919, on the grounds that it was a dangerous and diversionary tactic, proved particularly apposite. Although the Conference proposed a universal forty-hour week, an extension of the minimum wage system, and the establishment of a permanent Joint Council of employers and trade-unionists to advise the government on economic matters, the government did nothing to ensure the speedy implementation of any of the recommendations. It soon became obvious that both the employers and the government had used the Conference merely to take the steam out of the immediate threat of industrial disruption during February–April 1919. Neither side was prepared to countenance such a sudden transformation in the pattern and substance of industrial negotiations. Parliament itself was more heavily representative of business interests than had been the case immediately before the war. Industrialists were hardly reassured by union representations during the Conference that the first necessary condition of the removal of industrial unrest was 'the widest possible extension of public ownership and democratic control of industry'.[14]

In reality, the spirit of Whitleyism and wartime co-operation proved transitory. Their influence gave way to that of the free play of economic forces, a transition that had the full support of the N.C.E.O. The conciliatory posture adopted by the F.B.I. was quickly overshadowed by the more pragmatic, self-interested caucus within the Confederation, especially amongst the engineering employers. They resisted any notion of established minimum standards and government interference and sought freedom to meet overseas competition as best they thought fit.[15] In truth, the National Industrial Conference was one 'in which the trade unions were aware of their power and of the necessity of influencing national policy. In their efforts they met an unusual degree of response amongst the employers involved. Unfortunately it was not one that the real centres of power in employers' councils reflected.'[16]

(B) PATTERNS OF AUTHORITY IN THE EARLY 1920s

When the post-war boom broke in 1920 the balance of power shifted significantly in favour of business men. Abrupt deflation in 1921, the onset of large-scale unemployment, and a general and strong pressure on wage rates in face of declining trade and intense foreign competition found unionists defending standards rather than trying to raise them by threats of direct action. In this spirited defence lay the origins of the General Strike, not least because the employers' efforts to reduce wage rates, whilst they did not lead to open conflict in every industry, nevertheless seriously disturbed relations in essential basic trades and dictated the terms under which peaceful compromises could be attained in most others. They were conducted, furthermore, against the background of an official deflationary policy which, in its insistence on seeking stability through restoration of the gold standard at the pre-war parity, put a high premium on the reduction of domestic, especially labour, costs.

Nowhere was the employers' struggle to meet the challenge of changed economic conditions more clearly portrayed than in the coal industry. The government, in a calculated act of political expediency, relinquished its war-time control of the industry in March 1921, leaving colliery-owners to adjust to rapidly falling prices, high costs, declining profits, low productivity, and intense competition in overseas markets. Although the industry was in the throes of secular decline, due largely to excess world capacity and fuel econo-my and substitution, a number of fortuitous events—such as the United States coal strike in 1922 and the French occupation of the Ruhr in 1923—kept alive the employers' expectation of at least a partial return to their exceptional pre-war prosperity. Given the high proportion of labour to total costs of production, employers persistently attempted to reduce wages and to increase hours of work to meet the demands of interregional and inter-national competition. Their objective—to increase sales and profits by lower-ing costs—was complicated by the obligation they had undertaken from 1921 to pay a district minimum wage to labour as a first charge on the industry's proceeds. In practice, the decline in the demand for coal so reduced net pro-ceeds in the industry that employers had to forgo profits in order to meet minimum wages. As a result, labour's share of net proceeds in the later 1920s rose to levels higher than originally envisaged.

Low selling prices and high wage costs kept profits in the majority of coal-mining districts at a low level. From the early 1920s national agreements determined the structure of district wage rates and it was during the first half of the decade that the coal-owners were forced to retaliate vigorously against a highly organized mining labour-force intent at the very least on maintaining minimum standards and increasingly regarded by other key workers as in the forefront of the battle against wage reductions.

The Mining Association, representing the owners at national level, firmly rejected long-term schemes of capital reorganization, especially with the workers' demand for nationalization forever lurking in the background. It was uncompromising in its demand for wage-cost adjustments to vary according to the economic capacity of the different colliery districts.[17] Although the mine-owners expected to meet distrust, suspicion, and downright obstinacy amongst the miners, they were shaken by the Conservative Government's apparent willingness to avoid a show-down between the two sides when, in 1925, it offered to subsidize the existing level of wages for a period of nine months. Nothing, however, would deter the employers in their opposition to planned reorganization of the industry—indeed, they successfully warded off an official move by the German Government in 1925 to promote an inter-national coal agreement aimed at avoiding price competition, stabilizing coal prices, and dividing markets[18]—and they persisted in resisting government interference through subsidy, demanding freedom to impose wage cuts and to alter the length of the working day. In this they were supported by the N.C.E.O. and employers in iron and steel, shipbuilding, engineering, cotton and wool, to all of whom cheaper fuel offered the opportunity of lower prices and increased profits, not least because it had proved difficult in these industries to enforce substantial cost reductions.[19] The coal-owners' response to the uncertain economic conditions of the pre-1926 period had been to emphasize their right to pay wages in accordance with what they felt the industry could bear, free from government interference and regulation, and according to the dictates of national and international competition.

The engineering employers' forthright determination to meet economic contraction and heavy unemployment by policies which involved a reassertion of their authority over labour cast a shadow over the emergence of a new peacetime relationship within the industry. If their conflicts were less menacing and less politically explosive than those within the coal industry, they were nevertheless significant in their influence on the attitudes adopted by industrialists in other sections of the economy.[20]

From its inception in 1896, the Engineering Employers' Federation had sought to preserve the power to manage and to keep the peace. The creation of provisions 'for the avoidance of disputes' in 1898, whereby conciliation was kept within the industry and unresolved differences were submitted to local, and if need be national, conferences, had proved so acceptable to both sides in the industry that official moves to intrude upon the established machinery by Joint Industrial Councils had been promptly resisted. The employers' sensitivity to managerial authority, however, had already led to a lock-out in 1897 and predisposed the Federation to oppose any increase in the participation by unions in the control of industry at national or local level.[21] This reaction rested in part on the fact that the industry was characterized by continued growth and change and a need to adapt quickly to fresh techniques and methods of production. To this was added the fear, heightened by the wartime shop stewards' movement, that union intervention at workshop level could be a first step in the eventual obliteration of the private employer.

The engineering employers had reacted bitterly to the usurpation of their prerogatives and to the lack of consultation by the government during the First World War.[22] Their Federation played a leading part in mobilizing employers' organizations into new national bodies after the war. With an increase in its own membership and influence,[23] it forced through wage reductions during the deflation of 1921, adopting a policy which was a response to market pressures but was also shaped by the employers' central concern to re-establish managerial prerogatives within the industry. The pressures of war had forced many engineering employers to yield in their observance of the procedure for avoiding disputes and to establish a new formal relationship with the shop stewards' movement which they felt had reduced their ultimate power to manage the industry in accordance with their own wishes.[24] With renewed vigilance the employers continued, for most of the inter-war period, their long-standing refusal to allow trade unions the right to regulate the wages and conditions of apprentices, and sought to reduce demarcation disputes between skilled crafts which they maintained hindered management in its effective utilization of labour, especially in the manning of machines.[25] It is not altogether surprising, therefore, that a dispute with the Amalgamated Engineering Union over who should have the right to decide overtime working, which eventually led to the 1922 lock-out, was readily interpreted by the Federation as a key issue in the right of management to exercise its legitimate functions.

The employers' insistence on being the sole arbiters of working conditions during a time of large-scale unemployment indicated to the A.E.U. 'that they have learned nothing, that circumstances are of no account, that they still harbour the old idea of master and men'.[26] But the employers saw their fight as one to preserve the freedom of management, so essential to restoring British engineering to its pre-eminent position in world markets. 'In any organization for the direction of human effort', they claimed, 'it is necessary that there should be one directional authority.' This sentiment was successfully driven home in the formal peace settlement with the unions under which it was agreed that 'the employers have the right to manage their establishment and the trade unions have the right to exercise their functions'.

There is little doubt that the engineering workers' identification with the demand for workers' control and the marked sectionalism of union organization strengthened the employers' offensive, since it was able to be portrayed as a spirited defence of the existing system of ownership against those who appeared determined to destroy it. In practice, it merely spread bitterness and suspicion within the industry and hampered any moves towards a more positive reform of collective bargaining. But from the management's point of view the rights of trade unions had been closely defined whilst theirs remained satisfactorily vague. In the wake of their success the employers were able, in subsequent years, to resist demands for the restoration of wages to their pre-1922 level and, in some cases, to impose further wage reductions.[27]

A number of the factors which enabled the engineering employers to weather the storms of the early 1920s operated in favour of those in the cotton industry. Systematic consideration of the differences between employers and workers had been firmly entrenched within the industry since the end of the nineteenth century. The employers were organized into two main bodies—the Federation of Master Cotton Spinners and the Cotton Spinners' and Manufacturers' Association—and had managed to command a marked degree of discipline and co-operation from their members by adopting the same federal form as the union amalgamations in order to iron out conflicts of interest between firms of different size, locality, and structure. [28] The cotton workers were also strongly unionized though they failed to match the growth of employer strength and lacked any effective concerted policy in relation to their industry. Nevertheless, they remained successfully locked with the employers in a struggle to improve efficiency and prospects, though one in which neither side was able to provide an adequate solution outside of organized short-time working.

It would be rash to assume from the evidence presented so far that the transformation in the economic climate during the early 1920s seriously damaged relations between labour and capital in all or even the majority of industries. As might be expected, most employers in sheltered trades were not forced to adjust to such drastic changes in their market and competitive environment as those in the unsheltered basic sectors, and their policies, though dictated by deflation and cost-consciousness, often avoided the kind of abrupt changes in working conditions that would have invited extreme retaliation by labour. The reality of economic depression in a number of industries did not entirely obliterate the co-operation and respect fostered between the two sides in more prosperous, stable times.

Regular negotiations between the Shipping Federation and the seamen dated only from 1917 but subsequent relations proved exceptionally friendly.[29] Thus, although the Federation could not avoid imposing reduced wages during the early 1920s, it succeeded in March 1925 in gaining trade union support for a joint investigation of the cost structure of the industry as a preliminary to deciding the most effective means of meeting fierce international competition.[30] Relations between the Federated employers and the union representatives in the boot and shoe industry were noticeably peaceful throughout the 1920s.[31] The iron and steel employers, faced with a check in world demand for their goods and high internal costs, relied heavily on the legacy of mutual respect between them and the unions and did their utmost to preserve a flexible working relationship. They had little sympathy towards non-unionists or notions of company unionism. To their delight the conservative leadership of the main unions exercised a strong executive control over the membership and insisted on the sanctity of agreements entered into with the employers. Such co-operation was made easier by the fact that the industry contained a relatively large proportion of family firms which tended to perpetuate arrangements for settling disputes, shouldered labour costs which were a relatively small proportion of total costs, and through wage-price sliding scales had given the unions a vested interest in co-operating with price-fixing agreements.[32]

To their credit, the iron and steel employers refrained from any concerted attempts to weaken or damage the unions and sought to preserve the long-established and trusted collective bargaining machinery.[33] Their actions demonstrate the importance of recognizing the extent to which an employer's view of industrial relations is determined by the nature and effectiveness of the trade union body within the industry. The internal adjustments demanded by and conceded to the iron and steel masters were very much conditioned by the union leaders' willingness to educate their members into accepting co-operation as a norm rather than an exception. The unions organized work-teams with clearly defined levels of seniority and wide earning differentials linked to promotion opportunities through union membership. This developed a feeling of stability and security for those in employment which the employers were able to exploit in less favourable times: the Iron and Steel Trades Federation succeeded in gaining union support for the temporary amendment of the eight-hour day during 1922–6 for the purpose of reducing costs.[34]

The evidence of mutual co-operation in other industries, even if it is selective and conditioned by the particular economic problems facing representatives on each side, is nevertheless another reminder of how much the tarnished history of industrial relations in the early and mid-1920s arose very much from the problems of the coal and, to a lesser extent, engineering industries. Elsewhere employers were prompted by a habit of responsible negotiation to safeguard the collective bargaining machinery, even at the most critical moments in the progress of an industry. Wage adjustments in the tinplate industry were subjected to careful examination by both sides through the recognized negotiating machinery;[35] and a similar situation existed in the glass,[36] hosiery and knitwear,[37] printing,[38] biscuit,[39] and woollen and worsted industries.[40]

Where the dominant personality within an industry was fired with a sense of responsibility towards the well-being of his employees the results were even more encouraging. Lord Leverhulme, head of Lever Brothers, characteristically ensured that the wage reductions imposed during the 1921–2 downturn deliberately left rates above minimum union levels and that the blow was softened by the almost simultaneous introduction of unemployment, sickness, and benefit payments.[41] Such an enlightened attitude towards labour sprang from his firm conviction that economic circumstances should never be allowed to obliterate justice and humanity and that the major problems of industrial relations in a maturing economy could be solved only by sustained co-operation—not excluding labour participation in management—and respect for the rights and obligations of each side in industry.[42]

Such sentiments were rare amongst the majority of contemporary business men. Moreover, even when they existed their practical application was never entirely free of subtle means of asserting managerial authority. Leverhulme's generous wages and benefits policy, for example, was an obvious ploy to retain the loyalty of the workmen and to weaken the trade unions.[43] In addition, both Lever Brothers (later Unilever) and I.C.I. sponsored profit-sharing as an effective means of promoting better relations with labour. In essence, each scheme of 'co-partnership' entitled workers to ordinary shares allotted in proportion to wages. Since the value of the shares fluctuated with the profitability of the company it was hoped, by binding the labour-force to the firm's interest, to avoid undue loss and efficiency.[44] Both schemes served to weaken trade union solidarity. Employees at Lever Brothers stood to lose all their bonuses if they left the firm and went on strike.[45] For those workers at I.C.I.

with more than five years' service there was added the further incentive of possible promotion to a privileged staff grade at the discretion of the Directors. Works Councils representing management and men at factory and industry level were to enhance status and security amongst the work-force. The unions regarded the Councils as dangerous alternative means of making organized approaches to management. But in reality the Councils had little authority. They were purely consultative and discussions of wages and conditions were kept firmly under management control. Indeed, the Executive Committee of I.C.I. had decided privately that in its deliberations with the Councils 'any discussion of production costs should be limited to very general statements' and that 'it would be undesirable to give any figures of any kind'.[46] The company's policy towards labour, though fair and generous by contemporary standards, included elements of a 'cynical bargain by which "benefits" were traded off against hard cash . . . so that I.C.I. continued to gain a labour force both contented and comparatively cheap'.[47]

In the years before the General Strike, therefore, the majority of industrialists, faced with a sudden break in the economic climate which transformed both business prospects and the inherent power of organized labour, and preoccupied with the particular problems of their trade, sought as pragmatically as possible to safeguard their future viability and managerial authority. In this they were helped by the fact that employers' organizations at industry and national level had gained in strength and influence and had managed to retain a large degree of autonomy. No lasting procedural relationship had been established between the N.C.E.O. and the T.U.C. even though the latter was empowered after 1924 to co-ordinate in special circumstances the activities of its constituent members for the purpose of industrial action. Although on the employers' side a number of Confederation members had toyed with the idea of co-ordinating action to resist wage claims during 1919–20 nothing more came of the proposals. By 1924 the notion of central control over industrialists' action towards their employees had lost its attraction for a Confederation dominated by the leading representatives of the shipowners, engineers, and mine-owners, each determined to assert their managerial prerogatives.[48] As an organization it 'exercised little control over its constituent organizations and was always fearful of losing any one of them'. As a result, it pursued a consensus policy and moved at the rate of its slowest and most 'reactionary' members.[49] There is no evidence to suggest, for example, that either the F.B.I., the N.C.E.O., or their member associations were consciously planning a united attack on the trade union movement. But the employers' bargaining position had already been strengthened in a number of important ways. During the 1920s governments of both persuasions had sought to 'educate' labour into accepting changes in the social order through gradual constitutionalism, whilst the Labour Party actively reduced its radical plea for the complete transformation of industrial ownership and control to a search for a regulated form of capitalism which necessarily implied a distribution of effective power between 'captains of industry' and workers, not unlike the *status quo*. More obvious in its effect was the impact of industrial recession. The rapid deflation between mid-1920 and mid-1922 so reduced the trade-unionist's conception of the potentialities of direct action and his expectations of continually improving conditions that many were content to hold on to the gains they had already made. It was not so much that industrial relations had been transformed for the better by the extension of practical forms of joint consultation based on traditional voluntary procedures, as the fact that labour's prevailing attitudes and expectations were sufficiently inhibited by the economic *malaise* to suit the available machinery.[50] This was of small comfort to employers in basic industries where labour's rearguard action was more sustained if only because it was under greater pressure, but elsewhere it operated in favour of those trying to establish their market strength with the minimum of labour unrest.

(C) AFTER THE GENERAL STRIKE

It is not necessary to dwell on the more obvious effects on industrial relations of the outbreak of the General Strike and the ensuing coal stoppage in 1926. The facts are well documented. But since industrialists in a number of industries had already, as we have noted, taken a keen and selfish interest in the outcome of the coal-owners' offensive before 1926,[51] it is of some interest to examine how far the episode marked the sharp break in the general attitude of employers—for both good and bad—often ascribed to it.

Flushed with success after the collapse of sympathetic trade union support for the miners, the coal-owners pressed even more vigorously for the abolition of the national minimum wage, for district wage reductions, and for a longer working day. The Mining Association, which had only reluctantly assumed the role of national negotiating body for the owners in 1921, was relieved of such duties in June 1926 to enable district employers' associations to embark unilaterally on imposing their demands upon the work-force. The government, however, proved difficult in insisting that national negotiations should be resumed between the parties. Incensed at this further meddling in its affairs, the Mining Association, supported by employers in other trades, eventually succeeded in deflecting such interference. By now employers' organizations and trade associations within iron and steel, shipping, engineering, cotton, woollen and worsted, and chemicals were anxious to protect their collective interests in any agreement between the parties. In August 1926 the shipowners' organization, in consultation with their principal coal-consuming industries, had sought to persuade the Cabinet to yield to the mine-owners' solution to the crisis.[52] The N.C.E.O. was equally insistent that the government should allow the owners complete freedom to arrange the final terms of settlement.[53]

The coal-owners were to win their final victory. Despite government appeals and their public assurances to the contrary, they increased humiliation within the coalfields by open victimization, ruthless bargaining, and frequent attacks on the authority of local trade unions. Other industrialists, angered by the disruption of established procedures and agreements through the organized withdrawal of labour during the General Strike, joined in the clamour to restrict the effective power of the trade union movement. Workmen in the docks, printing, iron and steel, railways, and electricity supply were pressed by their employers to refrain from unconstitutional action. Both the government and the N.C.E.O. favoured a stronger legal control. The majority opinion within the Confederation sought a wholesale reconstruction of union law by the effective removal of the immunities regarding picketing and inducements to breaches of contract given to the unions under the 1906 Trade Disputes Act.[54] In the event, the government refused to implement the N.C.E.O.'s politically explosive suggestions, although the engineering employers and the National Union of Manufacturers, based on small-scale Midlands firms, had their demands for a reform of the trade union political levy vindicated under the 1927 Trade Disputes Act.

Despite the retaliation and recrimination practised by some industrialists after the 1926 dispute, it is customary to emphasize, almost as an antidote, the important shift towards closer collaboration between the two sides of industry as evidenced in the famous Mond–Turner talks.[55] These celebrated discussions sprang essentially from the culmination of a number of factors making for industrial co-operation after 1926. Some important employers recognized that to fight the powerful trade union movement was costly and to a large degree self-defeating, inasmuch as the essential need to boost exports through reduced unit labour costs and increased efficiency and rationalization demanded the assistance of the unions. Moreover, it was not unreasonable in the prevailing circumstances to expect such collaboration to be readily forthcoming. The employers' offensive since 1920 had weakened union strength, especially at shop-floor level, had effectively defused the workers' demand to be intimately involved in the commercial and financial decision-making process of business, and had convinced influential members of the T.U.C. General Council, notably Bevin and Hicks, that the industrialists' struggle to revitalize and rationalize industry in the face of contracting markets and falling profits needed the support of labour, if only to afford the latter some measure of self-protection.

The co-operative mood within some parts of industry was buttressed by a favourable movement of public opinion,[56] firm political support from the Prime Minister and the Minister of Labour, and the relatively favourable economic climate between 1926 and 1929 which improved the export performance of many industries, except coal and cotton, increased real wages for those employed, and raised the levels of industrial production, consumers' expenditure, and gross domestic capital formation.[57]

What is striking about the Mond–Turner episode from the employers' point of view is just how many of them fundamentally opposed the suppositions on which it was based. It is true that those involved conceded the unions' right to be consulted over questions of general industrial policy—no mean thing in itself. Indeed, much of the joint discussion had centred on devising permanent machinery for industrial co-operation representative of the T.U.C., the F.B.I., and the N.C.E.O.[58] But in point of fact, those employers within the Confederation and its member organizations were more intimately involved in labour matters than those within the Mond group and were more influenced by relationships and traditions at the industry and work-place level. Whilst the majority of the Mond–Turner employers represented large-scale science-based industries such as chemicals, rubber and oil, and the newer, domestically orientated and capital-intensive industries, those who were most influential within the F.B.I. and the N.C.E.O. were in basic industries. As such, they were particularly conscious of costs and, in important instances, of the objective of preserving managerial authority. They were equally anxious to resist any moves towards the national determination of labour's claim to a share in commercial and industrial decision-making through extended consultation and co-operation.[59] The more dominant employers in the economy were in fact less interested in espousing prophetic sentiments than in isolating labour problems from the total industrial scene and confining the trade unions to operating as collective bargaining agents in accordance with accepted economic doctrine. 'Whereas the mainstream of British trade unionism thinking in the 1920s moved towards co-operation in a far more positive form than ever before,' writes Charles, 'the employers who wished to reciprocate had to struggle against the tide of their own organizations.'[60] The central employers' organizations which existed had neither the will nor the ability to enter into a new procedural relationship with labour. Some of the keenest opposition came from the Engineering Employers' Federation, the most influential affiliate of the N.C.E.O., which saw the talks as a dangerous prelude to a trade union take-over of industry.[61]

(D) BASIC INDUSTRIES IN THE 1920s AND 1930s

As the Mond–Turner talks continued there was clear evidence in some industries that it would take more than a high-level conference to alter the basis on which employers responded to long-term depression. Despite the coal-owners' success in forcing a massive reduction in labour costs after 1926 the industry's finances remained in a parlous state and the short-run competitive advantage won over European producers rapidly dissipated. After district efforts to promote restriction of output and controlled prices the government stimulated the tendency towards imperfect competition within the industry by the 1930 Coal Mines Act. Its efforts to foster deliberate cartelization of the industry, to raise coal prices, and to promote reorganization merely resulted in spreading business amongst the efficient and inefficient alike. The Mining Association could not be roused into any more enthusiasm for planned amalgamations than it had shown for previous official efforts to promote voluntary action on similar lines under the 1926 Coal Mines Reorganization Act. Although voluntary pit closures and amalgamations did occur, the multiplicity of undertakings of varying size and efficiency continued to exist and the pace and character of technical improvement was hardly affected by the legislative meddling with the production, supply, and sale of coal.

Throughout the late 1920s and 1930s, therefore, the mine-owners were able to resist the demand by their work-force for national wage determination[62] and industrial reorganization and continued successfully to modify conditions to meet the needs of competition. It remained patently clear that industrial solutions were to be sought in accordance with the strict and narrow view of industrial relations which put the individual owners' managerial pre-rogatives—including the prerogative to determine wages—far above long-term and costly considerations of amalgamations and co-operative selling.

The blank refusal of the engineering employers during 1928–30 to consider granting wage advances even in the more profitable sections of the industry convinced the workmen that the issue was not one of the ability of the industry to pay or one that rested on 'the justice or efficiency of our case . . . or the cogency of our argument . . . it is a matter of power.'[63] Cotton operatives faced an equally painful reminder of who was to dictate industrial relations. The traditional flirtation with organized short-time working practised within the industry during the 1920s had by the end of the decade merely added to rising unit costs and had proved singularly inappropriate to conditions of a permanent decline in demand. All efforts to enforce price-fixing had failed, technological advance was virtually at a standstill, and cost-reducing improvements were conspicuously absent.[64]

As the cotton unions clamoured in the early 1930s for more amalgamation, mass production, standardization, and control of production and prices, the master weavers sought economies without capital outlay by increasing the number of looms attended by a single weaver, whilst employers in the spinning section terminated existing agreements over working hours in an effort to impose a longer working week in the industry.[65] Wage disparities in both the spinning and manufacturing sections bore witness to the employers' willingness to renounce existing collective agreements and peace was restored only through the intervention of the Ministry of Labour and the agreement of the weaving section to the imposition of legally enforceable wage lists in 1935. Clearly, in the face of open disunity amongst the separate trade union organizations and the apparent willingness of the government to rely on a revival of exports to provide relief to the industry, the employers were under little pressure to forego the more traditional means of cost reduction in favour of any schemes of industrial reorganization other than those that they themselves thought were necessary. Nor were employers in the woollen and worsted industry any less reluctant to give way to the spirited resistance of the unions to wage reductions during 1929–30 even at the cost of a breakdown in regular communication between the two sides.[66]

There is undoubtedly some truth in the view that the Mond–Turner talks not only improved relations at the higher levels of British industry but educated many employers in later years to accept the downward 'stickiness' of wages and to seek less painful ways of adjusting to economic decline.[67] In spite of the particular responses just outlined there was no general onslaught by employers' associations on either unions or their rights in collective bargaining. Indeed it is possible, even in the worst years of depression, to witness within particular industries a basic desire to preserve some continuing element of conciliation and compromise between management and men. Few trades escaped the mutual distrust, anger, and frustration which soured industrial relations in the immediate aftermath of the General Strike; but in the tinplate, soap, printing, and iron and steel industries, for example, industrialists appeared reluctant in later years to press their advantage to the extreme. Indeed, in the latter case, when unfavourable economic conditions fostered demands for national planning and conscious control of industry, both sides co-operated in seeking a solution to the industry's problems.[68]

But having said that, it is hard to deny that the ultimate and decisive rejection of the Mond–Turner Joint Interim Report by the F.B.I. and the N.C.E.O. was merely an expression of a more deep-seated hostility amongst nationally organized employers[69] to the promotion of formal industrial co-operation. This was particularly evident during the strained series of talks subsequently held between the two organizations and the T.U.C.[70] It was obvious from the time of the first tripartite conference in April 1929 that the national employers' organizations were keen to return the initiative in industrial relations to the individual employer. Exponents of co-operation faced a resurgence of the less enlightened and jealously independent views so clearly expressed by the N.C.E.O. and the F.B.I. in previous years. The fact remained that despite the efforts made since the formation of a National Industrial Council in 1911 no permanent relationship had been successfully forged at national level between the two sides of industry. There were those within the unions who were suspicious of such a development but it foundered largely because of the obstructive and belligerent attitude of important groups of employers, and a fundamental reform of British industrial relations between the wars was allowed to go by default.

It is arguable, in any case, whether the successful establishment of formal co-operation would have been of exceptional benefit. National bargaining with militant trade unions, wage and price instability, and large-scale industrial conflict had put employers on the alert during the immediate post-war years. With less price-fluctuation and a marked reduction in national conflict

after 1926[71] there was generally less managerial enterprise in industrial relations at either national or company level when its accepted purpose—the
avoidance of disputes—appeared less important.[72]

(E) CONCLUSION

The paucity of published material on the industrial relations activities of
individual or collective employers makes it almost impossible to provide a
chronologically complete or industrially balanced account of the factors
which influenced business men in their relations with labour between the wars.
This chapter has only traced the relationship in its barest outline and has
obvious limitatiohs. Much of the supporting material relates to the activities
of national employers' organizations. This is not surprising inasmuch as, for
most of the inter-war period, collective bargaining with labour was a fairly
minor interest of the managements of most industrial concerns. It was the
employers' federation or association that generally took the initiative in
industrial relations and only exceptionally the individual employer.[73] It has
been pointed out already that member groups severely restricted the ability
of the N.C.E.O. to co-ordinate their industrial relations activities.[74]

Nevertheless, this does not preclude the need for more empirical research at
the level of individual industries—especially amongst the newer growth sectors
so neglected here and amongst those trades which were unrepresented at
national level. It is clear, moreover, that we need further investigation at
industry level of the industrial relations activities of employers. This is particularly so in the case of coal and shipbuilding, which were nationally organized,
as well as those in other important areas such as chemicals, cotton textiles,
and railways. Until this has been done it will be difficult to judge how far our
present and scanty knowledge of employer reaction within the more dominant
sectors of the economy disguises important elements of conflict, compromise,
and contradiction.

Certain aspects of the employers' reaction to labour problems developed
here are worthy of further study. It is clear that employers in general sought
to exploit their position as profitably as possible by choosing a strategy best
fitted to prevailing circumstances and most likely to achieve an acceptable
outcome with the minimum of confusion and disruption. In view of the varied
and intractable sources of industrial conflict it is obvious, as one observer
has noted, that 'any general explanation of employers' labour acitivities
and their preference for particular types of bargaining arrangements must
include an examination of management's objectives, both commercial and
political, as pursued under different structural and economic conditions'.[75]
To this extent the variety of factors which predetermine the attitudes and
expectations which an employer brings to bear on an industrial relations
problem are of critical importance. The posture ultimately adopted could be
influenced amongst other things by the desire or otherwise to avoid industrial

disputes depending on known resources and tactical strength; by the need to equalize or minimize wage costs; by a determination to defend managerial authority; by the need to assist trade union development or to preserve the viability of collective bargaining when the institutional needs of both sides coincide; or by a general wish to influence the nature of non-wage items in substantive collective agreements, such as those governing dismissal, training, or promotion, which afford workers some protection from the free play of market forces.

In addition, the product and market environment in which the employer operates would need careful investigation. His reaction, for example, to centralized wage negotiations or the establishment of minimum working conditions in one firm or plant rather than another may well be determined by the degree of product homogeneity within the industry, the degree of potential competition, the pace and character of technical change, the income-elasticity of demand for the final product, or the difficulties such concessions might conceivably pose to the existing combination of labour and capital inputs or the allocation of labour and capital between firms.[76] To all these influences must be added such amorphous but no less important considerations as the employer's perception of the factual situation, his sympathy for and understanding of the other side, his skill in bargaining and persuasion, his motives, future expectations, and not least his judgement of the feasibility of obtaining his objectives.[77] Such constraints may rarely figure in an employer's public defence of his actions, if such is even made, but the temptation to reduce the causes of conflict to crude issues of class warfare, if never entirely misplaced, could nevertheless distort the picture and give undue weight to the claims and aspirations of the labour participants. In so far as research into industrial activity continues to cast doubt on the accepted judgements of entrepreneurial behaviour in the past it would be foolish to pretend that employers' relations with labour might not be influenced by factors held to be as just, rational, and defensible as those espoused by the unions.

To this extent it seems important that further investigation should seek to fill the gaps and imperfections in the existing historical accounts of industrial relations, so far as employers are concerned. The evidence presented here of the views of national employers' organizations and of federated groups within particular industries, for example, emphasizes how little is known about developments at workshop and establishment level and how much the systematic consideration of the relations between management and men in individual factories between the wars has been sadly neglected. In addition, the Mond–Turner discussions revealed how varied were the attitudes and expectations of different groups of employers. The obvious dichotomy between those who favoured and those who opposed co-operation with the unions surely masks a diversity of attitudes and ideologies within other industries which would be worthy of further empirical research.[78] Furthermore, in so far as the attitudes and expectations of employers were critically important it would be as profitable to examine, along similar lines to Erickson,[79] how far the growth of large-scale concentrated production eroded or reinforced traditional forms of ownership and control and to question, where appropriate, whether professional managerial groups, as paid labour, fostered particularly distinctive relations with the work-force. Nor is the role of tradition without some significance. The engineering and coal employers, if nothing else, strove desperately to defend what they believed to be established rights. How far, one might ask, were the industrial relations activities of employers in 'new' industries the product of their willingness to reject the traditional acceptance of an inherent conflict with labour in the face of their pressing obligation to communicate with large numbers of workers engaged in collective production?

Obviously, there are innumerable approaches to any study of employer behaviour and those aspects of their industrial relations activity suggested here as worthy of further thought are by no means exhaustive. One could speculate, for example, about the influence of government or the nature of trade union growth and organizational development on the changing attitudes of private industrialists—or, indeed, about the contribution business men themselves have made towards determining the framework in which industrial relations are conducted. But since (to select somewhat arbitrarily) industrial unrest, restrictive trade practices, resistance to technical change, and encroachments on managerial authority have so obviously forced employers to react towards the labour interest, it is only by fostering a more deliberate study of the motives, aspirations, strategy, and success of the employers[80] that we can hope to understand fully the past record of British industrial relations and with it a major factor in the growth and development of the economy.

NOTES

1 The author wishes to express his thanks to Professor Hugh Clegg for his comments on an earlier draft of this chapter.

2 See A. Flanders, 'Collective Bargaining—A Theoretical Analysis', *British Journal of Industrial Relations*, vi (1968).

3 H. F. Gospel, 'An Approach to a Theory of the Firm in Industrial Relations', *British Journal of Industrial Relations*, xi (1973).

4 For some this proved the beginning of an almost new phase of activity. Up to 1914, for example, shipowners and the railway companies had refused to accept collective bargaining with the unions.

5 G. W. McDonald, 'The Report of the Commission of Inquiry into Industrial and Commercial Representation—the Devlin Report of 1972: An Historical Background', *Business Archives*, xxxviii (June 1973). Further details can be found in H. F. Gospel, 'Employers' Organisations: Their Growth and Function in the British System of Industrial Relations in the Period, 1918–1939' (unpub. Univ. of London Ph.D. thesis 1974) which concentrates on the engineering, flour-milling, and electrical contracting industries. See also J. H. Richardson, *Industrial Relations in Great Britain* (1938 edn., Geneva), Chs. 3 and 4; H. Clegg, *The System of Industrial Relations in Great Britain* (Oxford, 1970) esp. Chs. 4 and 10; L. H. Powell, *The Shipping Federation, 1890–1950* (London, 1950); E. Howe, *The British Federation of Master Printers, 1900–1950* (London, 1950); A. Barker, *The Employers'*

Federation of Paper and Boardmakers (1953); J. E. Longworth, *Oldham Master Cotton Spinners' Association Ltd.* (Oldham, 1966); E. L. Wigham, *The Power to Manage: A History of the Engineering Employers' Federation* (London, 1973).

6 The Whitley Committee, *The First Interim Report*, State Papers, 1917–18, xviii, para 2.

7 The best detailed account is R. Charles, *The Development of Industrial Relations in Britain, 1911–1939* (London, 1973). See also J. Seymour, *The Whitley Council's Scheme* (London, 1932).

8 Charles, op. cit., pp. 117–19.

9 H. Clay, *The Problem of Industrial Relations* (London, 1929), p. 152.

10 Charles, pp. 121, 219–21.

11 Seymour, op. cit., p. 191.

12 J. H. Porter, 'Wage Bargaining under Conciliation Agreements, 1860–1914', *Economic History Review*, 2nd Ser. xxiii (1970).

13 *The Times*, 14 Feb. 1919, cited in Charles, p. 233.

14 Report of Provisional Joint Committee presented to meeting of Industrial Conference 14 April 1919, Cmnd. 501 (1920).

15 Charles, p. 252.

16 Ibid., p. 257. See also 'The National Industrial Conference, 1919–1921', in V. L. Allen, *The Sociology of Industrial Relations* (London, 1971).

17 G. W. McDonald, 'The Role of British Industry in 1926', in Margaret Morris (ed.), *The General Strike* (London, 1976).

18 Ibid., p. 295. There were individuals within the F.B.I. who felt the need for the government to assist in the reorganization of the coal industry to promote greater efficiency. (Ibid., pp. 138–9.)

19 G. W. McDonald, 'Insight into Industrial Politics: The Federation of British Industries Papers, 1925', *Business Archives*, xxxviii (June 1973), 26–7; McDonald in Morris (ed.), op. cit., pp. 296–8.

20 See below, pp. 256, 259.

21 Wigham, op. cit., p. 6. The Federation was known officially in 1919 as the Engineering and National Employers' Federation and from 1924 as the Engineering and Allied Employers' National Federation.

22 Ibid., Ch. 5.

23 Its membership increased from about 830 firms in 1912 to over 2,000 in 1922—it having been joined in 1918 by the National (formerly the Midlands) Employers' Federation. (J. B. Jefferys, *The Story of the Engineers*, London, 1945, p. 219).

24 Wigham, op. cit., pp. 110–11.

25 J. Hilton, *et al.*, *Are Trade Unions Obstructive?* (1935), pp. 141–3, 150–3.

26 Jefferys, op. cit., p. 221.

27 Wigham, p. 129; Jefferys, pp. 231–2.

28 H. A. Turner, *Trade Union Growth, Structure and Policy: A Comparative Study of the Cotton Unions* (London, 1962,) p. 375.

29 Powell, op. cit, Ch. 5.

30 Hilton, op. cit., p. 276.

31 Richardson, op. cit., pp. 130–2.

32 W. Campbell Balfour, 'Union–Management Relations in the Steel Industry from the Great Depression to the Second World War', in International Institute of Social History, *Mouvements ouvriers et dépression économique de 1929 à 1939* (Netherlands, 1966).

33 J. C. Carr and W. Taplin, *History of the British Steel Industry* (Oxford, 1962), p. 455.

34 Ibid., pp. 452–3.

35 W. E. Minchinton, *The British Tinplate Industry: History* (Oxford, 1957), pp. 225–7.

36 T. C. Barker, *Pilkington Brothers and the Glass Industry* (London, 1960), pp. 210 ff.

37 F. A. Wells, *The British Hosiery and Knitwear Industry* (London, 1972 end.), pp. 210–11.

38 A. E. Musson, *The Typographical Association* (Oxford, 1954), pp. 363–87; J. Child, *Industrial Relations in the British Printing Industry* (London, 1967), Ch. XV; Howe, op. cit., pp. 64–84.

39 T. A. B. Corley, *Quaker Enterprise in Biscuits: Huntley and Palmers of Reading, 1822–1972* (London, 1972), pp. 210–15.

40 Hilton, pp. 303, 306. The Joint Industrial Council worked well in this industry until 1925 when conflict arose over a wage claim, resulting in the first general stoppage of the trade as a whole. Peace was restored after a Court of Inquiry recommended the continuation of existing wage rates. (Ibid., p. 401.)

41 C. H. Wilson, *The History of Unilever* (2 vols., London, 1954), i, 277.

42 Ibid. i, 292–6.

43 Cf. A. E. Musson, *Enterprise in Soap and Chemicals, Joseph Crosfield & Sons Ltd., 1815–1965* (Manchester, 1965), p. 318.

44 Wilson, i, 142–3; W. J. Reader, *Imperial Chemical Industries: A History*, ii, (Oxford 1975), pp. 59–70.

45 Wilson, i, 296; Musson, *Crosfield*, pp. 316–17.

46 Reader, op. cit. ii. 61–2.

47 Ibid. 70.

48 Gospel, 'Employers' Organisations' 306–8.

49 Ibid. 352.

50 E. H. Phelps Brown, 'A Non-Monetarist View of the Pay Explosion', *The Three Banks Review*, 105 (Mar. 1975), 12–16.

51 See above, pp. 251–2.

52 McDonald in Morris (ed.), p. 304.

53 Ibid., p. 305.

54 Ibid., pp. 307–8.

55 For details of the origins and progress of the talks see Charles, Chs. 18 and 19, and G. W. McDonald and H. F. Gospel, 'The Mond–Turner Talks, 1927–1933: A Study in Industrial Co-operation', *Historical Journal*, xvi (1973).

56 For details see Charles, pp. 264–6.

57 McDonald and Gospel, art. cit. 810–15.

58 Ibid. 820.

59 Gospel, 'Employers' Organisations' 347–8.

60 Charles, p. 109.

61 Wigham, pp. 131–3; Charles, pp. 290–1.

62 In this, they received the support of other employers. Both the F.B.I. and the N.C.E.O. joined the Mining Association in resisting government efforts to constitute, under the terms of the 1930 Coal Mines Act, a National Industrial Board to deal with wages and other conditions in the industry.

63 Jefferys, p. 237.

64 G. C. Allen, *British Industries and their Organization* (London, 1959 edn.), pp. 238–9; Turner, op. cit., p. 346. This is not to deny, however, that there may have been some rationale in the employer's reluctance to radically alter the structure and technique of his methods of production. See L. Sandberg, *Lancashire in Decline* (Ohio, 1974).

65 Turner, pp. 328–9; Hilton, pp. 66–7.

66 Hilton, p. 310.

67 S. Pollard, 'Trade Union Reactions to the Economic Crisis', *Journal of Contemporary History*, iv (1969), 113–14.

68 Musson, *Typographical Association*, pp. 363–87; Howe, op. cit., pp. 101–17, 126–31; Wilson, ii. 381–4; Minchinton, op. cit., pp. 212–17; Carr and Taplin, op. cit., pp. 457–61; Report of the Import Advisory Committee on the Present Position and Future Development of the Iron and Steel Industry, Cmd. 5507 (1931).

69 It was estimated in 1938 that about one-half of British workers were employed by firms belonging to organized employers' associations (Richardson, p. 83.).

70 McDonald and Gospel, 825–8. Charles, pp. 292–4.

71 H. A. Clegg, 'Some Consequences of the General Strike', *Manchester Statistical Society* (1954).

72 G. A. Phillips and R. T. Maddock, *The Growth of the British Economy, 1918–68* (London, 1973), p. 85.

73 E. H. Phelps Brown, *The Growth of British Industrial Relations* (London, 1965), pp. 270, 293; Phillips and Maddock, op. cit., p. 82.

74 See above, p. 256.

75 Gospel, 'Employers' Organisations' 362.

76 Ibid. 352 ff.

77 Flanders, loc. cit. 16.

78 For further discussion see Gospel, 'Employers' Organisation' 368–9.

79 Charlotte Erickson, *British Industrialists: Steel and Hosiery* (Cambridge, 1959).

80 Much will depend on the success in obtaining the relevant primary and secondary material. In this respect see P. Mathias, 'Surveys of Business Archives', and J. Wecks, 'A Survey of Selected Business Archives', *Business Archives*, xxxix (Dec. 1973).